Resident Peoples and National Parks

Resident Peoples and National Parks

*Social Dilemmas and Strategies
in International Conservation*

Patrick C. West and Steven R. Brechin
Editors

THE UNIVERSITY OF ARIZONA PRESS
TUCSON

95 94 93 92 91   5 4 3 2 1

Library of Congress Cataloging-in-Publication Data

Resident peoples and national parks: social dilemmas and strategies
    in international conservation/Patrick C. West, Steven R. Brechin,
    editors.
        p. cm.
    Includes bibliographical references and index.
    ISBN 0-8165-1128-4 (alk. paper)
    1. National parks and reserves—Social aspects. 2. Nature
conservation—Social aspects. 3. Eminent domain. I. West, Patrick
C. II. Brechin, Steven R., 1953-   .
    SB486.S65R47   1991   90-11300
    333.78'14–dc20   CIP

British Library Cataloguing in Publication data are available.

Photographs in this book are credited as follows: Conrad Bailey,
p. 184 *center;* John Hough, p. 184 *top;* Susan K. Jacobson, pp. 2 and
232 *top;* Shishir R. Raval, p. 52; Mingma Sherpa, pp. 30 *bottom,* 88,
and 92; Sally M. Weaver, p. 232 *center* and *bottom;* Hung Taek Woo,
pp. 30 *top,* 184 *bottom,* and 236 *top;* Wood Buffalo National Park,
pp. 236 *bottom* and 360.

We dedicate this book to the human dignity of the many varied peoples who live in and near the many national parks and protected areas around the world. Many have suffered that we may have the assurance of the preservation of representative global ecosystems. The economic, social, and cultural impacts they have endured have received scant attention and little humanitarian concern on the part of the new ecological mandarins. Our "moral" concern for species everywhere has not extended sufficiently to our own species. Yet they are our common humanity and therefore ourselves. The Reverend Martin Luther King, in one of his last speeches, said that social justice is indivisible: that injustice anywhere is a threat to justice everywhere. We hope that this volume, more than any specific strategies we explore for more just treatment of resident peoples, will help to stimulate and mobilize a more deeply felt concern, a conversion of thinking from blind ecological imperative to more honest recognition of painful moral dilemma, and a sincere desire to help rectify the injustice of the past. Only then will our pragmatic search for specific constructive solutions take root and help to stimulate meaningful change. An open heart must precede a redirected mind and corrective action.

Their children and ours face a common destiny. In our efforts to ensure that they inherit an ecologically viable world let us also strive for an equity that will bind their common humanity in a world where justice, indivisible, shall prevail; a world where our children can face their children unashamed. Martin, you were dead right; Garrett Hardin, you are dead wrong. It is not that "injustice is preferable to ruin"; but rather injustice will lead to ruin, ruin of our precious ecological heritage that sustains us all, and ruin of our common human community, and of the human soul.

CONTENTS

COMMENT

PART FIVE

**Nature
Preservation
and
Ecodevelop-
ment:
Tourism**

PART SIX

**Planning and
Decision
Processes in
Social Change**

ILLUSTRATIONS

ACKNOWLEDGMENTS

We would like first to acknowledge the University of Michigan, School of Natural Resources, Wildland Management Center, and the Dana Chair Endowment for financial support that helped to bring this project to fruition. The Wildland Management Center and its former director, David Hales, provided $2000 to help in the preparation of the manuscript and to subsidize it's publication. The School of Natural Resources, Dana Chair Endowment has provided an additional $4000 to further subsidize the publication of the book so that our rather lengthy work can be sold at a more reasonable price to maximize its distribution and impact. Our thanks also therefore extends to Laurance S. Rockefeller, The University of Michigan, and School of Natural Resources contributors that collectively established the Dana Chair endowment, and to Samuel T. Dana (former dean to the School of Natural Resources), in whose name these monies were given to form the endowment. Our thanks also go to our current dean, James Crowfoot, who authorized both expenditures and provided constant moral support and encouragement in bringing this project to fruition. Steve Brechin would also like to acknowledge the support from The University of Michigan for a post-doctoral fellowship that helped to support his work on the book, among other activities, during the last several years.

Secondly, we would like to extend our deep appreciation to the many School of Natural Resources students who have done so much behind-the-scenes work on the manuscript over the years. Without your dedicated efforts this book would not have been possible. We also extend our appreciation to the University of Michigan, Rackham Graduate School's work-study program that provided the funding to hire these many student workers. Know that your funds were put to good use, and that the students' education here benefited from their involvement in this project.

Thirdly, we would like to thank all the chapter authors for their patience, support, and persistence in the long process of multiple revisions needed to bring this project to a successful conclusion. We would also like to thank the professionals at the University of Arizona Press, especially Barbara Beatty, the acquiring editor, for their sustained faith in the importance of this volume and their helpful guidance in shaping the manuscript into the best possible quality. Similarly, the Press's peer reviewers' valuable suggestions for revisions have greatly improved the quality and effectiveness of the book. Also, several chapters have been adapted from or are revised from previously published materials. We acknowledge the specific publishers in the notes of appropriate chapters.

Finally, we would like to thank our wives and families. They have been hearing about the ups and downs of "the book" for a long time. Their support and faith have been invaluable to us both.

P.C.W.

S.R.B.

INTRODUCTION

Patrick C. West

In this book we assemble state-of-the-art writing and research with respect to the thorny dilemmas posed by the impacts of national parks and other protected natural areas on
local resident peoples in developing nations. We seek to address this dilemma by searching for ways to balance the values of conserving world ecosystems against the survival
needs of resident peoples, both traditional tribal societies and
modernizing peasant populations, in rural poverty.

Contributions to the volume span many disciplinary and
professional orientations including sociology, anthropology,
geography, history, resource policy, planning and management, conservation biology and ecology, wildlife ecology and
management, land use planning, fisheries and marine ecology and management, human ecology, conflict management,
social and environmental impact analysis, rural development
economics, and others. They include contributions from both
academic scientists and researchers and practicing wildland
management, cultural survival, and rural development
professionals.

We have not imposed any particular ideological perspective on these contributions other than a sincere concern for
the fate of resident peoples in the course of efforts to achieve
wildland conservation in representative global ecosystems.
Thus, different views and perspectives are included with respect to how far, and in what ways, conservationists should
bend to meet the legitimate needs of local peoples and cultures. Overall we have sought to represent a range of views
and a balance among them. The great conservationist Gifford
Pinchot once said that the greatest challenge in resource
management was a "search for balance." Perhaps if we manage to annoy readers of all persuasions on this issue we will
have succeeded in the search for balance. But we hope you
will put aside disagreements with this or that point or perspective and engage with us in the important task of devel-

oping constructive solutions to the important dilemmas among natural preservation, cultural preservation, and local rural development for resident peoples in and around national parks and other protected areas in developing countries.

Organization of the Book

The book is divided into seven thematic parts. Part 1 is a conceptual introduction and overview of the book, providing a framework for considering the local resident people and protected area debate. Part 2 investigates the historical and institutional context of the resident people issue with examples from Great Britain and India. Part 3 focuses on the issue of displacement of people from national parks. Case studies from Uganda, Swaziland, and India contrast the complexity of this critical issue. Part 4 consists of case studies of ecodevelopment and sustained natural resource use by local peoples. Chapters in this part focus on resource utilization and impacts on diversity; the resource management debate regarding human rights; and various types of resource extraction and restrictions and their effects on local people and conservation. Part 5 again uses a case study approach to analyze tourism and its effects on conservation, ecodevelopment, local people, and their cultures. Case studies and general essays in part 6 focus on the critical aspects of planning and decision processes essential if local resident people are to be involved in planned social-change activities that result from the introduction of conservation practices. Part 7 concludes the book with an integrated analysis of the issues of resident peoples and protected areas, assessing various perspectives and key dimensions discussed throughout the volume.

Origins and Perspectives

The idea for this book was born some years ago in La Mauricie National Park in the Canadian Province of Quebec. For three years I was a staff member on the International Seminar on National Parks and Equivalent Reserves, cosponsored by the University of Michigan, School of Natural Resources, the United States National Park Service, and Parks Canada. Each year for the past two decades, park managers, planners, and administrators from all over the world have come to study American and Canadian national parks in this traveling seminar held in these parks. As a natural resource sociologist, I was especially mindful of the dangers of participants directly adopting our policies and management strategies that may be appropriate in our culture and society but not in theirs. One could sense the hungry eyes, ears, and minds soaking up our way of doing things and, with almost missionary zeal, returning to the Thailand jungle to develop an RV (recreation vehicle) campground just like the one in whatever park we were in that day.

This problem was especially acute with respect to the problem of resident peoples and national parks in developing countries. It is one thing to displace upper middle-class, summer-home people from Sleeping Bear Dunes National Lakeshore; it is quite another matter to displace a primitive tribal society having little prior contact with the outside world, or a marginal impoverished peasantry on the bare edge of survival. However, the United States notion of national parks embodied in the International Union for the Conservation of Nature (IUCN 1975) definition identifies a national park with exclusion of resident peoples from residence in and use of resources from national parks. A national park is narrowly defined as a large area:

1. where one or several ecosystems are *not materially altered by human exploitation and occupation*, where plant and animal species, geomorphological sites and habitats are of special scientific, educative and recreative interest or which contains a natural landscape of great beauty;

2. *where the highest competent authority of the country has taken steps to prevent or eliminate as soon as possible exploitation or occupation in the whole area* and to enforce effectively the respect of ecological, geomorphological or aesthetic features that have led to its establishment. [emphasis added]

The United States National Parks model has been liberalized in recent years (especially in Alaskan parks) and recent revisions and supplemental policies have opened some loopholes in IUCN's exclusionary definition (Kutay 1984). However, the real tragedy is that, based on such definitions alone, resident peoples in developing countries have been displaced or blocked from traditional uses of park resources and left to suffer severe deprivation and social impacts without any documented proof that they were harming the resources of the park. The international conservation movement has perhaps too eagerly proselytized this concept

in an attempt to save natural wonders, wildlife, genetic resources, and ecosystems around the globe; and developing
country conservationists and resource managers have too
often eagerly embraced these notions without questioning
their relevance to their own economic, social, and cultural
contexts. While these tendencies have been stimulated more
recently by the IUCN, they are also rooted historically in
colonial systems, particularly in Africa and Asia.

During the three years I was on the national parks seminar numerous representatives of developing nations repeatedly raised the painful problems of dealing with resident
peoples in their countries. Some were simply eager to hear
ways for "getting rid of the people" and controlling their subsequent "illegal" uses of their parks. Others, however, began
challenging the United States national park paradigm and
asserting the agendas of Aboriginal land claims, cultural
preservation, rural development, and human rights. While
claims of compatibility through "ecodevelopment" in wider
conservation circles began to be heard, international rural
development and cultural survival social scientists began
viewing the international conservation movement in terms
of "cultural imperialism" (e.g., Thompson et al. 1986:55).
Others began documenting the harmful social, economic,
and cultural impacts this movement was having on resident
peoples and cultures in developing nations.

Stuart Marks (1984:5–6) has perhaps stated these concerns most bluntly, yet most eloquently, in his book *The
Imperial Lion*, based on his anthropological fieldwork in Central Africa:

> Many Romantic and Arcadian ideas survive, promoted in the
> tourist industries of today. Materialistic Northerners have
> sought to preserve African landscapes in the only way they
> could, by separating them from daily human activities and
> setting them aside as national parks where humans enter on
> holiday. . . . The creation of most national parks has incurred
> restrictions on the rights of local human populations without
> compensatory actions on the part of government. . . . Wildlife
> protection, like other imposed policies, has always carried
> with it the implications of force, of quasimilitary operations,
> and of sanctions. It is my contention that for the West to per-
> sist in its support of preservationistic policies that hold vast

acreages of land hostage to its myths is to ensure their certain destruction through African needs and perspectives.

The International Parks Seminar was ill prepared to deal adequately with this growing debate that was coming most immediately from the participants themselves. This book was born in the cauldron of that rising debate. It is our hope that it will contribute to a more reasoned, analytical, appropriate, and constructive resolution of these issues in the developing world. It is vitally important both for the fate of resident peoples and, we believe, for the fate of the international conservation movement that these wrenching issues be faced more directly, and with an openness to changing the ways in which these issues have been dealt with (or not dealt with) in the past.

A famous philosopher once said that the greatest and most troubling conflicts are not between good and evil, but between good and good. In conflict between good and evil the solution is simple—seek the triumph of good over evil. But in the conflict between good and good the balancing of conflicting moral imperatives is painful and trying, and without clear implications for a correct course of action. The resident peoples issue is clearly in this latter category. The preservation of representative world ecosystems, species, genetic diversity, and natural wonders is indeed a noble and important goal; but the protection of local human cultures and the opportunities for economic improvement through appropriate rural economic development in the face of stark rural poverty is also a critically important goal and moral imperative.

Our initial concept for the book focused on a perceived need to document the negative social impacts of the insensitive treatment of local peoples, because, at the time, all too many in the international conservation community viewed resident peoples as a clear evil, a "weed" to be plucked from the purity of wild nature. However, the rising debate over resident peoples has, in recent years, led to a much wider acknowledgment of this issue as a legitimate and important moral dilemma, and to a growing perception that the fate of protected areas is tied to the support, and hence the fate, of local peoples.

The conservation movement has increasingly adopted concern for cultural preservation and ecodevelopment and expanded its repertoire of types of protected areas to include biosphere reserves and other designations that are not as exclusionary in their concept and definitions as the traditional United States model of national parks. European, Japanese, and more recently, new concepts of Canadian national parks in its northern territories are increasingly seen as potential alternative models of national parks that are more permissive of local occupation and use by resident peoples.

Thus, our concept for the book has changed from one of documenting the wreckage of the past, to one of documenting and integrating new approaches and hopes for better ways of dealing with this issue. While we include numerous cases of continued negative social impacts from protected area policies and management, our primary emphasis has been to seek general essays and specific case studies of creative attempts to deal with ways of accommodating the cultures and rural development needs of local peoples in the developing world. The pressing issue has become not whether this is an important dilemma, but rather, how can this dilemma, and the conflict it engenders, be creatively and constructively dealt with in a way that respects the multiple objectives of conservation, cultural preservation, and local rural development. It is this question that drives the concept and organization of the book and criteria for the material included.

Fundamental Questions

There are four fundamental issues that we focus on in the book:

1. Under what conditions should resident peoples be displaced, and under what conditions should this not be done? If resident peoples are to be displaced, how should this be done to minimize negative social impacts?
2. To what extent and in what ways should resident peoples residing in or near protected areas be permitted to utilize natural resources of the area?
3. Under what conditions (if any) is the preservation of natural ecosystems, without allowing human use, important for *local* rural development (i.e., local ecodevelopment) and cultural preservation, and if so, in what specific documented ways?
4. What types of planning, conflict resolution, and decision processes have or should be established for dealing with these issues on a case-by-case basis?

The implications of these basic questions for the dual objectives of cultural preservation and rural economic development are emphasized. The specific case studies all deal with various aspects of these basic questions.

In the concluding chapter we return to these basic questions and their implications for cultural survival and rural development as we seek to set the general essays and specific country case studies in comparative perspective and integrate their findings and implications for national park and protected area policy and management.

Revolutions in the International Conservation Paradigm

As we sought materials for the book we began to observe a fascinating revolution in the tenor of conservationist writings on this subject. In the past, "man" (including woman) was treated as a terrible threat, totally incompatible with the objectives of species and ecosystem preservation. In the short span of ten years, recent writings now resound with assurances that the objectives of nature conservation and needs of resident peoples (especially indigenous tribal peoples) are compatible and harmonious through the vehicle of "ecodevelopment." And yet to date, while there are grand and noble plans and many initial experiments in merging conservation, culture, and development, there are few rigorous evaluation studies that can actually document these claims. One suspects, that with the conservation movement on the defensive, it has sought to take the moral high ground with the rhetoric of "ecodevelopment" as its watchword, and let the details work themselves out later. Whereas, in the past, resident peoples' concerns were swept under the rug as being irrelevant, today they are frequently swept under the rug in glowing praise of ecological compatibility, still coupled with rigorous, exclusionary preservation.

There has been much written about ecodevelopment but few actual documented cases where ecodevelopment has benefited local people, especially in the sense in which natural area preservation (as opposed to use) is functional for local rural development. Ecodevelopment conserves watersheds and helps prevent downstream siltation of dams. This helps broader regional and national development but leaves local people in the hill lands wondering when they get their piece of the pie purchased at the expense of their welfare. The conservation of gene pools is lauded as a critical resource for sustainable economic development, yet if Colgate is able to make a better toothpaste from some yet unrealized genetic resource, this is wonderful for us but does not help local people very much. In other words, as Bailey (this volume) asks "development for whom?" These are hard questions that have not always been squarely faced.

This is not to discount the sincere and dedicated efforts on the part of many people, including many of our authors in this volume, to breathe real life into the rhetorical principles of ecodevelopment. There are early signs of promise in specific cases documented here and elsewhere. But for the most part, it is too early to tell. Many of our chapters are based on prescriptive hopes, plans, and dreams; others on impressionistic, qualitative judgments after early steps in initial implementation.

We had hoped to have more rigorous hard scientific evidence that such new innovations were working or not working after years of implementation. But the state of the art in developing, testing, and evaluating these new innovations is simply not advanced enough, as of this writing, to be able to report definitive results. Therefore, we all need to be cautious about succumbing to the all too human tendency in the absence of hard data to assume things are working out better than they really are.

There is some evidence of this from comparing impressionistic accounts with the few good evaluative studies we have located and included in the book. While such errors are surely unintentional, we will see numerous cases where the claimed benefits of tourism to local people are not borne out in practice. We will also see that local control of management planning and policies by Aboriginals is highly touted in conservation circles but an empty promise on the ground. We had one draft chapter that spoke in very upbeat terms about the success of new concepts for merging conservation and development in a protected area. But when we asked for an update revision, the authors chose to withdraw their chapter because they did not want to put in print the fact that things were not really working out so harmoniously with local people as previously indicated.

What we suspect is that the international conservation movement is in for a second major revolution based on shock therapy in the face of harsh reality. It is not quite so easy to harmonize natural area protection, cultural preservation, and true rural development for resident peoples. The gap between rhetoric and reality is not so easily closed. Tragic dilemmas and hard wrenching choices will not go away.

Once we have come to that realization, then perhaps we can truly proceed to both build and rigorously evaluate new alternatives, firmly rooted in the integrated use of the natural and social sciences, and using participatory planning and conflict management processes. This will need to be merged with a sense of balanced moral responsibility for the human and ecological consequences of our actions, and the political will to support real implementation of concepts such as local control and co-management that will be politically threatening to a variety of powerful interests, not the least of which is the autonomy of the international conservation movement itself. This will be a hard pill to swallow for the conservation movement, but, as we argue throughout, it may be the only way to salvage a pragmatic and responsible course of action. Otherwise, the prophecy of Stuart Marks cited above may come to pass.

In this book, therefore, we cannot document the resolution of these issues because they have not been resolved, or even rigorously tested yet. What we are able to do at this stage is to assess where we are, analyze promising concepts and preliminary findings, point out where there is insufficient natural and social science assessment, and suggest where we need to go from here. To begin this assessment we need to acquire an interdisciplinary and integrated perspective.

The Need for an Integrated and International Perspective

As you wander through the many journeys to various lands and peoples represented in this book, we hope you will come to appreciate not only the complexity of the problems involved in merging and integrating conservation, culture, and rural development, but also the importance of an integrated, interdisciplinary approach to these problems and issues. As a natural resource sociologist by trade, I often find myself immersed in the interconnecting pathways of insights and debates in other disciplines in order to figure out my piece of the puzzle. Nowhere has this task of integration been more challenging, demanding, and important than on this project. While seemingly a sociological "people problem" issue, the specific solutions to particular resident peoples issues often

rest on improved knowledge needed in the dynamics of conservation biology and their interaction with sociocultural dynamics. Many of our chapters illustrate this, but perhaps the
chapter by Raval on Gir National Park in India illustrates it
most poignantly and tragically. But then, nobody ever said
that interdisciplinary integration was easy. Yes, it is difficult; we have not always done it as well as we might, but
interdisciplinary integration can and must work if we are to
face adequately the challenges of natural resource planning,
policy, and management problems—as in this very complex
and difficult resident peoples issue—that are only going to
get more difficult in the years ahead. We hope you will join
with us in that search.

Part One CONCEPTUAL OVERVIEW

Local produce for
sale near
Kinabalu Park.

Introduction   To date, no comprehensive overview has been assembled on one of the most difficult topics facing conservation efforts in the world today: protecting the Earth's environmental integrity and biodiversity, while at the same time protecting the rights of people who live in and around parks and reserves. Some may suggest it is not possible to do both, that we must choose between one or the other. In our view, however, it is precisely the union of these two missions that is essential if both socioeconomic development and biological conservation are to become sustainable. Development for all people and all generations depends upon conservation. Likewise, the success of conservation itself depends upon how well its strategies serve people—especially those most directly affected by them, in particular the masses of the rural poor. One of our central points is that the fates of rural people and of conservation are inextricably woven together. This is especially true in the tropics, which serve as the principal geographic focus for the book.

1   Resident Peoples and Protected Areas: A Framework for Inquiry

Steven R. Brechin, Patrick C. West,
David Harmon, and Kurt Kutay

The purpose of this chapter is to establish a systematic framework for inquiry. We begin with a review of several key background issues: (1) a definition and typology of resident peoples in protected areas; (2) a classification of protected areas; and (3) an analysis of basic concepts in cultural preservation and rural development. Then the book's five major themes are reviewed: the historical and institutional context of the protected-area movement; the displacement of resident peoples; ecodevelopment and local-level sustained-yield utilization; ecodevelopment and tourism; and planning and decision processes of natural resource management and social change. First, however, let's begin with some definitions.

Resident Peoples: Definitions and Typologies

One of the major inadequacies of the current approach to the issue of residents in protected areas is the limited context in which the debate is taking place. Throughout the recent literature on the subject, emphasis is placed on "traditional societies," "native peoples," and "indigenous peoples." The terms are usually not defined and are often used interchangeably.[1] When people in the conservation community use these terms, the distinction they seem to want to make is between those who live harmoniously, in an ecological sense, with their immediate environment, and those who do not. In the recent conservation literature, it is often presumed that traditional societies, native peoples, and indigenous peoples do live in harmony with the environment; modern societies, colonists, and other nonindigenous peoples do not. Reality paints a more complicated picture, however. There are examples where members of traditional societies have harmed the environment of specific regions, just as there are examples where members of modern societies have coexisted rather well with their surroundings. These presumptions are diverting attention away from more central concerns:

whether human residency in protected areas is ecologically incompatible with most conservation objectives; and whether it is politically unavoidable, given the realities faced by many developing countries.

In this volume, resident peoples are simply those individuals, families, and communities—"traditional" or "modern"—that occupy, reside in, or otherwise use, on a regular or repeated basis, a specific territory within or adjacent to an established or proposed protected area.[2] The term "resident peoples" has several advantages. It carries no political connotations. It is also a term defined by space and not by time (as is the term "indigenous") nor as a cultural label.[3]

To help clarify our discussion of resident peoples, we present the following typology. It will be used to identify the type of residents found in the book's case study chapters:

Tribal peoples are those individuals and communities that are relatively isolated and politically autonomous kinship societies. An example would be Amazonia rain forest Indian peoples.

Acculturated tribal peoples are culturally and ethnically distinct groups, but acculturated to modern society. Native Americans are included in this category, as are Australian Aboriginals, the Kuna Indians of Panama, and others.

Peasant peoples are subsistence agriculturalists, with or without agricultural surpluses. People of this category may be engaged in a limited amount of cash cropping if the emphasis of their agricultural practices is on subsistence production. They may be ethnic or culturally distinct peoples with kinship ties, but are formally incorporated into state activities (such as taxation). Agriculturalists in most developing countries provide examples.

Farmers and rural citizenry are those who produce primarily for commercial markets (or assist others in doing so). Farm laborers as well as local farm suppliers are included in this category. The scale of activities may range from small to large. Examples include most agriculturalists in developed countries.

Local entrepreneurs are persons engaged in commercial activities as a result of the protected area's establishment. Examples include those who run inns and restaurants, guide tourists, keep supplies, shops, and so on, and can be found in developing as well as developed countries.

Protected Area Categories and Alternative Models

Over the last several decades or so, the International Union for the Conservation of Nature and Natural Resources (IUCN which recently changed its name to the World Conservation Union) has been developing and refining management categories for the world's protected areas. IUCN's Commission on National Parks and Protected Areas (1984) describes a comprehensive system of protected area categories. A matrix of these categories (adapted from Miller 1978) is in Table 1.1. Each category is defined by its conservation objectives. An essential difference between categories is the acceptable level of human use and alteration of the natural environment. For the purposes of this book, we define a protected area as any finite area of land or water that comes under a systematic managerial regime which itself includes some set of basic objectives to be accomplished.

More strictly protected natural areas, such as a natural monument, scientific reserve, or national park, may, by design, severely limit human intervention. The exception is where human interference is deemed necessary to perpetuate a desired species, biotic community, or physical feature that would otherwise disappear (Dasmann 1975; and Vin, this volume). For example, fires may be a necessary management strategy for maintaining particular desired species. In other cases, it is not uncommon to find human populations which have evolved as an integral part of an ecosystem, such that their continued interaction in the natural environment (grazing, farming, hunting, etc.) is necessary to maintain desired ecological conditions.

The objectives of other categories on the continuum place increasing emphasis on more direct human use and resource development. These include, for example, Protected Landscapes (Category V). Most often found in Europe, Protected Landscapes encourage controlled human use and alteration of the environment to perpetuate semi-natural ecosystems (IUCN 1987). Multiple-Use Management Area (Category VIII) is another category emphasizing managed human use of nature. National Forests in the United States provide an example where multiple-use principles allow exploitation of timber, forage, and wildlife, as well as host recreation, which may substantially alter the natural ecosystem. For this book, we have included an additional category. Category IX represents the planned use of resources by resident (includes those

Table 1.1 Alternatives for Management and Development of Natural and Cultural Resources

	Alternative Management Categories										
Conservation and Development Objectives	Scientific Research	National Park	Natural Monument	Nature Conservation Reserve	Protected Landscape	Resource Reserve	Anthropological Reserve	Multiple Use Management Area	Protected Area for Local Use	Biosphere Reserve	World Heritage Site
	I	II	III	IV	V	VI	VII	VIII	IX	X	XI
Maintain sample ecosystems in natural state	●	●	●	●	◐	○	●	⊘	◐	●	●
Maintain ecological diversity and environmental regulation	○	●	●	◐	◐	◐	●	◐	◐	●	●
Conserve genetic resources	●	●	●	●	◐	○	●	○	○	●	●
Provide education, research and environmental monitoring	●	◐	●	●	◐	○	◐	◐	◐	●	●
Conserve watershed production	○	○	○	○	◐	○	○	○	○	○	○
Control erosion and protect downstream investments	○	○	○	○	○	○	○	○	○	○	○

Provide sustenance and/or sport hunting and fishing

Provide for recreation and tourism

Produce timber and forage on sustained yield basis

Protect important cultural, historic and archeologic sites

Protect scenic resources and green areas

Maintain flexibility through multipurpose management

Support rural development through rational use of marginal lands and provide stable employment opportunities

KEY: ● Primary Objectives ◐ Secondary Objectives ○ Lesser Objectives ⊘ Not Important or Applicable
(adapted from K. R. Miller 1978, modified)

living next to protected areas) and local peoples. This multiple-use category differs from Category VIII by its designation for use and management by local peoples, yet provides for the protection of the area's special resources. The present Biosphere Reserve category would be a more restrictive sub-category.

In spite of this detailed and comprehensive system, one category, "national park," is the most frequently used in developing countries (IUCN 1985). The over-use of this category and the emulation of the United States park system in developing countries has added to the complexity of the resident peoples issue. The ideas that people should not live in protected areas or consume their resources are virtually synonymous with the national park ideal. This raises a major question of definition. Would there be a resident peoples issue if the accepted notion of what constitutes a national park changed, or some of the multiple-use categories attained the same status and political appeal? Would the problem exist at all if developing countries had adopted the British model, which has always included people (see Harmon, chapter 2), rather than the American model, or if the United Nation Educational, Scientific, and Cultural Organization's (UNESCO's) Man and the Biosphere program were better understood and more popular (Kellert 1986)?

There has been much debate among conservationists and others over the appropriateness of protected area categories across cultures. It has become quite clear that the categories as described in Table 1.1 are an ideal, while the management practice of conservation remains a much more muddled affair. To help sort out the matter, the first page of each case study chapter (chapters 2–27) in this volume lists the categories used. First is the official label, that is, the one used in its title (e.g., Exmoor National Park). Listed next is the type of category that best fits how the protected area is actually being managed, as characterized by the IUCN system (e.g., Exmoor is actually considered a protected landscape rather than a national park).[4]

We continue our background discussion on the resident peoples issue with an overview of concerns related to cultural preservation and rural development.

Cultural Preservation

Another way of viewing the resident peoples issue is not from the perspective of humans creating problems in natural heritage preservation, but from an integrated perspective of natural and cultural heritage preservation. Cultural heritage preservation has been a part of the national parks movement for many years, but usually merely as an interpretation of historical peoples or the physical remnants of removed populations. In the latter case there is a particularly strange irony in the policy of first removing a local people because they are "incompatible" with the park ideal, and then interpreting the culture using the now empty structures. Until recently this was the statutory policy of Parks Canada. For instance, in a Newfoundland park a traditional fishing village was removed at great financial expense, and local residents resented it greatly. The old, empty village buildings were used to interpret the cultural heritage of the area. What would have been lost, one wonders, if they had simply let the village exist as living history?

In many areas of the world today, cultural heritage preservation, in the form of protecting the rights of tribal and acculturated tribal peoples, is taking its place alongside natural preservation as a legitimate policy of the national parks movement. In Honduras, for instance, cultural preservation areas along with biological reserves are being created so that tribal peoples are able to maintain their traditional ways of life. In the Northern Territory of Australia, Kakadu National Park was established on Aboriginal lands in cooperation with the tribal council. The discovery of valuable uranium in the area has led to severe conflicts over resource extraction, nature preservation, and Aboriginal rights. Nevertheless, the presence of Kakadu has been an important institutional buffer at the federal level which has helped to protect Aboriginal rights in the face of the economic power of the uranium companies.

Other examples of convergence between protected-area establishment and cultural preservation can be found throughout the world: the Kuna Indians in Kuna Yala Biosphere Reserve in Panama (Gradwohl and Greenberg 1988); tribal peoples in the Xingu National Park in Brazil (Bodley 1982); Eskimos and the Kobuk Valley National Monument in Alaska, the United States (Bodley 1982); and Ozark cultures in Arkansas, the United States (Sax 1984).

It must be recognized, however, that cultural preservation will be a more important concern for some resident peoples than others: more for tribal cultures than peasants (or farmers) who are more integrated into the dominant society; more for Australian Aboriginals than residents of the New Jersey Pinelands. Cultural groups for whom this is an important issue are concerned not so much about being kept statically in what has been termed "enforced primitivism" (see Goodland, this volume). Rather, they desire the freedom to choose for themselves the extent to which they preserve the old or assimilate the new, and at what pace. Conservationists must work to preserve the right of self-determination, rather than some romantic ideal of primitivism—people with quaint grass shacks and the like. This entails dynamic, adaptive cultural change, including changing material culture, technology, and resource utilization patterns. This is a highly controversial issue in international conservation circles, but it is precisely the ability of humans to change that has made Homo sapiens the adaptive wonder of fauna species. It is because of this ability that the Earth is dotted with cultures as diverse as its biota.

The basic prerequisites for this broader conception of cultural preservation are detailed systematically in the chapter by Goodland (this volume). Based on anthropological research, Goodland's chapter documents four key "prerequisites" for cultural and ethnic survival in the face of externally imposed change, whether it be a hydroelectric project or a national park. These are particularly relevant for isolated tribal cultures but also for other cultural groups in varying degrees. These key factors are:

1. recognition of territorial rights
2. protection from introduced diseases
3. time to adapt
4. the right of self-determination

Those familiar with the history of international protected area policy and practice will immediately recognize that the first and fourth factors conflict with the traditional way conservationists have done business with local peoples in the international conservation movement.[5] Time to adapt has also been frequently ignored by planners eager to save the dwindling wildlands of the Earth. Less common are examples where the failure to protect resident peoples from introduced diseases has proved harmful, though there are cases involving tribal people. For instance, the highland Phoka peoples were displaced from Myika National Park in Malawi and resettled in lowland areas, where they were decimated by malaria to which they had no resistance (McNeely 1985).

It will be important to keep these four prerequisites in mind as you read through this book. They are a key part of the integrative comparative analysis in the book's final chapter. Those with a particular interest in cultural preservation may want to read Goodland's chapter first before going on to the case studies.

Rural Development

Another concern throughout the book is the implications of protected area policy, planning, and management for rural development among local people to help alleviate the rural poverty which is often present near protected areas. Here, as in the case of cultural preservation, concerns about rural poverty and rural development will vary according to the types of resident peoples. It should be the expressed desires of the peoples themselves that determine the degree of emphasis put on rural development and what relationship this has to cultural preservation.

Recently, IUCN's Commission on Ecology (1980b) and the *World Conservation Strategy* (IUCN 1980a) have emphasized the importance of alleviating rural poverty as an important consideration in conservation planning. From this, the concept of joining economic development with conservation, along with the phrase "ecodevelopment," emerged.[6]

The focus of this book is not economic development in general, but rather local rural economic development efforts directed at the poorer members of the community. These are the people who are most vulnerable and often most heavily affected by exclusionary policies of national parks and protected areas. Our particular concern is not so much for the large cattle rancher who has the resources to adapt—not to mention the power to demand—but rather for the peasant or tribal peoples whose daily subsistence and domestic commodity production needs have traditionally been met using park resources. It must be emphasized again that national and regional economic development do not always (or even

often) imply local measures aimed at benefiting the poorer
strata of resident peoples.

With respect to these peoples, we have adopted, as a provi-
sional orientation, Hough and Sherpa's (1989) recent cate-
gorization of rural development strategies in relation to
protected-area management. Hough and Sherpa distinguish
between three basic rural development strategies: "top-
down," "basic needs," and "bottom-up." Top-down models emphasize centralized, often highly capitalized programs where
investments and profits are externally controlled (Korten
and Klauss 1984). Most tourism development follows this approach. The centralized, top-down approach assumes economic benefits will trickle down to the poorer strata from the
efficient production of wealth in the national economy. The
problem with this strategy is that frequently few, if any,
benefits trickle down. Instead, one might say that the benefits drip down and evaporate before they reach the poor.
Moreover, as Nugent and Yotopoulus (1984) observe, there is
not infrequently a reverse trickle up, widening of the gap between rich and poor when the top-down approach is adopted.
We will see this phenomenon repeatedly throughout this volume with respect to certain forms of tourism development.
Not only do the local poor not benefit, they also suffer economic hardship (in terms of inflation) and negative social
and cultural impacts.

A second model, which stresses the provision of "basic human needs" (Leipziger 1981), would seem to be more appropriate at first glance as a humanitarian way of compensating
local people displaced by protected areas. Instead of letting
them use park resources, this approach advocates giving
them medical facilities, cash to meet their needs, and surplus
agricultural export food to compensate for the farming production which has been excluded from the park. Though
somewhat seductive, this strategy is deceptive. It substitutes
unproductive welfare services for a productive, possibly sustainable, economic base. It undermines self-sufficiency and
self-determination; it creates dependency and erodes cultures; it provides an entree for the penetration of consumer
markets, thereby increasing the addiction to modern goods
while undermining the long-term economic ability to pay for
that addiction. In short, it confuses "modernization" (Inkeles
and Smith 1974) with "development." A poignant case of this

is in Shkilnyk's (1985) already classic book, *A Poison St*
than Love. Shkilnyk presents a detailed study of the destruction of an Ojibway tribe in Canada following displacement
from their traditional reserve. In this relocation basic human
needs and modernization, as defined from the perspective of
the dominant culture, were stressed over productive rural
economic development within the boundaries of their traditional economy and culture.

Ironically, welfare reformers from both the left and right
seem to be converging on the same set of conclusions with
respect to the inadequacies of this approach to poverty. There
are elements that may be beneficial, such as improved medical services, but these elements alone without a sustainable
productive economy may represent a cruel deception.

The third perspective, the one which is emphasized in this
volume, is the "bottom-up" approach. It stresses appropriate
scale improvements in existing, productive local economic
systems. It encourages self-sufficiency, using sustainable resource bases for subsistence and small-scale market development. It entails full participation and control by local people
in planning for and implementing rural development projects
(Cernea 1985; Korten and Klauss 1984). While often incompatible with traditional exclusionary policies of national
parks, it will be argued that this strategy can work with a
revised model of protected-area management. Such a model
permits careful sustained extraction of selective resources
from within protected areas, combined with coordinated sustainable resource development, cottage industries, and the
like in buffer zones and the surrounding region.

The Integration of Cultural Preservation and Rural Development

Another important consideration in the selection of appropriate strategies is the effect rural development can have on
cultural preservation. On the one hand, viable rural economies are essential to cultural preservation; on the other, ill-
advised development can be highly detrimental to it. With
respect to resource development on American Indian reservations, West (1982b) has labeled this concern the "Identity-
Poverty Dilemma." Economic development projects can be a
two-edged sword. Thus, enlightened protected-area policy
and planning ought to be concerned with cultural preservation and rural development in an integrated sense, considering their mutual dependence and impacts on one another.

West (1982b) has also argued that the conditions most conducive to this mutual compatibility are local control of property rights, full participation in planning, and self-determination. As a working hypothesis, we believe that the bottom-up model of rural development is the one most likely to create these conditions. Note that this accords with Goodland's four prerequisites for ethnic identity and survival.

Bottom-up rural development, however, will not easily emerge on its own. Political will and financial resources will need to be mustered from the top down to support bottom-up activities (see Ayres 1981; Annis 1987; Brechin and West, 1990). International funding agencies and national governments will need to make bottom-up development a priority and give it substantial support if it is to be widely successful.

We turn next to an overview of the book's five major themes, beginning with the historical and institutional context of the resident peoples debate.

Theme 1: Historical and Institutional Context

The complex issue of the historical and institutional context of conservation is explored in part 1. The idea of a national park is, by and large, an American one (Nash 1970; Runte 1979). It grew from the American experience. Nash, as well as Harmon (1987:149), reflects that national parks are the product of an affluent culture, and that they emerged from a "context of boundless wealth, under the expectation that the natural resources left outside them were inexhaustible." Conservation needs and patterns are inseparable from any culture (Harmon 1987; Garratt 1984; Nietschmann 1984; Tucker, this volume), but the American national park ideal has become the model system of conservation for a large part of the world, enthusiastically imported by many countries.[7]

Unfortunately, the American ideal carries implicit meanings, political mandates, and management objectives that do not always fit circumstances elsewhere. The United States has always been a country with vast, sparsely settled lands. It is also a wealthy country where most of the population is now urban-based and does not need to subsist directly from the land. Also, the basic preservationist objectives of national parks fit nicely into our overall system, in which other protected areas are given over to multiple uses and managed for sustained-yield production in support of economic growth and development. Many developing countries lack this larger context.

The effects of colonialism on conservation also need to be considered. The establishment of large game parks in Africa and elsewhere for the pleasure of the elite, usually at the exclusion of others, has left its mark. Conservation, particularly parks, often represents to the poor majority the power and privileges of the wealthy and of outsiders. This has helped to separate parks and conservation from the daily activities and concerns of the poor majority, often making them the objects of scorn. Tucker (this volume) explores this perspective in an overview of conservation history of India.

The heart of the debate on conservation priorities and resident peoples lies with which resource management objectives should be emphasized, and how these can be chosen to fit a given country's history and culture. If the principal object of a protected area is strict resource protection, then the presence of residents may be incompatible—though not necessarily. On the other hand, if the object is to help maintain sustainable resource use for rural development, the presence of people within the protected area could be essential (see Harmon, this volume).

Theme 2: Displacement of People from Protected Areas

Until very recently, the establishment of national parks in the United States generally assumed the absence of human residents. In national parks, particularly, the government required the relocation of residents. The American park ideal exemplifies the notion of protecting intrinsic resource values over consumptive uses by local people, whatever the scale. What is too little understood, both by professionals and scholars alike, is the social impact of displacement and relocation. When resident peoples are forced to move, certain general impacts can be expected, but the collective social impact on the community (or other social organization) differs widely from case to case; to date, no model exists to predict the cumulative effect.

Although various forms of compensation can be used to soften the blow of dislocation, the concern here is the negative effects it can have on the rural poor. Relocation may place the cultural integrity of a group in jeopardy, as in the case of the Ik people of Uganda (Turnbull 1972; Calhoun, this volume). In addition to concerns of human rights, conservationists need to be aware of the effect that protected-area establishment, subsequent relocation, and denial of access to resources might have on the attitudes of local people toward the protected area itself. Stirring up discontent among the people at the doorstep of a protected area does not bode well for its future.

Many adverse social impacts on residents and consequential threats to protected areas can be avoided simply by discarding the notion that wholesale removal of residents is always necessary (see Raval, this volume). There is much evidence to suggest that resident peoples can live in harmony with the environment and in consonance with (and even furthering) management objectives. In cases where relocation is the best alternative, the social impacts on residents can be lessened considerably by involving them in the planning and relocation process. Meaningful participation of resident peoples in such matters should be facilitated when removal becomes necessary, always done with great circumspection, and avoided whenever possible.

When considering displacement, major consideration should be given to the social and economic structure of the region. Displacement in some societies might have greater impact on local people than in others. In areas where population densities are high, poverty extreme, social services and social welfare institutions weak or lacking, comparable replacement lands unavailable, and alternative employment opportunities restricted, the policy of displacing local residents may be much more harmful and thus less advisable. Social impacts may not be as great in areas where population density is low and alternative replacement lands as good as or better than those currently occupied (see Ntshalintshali and McGurk, this volume). The issue of displacement is discussed in chapters 4, 5, and 6 of part 3.

Theme 3: Ecodevelopment Based on Sustained Yield: Local Resource Utilization

National parks and other protected areas make up only a very small part of the world's land mass. One source lists the percentage of land in national protection status at 2.9 percent (WRI and IIED 1988:294).[8] A basic question asked by many preservationists is: Is it too much to ask to leave intact these very special areas and instead focus our attention on making the remaining nonprotected areas more sustainable and productive? There is a righteous appeal to this argument, but realities in the developing world force us to take a closer look at its validity. Certainly, securing improved productivity from land already in use is essential if development is to be rationally pursued and poverty reduced. This course of action should be followed vigorously. Yet, in many developing countries, poverty is deep and persistent. The rural poor constitute anywhere between 40 percent and 90 percent of these countries' populations, with actual numbers rapidly increasing (World Bank 1988). Can we realistically lock away precious resources in protected areas while poverty and starvation abound nearby? Or expect political support from governments to protect reserves under these circumstances?

Although the world average of nationally protected land is 2.9 percent, it obviously does not mean that the 97.1 percent that remains is available for productive use in general, let alone for the rural poor.[9] Arable land is scarce in many countries, and in some regions like Latin America what is available is often controlled by the wealthy few (see Barry 1987).

Where arable land is scarce and poverty deep, it is essential to find ways for protected areas to serve local needs. There is a growing list of examples where this is being done already. Thatch grass is harvested legally yearly by local people from the Royal Chitwan National Park, Nepal (Mishra 1982; Lehmkuhl et al. 1988). Used for roofs of huts and other domestic needs, the grass is scarce outside the park because of development. The Mapimi and La Michilia biosphere reserves in Mexico have provided tangible benefits to local residents, from improved grazing for ranchers to fruit production for local farmers (Halffater 1981; Halffater and Ezcurra 1987). Machlis and Tichnell (1985:19) list similar benefits to local people, ranging from bush meat to employment. A wide range of substantial benefits from the Annapurna Conservation Area in Nepal are being obtained by residents (Bunting et al., this volume). This unique protected area has been designed with resident people just as much in mind as the natural ecosystem and the paying tourist.

Local utilization of protected-area resources produces a number of thorny issues, however. How much use is too much? Which kinds of uses are appropriate? How should use be regulated over time, especially in those areas established specifically for the protection of tribal peoples? If management restrictions are inappropriate, the resource can become overused, or resident peoples can be subjected to enforced primitivism.

Attempting to distinguish between natural and introduced acculturation is also a difficult problem. Protected-area officials can adopt policies that allow for voluntary residency among a population in a protected area, with residents themselves deciding whether to retain their culture intact. The Kuna Indians of Panama have been very successful in this way (Wright et al. 1985; Chapin and Breslin 1984). Those who prefer a different approach to life can leave to fulfill those aspirations. This suggests the desirability of "elective primitivism," where a tribal people itself decides and controls the acculturation process (Clad 1982).

Ironically, elective primitivism may require the "traditional" society to possess a considerable degree of power and control over its affairs and have the sophistication and resources to negotiate with the dominant culture. These requirements may limit the elective primitivism option to highly acculturated tribal groups. Another drawback to elective primitivism is that the departure of members from an established community may alter the community's character and even diminish its viability. Regardless, the concept of elective primitivism does provide important and voluntary alternative courses of action for at least some tribal societies.

Theme 4: Nature Preservation and Ecodevelopment: Tourism

Wildlife and nature tourism is a big business, especially in Africa. In 1985 alone, Kenya netted $300 million from wildlife-associated tourism (IIED and WRI 1987:80). In some countries, there is intense pressure to link tourist-related income to park preservation. One case can be found in eastern Rwanda where the future of the relatively isolated Akagera National Park, which composes 10 percent of the country's land mass, is very much in question (Perlez 1988). Without tourism and the revenue it would generate, there will be too much political pressure to turn the park over for cultivation. Rwanda is one of Africa's most densely populated countries.

Although there are specific economic and political realities reflected in this example, they emphasize national-level issues and interests. Local resident peoples often do not benefit from tourism (Machlis and Tichnell 1985:18). In Kenya, most of the tourism-generated revenue remains in Nairobi where the safari companies are located (IIED and WRI 1987:81). A similar situation exists in the Galapagos Islands, where most of the profits remain on the Ecuadoran mainland or with expatriate companies (Bailey, this volume).

Tourism, however, does not have to be "big-time" to aid both local people and conservation. Perhaps residents benefit more when it is not. The Air and Tenere National Reserve in arid northern Niger provides an example where resources are being protected and the conditions for resident peoples bettered from a tourism development intervention (Newby and Grettenberger 1986; Brooke 1988). To protect the endangered addax antelope (*Addax nasomaculatus*), conservationists have collaborated with development experts to regulate tourist activities and improve the lives of the Toureg people in environmentally sensitive ways. Visitors are required to pay entrance fees and must hire local guides to see the addax. Previously, visitors were free to chase the swift animal, sometimes to its death, in their vehicles. Local guides enforce the park rules. It was also recognized that tourism will affect only a portion of the region's estimated 7,000 Touregs, so development programs are underway to work with them in conserving wood, water, and pasture land in the harsh Sahara Desert (Brooke 1988).

Tourism and development together may be sufficient to manage a unique species while improving the lives of resident peoples. In the Air and Tenere, a National Reserve category rather than a National Park category was intentionally selected to avoid any confusion. Helping the resident people was considered equally important to protecting the addax (Newby and Grettenberger 1986).

Tourism, however, can seriously affect natural resources. With the advent of the global village, recreation and tourism have come to have a considerable effect on many protected areas, even the most far-flung. Today's traveler can attest to the denuding of Sagarmatha National Park in Nepal by its residents in order to supply expeditions to Everest with fuel wood. Set in motion by a combination of political and institutional factors, a vicious cycle has emerged wherein the residents, made wealthier by illicit sales, have been able to better themselves materially by building larger homes—requiring ever-increasing amounts of fuel wood to heat (Jefferies 1982;

Weber, this volume). Tourism can be most damaging to local people when it is used as a panacea for their problems.

In Benin, modern tourist facilities in the Pendjari and "W" national parks have been touted as an answer to the chronic poverty of local people. The two parks currently receive low visitation to the existing primitive visitor facilities, which are built with endemic materials and maintained by residents of the park. Properly planned modern infrastructure, it is claimed, would not necessarily be detrimental to the surrounding ecosystem (Sayer 1981). If so, here would be a perfect opportunity for ecodevelopment through tourism. However, the opportunity appears lost. The atmosphere of consensus, so vital to ecodevelopment, has been hopelessly soured because residents have been denied the use of the park for hunting, a primary source of meat for their diet, while park rangers tolerate hunting by political elites (Hough 1989). Local residents are now no longer receptive to arguments about the benefits of tourism. Even if controlled hunting were restored to them, it seems likely their distrust of the park authorities would continue unabated (Sayer 1981; Hough 1989).

This example shows the futility of depending solely on the promise of tourism to correct past mistakes. If the park authorities had taken time to learn local desires and needs, they might have maintained limited access for local people to meat sources within the park and thus established an atmosphere of trust. Instead, they alienated the local people, hoping to redeem themselves by promoting tourism.

Similarly, it would be a mistake to use tourism as an economic stopgap. In Oceania, many communities formerly dependent on local fisheries now rely almost entirely upon foreign aid because their clan-based rights system collapsed. It has been suggested that traditional fishing practices can and should be preserved because they are of interest to tourists. Tourism based on these practices would be used as a bridge until economic considerations (such as a decrease in foreign aid) force the residents back to a self-sufficient fishing economy (Johannes 1982).

Behind this proposal lies the presumption that tourism can be turned on and off like tap water. Such thinking ignores the fact that when the end of the "bridge" is reached, many Oceanians will have developed a vested interest in the new tourism. The intended effect—the preservation of long-standing fishing techniques and knowledge—would be achieved, but only in the most superficial way.

Before any tourist schemes are introduced in the hope of benefiting the residents of a protected area, all the consequences must be thought through. Tourism, or the rejection of it, must be considered as an integral part of the protected area's management plan. In Benin, two seemingly unrelated managerial considerations, subsistence hunting and tourist infrastructure, turned out to be vitally linked. Some of the intricacies of ecodevelopment and tourism are discussed in part 5.

Theme 5: Planning and Decision Processes for Resource Management and Social Change

If conservation is to become sustainable, approaches and methods must be developed that more actively involve resident peoples in the planning and decision-making process. And since governments and outside funding organizations have considerable power in establishing conservation policies and implementing strategies, responsibility rests squarely on their shoulders to involve resident peoples.

There are a number of ways to accomplish this. They range from a nominal to an integral level of involvement. Examples of many of them are presented in part 6. Here, we review three major approaches: social impact assessment, conflict management, and co-management.

Social Impact Assessment. Social impacts generally refer to consequences, anticipated or not, of some preceding event or action that has altered the ability of a social unit (ranging from an individual to a community) to function as it has in the past. Consequently, social impacts, which can be physical or abstract in form, can either be negative or positive, depending on what has been altered, and its social value, as determined by the affected social unit. Discussions of social impacts usually center around negative consequences.

Social impacts have profound implications for the planning and management of protected areas. Park establishment and management procedures can severely affect the livelihoods and integrity of resident peoples—families, communities, and even entire cultures (see Calhoun [chapter 4]; Woo [chapter 22]; and Hough [chapter 23], this volume). The negative effects can also severely erode local support for the protected area. Without some minimal level of local support, managing a protected area, especially in heavily populated regions, is almost always a futile endeavor.

Social-impact assessment (SIA) can provide a framework to help determine the effects of conservation strategies on people. Freudenburg (1986:452) defines SIA as "assessing (as in measuring or summarizing) a broad range of impacts (or effects, or consequences) that are likely to be experienced by an equally broad range of social groups as a result of some course of action." Among its dimensions, most relevant to our discussion on resident peoples is that SIA can be used as a prospective planning tool. The goal is to "foresee and hence avoid or minimize unwanted impacts" (Freudenburg 1986: 452). Consequently, SIA can be used to weigh the impacts of various conservation plans on resident peoples before they are implemented. Although the SIA approach may or may not directly involve local people in the planning and decision-making process, it can provide a mechanism for those with power to consider alternative courses of action. The opportunity, at least, exists for decision makers to select alternatives more sensitive to the needs of the resident peoples. The chapter by Hough reviews further the applicability of SIA to the resident peoples debate.

Conflict Management. A normative protected-area model, which attempts to integrate local cultural values into natural area conservation, may be very difficult to achieve whenever tradeoffs between competing interests for use of the area cannot be avoided. Traditional methods of resolving conflicts over the use of public lands (at least in Western developed countries) often fail to reconcile conflicting claims of contending interest groups.[10] Susskind and Ozawa (1983:5) point out why this is especially a problem in environmental resource allocation decisions:

> Environmental disputes are characterized by substantial complexity, often heavy reliance on technical data and analysis, diffuse and unrepresentable interests (such as the interests of future generations), and substantial "externalities." Power relationships among interested parties may vary considerably, especially in terms of access to sources of information, ability to manipulate the media and public opinion, and availability of resources to garner support.

New approaches for resolving environmental disputes are necessary if conservation authorities are to involve local people in creating joint solutions to meet their needs, protecting traditional rights, and maintaining communication for mutual cooperation. Western approaches, such as litigation and other adversarial methods, may, however, be inappropriate for use in many developing countries.

What appears to be required is an interactive, consensus-agreement strategy. Conflict management techniques involving mediation and negotiation may work best (see Bidol and Crowfoot, this volume). At the same time, participating in mediation carries some risks for parties with very limited power, such as resident peoples. In order for this type of alternative to work, conservationists and resident people must seek out areas where their interests converge on a range of issues (see Clad 1982). But as noted by Hough (1988), the burden for action rests on those with power (i.e., conservationists and other government officials) to take the first substantial steps in a consensus-agreement approach.

Co-management. Co-management refers to the substantial sharing of protected-area management responsibilities and authority among government officials and local people. This arrangement contains inherent tensions. Conservationists fear sacrificing their ideals to local interests, while local people fear losing their control over resources to others. Obviously, compromise and consensus are essential ingredients to this approach. Although difficult to implement, the advantages of co-management can be significant, especially when conservation arrangements depend on local-level support. As noted by Pinkerton (1987), conservation strategies, when agreed upon in a true co-management framework, will be viewed as more legitimate by local people, and consequently will be supported by them. True co-management, however, seems to be difficult to find (Lawson 1985; Weaver, this volume). Various forms of cooptation may be more common. East (this volume) believes that Canada, at least in its northern territories, is making important strides in sharing control over natural resource management issues (see Griffith 1987; P. J. Usher 1987; Osherenko 1988). The topic of co-management and the controversies that surround its use are discussed in several chapters of part 6.

Conclusion   In this chapter we have reviewed briefly the contents of the book and, in the process, established a framework for inquiry. If this book has one central point, it is that if conservation is to become sustainable the interests of local people and conservationists must converge. Protected areas will not survive for long whenever local people remain impoverished and are denied access to needed resources inside protected areas. Likewise, local people will sink further into poverty unless they manage wisely and conserve their natural resources. But, for local people to support protected areas, park management must make some concessions to their interests. As a consequence, whenever possible, resident peoples should be allowed to remain and have access to resources on a sustained-yield basis. Displacement should be an act of last resort because of the social disruption that can result and the resentment of the park and conservation efforts that it will engender. However, if residents are displaced, how they are displaced is critically important.

It is interesting to note that while many developing countries have been busy emulating the American ideal of excluding people from national parks, some other developed countries have never had such policies, most notably Great Britain (Harmon, this volume). Others have been backing away from the ideal as well. For example, in Canada most new park expansion is taking place in the northern territories, impinging on Inuit and Indian populations. Recently, Parks Canada has made an about-face, and now stresses the importance of protecting living cultural heritage as part of the national park mandate. Revisions in the National Park Act of 1974 state that traditional communities are to be allowed to remain and their resource extraction to continue. Recent policy statements by the Director of Parks Canada (Kun 1979) and the Department of Indian and Northern Affairs (1978) also reflect this change.

Perhaps we are on the verge of a major shift in protected-area philosophy. The Western effort to protect, revere, and interpret the natural wonders of "our" national parks might have been an attempt to show, in part, that the old Christian ethic of at least spiritual separation of people and nature was faulty. But in so doing, we fell into the trap of buying the old dichotomy by physically separating and removing people from selected natural areas. Now, in the developed world, we may even be on the verge of seeing people truly as a part of nature. In Burch's (1971) words, perhaps, instead of viewing Homo sapiens as a noxious weed, our species may turn out to be an unappreciated wildflower.

NOTES

1. An exception is Goodland (1982), who provides more precise definitions of these terms.

2. The term "resident peoples" is meant to include those who live next to protected areas as well as in them. At times, when it seems useful to distinguish between these two groups, we use the term "local people" to denote those who live in the immediate vicinity.

3. We do not wish to appear insensitive to issues of minority rights or to the problems of cultural genocide that are occuring in some countries. Nor do we dismiss the primitivist-environmentalist approach (using conservation strategies, especially the creation of protected areas, for purposes of preserving "traditional" cultures from destructive acculturation—see Bodley 1982). In fact, we share similar concerns. Rather, we advocate supporting *all* people who are struggling to survive, particularly the rural poor (including those of the dominant culture).

4. For example, a protected area may be called a national park, but its actual management may better fit the protected landscape category.

5. There is some evidence that this approach is beginning to change. The World Wildlife Fund's Wildlands and Human Needs program provides a good example where conservationists are explicitly focusing attention on local needs and concerns. See chapter by Bunting, Sherpa, and Wright, this volume, for a description of the Annapurna Conservation Area.

6. More recently the term "sustainable development" has emerged and appears to be replacing "ecodevelopment." Sustainable development also denotes the union of conservation practices with economic development. While not universally accepted, the term has been embraced by many influential international bodies, most notably the World Commission on Environment and Development (WCED). The clearest explanations of sustainable development can be found in the WCED's report *Our Common Future* (WCED 1987) and in the 1988–89 *World Resources Report* (International Institute for Environment and Development and World Resources Institute 1987). Brechin and West (1990), however, see subtle differences between the two terms, at least in how ecodevelopment has been largely practiced to date. Sustainable development requires, by definition, a local-level focus and support. Ecodevelopment has mostly been practiced at the national level, often ignoring local interests and concerns.

7. The United States national park ideal is, of course, the notion of preserving vast pristine wilderness void of human presence. Not all United States parks live up to this ideal. As noted by one author, the parks in our system are a "motley collection" (Foresta 1984:9). Although it can be argued that our ideal notion of a national park has changed little over time, the model employed certainly has changed, beginning

with Canyon de Chelly in 1931 where, in cooperation with the Navajo Tribal Council, the Park Service manages the historic resources but owns none of the land. More recently, all Alaskan parks allow hunting, fishing, and trapping by local rural residents.

8. This particular figure represents those terrestrial, marine, and coastal parks and protected areas that form part of national-level protection schemes throughout the world. The figure is, however, only an average. A number of developing countries have more than 10 percent of their country in parks and protected areas.

9. Of course, not all protected areas contain arable lands. Some are remote mountain ranges, deserts, or other "less-productive" land and, consequently, they are not under as much pressure as is other, more arable land. This observation, however, does not detract from the central point made here.

10. For the sake of simplicity, this discussion describes a two-party dispute between park authorities and local people. Actually, there are often many competing interests within a local community, as well as between other outside parties, including those interested in commercial development.

Part Two   HISTORICAL AND INSTITUTIONAL CONTEXT

Natural beauty created by traditional agricultural activities *(above)*, Grasmere, Lake District National Park, England. *(Below)* Sickles, a village with a population of ca. 3,000, is just one of several villages within Annapurna Conservation Area, home to 40,000 residents.

Introduction   The growing conflict between national parks and resident peoples has been rooted largely in the basic conception of national parks as areas devoid of human habitation. This conception has been spread to the developing world in recent years by the International Union for the Conservation of Nature and Natural Resources (IUCN), which in turn borrowed heavily from the United States model of national parks.

In chapter 2 we learn that the developed countries could have spread a different model of national parks that is more sympathetic to human habitation and resource use. Harmon describes how the British concept of national parks in Great Britain differs radically from the United States' and IUCN's. People and their activities have, over centuries, shaped the landscape with a distinctly human touch. The British parks are not wilderness preserves as commonly found in the U.S., but rather protected landscapes. But to the British they are equally awe inspiring. Here, the people and the land have become inseparable and very worthy of protection. There are other important differences as well. Government ownership of land is pursued only for small areas within designated parks. The parks of the United Kingdom have always incorporated the principles of ecodevelopment involving sustainable resource use and rural development. A central mission has been to create and protect healthy rural economies. While parks in the developing countries fight against the onslaught of expanding agricultural production, British national parks seek to promote it and indeed worry about the decrease of the agricultural population within their national parks. In a comparative contrast, then, we see that the spread of the national parks concept to the developing world was a historical outgrowth of a particular cultural conception of a national park. It stems from the cultural and institutional forms of U. S. national parks, and thus is not a universal model.

Ironically, even regions of the developing world that were dominated by British colonialism tended to adopt a more exclusionary model of national parks and protected areas. A major case in point is the protected areas in India. In chapter 3 Tucker traces the origins of wildlife and forest conservation among the Indian elite and colonial British rulers of India. The historical origins of protected areas were rooted in

exclusionary preserves of the Indian elite prior to any impor-
tation of western notions of national parks. British colonial
rulers formed coalitions with indigenous elite in the founding of natural reserves long before the first British national
park was created. While later in their development Indian
national parks and protected areas were influenced indirectly by the early national parks movement in the United
States, with its policies of displacing resident peoples, it is
important to emphasize that these exclusionary policies were
historically rooted in indigenous elite attitudes toward agricultural peasants and tribal peoples within India itself.
Hence we cannot blame the United States model of national
parks for the exclusion of resident peoples in all cases. We
learn that the cultural and institutional preconditions within
the developing countries themselves are important in shaping the nature of modern policy debates over the role of resident peoples in protected areas.

2 National Park Residency in Developed Countries: The Example of Great Britain

David Harmon

PROTECTED AREA	National Parks
CLASSIFICATION	Labeled as: National Parks Managed as: Protected Landscapes, IUCN Category V
RESIDENT PEOPLES	Farmers and Other Rural Citizenry

The inherent difficulty of designating protected areas in Great Britain (as in all of Europe) is that they must be superimposed on a long-established order of land tenure. In Britain, even the remotest districts have known settlement for centuries, and displacement of residents is simply not a possibility in protected-area proposals.[1]

Over the years, the British people have become highly aware of the lay of the land and how they shaped it. Humans and landscape converge in the British eye, and national parks are no exception. "The richly varied landscape of our country is a joint creation of natural growth and man's cultivation," said an early park planner (Hobhouse 1947:9). Most recent observers have assented to this view. "The keynote," said one, "is continuity and gradual change, with man at the center of and integral to the rural landscape" (Blacksell 1982:14). This is a strong contrast to the conception of national parks in the United States, where residents are almost always excluded.

John Dower, the architect of the national park system in England and Wales, recognized the contrast.[2] In his pioneering 1945 report, "National Parks in England and Wales," he devised a definition to accord with conditions in Britain:

> A national park is an extensive area of beautiful and relatively wild country in which, for the nation's benefit and by appropriate national decision and action, (a) the characteristic landscape beauty is strictly preserved, (b) access and facilities for public open air enjoyment are amply provided, (c) wildlife and buildings and places of architectural and historical interest are suitably protected, while (d) established farming use is effectively maintained (Dower 1945:44).

The British national park need only contain "relatively wild country" rather than vast tracts of pristine land. And nowhere in the definition is public ownership called for.[3] Dower goes on:

> I do not regard the public acquisition of all or any great part of the land in National Parks as in any way *essential*. Indeed, except as part of some scheme of public acquisition of the freehold, or of the development rights in all land or at least all rural land, I should be opposed to the public acquisition of all or most land in National Parks, as certain to entail in practice a crippling limitation on the number and size of Parks to be secured [emphasis in original].

Dower envisioned a governing authority that would primarily use scenic control measures rather than outright acquisition to manage the park lands. He did want this authority to have a few powers of purchase. It should, he thought, be able to buy small, heavily used recreation sites and prominent "beauty spots," and be able to spend money to efface landscape disfigurements (Dower 1945:45–47). A later advisory panel—whose recommendations immediately preceded the creation of the Countryside Commission, Britain's overall national park authority—concurred in both his definition and analysis (Hobhouse 1947:40).

The Dower prescription has been followed ever since. Most

of the land in the ten national parks in England and Wales is
owned privately; only a tiny fraction belongs to the Countryside Commission (Leonard 1980:373). Each park is overseen
by a local authority. For two parks (Lake District and Peak
District), the authority is an independent planning body; for
the rest, the authority is a standing committee of the County
Council (Poore and Poore 1987:11).[4] (see Map 2.1).

This is not extraordinary, for national park development in
Britain has always given way to the needs and desires of the
local populace. The success of the parks is measured by how
well they invigorate the economy—and particularly the farm
economy—within them. Once again Dower set the tone, declaring that "the well-being of those who live and work in
[the national parks] must always be a first consideration"

Map 2.1

Protected Areas
of Great Britain

(Dower 1945:8). Others specifically identified farming as one of the "essential industries" that must flourish, unhampered by unnecessary controls or restrictions and protected as far as possible from inconveniences that might arise from an increased number of visitors" (Hobhouse 1947:8:21). In 1974, a blue-ribbon panel urged even more "recognition of the importance of farming to the purposes of national parks . . . and the need for measures to protect farmers from, and help them cope with, visitor pressure, so that recreational use of the national parks will not be at the farmers' expense" (Countryside Commission 1977:7).

Has this outlook fostered viable, genuine farming communities within the national parks? Recent statistics show a resident population of slightly more than 240,000 in the ten parks (see Table 2.1). Densities range from 2.4 per square kilometer (Northumberland) to 37.7 per square kilometer (Pembrokeshire Coast, the only lowland national park), with an average of 17.8 per square kilometer (Poore and Poore 1987:13, 16–46). These figures may suggest a healthy agricultural economy, but the Countryside Commission has its doubts:

> The popularly held view of a static and traditional system of upland farming is everywhere contradicted by the increasing numbers of sheep and cattle being kept on hill and upland farms by a declining number of farmers and farm workers: three-quarters of the farm employees have been lost from Snowdownia National Park in the last decade; two-thirds of the farmers and farm workers have left Northumberland National Park in the twenty years of its existence.

Yet the number of people living in the parks has remained almost constant; the apparent anomaly "is explained by the growing number of holiday and second homes which now account for up to 30 percent of the dwellings in some parishes" (Countryside Commission 1978:4–5; see also Leonard 1980: 370–375).

According to some critics, the declining number of farm workers in the parks can be attributed to the government's own agricultural policies, and they point to Exmoor National Park as a prime example. There, the Ministry of Agriculture, Fisheries and Food has given grants to landowners to modernize buildings, clear ground cover, and drain moorland.

Table 2.1 Resident Populations in Great Britain's National Parks

Park	Area (sq. km)	Residents	Density/ sq. km
Brecon Beacons	1,350	32,000	23.7
Dartmoor	945	30,000	31.7
Exmoor	686	10,000	14.6
Lake District	2,280	40,000	17.5
Northumberland	1,031	2,500	2.4
North York Moors	1,432	25,000	17.5
Peak District	1,404	40,000	28.5
Pembrokeshire Coast	583	22,000	37.7
Snowdonia	2,170	25,000	11.5
Yorkshire Dales	1,761	16,800	9.5
TOTALS	13,642	243,300	17.8

Source: Poore and Poore, 1987:13, 16–46.

Not only do these grants lead to the destruction of the moors—the very reason for the park's existence—but they also discourage traditional farm communities in favor of agribusiness (Mills 1982:33; McCormick 1982:34). As farmers continue to mechanize and consolidate, and as the government more vigorously promotes tourism in the park, the Exmoor labor force is transformed: there are now about 1,000 more full-time workers in the tourist industry than in farming (Poore and Poore 1987:24).

It was suggested, as part of a study of the Exmoor problem, that the Countryside Commission be given the power to issue "moorland conservation orders," that is, to impose conservation easements on resident farmers through a sort of condemnation process. The idea was discarded. Voluntary easements negotiated between residents and the park authorities were recently made legal, but few now exist. So far, the government has not abridged the rights of landowners in the parks in any way (Phillips 1988:40). The Countryside Commission and its local authorities cannot force an unwilling owner to do anything. Such powers were proposed as part of the Wildlife and Countryside Act of 1981 but dropped from the final law (Leonard 1980:379–381; Cherry 1985:136–137).

Landscape protection is the dominant concern of British protected areas because of the way they are set up in the law. The Countryside Commission is not legally required to protect park ecosystems. Still, anything it can accomplish along this line is incidental to the preservation of landscape value. Environmental conservation at the national level in England and Wales is officially the province of the Nature Conservancy Council, an entirely separate organization.[5] The Nature Conservancy Council and County Conservation Trusts have the power to designate strict National Nature Reserves and Local Nature Reserves, respectively, including lands they own within national parks. The extent of nature reserves within the parks is very small, however, amounting to less than 5 percent of the total area (estimate based on Poore and Poore 1987:16–46). The Nature Conservancy Council also has the power to protect important natural areas under the category "Site of Special Scientific Interest." The amount of land so designated within the national parks is somewhat larger—roughly 1,800 square kilometers all told, or a little more than 13 percent of the total area (Poore and Poore 1987:11).

At first glance, it seems that the failure to ascribe any strong environmental purpose to the national parks prevents them from reaching their potential as protected areas. This would indeed be the case if one of them were to hold the parks to IUCN's definition of a "national park" (its "Category II"): an area not materially altered by humans, which is also of outstanding scientific or natural interest (IUCN 1985:6). But the Countryside Commission acknowledges that the national parks are in fact Category V areas; that is, "protected landscapes" (Phillips 1988:38). The hallmark of a protected landscape is a special aesthetic quality which has resulted from human interaction with the land (IUCN 1985:8). Set against this measure, the British national parks are achieving much, though by no means all, of their potential. Yet by the same token, if they are truly to conform to IUCN's criteria, they should be formally redesignated as "national protected landscapes."[6]

The fact that landscape value predominates over nature conservation value in the national parks is not a consequence of their having residents, however. Rather, it is the price of a characteristically British "heritage approach" that

"seeks to conserve traditional qualities and national and regional characteristics in a living, in-use way rather than in a
museum sense" (Foster 1979:4).[7] This *has* resulted in large
resident populations, though more vacation homes and fewer
farmers can hardly be counted a success in conserving traditional rural characteristics. The goal is eminently worthy.
Nevertheless, exclusionary, publicly owned national parks
lack the flexibility to fulfill it. The example of Britain shows
that resident peoples in protected areas can be desirable in a
conservation system that prizes, above all else, a venerable
rural landscape.

NOTES

1. As of 1988, there were forty-nine national-level protected areas in
the United Kingdom, covering more than 1.5 million hectares or 6.4 percent of the national land area (World Resources Institute et al.
1988:295). Ten of these protected areas are national parks; all are in
England and Wales. Despite having much land amenable to designation,
Scotland has no national parks. There are a number of reasons for this,
but the most important is that the Scottish people rejected the call of the
original planners for public ownership of park land—a proposal never
made in England and Wales (Ramsay et al. 1945:21–26; Blacksell
1982:15; Foster et al. 1982:4).

2. A summary of the history of the park movement in England and
Wales before Dower may be found in Cherry (1985:129–131).

3. For a telling difference, see the definition proposed for Scotland
(Ramsay et al. 1945:24).

4. Each park is overseen by a local authority, two-thirds of whose
members are chosen by the County Council, with the remainder appointed by the secretary of state for the environment. Through a variety
of means the County Councils often achieve their purposes in the parks
(Brotherton 1985:48–56; Brotherton 1982:87; Leonard 1980:370).

5. The consequence, as one analyst puts it, is that when "the scientific
'service' went its own way in the form of the Nature Conservancy," the
national parks were left to become "the 'soft-centered' target for the
amenity conscious and the recreationists, attracting that irrational, in-
constant blend of emotion, sentiment, polemic, and fervor which has
proved both difficult to handle and vulnerable to political manipulation"
(Cherry 1985:131).

6. The Nature Conservancy also has the power to designate similar
reserves under the category "Site of Special Scientific Interest." Again,
however, the Conservancy has not placed any special emphasis on designating SSSI's within the national parks (Brotherton 1982:97–99).

7. For an interesting comparison, see the description of France's "intermediate nature parks" in Sax (1982).

3   Resident Peoples and Wildlife Reserves in India: The Prehistory of a Strategy

Richard P. Tucker

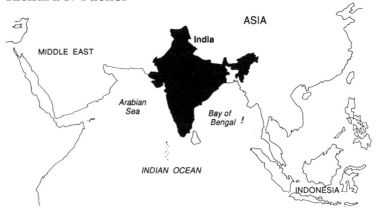

Systematic integration of local people into wildlife planning is a relatively new effort. Yet in most of the world there is very little true wilderness where wildlife does not coexist with human and domestic animal populations. Given this elementary fact, it is puzzling that a strategy that encompasses domestic as well as wild animal populations has taken so long to evolve. We are compelled to review the history of the conservation movement in each country to see the political, cultural, and natural setting in which the movement developed and to determine which constituent groups have played important roles in the movement, and what their priorities and preoccupations have been.

Many dimensions of wildlife conservation were constructed first in India and later adopted in other parts of the British Empire. The struggle to preserve India's wildlife heritage began more than a century ago, at the height of the imperial era, when its wildlands were coming under severe pressure from an ever denser population of humans and livestock. Under siege, the early conservationists favored only wildlife, and not until well after India became independent in 1947 were resident populations, either human or livestock, considered in detail. By then a series of attitudes toward peasants, tribes, and their livestock in relation to wildlife had evolved, providing the basis for more elaborate discussions of resident peoples in recent years.

The subject encompasses both agencies of the imperial regime and private civic associations; it includes both forest officials and hunter-naturalists, and both British colonialists and Indian aristocrats. Together their first priority over the years after approximately 1870 emerged as the effort to stave off extinction for big game species, which centered on the design and enforcement of laws controlling hunting and poaching. Until recently, it left little room for detailed understanding of the peasant and tribal communities' local needs in wildlife areas. Research focused on wildlife and habitat and was rarely integrated with the human and livestock population.

Following the colonial era, India went to war and succeeded in gaining self-rule in the 1940s. With their departure in 1947 the British also left principles for integrating the rhythms of wild and domestic life deeply embedded in India's approach to wildlands management.

The Rise of Modern Forestry and Game Management

Fundamental to the course of British rule in India was the inexorable expansion of arable land, at the expense of natural vegetation cover (Tucker and Richards 1983; Richards et al. in preparation). The achievement of increased agricultural production was a guiding moral and even the Forest Service maintained throughout the era that in any conflict between forest preservation and agricultural expansion, the food needs of the rural populace must have precedence.

Agriculture and urbanization expanded at the cost of massive forest depletion from the late eighteenth century onward (Stebbing 1922–1926). In each region the British quickly constructed military cantonments, civilian settlements and new transport facilities all providing commercial markets for timber. Then, in 1854, the great era of railway building commenced. Over the next thirty years Asia's finest railway network was constructed, consuming vast tracts of hardwood forest for supporting the rails and fueling the engines (Guha 1983; Tucker 1982).

In response to the massive cutting, high ranking officials established the Indian Forest Service in 1865, marking the first step toward wildlands conservation in the subcontinent. Foresters' three functions were profitable timber cutting, preservation of remaining forests, and providing for villagers' subsistence needs. The commercial function was the most successful, due to the high profits, praise from the higher reaches of government, and promises of more adequate departmental budgets. The third charge, to understand and meet the needs of resident peasants and tribals, was the function that the forest service was least equipped to carry out. In part this arose from the colonial character of the regime.

The heart of the issue, for forests and later for wildlife, was the system of Reserved and Protected Forests established in 1878. These reserves were given to the Forest Department to cut selectively or, in more remote and fragile areas, to preserve without cutting. The forestry hierarchy was empowered to establish restrictions on local use of the forests wherever necessary to assure regeneration of timber supplies. Thus emerged a competition between peasants who had never before been restricted in their access to fuelwood and fodder, and officials imbued with a tradition of enforcing detailed regulations. Management by restriction was expressed in many ways, including the standardized forms in departmental annual reports that compiled statistics of each year's forest offenses, fines imposed, cases brought to court, and cases resolved (Tucker 1986).

The preoccupation with legal forms and illegal actions bore heaviest on the forest rangers and guards. Of low rank, they had little motivation for controlling forest offenses; they could be tempted to blackmail other peasants with threats of punishment, or could easily be bribed. Later as gun licensing and anti-poaching laws were set into place, poachers learned the unwritten rules of the game against the forest guards as quickly as firewood gatherers had.

By 1900 the Forest Department regulated access to the Reserved Forests not only for wood and fodder but also for game. It issued gun licenses to villagers (as distinct from sport hunters from outside) explicitly to defend their fields and livestock from predatory wild animals. In these and other ways the foresters' relations with the village economy were complex, not entirely adversarial.

The Nongovernmental Conservation Movement

In the same years a movement was launched to declare certain Reserved Forests closed to all human exploitation, so as to preserve endangered game species from extinction. This fledgling national parks movement saw little legitimate place for any human or livestock residents in the vicinity of endangered game. From its inception, major impetus came from voluntary organizations outside official government agencies.

In 1883 the Bombay Natural History Society was founded, providing a meeting place for wildlife enthusiasts both Indian and Western, both private and official. Sponsoring field studies of animals, fish, and birds of the subcontinent, the Society quickly established standards respected internationally for the recording of natural history. Equally important, it became a hunters' club and emerged as imperial India's national lobby for controlled hunting.

Provincial game associations appeared in the same years, the first and most influential being the Nilgiri Game Association, founded in 1879 in the hills of south India and dominated by tea planters. More than one important nature reserve in the Nilgiris today was formerly a tea-planter's reserve whose wildlife habitat was protected by the Nilgiri Game Association (Bedi and Bedi 1934; Phythian-Adams 1893, 1927, 1929, and 1939).

By 1900 another powerful Indian component of the conservation movement emerged: several leading "Native Princes," rajahs who began to realize that game species were being rapidly depleted in the ancestral hunting reserves. In close parallel to European aristocratic tradition, an essential element of Indian courtly life was the social ritual of *shikar*, the aristocratic hunt, which re-enacted both the warrior's fighting prowess and his social dominance in peacetime (MacKenzie 1988). In the nineteenth century important rajahs regularly hosted British hunting parties, a social and diplomatic coalition that produced appalling slaughter of game because improved technology was now available from Europe (Burton 1952; Phythian-Adams 1939).

Several major rajahs began adapting British India's game laws to their own hunting reserves; some hired professional game managers. But there was a difference from British India. Most rajahs held unfettered personal authority to frame and enforce laws in their domains. Being autocrats, rooted in medieval times, they tended to levy harsh and instant punishment on poachers in their personal reserves (Stracey 1963). One of the most powerful, the Maharajah of Kashmir, summarily removed the human population from the Dachigam deer reserve in the high mountains in about 1910; in British India the government had no such power (Holloway et al. 1969).

The movement primarily emphasized avoiding extinction of endangered quadrupeds, and secondarily regulating hunting of those birds and animals that still flourished in safe numbers. The legislative means to achieve this were laws linked to the forest laws. First, they prohibited taking valuable animals and provided penalties for breaking the new restrictions. Second, they provided a licensing system which for a fee legitimized a hunter, like a fuelwood gatherer, in claiming the resource if local foresters considered it to be in adequate supply.

For British India as a whole, the Forest Law of 1878 enshrined many provisions regulating shooting. In the same year several provinces put in place complementary legislation designed to protect specific endangered species, including elephants and one-horned rhinoceros (Phythian-Adams 1939; Gee 1950). Enactment was one thing, however; implementation was far more difficult.

The Acceleration Movement, 1918–1939

World War I and its aftermath brought fundamental changes to India. Among them were greatly accelerated threats to its wildlands and consequently new initiatives from the nature protection movement. The war led immediately to a dramatic rise in commercial game poaching because of greatly increased access to sophisticated breechloading rifles (Phythian-Adams 1939). The war also brought the automotive era to India, constructing new road networks into forested areas previously accessible only by foot, horse, or elephant. By the early 1920s many new cars appeared in India; the era of the townsman-hunter was beginning, and new technologies made possible more wanton killing than even the mass shikars (Seshadri 1969).

In these years India drew heavily from other continents in shaping its strategies, and, in turn, contributed considerably from its own path-breaking experience, for its leading conservationists had close ties at high levels in Europe. The international parks movement began with the creation of Yellowstone National Park in 1872, but after the virtual elimination of the native population in North America, parks were never faced with the problem of resident human and livestock populations to nearly the degree that park planners would face elsewhere. The North American model in this way was a risky one to adopt in the colonial countries of the tropical world, but this became evident only slowly.

In 1900 the European colonial powers launched a series of international conferences to plan wildlife reserves (Boardman 1981). The first conference, held in London, produced the first wildlife convention for Africa, stressing the need for more effective regulation of hunting. In 1933 conservationists met again in London to design the landmark International Convention for the Protection of the Fauna and Flora of Africa. The links between that conference and India led in both directions: Indian models for colonial wildlife management were used in the conference discussions, and the new convention spurred two years of major changes in India itself.

In 1934 the Indian National Parks Act became law, embodying many years' experience of game laws and their implementation. Regarding resident peoples in protection areas, the act defined which human visitors could enter the game reserves, with which licenses and at which seasons. But this focused on sport hunters; regarding resident tribal and peasant populations, it was almost silent.

A year later Corbett Park, India's first modern national park, was established, covering ninety-nine square miles of prime tiger habitat in the Terai jungles at the foot of the Himalayas (Burton 1951a). The problem of resident human and livestock populations there was not severe, for the incidence of malaria was so high that only a scattering of Tharu tribals, immune to the anopholes mosquito, could survive the monsoon rains there (Ford-Robertson 1936).

The new law and its first park came at a difficult time for wildlife management, for funds to administer forests and game reserves were shrinking in the Depression years, making it ever more difficult to guard against poachers. In response the United Provinces Wildlife Preservation Society, assisted by the BNHS, organized a major conference in New Delhi in 1935 (Burton 1953).

The familiar conservationist theme dominated each province's report. Endangered species must be preserved at all costs. More national parks were needed. Budgets for control of poaching must be increased. In addition, leading wildlife enthusiasts were beginning to explore the implications of how habitats could be reconciled with a human presence, and in particular, what the economic implications might be for villagers in and near the new game reserves.

First were the universally accepted principles that gave farmers rights of subsistence and self-protection near forests, and access to wood and grasses. But their licensed guns, used for crop protection in the nights before harvest, enabled the farmers to turn into predators in other seasons. One forester urged more sport hunters to hire the best local *shikaris* to guide them in the wilds, arguing that this would give an income to poachers and establish at least momentary control over them.

The question of poaching for subsistence, and beneath it the issue of resident peoples in wildlands, often concerned the habitats of the tribal peoples who had long been the primary inhabitants of India's hill regions. Though their subsistence patterns varied widely with the ecological setting, many were bird and animal hunters. With the fast-accelerating market for bird meat at elite dinner tables and bird feathers on international markets, many tribes had their first access to cash incomes from snaring game birds and selling them to urban-based traders. By the 1920s this commercial trade had gained massive proportions, endangering many species of game birds (Abdulali 1942; Ogden 1942).

Conservationists alarmed at this trend blamed not the tribals themselves, for many British held a romantic and paternalistic view of the tribals. Instead, they centered their wrath on the urban traders and exporters who callously exploited both the game and the hunters. The New Delhi conference reflected this in declaring that traders in birds must be stopped; if the market for bird poaching could be curtailed, tribals would no longer be corrupted (Burton 1953).

Shifting cultivation, the other aspect of tribal life that had a direct impact on wildlife habitat, was a very different problem, and British officials had long insisted with near unanimity that it had reached a dangerous scale. Tribals must be encouraged or pressured to settle into permanent tilling of individually owned plots. In sum, foresters and conservationists were confronting the intricate web of tribal life as the market economy, and population increase began to change the basis of tribal subsistence.

Peasants presented a very different set of dilemmas, not the least of them the regulation of their livestock. The New Delhi conference in 1935 repeatedly raised the dangers of epidemic cattle diseases spreading to hoofed wildlife. Conference participants were convinced that these epidemics, of both domestic and wild cattle, were becoming more severe and frequent as India's domestic cattle population inexorably increased.

Two broad approaches arose to confront the challenge of cattle disease. First was to organize large-scale vaccination campaigns (Burton 1953). This approach assumed that limiting the cattle population was virtually impossible, and it implied a willingness to improve the conditions of domestic populations in or near important wildlife habitats. But the principle was not pursued in any detail; no study resulted on how resident peoples' subsistence systems could be balanced with the remaining wildlife.

The second approach to the livestock problem at the New Delhi conference was more fully consistent with the conferees' largely negative approach to the claims of resident villagers. Several speakers urged strict limitations on the number of cattle allowed to graze in the sanctuaries during the hot, dry months and then the monsoon rains, when grass resources were at the most delicate stages of their growth cycles. Only as many cattle should be admitted as would not endanger the fodder needs of the wild ungulates. This principle gave the needs of wildlife precedence over those of domestic cattle, in contrast to the accepted principle that humans in the villages must have access to reserves for legitimate subsistence needs.

In sum, by 1935 the conservation movement had achieved mature studies of wildlife species and their habitats, had designed detailed laws to assure the preservation of rare fauna, and was increasing its awareness of the full range of life in critical ecosystems. Serious attempts at a detailed understanding of adjacent human and livestock populations, or their interactions with wildlife ecology, had hardly begun.

**World War II
and the
Transition to
Independence**

The decade of the 1940s was a difficult time for total self-rule
to come to India. The Second World War brought devasta-
tion to wildlife interests as great as the first had done. Once
again guns by the tens of thousands flowed into rural India
as a consequence of the war, enabling many more peasants to
become hunters and poachers than ever before (Stracey
1963).

During the war the Forest Service was stretched to the
limit of its resources of money and men. All its energy had to
be turned to harvesting timber as war material, wherever
possible, by accelerating rotational cutting schedules. Some
foresters departed for the war, leaving the management of
forests severely understaffed, and wildlife protection had to
remain an afterthought for the next six years.

The end of the war led quickly to independence under the
new Prime Minister, Jawaharlal Nehru. Two major segments
of the subcontinent became Pakistan, but what remained in
India encompassed most of the major wildlife areas of the
subcontinent. The tensions of these transitions had discouraging effects. In the Terai jungles of the north, Corbett
National Park had been clearly delineated, and no part of it
could now be alienated for the plow. But new lands had to be
found for resettling masses of Sikh and Hindu refugees from
West Pakistan, and only some of them could take farmland
from which Muslims had been evacuated; therefore Forest
Department lands were designated (Anonymous 1947). Today, four decades later, large areas of what had been Terai
forests support extremely successful ex-Punjabi farmers,
across the border from similarly cleared foothill jungles in
Nepal.

Clearing forests for settlement of Sikh refugees was at
least an administratively orderly operation; other events
were not. In many parts of India, game was besieged by
hunters. In both British and Princely districts, peasants
went on a rampage of poaching, for the old regimes were
dead; what better way to celebrate than to violate their most
galling laws (Seshadri 1969; Stracey 1963; Prakash and
Ghosh 1976).

The first decade of India's independence brought a fundamental shift in her economic and political priorities, toward
accelerated economic development both rural and industrial.
The 1950s saw a major expansion in the acreage under crops;

by the end of the decade virtually all viable agricultural soils
and much marginal land came under the plow (Farmer
1974). In addition, regional marketing networks and expanding urban centers, particularly in hill areas, placed new pressures on forest and wildlife zones.

Closely linked with agricultural expansion in a monsoon
climate with its long, dry season was the launching of India's
great multipurpose hydropower dams. In the Himalayan
foothills, the first of the great dams, at Bhakra, was completed in 1960, inundating farm and forest land. East of
there the Ramganga River flowed into the Ganges through
part of Corbett Park. When its dam was completed in 1972,
the finest grazing area for the park's wildlife was lost in
order to meet the human needs of the plains district down-
river (Kandari and Singh 1982).

Wildlife planners and foresters watched the construction of
the high dams with mixed emotions, recognizing the need to
harness the power and regulate the rivers, yet seeing more
clearly than the engineers the threat to watersheds and wildlife. In this setting, the arguments for the economic benefits
of wildlife habitat took on new sophistication, for as Burton
argued for the BNHS, reforestation would benefit not only
wildlife but village agriculture and hydroelectric dams'
watersheds as well (Burton 1951b).

Fortunately, Nehru, who exercised enormous power until
his death in 1964, understood the urgency of preserving India's compromised wildlands. As an urban and cosmopolitan
man he cultivated a romantic vision of the potential harmo-
nies of peasant and tribal life. The leading Indian conservationists, whether the rajahs or the urban-based naturalists in
Bombay and elsewhere, had personal access to Nehru. The
social basis of the pre-independence movement had survived
the difficult years largely intact, and also remained influential in the international conservation network through the
IUCN (Burton 1950). Together with Nehru they constructed
a new and far more ambitious legal and administrative
structure for wildlife preservation.

In 1949 Nehru established a National Wildlife Board. Its
constitution charged it "to preserve the fauna of India and to
prevent the extinction of any species and their protection in
balance with the natural and human environment" (Burton
1953:ix). The emphasis was still on preservation of endan-

gered species, but the board's principles could be understood
to encompass the needs of resident peoples' in the vicinity of refuges. In the 1950s many additional national parks
and wildlife refuges were established; their administrations
posed difficult questions of priorities. Wildlife management
remained a secondary branch of the Indian Forest Service.
There was no separate professional track for wildlife biologists, and Forest Department budgets remained chronically
inadequate to support wildlife research and management. Finally, shortly after 1980 the central government resolved
that wildlife management should be separated from forestry
and made an autonomous agency (Saharia 1982). The conservationists' desire for greater professionalization of wildlife
managers was achieved, but at the cost of adopting a more
fragmented approach to balancing wild and domestic life.

The growth of more aggressive rural political lobbies in recent years has led in that direction, for rural and "backward"
constituencies have increasingly learned to exercise their
leverage in India's structurally democratic system. Because
many major wildlife habitats are also tribal areas, the rise of
tribal political movements has great potential significance
(Singh 1982). As tribal habitats have become degraded in recent decades, the conflict between tribals and state forest departments has intensified. In this political setting it has
become less adequate for any forester or wildlife manager to
stress merely the destructive aspects of tribal hunting traditions, although P. D. Stracey's wildlife textbook for forestry
trainees in 1963 still took that perspective, reflecting the dis-
couragement of his long years in the service. "Forest dwelling communities are invariably inveterate hunters and have
in most areas practically annihilated the game animals and
birds by indiscriminate hunting and snaring. It is surely
time to instill in the tribal mind a respect for the basic game
laws of the country" (Stracey 1963).

By the 1960s the old ambivalence of hunters, foresters,
and conservationists toward the tribals was hardening into
an almost total hostility as the habitat inexorably declined.
This in itself was reason to search for fuller understandings
of the forest peoples' subsistence as they struggled to avoid
cultural extinction.

Part Three   **DISPLACEMENT OF PEOPLE**
             FROM PARKS

Maldhari
children in a
resettled
Maldhari
settlement near
Talala Village,
Gir National
Park, Gujarat
State, India.
Below: Typical
Maldhari house
and yard.

Introduction   In part 3 we present three cases involving displacement of resident peoples from national parks in developing countries. The removal of resident peoples has become standard procedure in national parks and protected areas in developing countries. Yet this policy has usually been followed with little regard for the negative social impacts it can have on the displaced people and their social and cultural organization.

The degree of negative social impacts that will occur from forced displacement depends upon a variety of social, economic, and cultural conditions. In our first case study (chapter 4) we see that the displacement of the Ik tribe with the formation of a national park in Uganda had disastrous impacts on the Ik, leading to a total unraveling of their culture and social organization. Calhoun's chilling account is based on the work of anthropologist Colin Turnbull and his book *The Mountain People* (1972). This case represents, perhaps, the worst case scenario of the negative impacts that forced displacement can have on local people. Because of the extreme nature of this case we must be careful that we do not dismiss it simply as rare or atypical. The differences in this case from others may be only a matter of degree, not of kind; all resident peoples may feel the negative effects of forced displacement in varying degrees.

At the same time, we should recognize that there are some combinations of social conditions under which sensitive programs of displacement can be done carefully with a minimum of negative social impacts. In chapter 5, Ntshalintshali and McGurk describe a case in which the displacement of resident peoples from a national park in Swaziland had few negative impacts on the displaced peoples. They describe a number of social conditions that stand in stark contrast to the case of the Ik's displacement that make this case highly successful in minimizing negative social impacts. We present a systematic comparison of these contrasting factors (drawing also on other comparative cases) in our comparative conclusion to the book. This represents the beginnings of a comparative theoretical model that can help predict the degree of negative social impacts that any given displacement from a protected area may have. From this model we also derive a policy guideline that displacement should only be considered where social conditions are favorable for successful displacement.

Standing between these extremes is the case of the displacement of the Maldhari herders from the Gir National Park in the state of Gujarat India (chapter 6). While no detailed social impact analysis has been done on this case of displacement we expect that negative social impacts will be greater than the Swaziland case but less severe than in the case of the Ik.

The Gir case also illustrates our second major policy guideline with respect to displacement—that displacement should only be considered where there is convincing evidence that resident peoples are seriously affecting the resources of the park. In the Gir there is significant scientific doubt about the effect of the Maldhari's cattle and buffalo grazing on the food supply of the Asiatic Lion. Berwick's (1976) research argues that the Maldhari's cattle and buffalo do not displace habitat for the wild ungulates that are the source of the lion's diet. The evidence from this research is clearly strong enough that, at least, the park authorities should have conducted research to test these findings further before they moved unilaterally to displace the Maldhari.

4 Plight of the Ik

John B. Calhoun

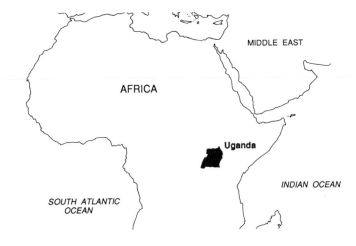

PROTECTED AREA	(Kidepo Valley) National Park

CLASSIFICATION	Labeled as: National Park
	Managed as: National Park, IUCN Category II

RESIDENT PEOPLES	Tribal Peoples

The Mountain—how pervasive in the history of man. A still, small voice on Horeb, mount of God, guided Elijah. Earlier, Moses stood there, before God, and received the Word. And Zion: "I am the Lord your God dwelling in Zion, my holy mountain."

Then there was Atum, mountain, God and first man, one and all together. The mountain rose out of a primordial sea of nothingness—Nun. Atum, the spirit of life, existed within Nun. In creating himself, Atum became the evolving ancestor of the human race. So goes the Egyptian mythology of creation, in which the Judaic Adam has roots.

And there is a last Atum, united in his youth with another mountain of God, Mt. Morungole in northeasternmost Uganda. His people are the Ik, pronounced "eek." They are the subject of an important book, *The Mountain People*, by

Colin M. Turnbull (1972). They still speak Middle-Kingdom
Egyptian, a language thought to be dead. But perhaps their
persistence is not so strange. Egyptian mythology held that
the waters of the life-giving Nile had their origin in Nun.
Could this Nun have been the much more extensive Lake
Victoria of forty to fifty millennia ago when, near its borders,
man groped upward to cloak his biological self with culture?

Well might the Ik have preserved the essence of this ancient tradition that affirms human beginnings. Isolated as
they have been in their jagged mountain fastness, near the
upper tributaries of the White Nile, the Ik have been protected from cultural evolution.

What a Shangri-la, this land of the Ik. In its center, the
Kidepo Valley, 35 miles across, home of abundant game;
to the south, mist-topped Mt. Morungole; to the west the
Niangea range; to the north, bordering the Sudan, the Di-
dinga range; to the east on the Kenya border, a sheer drop of
2,000 feet into the Turkanaland of cattle herdsmen. Through
ages of dawning history few people must have been interested in encroaching on this rugged land. Until 1964 anthro-
pologists knew little of the Ik's existence. Their very name,
much less their language, remained a mystery until, quite by
chance, anthropologist Colin M. Turnbull found himself
among them. What an opportunity to study pristine man!
Here one should encounter the basic qualities of humanity
unmarred by war, technology, pollution, and overpopulation.

**The New
Meaning of
Laughter**

Laughter, hallmark of mankind, not shared with any other
animal, not even primates, was an outstanding trait of the
Ik. A whole village rushed to the edge of a low cliff and
joined in communal laughter at blind old Lo'ono who lay
thrashing on her back, near death after stumbling over. One
evening Iks around a fire watched a child as it crawled
toward the flames, then writhed back screaming after it
grasped a gleaming coal. Laughter erupted. Quiet came to
the child as its mother cuddled it in a kind of respect for the
merriment it had caused. Then there was the laughter of in-
nocent childhood as boys and girls gathered around a grand-
father, too weak to walk, and drummed upon his head with
sticks or pelted him with stones until he cried. There was the
laughter that binds families together: Kimat, shrieking for
joy as she dashed off with the mug of tea she had snatched

from her dying brother Lomeja's hand an instant after Turnbull had given it to him as a last token of their friendship.

Laughter there had always been. A few old people remembered times, twenty-five to thirty years ago, when laughter mirrored love and joy and fullness of life, times when beliefs and rituals and traditions kept a bond with the "millions of years" ago when time began for the Ik. That was when their god, Didigwari, let the Ik down from heaven on a vine, one at a time. He gave them the digging stick with the instruction that they could not kill one another. He let down other people. To the Dodos and Turkana he gave cattle, and spears to kill with. But the Ik remained true to their instruction and did not kill one another or neighboring tribesmen.

For them the bow, the net and the pitfall were for capturing game. For them the greatest sin was to overhunt. Mobility and cooperation ever were part of them. Often the netting of game required the collaboration of a whole band of one hundred or more, some to hold the net and some to drive game into it. Between the big hunts, bands broke up into smaller groups to spread over their domain, then to gather again. The several bands would each settle for the best part of the year along the edge of the Kidepo Valley in the foothills of Mt. Morungole. There they were once again fully one with the mountain. "The Ik, without their mountains, would no longer be the Ik and similarly, they say, the mountains without the Ik would no longer be the same mountains, if indeed they continued to exist at all."

In this unity of people and place, rituals, traditions, beliefs, and values molded and preserved a continuity of life. All rites of passage were marked by ceremony. Of these, the rituals surrounding death gave greatest meaning to life. Folded in a fetal position, the body was buried with favorite possessions, facing the rising sun to mark celestial rebirth. All accompanying rituals of fasting and feasting, of libations of beer sprinkled over the grave, of seeds of favorite foods planted on the grave to draw life from the dust of the dead showed that death is merely another form of life and reminded the living of the good things of life and of the good way to live. In so honoring the dead by creating goodness the Ik helped speed the soul, content, on its journey.

Such were the Ik until wildlife conservation intruded into their homeland. Uganda decided to make a national park out of the Kidepo Valley, the main hunting ground of the Ik. What then happened stands as an indictment of the myopia that science can generate. No one looked to the Ik to note that their hunter-gatherer way of life marked the epitome of conservation, that the continuance of their way of life would have added to the success of the park. Instead they were forbidden to hunt any longer in the Kidepo Valley. They were herded to the periphery of the park and encouraged to farm on dry mountain slopes so steep as to test the poise of a goat. As an example to the more remote villages, a number of villages were brought together in a tight little cluster below the southwest pass into the valley. Here the police post, which formed this settlement of Pirre, could watch over the Ik to see that they did not revert to hunting.

These events contained two of the three strikes that knocked out the spirit of the Ik. Strike No. 1: The shift from a mobile hunter-gatherer way of life to a sedentary farming way of life made irrelevant the Ik's entire repertoire of beliefs, habits, and traditions. Their guidelines for life were inappropriate to farming. They seemed to adapt, but at heart they remained hunters and gatherers. Their cultural templates fitted them for that one way of life.

Strike No. 2: They were suddenly crowded together at a density, intimacy, and frequency of contact far greater than they had ever before been required to experience. Throughout their long past each band of 100 or so individuals only temporarily coalesced into a whole. The intervening breaking up into smaller groups permitted realignment of relationships that tempered conflicts from earlier associations. But at the resettlement, more than 450 individuals were forced to form a permanent cluster of villages within shouting distance of each other.

These problems are what Dr. Turnbull's book on the Mountain People is all about. Just before Turnbull arrived, Strike No. 3 had set in: starvation. Any such crisis could have added the coup de grace after the other two strikes. Normally, the Ik could count on only making three crops every four years. At this time a two-year drought set in and destroyed almost all crops. Neighboring tribes survived with their cultures intact. Turkana herdsmen, facing starvation and death, kept their societies in contact with each other and continued to sing songs of praise to God for the goodness of life.

By the beginning of the long drought, "goodness" to the Ik simply meant to have food—to have food for one's self alone. Collaborative hunts were a thing of the past, long since stopped by the police and probably no longer possible as a social effort, anyway. Solitary hunting, now designated as poaching, became a necessity for sheer survival. But the solitary hunter took every precaution not to let others know of his success. He would gorge himself far off in the bush and bring the surplus back to sell to the police, who were not above profiting from this traffic. Withholding food even from wife, children, and aging parents became an accomplishment to brag and laugh about. It became a way of life, continuing after the government began providing famine relief. Those strong enough to go to the police station to get rations for themselves and their families would stop halfway home and gorge all the food, even though it caused them to vomit.

The village reflected this reversal of humanity. Instead of open courtyards around each group of huts within the large compound, there was a maze of walls and tunnels booby trapped with spears to ward off intrusion by neighbors.

In Atum's village a whole band of more than one hundred individuals was crowded together in mutual hostility and aloneness. They would gather at their sitting place and sit for hours in a kind of suspended animation, not looking directly at each other, yet scanning slowly all others who might be engaged in some solitary task, waiting for someone to make a mistake that would elicit the symbolic violence of laughter and derision. Homemaking deteriorated; feces littered doorsteps and courtyard. Universal adultery and incest replaced the old taboos. The beaded virgins' aprons of eight- to twelve-year-old girls became symbols that these were proficient whores accustomed to selling their wares to passing herdsmen.

One ray of humanity left in this cesspool was twelve-year-old, retarded Adupa. Because she believed that food was for sharing and savoring, her playmates beat her. She still believed that parents were for loving and to be loved by. They cured her madness by locking her in her hut until she died and decayed.

The six other villages were smaller and their people could retain a few glimmers of the goodness and fullness of life. There was Kuaur, devoted to Turnbull, hiking four days to deliver mail, taunted for bringing food home to share with his wife and child. There was Losike, the potter, regarded as a witch. She offered water to visitors and made pots for others. When the famine got so bad that there was no need for pots to cook in, her husband left her. She was no longer bringing in any income. And then there was old Nangoli, still capable of mourning when her husband died. She went with her family and village across Kidepo and into the Sudan where their village life turned for a while back to normality. But it was not normal enough to keep them. Back to Pirre, to death, they returned.

All goodness was gone from the Ik, leaving merely emptiness, valuelessness, nothingness, the chaos of Nun. They reentered the womb of beginning time from which there is no return. Urination beside the partial graves of the dead marked the death of God, the final fading of Mount Morungole.

My poor words give only a shadowy image of the cold coffin of Ik humanity that Turnbull describes. His two years with the Ik left him in a slough of despondency from which he only extricated himself with difficulty, never wanting to see them again. Time and distance brought him comfort. He did return for a brief visit some months later. Rain had come in abundance. Gardens had sprung up untended from hidden seeds in the earth. Each Ik gleaned only for his immediate needs. Granaries stood empty, not refilled for inevitable scarcities ahead. The future had ceased to exist. Individual and social decay continued on its downward spiral, in the wake of the National Park. Sadly Turnbull departed again from this land of lost hope and faith.

NOTE
1. This chapter has been adapted, with permission, from an article with a similar title published in 1972 by the *Smithsonian* 3 (8): 19–23.

5   Resident Peoples and Swaziland's Malolotja National Park: A Success Story

Concelia Ntshalintshali and Carmelita McGurk

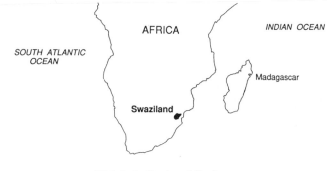

PROTECTED AREA	Malolotja National Park
CLASSIFICATION	Labeled as: National Park Managed as: National Park, IUCN Category II
RESIDENT PEOPLES	Peasant Peoples

High in the northeastern part of the Drakensburg Mountain Range is a unique national park in Swaziland; it is a success story in which the conflict between resident peoples and parkland seems to have come to a mutually satisfactory settlement. There are some factors in this case study that could have existed only in Swaziland, but many strategies could be applied to other countries. To understand the complexity of this situation, the park itself will be described first, followed by the history of its establishment, the important participatory role of the king, his control over landownership, and how the culture of the people plays an integral part in the story.

Malolotja National Park Area

Malolotja National Park lies in northwestern Swaziland in the ecological region known as the Highveld. The Highveld is predominately grassland with evergreen hardwoods along the river valleys. Because of the high rugged mountains, this

cool area is poor for farming, although it has the highest
average rainfall in Swaziland (1270 mm per annum). The
area that is now the reserve includes 175,000 hectares of
spectacular mountain scenery and the mountain of Ngwenya
(1828 m)(see Map 5.1). The park is named after the Malolotja
River, which tumbles over numerous waterfalls including
Swaziland's highest, the Malolotja Falls (with nearly a 100 m
vertical drop).

The creation of Malolotja National Park ensured the pre-

Map 5.1
Malolotja
Nature Reserve,
Swaziland

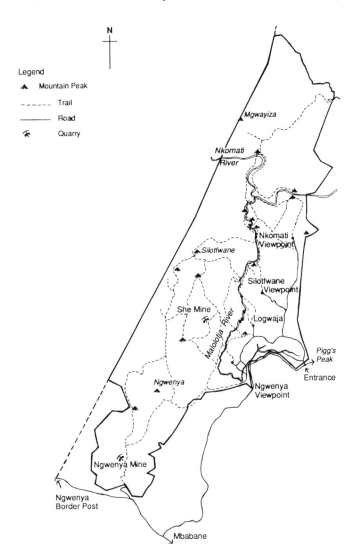

servation of an area which has unique flora, fauna, and geology. Significant populations of impala, wildebeest, besbuck, zebra, and rhinoceros have been established as a result of wildlife reintroduction schemes. Over 230 species of birds have been recorded: the Park is particularly important habitat for blue swallow and blue crane; and there is a flourishing bald ibis colony on the cliffs above Malolotja falls. The flora of Malolotja is perhaps its greatest attraction—throughout the year there is a variety and abundance of wildflowers.

The entrance fee at Malolotja is reasonably affordable for most Swazi citizens. The Park entrance is located near a bus stop, making it accessible to the many people who do not have cars. Just inside the entrance is a small office area and visitors center that has displays on the flora, fauna, and geology of the Park, and on the trails to be hiked. Currently, there are plans to establish an environmental education center in the Park that will include overnight accommodations for school groups. The funds are being raised by the Malolotja staff and Peace Corps volunteers.

History of Malolotja's Establishment

The situation could have been much different had the Park not been established. The rich natural resources undoubtedly would have suffered from further exploitation, as was the historical trend. At one time the whole area was filled with wildlife, but in the 1800s the Boers and English spread through southern Africa. They encouraged the harvest of wildlife by trading goods for skins and furs. Later, sport hunters and poachers contributed to the decline of wild populations.

A rich mineral potential has long been recognized in this area. The 1886 Transvaal Gold Rush reached Swaziland in the 1890s. Gold mining took place at Forbes Reef, along the southeastern border of the park. Several small abandoned mining sites are located within the park boundaries. Asbestos deposits were discovered at Havelock, just north of the Park, in 1919. Commercial mining has been going on at Havelock since 1939 and continues today.

As early as 1959 requests were made to the then British Colonial government to create a national park system for Swaziland; Malolotja was selected as one of the most suitable areas. This decision was based on extensive investigation of both the habitat and the problems associated with displacing

already established Swazi families. Proposals for the procla-
mation and development of Malolotja were then submitted to
the British Colonial government. These were turned down on
the grounds that they were too extravagant.

In 1972, four years after national independence, the Swazi
people established the Swaziland National Trust Act, which
included the establishment of the Swaziland National Trust
Commission. The function of the Commission included the
creation and promotion of national parks, nature reserves,
monuments, sacred places, and the National Museum.

King Sohbuza II was actively interested in forming the
Park. In the same year, he appointed Prince Bhekimpi, Chief
of Enkaba, to buy private farms from those freeholders in the
Malolotja area who were willing to sell, so that these lands
could be turned into a national park. Interestingly, Prince
Bhekimpi was one of the chiefs whose land was also to be
incorporated into Malolotja. This was a strategy of the king;
getting the local chief involved in the project would make
him feel he had an important responsibility and lessen his
resentment of losing land. J. S. Matsebula, from the Swazi
National Trust, was also involved in the negotiations, which
took place from 1972 to 1978.

Negotiations for the national park took place between
1972 and 1978, a long time because of the many details involved in the transfer of land. Sixty-three Swazi families,
mostly under Chief Bhekimpi, had to be removed. Understandably, these families resented the move. The king personally gathered these families together and asked if their
farmland was good. They answered that basically it was not;
it was too rocky and cold. To defuse the situation and as an
incentive to cooperate, the king offered to move these people
to a better area.

The king bought the Hawana Farm in the Middleveld for
the resettlement of these people. In addition to good soil and
more arable land, this farm had the advantage of a fairly
well developed infrastructure of roads and water. The move
provided economic and health improvements for the families
who moved. There was no resistance mainly because of the
peoples' inherent trust in the king. The king's involvement
created a smooth transition and Malolotja National Park
opened in 1979.

Today, families that remain located near the park can buy

inexpensive game meat, which is sold by the Park to control the animal population. The meat, sold throughout the year, includes wildebeest, impala, duiker, and warthog. This is important to the people's diet, and helps to minimize the problem of poaching. The park also contains lakes which are stocked with fish, although this is of secondary importance. Fish is not a major source of protein for the Swazi people: living in a landlocked country, they do not traditionally eat fish.

Elements of Management Success

Land Tenure and the King

In order to understand how the Park has successfully handled resident peoples, it is important to look at the Swazi culture and society. The king's control over property rights was an important factor. In Swaziland there are three types of landownership. During the British reign until 1968, urban administrative centers were known as "Crownlands." Today these lands may be privately owned, but they are now under the authority of the local Town Councils.

On Freehold land people must own title deeds. This portion of the land belongs primarily to whites, most of whom are absentee landowners. Swazis, however, are gradually buying this farmland. The Hawana Farm, which the king bought for relocating the people, was this type of land.

The third type of landownership is Swazi National Land. It comprises approximately 66 percent of Swaziland. Much of Malolotja National Park was settled as Swazi National Land. Swazi National Land is communal and belongs to the people; there is a hierarchy that exists in its administration. Basically, the king "owns" the land for the benefit of all the people. The chiefs are the eyes of the king and distribute the land for him. In theory, the people "own" the land, too, since they are Swazi people and have user-rights on the land distributed to them.

The people who were moved from the Malolotja area had lived there for many generations. The Swazi National Land on which a family lives was inherited from their forefathers; however, they do not own the title deeds. It is possible to ask for more land, or for good reasons the land could be taken away from a family. Therefore, technically, the families of Malolotja knew they did not own the land. If a family wants to move from one place to another, they have to inform their current chief that they will be leaving. They must also apply to the new chief and his *Libandla* (men's council). The council will ask questions, such as why the family is moving. When they are satisfied of legitimate need they may grant the family land on which to build a home and plots for farming. Anyone can use the communal grazing land.

King Sohbuza II set up the *Lifafund* (literally, inheritance fund—for future generations) to buy land for the Swazi people from foreign landowners. The money was raised by each homestead donating one of its herd. The cattle were sold and the money was used to buy back the land. This was how the king was able to purchase the Hawana Farm in the Middleveld for the resettlement of the people. Gaining more land for the Swazi people is recognized as one of King Sohbuza II's great accomplishments.

Culture   Three major elements of Swazi culture and tradition were very important in relocating the families from the park: the language, the king, and sacred beliefs. The Swazi people are part of the Ngunis of southern Africa; this allows for easy communication between Swazis and other Ngunis, such as the Zulus who are the neighbors in the south and as far north as the Ndebeles in Zimbabwe. Therefore, one aspect, which is uncommon in many countries of the world, is that all the people of Swaziland speak one language (*siSwati*) and follow one leader, the king. This universal language provides easy communication throughout the country even though many older people may not be literate. When the families of Malolotja were relocated from the Highveld to the Middleveld, the language and culture of this new area were the same. In many countries moving families to a new region would not work as well because of different ethnic groups, languages, and cultures.

King Sohbuza II (called Ngwenyama, "the Lion" in siSwati) was the longest reigning monarch in the world. He reigned from 1921 until his death in 1982. Even while under the British rule, the people of Swaziland considered their king's word more important than that of the resident commissioner, who represented the British throne. In 1973 the king repealed the Westminster Constitution, which was not well understood and was not in keeping with the Swazi way of life. The king leads the nation in preserving Swazi customs and traditions, and the people honor and trust the king.

King Sohbuza II was a very strong supporter of wildlife conservation; his personal support for the park as an asset for the entire country made it more acceptable for the people who were displaced. A son of King Sohbuza II, Prince Makhosetive, was crowned King Mswati III in April of 1986.

The traditional beliefs of Swaziland revolve around ancestral spirits. The spirits are considered to be sacred, and their powers are believed to be extensive. The fact that Malolotja contains many burial sites was an issue of great cultural sensitivity. In other areas of the country it has been necessary to move the remains of the ancestors before beginning new projects. However, in setting up Malolotja, the decision was to leave the remains in the Park, so that they would not be disturbed in any way. If one of the elders or family members wishes to visit a grave site, they ask permission to enter the park and do not have to pay. This action has removed a potential source of conflict between the resident peoples and the park.

Conclusion

Conflict and local dissent frequently occur when homesteads are suddenly designated as parkland. A solution was possible in the case of Malolotja because 1) the displaced families were not left on their own to find new areas for settlement; 2) they knew that the land belonged to the king; 3) the special personal interest that the king displayed for the people softened the hardship of leaving an area where all forefathers originated and were buried; 4) the move was to an area which was culturally similar and where the farmland was better; and 5) there was an understanding that the park was for the benefit of the whole nation, including those displaced.

In the larger context, this case study illustrates the very important role that opinion leaders play in the establishment of new parkland. Both the king and the local chief in this case were genuinely concerned about the welfare of the people and did everything they could to help. Also, the incentives of a park, if possible, should be for the long-term betterment of the people. In some cases this may involve an ongoing process, as with the situation of selling game meat to the nearby residents. The area where the people were relocated contained better farmland and a more sophisticated infrastructure—providing positive long-term effects for the people.

6   The Gir National Park and the Maldharis: Beyond "Setting Aside"

Shishir R. Raval

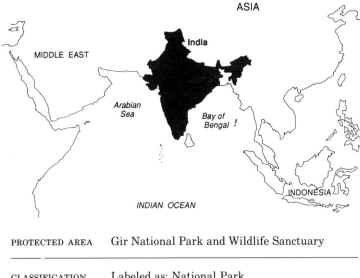

PROTECTED AREA	Gir National Park and Wildlife Sanctuary
CLASSIFICATION	Labeled as: National Park Managed as: National Park, IUCN Category II
RESIDENT PEOPLE	Acculturated Tribal Peoples (Indigenous Cattle Herders)

The issues concerning protected areas in the Third World countries transcend mere matters of "enjoyment" primarily by the rich and privileged visitors to such areas. Political and economic considerations tend to take precedence over virtues of conservation of natural and cultural resources. One of the most crucial issues is that while achieving short-term economic benefits, through tourism or timber harvesting, a healthy and long-term sustenance of the local resident peoples and their culture has often been overlooked. The adopted management actions frequently result in displacement of the resident peoples on the grounds that they over-exploit and damage the natural resources of a park that should remain undisturbed by human actions. The land is then "set aside" so that recreational, educational, and scientific benefits can be enjoyed by the people—who are often outside visitors.

While this concept may seem adequate enough for most of the protected lands in the developed countries, it may not yield desired results in many less-developed countries. Historical factors, such as old land tenure systems, colonial exploitation, and a higher rate of population growth combined with intrinsic cultural values, uses, perceptions of natural landscape, and economic considerations, give rise to unique concerns and management problems that may go well beyond the physical boundaries of a designated protected area.

This chapter examines cultural implications of national park concepts and management actions for the resident peoples of one of the most unique designated protected areas in the western plains of India—the Gir National Park and Wildlife Sanctuary in the State of Gujarat. The historical background, physical characteristics, resident peoples, management practices, and the resulting issues are discussed. Finally, relevant future directions are suggested for better understanding and management of the Gir and similar areas in India and other Third World countries.

Background

Historical Setting

India is one of the oldest civilizations with a rich heritage of cultural values that helped to evolve and maintain some of the best traditions of adoring and conserving Nature (Bandyopadhyay et al. 1985; and Chaitnya 1982). Conservation efforts are as old as the history of India itself. In ancient India, every type of life form was protected in the *ashram* (a sanctuary to learn and work in a natural setting) and the *abhayaranyas* (the "protected" or "no-fear" forests). Interwoven with the Hindu religious belief that all life forms are created equal is a respect for all forms of life. This tradition was further reinforced by sincere patronage provided by the kings for protecting the wildlife, forests, rivers, and hills.

It seems ironic that in spite of having rich cultural heritage and knowledge for conserving the natural resources, India in the modern times of today has to relearn and adopt external models for nature conservation. Perhaps these values have eroded from most parts of the country; however, they are still alive but remain limited mainly to rural and tribal India. These areas and their people, especially those who exist within or near a national park or other types of protected areas, are affected most frequently by the implementation of national park management goals and methods that are primarily developed in the western world.

During the Moghul dynasty and later under British rule, India suffered a great loss of wildlife primarily due to rampant hunting. The first relatively recent and explicit effort to protect a natural landscape was made in 1935 when the first national park was established in the foothills of the Himalayas, called the Corbett National Park (Sankhala 1969). The post-independence surge for development and, in turn, the shrinking of natural habitats prompted the establishment of the Indian Board for Wildlife Preservation in 1952, the Department of Environment in the mid-seventies, and the Ministry of Environment and Forests in 1985. Wildlife is given legal protection by the central government, and the state's forest management practices have to comply with the National Forest policy. Management of the forests, wildlife, and related tourist facilities within a national park is primarily the responsibility of the respective State Forest Department. These efforts mark the beginning of the planned governmental crusade for management of parks in India (see Tucker, this volume, for details).

To suit political and economic interests of the state, the policy makers and management agencies seem to interpret and modify the broad IUCN guidelines for the management of designated protected areas. Most of the efforts for conservation seem reactionary, fragmented, and on an ad hoc basis. There is a general lack of comprehensive policies, concerted effort, and accountability to conserve ecosystems as well as to cater to the needs of the resident peoples within or along the periphery of a protected area. For example, for the Gir Sanctuary area a rubble wall, one meter high and about 400 kilometers long, was built in the mid-seventies in order to keep the outside people and their unauthorized livestock out of that area, and to clearly demarcate the boundary. While such measures may help achieve the major management objectives to conserve and protect natural forest ecosystems, and to save the Asiatic lions from extinction, they also show a lack of integrated policy planning that takes into account the long and wide-ranging needs of, and impact upon, the people living in and around the sanctuary.

Physical Factors   The Gir National Park and Wildlife Sanctuary are located in parts of Junagadh and Amreli districts in the Kathiawad (also known as Saurashtra) Peninsula of Gujarat State (see Map 6.1). The total area of the Gir is 1412.13 square kilometers. It is approximately 77 kilometers east-west and 45 kilometers north-south. This area was constituted as the Gir Wildlife Sanctuary in 1965. A core area of 258.71 square kilometers was declared a national park in 1974 (Saharia 1982). It is one of the largest contiguous tracts of designated protected area in India serving primarily for the conservation of its native fauna.

Physiographically, this area is hilly with moderate valleys and plateaus. It rises above the flat semi-arid agricultural lands, with elevations ranging between 225.8 and 648.6 me-

Map 6.1
Gir Wildlife
Sanctuary and
National Park
in the State of
Gujarat, India

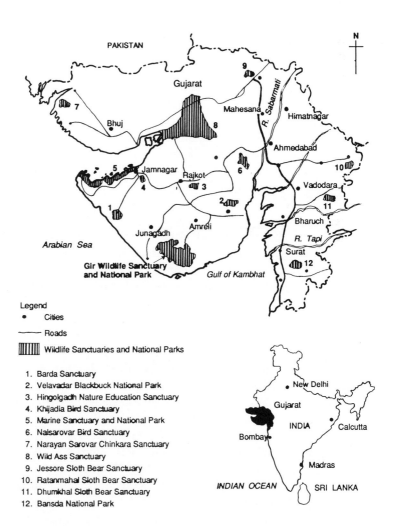

Legend

• Cities

—— Roads

|||||| Wildlife Sanctuaries and National Parks

1. Barda Sanctuary
2. Velavadar Blackbuck National Park
3. Hingolgadh Nature Education Sanctuary
4. Khijadia Bird Sanctuary
5. Marine Sanctuary and National Park
6. Nalsarovar Bird Sanctuary
7. Narayan Sarovar Chinkara Sanctuary
8. Wild Ass Sanctuary
9. Jessore Sloth Bear Sanctuary
10. Ratanmahal Sloth Bear Sanctuary
11. Dhumkhal Sloth Bear Sanctuary
12. Bansda National Park

ters. Nine small rivers flow from the hills supplying water to the surrounding agricultural fields and settlements. Fertile black soil of volcanic origin is found on the gentle slopes leading into the plain agricultural lands where groundnut, sugarcane, cotton, mango, and coconut, the most productive cash crops, are grown.

Climatically, the Gir lies in a semi-arid tract, and on average every third year is a drought year with less than 50 centimeters of rainfall. A cool, dry season prevails from late October to February with lowest temperatures around 10°C, and a hot dry season prevails from March to June with high temperatures reaching 43°C. The average rainfall varies from 80 centimeters in the extreme east to 100 centimeters in the west. The vegetation type is tropical, mixed dry deciduous forest dominated by teak (*Tectona grandis*) and its several associations, especially with grassy scrubland.

Wildlife

All these factors have given rise to a set of physical conditions that are conducive for diverse wildlife and particularly the Asiatic lions (*Panthera leo persica*) for which the Gir is the last natural abode in the world today. Major predators are panther, jackal, jungle cat, and hyena. Ungulates include spotted deer, Indian gazelle, nilgai, antelope, and four-horned antelope. Wild boars and langoor monkeys are also abundant. In addition, twenty-four reptile and 310 bird species have been recorded.

Historically, the Gir has been treated as a critical wildlife refuge. The pre-independence hunting of the wild species; the post independence population, agricultural and urban expansion; and a general development surge have all caused a decline in the quality and quantity of wildlife and their habitat. However, in the recent past, the causes for such a decline in the Gir have often been attributed to the local resident people, their cattle, and their lifestyle. Although this is partially true, this is not the whole story. Forces external to the Gir National Park affect the protected area in more subtle ways. The local resident people have become largely scapegoats in the broader context of the mismanagement of the natural and cultural resources and inadequately planned, short-sighted development programs. Therefore, it is important, first, to understand the local resident people, their ways of life, and how the park management practices affect this population.

The Maldhari

The "Maldhari," as they are locally known, are the main residents in and around the Gir; they lived there before and after the establishment of the National Park. Since ancient times the main occupation of these pastoral communities of tribes, such as the "Charan" and "Rabari", has been cattle herding. These pastoral communities that once extended throughout the grass and scrub forests of the Kathiawad region were forced to confine to the Gir, the Barda, and the Alech forests as the agricultural, urban, and industrial expansion began in post-independence India. There were about 845 families of Maldhari, with a total population of about 4,800, and 17,000 cattle living in 129 *nesses* (semipermanent settlements made with vegetative products, dung, and mud) in the Gir (Government of Gujarat 1975 and Desai 1976). In 1989, there were about 60 nesses existing in the sanctuary area.

The Maldharis are kind, hospitable, and courageous folk. Some of them are bards and poets. Their life is closely woven with the natural cycles, the wildlife, and their cattle. This bond with the place, the events, and the wildlife is manifested in innumerable folk legends and songs famous in the region. The Maldharis have very strong family bonds. They are poor and their worldly belongings are few. They have dedicated themselves to husbandry of the regionally famous Gir buffaloes and cattle. Their economy is based on the milk of these cattle from which they make *ghee* (refined butter) which they sell in nearby villages. Some sell milk directly to the dairy and earn more profit. Being vegetarians they cause no direct harm to the wildlife. Through years of close association with the wildlife they have become very perspicacious judges of lion behavior and are known for their traditional ways of living alongside the wildlife of the Gir.

Conflict Between the Maldhari and the Park: Assertions and Reality

There have been two main factors related to the Maldharis that are often cited as the major causes for the deterioration of the natural conditions of the Gir and the decline of the lion population. First, the cattle of the Maldhari overgraze the forest area and thus accelerate habitat deterioration; second, the lion population declines due to poisoning of the lions by the Maldharis. Both these factors represent a serious and grim threat to the existence of the national park. However, this is not the full story because many external forces beyond the domain of the Maldharis of the Gir affect the protected area.

It is true that overgrazing by cattle is a serious problem in some parts of the Gir; it can reduce the regeneration capacity of the native flora because of continuous trampling of the soil. But the government agencies and the experts who reviewed this situation in the late sixties and early seventies may have misjudged the implications of this phenomenon. They seem to have believed that overgrazing by domesticated cattle reduces the natural forage for the wild ungulates, thereby reducing their population size and in turn affecting the availability of natural prey for the lions. Therefore, the presence of the Maldharis and their cattle is conceived as the root cause for the deterioration of the habitat quality and the size of the wildlife in the Gir—a sure reason to displace the Maldharis from the protected area.

Indeed, the studies conducted by Stephen Berwick (1976) in the early seventies showed that grazing does deteriorate the regeneration capacity of the forest, that this does result in displacement of quality native flora, and also that if protected from extensive grazing the forest can return to its natural mix of rich native flora. This indicates a need for better management practices that, while closing the critical wildlife habitat from human influences, provides for the fodder needs of the cattle upon whose healthy existence the subsistence of the Maldharis depends. However, one of the most important findings of Berwick, overlooked by the decision makers, is that grazing by the cattle does not create a competition for forage between the wild ungulates and the domesticated cattle. Berwick clearly stated that the vegetation species and therefore the niche for the ungulates are clearly different from the ones for the cattle. The ungulates primarily browse and do not graze like cattle. Hence, the notion that the presence of cattle in the Gir affects the availability of forage for the ungulates and thereby reduces growth of the natural prey population for the lions may be largely misconceived.

Moreover, the circumstances that really accentuate the overgrazing and the resulting deterioration of the natural conditions within the protected area are mainly external. In the Gir area there occurs a frequent and extensive influx of the pastoral people from the distant surrounding plains during periods of drought. This happened most recently during the severe drought of 1986 and 1987. During this drought, hordes of cattle descended on the park area when about four hundred forest staff, who help protect the park, were on strike, demanding higher wages. This caused severe damage to the wildlife and the forest. The Maldharis were forced to lob the trees to support their own cattle.

It is indeed sad that instead of effectively catering to the fuelwood and fodder demands outside the protected area to resolve this seasonal influx of the migrating cattle and people, the Gujarat Government has taken steps, apparently in good faith, to displace the indigenous resident people of the Gir. However, the State Forest Department officials seem to have done a commendable job during the 1986–87 drought years by organizing cattle camps, with the help of Maldharis, outside the sanctuary boundary. Many Maldharis look back upon the help positively. At such camps, their milching cattle were saved by stall feeding and watering. Maldharis learned a new method of keeping cattle healthy and profitable. The Forest Department came to know the Maldharis' culture and problems more closely, which would be of help to them in formulating new schemes for the Gir and the Maldharis.

There are several other external forces that cause habitat deterioration for which the Maldharis are not directly responsible. The Maldharis use all forms of available biomass for their subsistence, including dung. Increase in agricultural areas and activities caused by an influx of outside farmers in the peripheries of the sanctuary created a demand for rich forest soil and manure. The Maldharis found this a new way of generating more income by selling cattle dung mixed with soil. They collect the dung mainly from the "ness" area and leave the dung that drops in the forest while they are grazing their cattle. This takes away an important source of organic matter from the forest soils. However, if the Maldharis are removed from the area entirely then this source of organic matter that adds to the fertility of the forest soils will be totally lost.

The second problem attributed to the Gir's Maldharis was the decline in the park's lion population. Occasional instances of lion poisoning by the Maldharis are recorded. The root cause for this can be traced to a management decision that did not consider long-term ecological or behavioral implications of predator-prey linkages: the famous 'Gir Lion

Show'. The show was conceived primarily to cater to tourists, so that they could enjoy a close view of the wild lions in their natural habitat. The show was arranged by tying cattle as bait at a certain place to attract the lions. It boosted tourism and in turn the income for the government, but it affected the lions' behavior.

Cattle have been a part of the lion's diet in the Gir as they would occasionally kill an animal that might accidentally stray beyond the surveillance of the Maldharis. When the lion shows became a regular feature of the sanctuary's tourist activities, the predator gradually became bolder and started killing the livestock instead of its natural prey of wild ungulates. The other reason for the increase in lion boldness could be the sudden rise in the scattered cattle population when pastoral communities from the surrounding plains used to take refuge in large numbers for fodder and fuelwood in the Gir. This resulted in the rise of availability of easy prey. The lions otherwise are known to be scared off by the legendary Gir cattle and would never find it easy to attack an animal. The loss of domesticated cattle to the lions is a serious economic loss to the already poor Maldharis. Some Maldaris retaliated by poisoning lions. The shows were stopped in mid-1987, but the cats' interest in livestock continues today with lion attacks common in certain areas. Debate is ongoing about how to deal with this problem.

Past Management Actions and Implications

There are no easy solutions to the problems described above. In the early seventies the Gujarat State Government took certain drastic steps to protect the lions and their habitat. Studies relating to the lions, the Maldharis, and their cattle were primarily conducted by eminent western experts such as Berwick (1976) from the United States, Joslin (1969) from Canada, and Hodd (1969) from the United Kingdom. These studies, collectively known as the Gir Ecological Research Project, were instrumental in helping the managers and experts in India to take some quick management actions. All these studies found the domesticated cattle population to be the main culprit for the degradation of the Gir ecosystem. Primarily based on these western experts' suggestions and in order to meet the international standards of park management, the state government through the Forest Department took the following actions (Government of Gujarat 1975 and Desai 1976):

1. Closed the Gir sanctuary to grazing by domestic cattle from outside.
2. Moved the Maldharis and their livestock out of the sanctuary and resettled them on the peripheral areas in the government wastelands.
3. Prevented the re-entry of the Maldharis and their cattle, after they were relocated outside the sanctuary.
4. Obstructed all the watercourses crossing the sanctuary periphery by the construction of special types of barricades.
5. Strengthened protection measures with the help of check posts, patrolling vehicles, and a wireless communication network.

All these actions are said to have been formulated in consultation not only with the wildlife experts but also the Maldharis. The main aims were to "break the vicious circle which had been responsible for the disturbance to the lion and also to ameliorate the poor social and economic condition of the Maldharis" (Desai 1976). By 1980, 455 out of a total 845 Maldhari families had been moved to resettlement sites. These families have been given land, health care services, a primary school, a drinking water supply, and agricultural implements to get them started in farming. The painstaking work of the State Forest Department with the support of the central government resulted in improved vegetation cover and increase in wildlife population of the Gir (Saharia 1982).

The solutions to one set of problems, however, lead to other problems. The above mentioned actions, implemented with tremendous faith in external expertise, overlooked the grim social and subtle wildlife management consequences. They have adversely impacted the social and cultural values of the Maldhari community. These actions also illustrate the classic "setting aside" approach to national park management that has been adopted by many Third World governments without consideration of the inherent cultural patterns of the resident people of a protected area.

The management plans seem to have been developed without clear value-oriented goals. Dharmakumarsinhji (1982) provided a candid and lively insight into the problems of the

Gir National Park management and the fate of the Maldharis. Backed with fifty years of experience of living and
working in close proximity to the Gir, he stated that moving
the Maldharis to peripheral regions results in the lions following their easy prey; and that the government did not always adequately compensate the lion predation because
many kills were made away from the sanctuary area. The
resettlement of the Maldharis in the peripheral buffer area
attracted new settlers to this government land. This land
was already used or settled, although its quality for
agriculture was questionable. Gradually, such areas came
under more extensive agricultural operations. The rubble
wall, built to restrict the cattle outside the Park, does not
confine the ungulates within it; hence animals such as the
nilgai and wild boar bound over and readily take to crop-
lands in the peripheries of the park. The lions who follow
them also come into conflict with the settlers. However, crop
damage by wild ungulates is not a problem for the Gir at
present.

There are people, especially in the local community, who
argue that the presence of the Maldharis in the sanctuary is
actually beneficial to the forest. The Maldharis have been
living along with the lion and other wildlife quite peacefully
for decades. The pro-Maldhari people argue that the Maldharis have helped protect them from the roving poachers of
timber and wildlife. Maldharis help prevent forest fires, and
grazing routes of cattle create dry tracks that act as fire
lines, thus helping to prevent the spread of fire. It is believed
that the seeds of vegetation species germinate better after
they get through the digestive system of cattle and drop with
the dung on the forest soil. Their presence, they believe, also
kept the lions from going out of the sanctuary.

However, such benefits to the forest of the presence of the
Maldharis in the sanctuary are debatable, especially from
the point of view of the Forest Department. They fear that if
the remaining Maldharis are allowed to stay in the sanctuary, their population, along with that of their cattle, is bound
to increase. The demands of the Maldharis, such as better
road access to dairies and installation of electricity in the
nesses, would result in further fragmentation and degradation of the sanctuary area.

The dilemmas and issues on both sides are crucial and solutions are not easy. However, there seems to be a general consensus that the government scheme to resettle the Maldharis in the mid-seventies was neither well conceived nor well implemented. It is believed that the criteria used for selecting which Maldhari family was to be resettled were not fair enough. They required the families to possess the government's permit for ten continuous years, from 1963 to 1973. Many did not have such permits for each of the ten years but had been living in the Gir for many decades. Moreover, the land allotted to many for agricultural activities is not of good quality. Some Maldhari families with political connections got better quality lands. Yet many lead a life in a socio-economic order that is alien to them. They have not been able to adopt the new imposed profession of an agriculturist. They have lost their cattle and with that their way of life. Many promises made have not yet been fulfilled. Some Maldharis have come back to the Gir Sanctuary area and live illegally with their adult sons. In short, as reported by one state government evaluation, the schemes of the mid-seventies might have helped the habitat (and even that is debatable), but they have not been successful in uplifting and maintaining the socio-economic status of the Maldharis.

The Gir has become an island surrounded by towns and farmland. Because of improved protection, wildlife populations, including the lions, have increased. There are parties with diverse and often conflicting interests. Solving the problems of the local residents and achieving wildlife management objectives will require enlightened political leadership, greater financial and human resources, and cooperation of all the concerned parties. If resettling the remaining Maldharis is imperative, lessons learned from the earlier schemes of resettlement and the cattle camps of the drought year will have to be kept constantly in mind. Relocating the Maldharis and finding a suitable alternative habitat for the lions are both difficult tasks. Unless effective stall feeding of fodder and needs of water and firewood are taken care of at heavy economic costs to the government, the forceful deprivation of the forest resources to the Maldharis can cause socioeconomic costs to them and the whole society at large. The new resettlement scheme proposed by the Forest Department is likely to be more comprehensive and it would at least not force the Maldharis to change their profession.

One of the other critical drawbacks of the management actions described earlier is the assumption that removing cattle will improve the potential for increasing the population of the wild ungulates—the natural prey of the lions. The most authoritative study in this regard was done by Berwick (1976), who clearly stated that removing the cattle will necessitate introduction of a native feral cattle, to add to the diet of wild predators and fill in the niche of a grazer. The study also found that the population of the wild ungulates will not increase to a number sufficient for the wild predator population, even if the cattle of the Maldharis are removed.

However, more recent government data and research on wildlife show that vegetative cover has improved and that population of the lions, other predators, and wild ungulates has increased considerably. Yet it is questionable whether the policy of total protection and allowing nature to take its own course (as is done in the smaller national park area within the sanctuary) is good for all species of wildlife. The grasses become dense and succession takes place: whether that will be a good habitat for the lions; whether removing a grazing population such as the cattle will be ecologically sound for the lions and the Gir; whether the Gir can support large wildlife populations for a long period of time are all questions being considered.

More recent preliminary studies for a minimum viable population based on historical lion population censuses, environmental stochasticity, and genetic factors indicate that the Asiatic lions may face extinction within a hundred years or less. This is due not only to habitat degradation but also to inbreeding and other related genetic factors (Pers. Comm. Michael Soule 1986 and Raval 1986). The habitat size seems very inadequate to support a total lion population of approximately 200 to 250 (the Gir has the highest density of lions in their natural habitat). This may also cause density-dependent diseases (Pers. Comm. Stephen Berwick 1989). There is need for more detailed analysis and research to understand all these issues. The results of the research conducted by the Wildlife Institute of India researchers in the late 1980s should become useful for future management actions for the Gir.

The resettlement of the Maldharis partly solves the problem of habitat quality but creates adverse social effects. What may matter then is preserving and restoring suitable large habitats similar to the Gir so that the wildlife population can be effectively re-established and thus relieved of genetic deterioration.

Lastly, one of the most famous resource management projects of the Gujarat government that has been projected for resource management in this era is worth mentioning in the context of the Gir National Park: the social forestry program of the Gujarat government. The program was conceived in the early seventies as a program "of the people, by the people, and for the people" (Government of Gujarat 1981). Begun in 1980, this program was aided by a financial loan from the World Bank. The main objective was to meet the statewide challenge for fuelwood and fodder demands in the remote rural areas. After years of experience and the application of technical expertise, this program has had some success at raising plantations on public, semi-public, and private lands.

What has happened, however, is that the effective healthy forest cover (much of which is concentrated in the Gir forest area) has actually dwindled from 0.95 million hectares from 1975 to 1979 to 0.51 million hectares in the mid 1980s in Gujarat State (Centre for Science and Environment 1985). In light of this, the periodic influx of the poor pastoral people into the Gir and other scattered green pockets of the state, especially during the drought periods, is hardly surprising. It indicates that the real goals of the social forestry programs are not met in spite of more than ten years of extensive implementation. This may be partly due to the fact that the program promoted quick-growing exotic species such as eucalyptus that have become more popular with the rich farmers who could afford to plant such economically beneficial species in place of agricultural crops. The government frequently plants eucalyptus on its waste lands.

In order to be more beneficial to the rural poor, the program needs to come out of its limited, commercial, profit-based implementation modes and policies. Perhaps then if the program is effectively incorporated into the overall Park management goals, the displacement of the Maldhari can be avoided. It may also help develop sympathetic land uses and promote biodiversity along the periphery of the Gir, which ultimately should be beneficial to the local residents and the sanctuary.

Management Suggestions

In India, the experts and decision makers of various fields evolve and implement ideas in glorious isolation and without adequate regard for either the environment as a whole or for social factors. Anil Agarwal (1986), a famous Indian environmental journalist, aptly describes the situation. He states that foresters do not have interest in farmlands, agriculturalists do not care for animal habitat or grazing land, and the animal husbandry and wildlife people concentrate on single-species management and do not suggest growing more fuel and fodder banks. The actions taken by government officials and experts seem well intended and suitable for particular problems at a particular time. However, while doing so they tend, or are forced, to overlook the need for a comprehensive approach to planning, and particularly the problems and concerns of the local residents of the park area. The following measures are suggested to resolve some of the larger issues and particular problems of the Gir.

At the national level the government of India should strive to create and effectively implement a national resource conservation policy giving priority to the cultural values and natural systems as opposed to conventional wildlife or tourism-based management programs for the protected areas. The National Wastelands Development Board was established in early 1985 to promote reforestation of degraded land in the country; its major emphasis is on plantations of fuelwood and fodder to meet subsistence needs of the poor (Government of India 1986). However, past experience with the established forestry programs for Gujarat State show that short-term economic considerations such as selecting commercially viable, fast-growing, exotic species soon defeat the primary goals of such programs. It has often been argued that a densely populated and resource-hungry country like India cannot afford to have the luxury of not planting fast-growing species. However, planting such trees meets initial goals, but unfortunately the practice perpetuates the problem and in the long run proves to be costly both ecologically and economically. Scarcity and mismanagement of water and large populations of roving cattle, goats, and sheep also cause problems for the plantations.

However, the focus should be shifted from short-term, single-objective resource management to long-term, multiobjective resource management for natural and cultural systems. For instance, it is acknowledged that the lions are an important component of the Gir and their presence generates tourism revenues; but concentrating only on management of the lion population or tourism will not be a healthy practice for the whole eco-region, which extends much beyond the physical boundary of the protected area. A national education policy that effectively incorporates environmental education programs suitable to the needs and concerns of different target groups should also be developed and implemented for different regions. In the case of the Gir, the Forest Department has done a commendable job for the last four years by organizing nature-education camps and forest youth clubs for the people of the surrounding villages and towns. In the long run, such programs are bound to be beneficial for the whole region.

It is also necessary that the resident people understand larger issues and comply with some restrictions that may not be suitable to their traditional way of life. They ought to realize that there are many tangible and intangible benefits that they derive because of the protection given to the Gir Forest. However, it is wrong to portray the resident people as the only culprit for the resource degradation of a protected area; the degradation often results from wrong decisions and actions taken elsewhere. At the state level it is encouraging to know that all commercial harvesting has been stopped in the Gir and the lion shows have been stopped completely since mid 1987. Social forestry programs can adopt native species that are more suitable to the natural conditions and visual quality of the region. The social forestry program could be combined with the goals of park management to evolve sympathetic land-use and management practices that eventually become mutually beneficial for the protected area and the resident peoples.

The current political and economic situation may not be conducive for treating the whole of the Gir and its periphery of say up to 10 kilometers, as a special management and development regime. Such a regime would help meet the national and local objectives for conserving the Gir. The management of such a regime should concentrate on programs that strive to provide and maintain viable and culturally acceptable alternatives for income generation. No boundary walls can effectively save a protected area if the local human population is not given opportunities for alternative sources to survive and grow. Experience of protecting the tiger population and its habitat through the centrally run and famous "Project Tiger" of India supports this point. Forest-based cottage industries, local dairies, and fodder farms are some of the ways more income could be generated.

Many additional management actions to help resolve some of the crucial resource management problems in the Gir are suggested throughout this chapter. Some of the more critical ones are:

Detailed studies and monitoring on interrelated environmental and cultural factors related to resource management.

Comprehensive range and agricultural land management practices in the surrounding plains.

An effective environmental education program and curriculum for the Maldharis and the people of the surrounding periphery.

A nature center for effective education and involvement of the local and visiting people so that the awareness and concerns for the fragile links of the habitat quality and human actions can be increased.

Organic manure production outside the protected area, to maintain the fertility of the soil, if the Maldharis are removed.

Options for creating and maintaining viable sources of income for the Maldharis in the Gir.

Assurance that efforts at boosting tourism do not adversely affect the natural and cultural fabric of the protected area.

Most important and fruitful will be to study social factors of the Gir. Incorporating social impact assessment studies into the planning process will be beneficial to all the parties involved. A positive perception by the target population of any management program is essential for its success. Participation of the resident peoples in program conception, implementation, and subsequent evaluation is also very essential. Participation should not mean inclusion of the local people for cheap labor but sharing the decision-making authority as well as the benefits. Some of the Central American as well as the Asian countries like Nepal and Bhutan offer some good examples that can be studied and implemented elsewhere with proper modifications and care.

Conclusion   The last natural abode for the Asiatic lion—the Gir National Park—and its indigenous people represent microcosmic realities of what is really happening in and around most of the protected areas of India and perhaps other Third World countries. The management efforts have been, at least in part, guided by western concepts of protected-area management that eventually prove less suitable for the cultural fabric found in the Third World countries.

The degradation of natural habitat and the resulting decline in the wildlife population of the Gir most often result because of external factors such as unplanned or inadequate land use and forest and wildlife management practices and policies. Natural factors such as erratic monsoons also add to the problems. The Maldharis of the Gir have traditionally been a pastoral community with strong bonds and a rich cultural heritage. They have developed a keen sense of understanding for behavior of the lions and have lived with this majestic cat and other wildlife in the Gir for many years. The cattle of the Maldharis do contribute to the degradation of the environmental conditions to a certain degree, but most often they have been victims in the larger context of diverse economic and political issues. The management actions, partly guided by external expertise, mandated displacement of the Maldharis from the Park; but the long-term social consequences of this action were not given serious consideration by the decision makers. Gir has been under the intense pressure of human use and cattle grazing. However, this chapter indicates that resettling the Maldharis on the peripheries of the park without adequate planning and evaluation would not necessarily yield beneficial and effective outcomes. As there is no single solution to the complex problem of protected-area management there is also no single cause of the problem. The managers of the protected areas in the Third World countries often face more serious dilemmas and financial and administrative constraints than their counterparts in the more developed world.

Gir and its adjacent lands are big and rich enough to allow peaceful coexistence of the wildlife and the resident people. India has enough technical expertise and human power to achieve this goal. The critical need is for value-based efforts and wise use of funding for management of natural and cultural resources within and beyond the protected area. Gir can then meet the challenge of sustaining a healthy survival and maintaining the availability of long-term options that may benefit the future generations of all the life forms.

NOTE

I wish to acknowledge the late Mr. Dharmakumarsinhji, whose article, "The Gir Forest," provided relatively more recent and authentic information about the Gir that was very useful for writing this chapter. I am also thankful to the people in the Forest Department of Gujarat State and outside of it who provided valuable information about and insights into the issues and possible solutions to problems for the Gir area.

Part Four ECODEVELOPMENT BASED ON SUSTAINED YIELD LOCAL RESOURCE UTILIZATION

For 98 percent
of the people in
Nepal's Conser-
vation Area, fire-
wood is the main
source of heating
and cooking.
Firewood and
fodder seedlings
are grown and
tended in nurs-
eries by locally
trained Anna-
purna women
and men.

Introduction   Ecodevelopment for local people in protected areas can occur in one of two ways: through the environmentally sustainable utilization of protected-area resources and through eco-development based on the protection of park resources (e.g., tourism). In part 4 we consider the first way. Discussion is divided into four subtopics: (1) case studies in which resource utilization is necessary for protecting biological diversity; (2) the debate over primitive harmony vs. human-rights based resource utilization within protected areas; (3) case studies of sustained-yield resource utilization of protected area resources; and (4) a review of literature on the potential danger of exotic tree species planted for local ecodevelopment escaping into protected-area ecosystems.

In chapter 7 we learn that removing grazing and charcoal forestry from a nature reserve in Israel led to the decline of various species of rare orchids. The biological diversity of the area had evolved over thousands of years in conjunction with human-resource utilization. Elimination of these human land uses altered the ecosystem interdependence of biological diversity and human use. Thus to maintain biological diversity the nature reserve authority had to reintroduce grazing and charcoal forestry production on a controlled basis.

A similar pattern of symbiosis between human uses of resources and biological diversity is found in chapter 8. In the Cévennes National Park in France there has always been agricultural use of the park, similar to British national parks (chapter 2). Just as in the British parks, the Cévennes National Park is experiencing a decline in the agricultural population. This population decline is causing a decline in biological diversity similar to the loss of species diversity in the Israeli nature reserve. These cases demonstrate that human utilization of protected-area resources is not always in conflict with nature preservation objectives of protected areas. Indeed the achievement of these objectives may often depend on continued human use of park resources.

In chapter 9 Polunin examines the important debate over the degree to which traditional island cultures evolved a conscious "conservation ethic" that could be the basis for resource utilization of marine-protected areas by local people. An essay by Nietschmann (1984), based on multiple cases of ethnographic research, argues that island cultures do have a tradition-based "conservation ethic." Also, based on a solid array of ethnographic research, Polunin argues quite the opposite:

> The rationale for the inclusion of resident populations in marine national parks should not be based on some romanticized view of primitive ecological wisdom embodied in traditional tenure systems that regulate resource extraction practices. . . . It is hard to escape the conclusion that the concern for traditional ownership is a human rights issue and that the concept of there existing a "traditional conservation ethic" has been commonly a political argument in support of those human cultures.

Burch's (1971) comparative essay (related more to terrestrial ecosystems) agrees with Polunin's critique of a romanticized ecological harmony, especially under conditions where culture contact and diffusion tend to convert cultural elements that may have been adaptive under previous conditions into a cultural continuity that becomes maladaptive under changed conditions. Polunin argues that traditional marine tenure was exercised not for conservation but for monopolization of resource exploitation rights. Nietschmann, on the other hand, argues that such exclusionary property rights schemes functioned also as a prime strategy of conservation that averted the logic of Hardin's "tragedy of the commons." It is possible that they may both be right with respect to marine tenure systems. The distinction between "latent" and "manifest" functions common to both anthropological and sociological functionalism may be important here. If such property rights' systems excluding outsiders were designed manifestly (i.e., as a clear, conscious motivation) to exclude outsiders and not to conserve resources per se, it may still have had the "latent function" of conserving resources. Those cultures that practice this method of exclusionary property rights may have selectively survived over those who did not; and thus, those who selectively survived may seem to have had a conservation ethic because they and their supporting ecosystem survived, even if conservation was never explicitly conceptualized in their culture (see West 1986:220–223, for a theoretical essay on functionalism in Max Weber's human ecology).

Thus, the key question for protected-area policy and planning may not be whether traditional cultural systems were intentionally ecologically virtuous or not. Rather, following Burch's (1971) argument, the key question may be the degree to which cultural contact and commercial market penetration have made their adaptive patterns of the past (whether latent or manifest) maladaptive in the present.

Chapters 10–14 present case studies of protected areas that permit varying degrees and kinds of resource use of protected-area resources. They also illustrate the strategy of providing intensified sustained-yield production of replacement resources in peripheral zones or adjacent lands for local people where exploitation of core protection zones have or need to be terminated. In chapter 10 Kutay argues that if protected areas in developing countries are to remain viable, national parks must attempt to accommodate the cultural values and economic needs of the local people. Recommendations of a park master plan call for controlled use of marine and freshwater fish resources and the sustained yield harvesting of coconuts in certain sections of the park.

In chapter 11 Hough discusses the development of a local integrated land-use management program for Michiru Mountain in Malawi. The program included provisions for sustained dairy farming grazing within the area. While local access to firewood was restricted, community forestry plantations were established and portions of the area remained open for firewood gathering on a rotating basis. Hough's chapter also describes in some detail the political and organizational difficulties of developing an integrated plan involving protected areas with multiple jurisdictions. The development of a local coordinating body, which received support from the high government officials and the local people, proved critical in the plan's eventual implementation.

In chapter 12 Croft discusses the incorporation of local resource uses in a comprehensive plan for Lake Malawi National Park, and the surrounding region in Malawi (Africa). The plan included provisions for the careful, sustained yield of fishery resources from the protected area and the establishment of community forestry plantations to compensate local people for the closure of certain zones in the park to firewood gathering. This case study also illustrates the careful use of detailed social and ecological assessment studies to determine the best way to reconcile park protection objectives with the needs of local people for the selective use of park resources.

In chapter 13 Glick and Orejuela discuss the integration of protection objectives and local resource utilization needs for the La Planada Nature Reserve in Columbia. They argue that resource protection and other environmentally related measures will not be well received by the local people until certain degrees of economic and social well-being have been achieved. The plan for this area included leaving agricultural plots farmed by indigenous Indian groups within the protected area and establishing community forestry plantations to compensate local people for the closing of inner protection zones to wood extraction. Other educational programs were directed at improving forage production and power generation using a sustainable mini-hydropower project as a local energy source.

In chapter 13 Bunting, Sherpa, and Wright present one of the most exciting models for merging protected-area objectives with local sustainable-resource utilization by local people. Because of its unique independent administrative status as a private trust the Annapurna project was able to innovate with new approaches to management and local par-

A group of high school children carries a poster proclaiming cleanliness is healthiness during one of the many environmental clean-up campaigns organized by ACAP.

ticipation. For instance, because of the importance of grazing for the local economy, grazing was permitted on a controlled basis. The plan also recognizes the importance of local institutions of social control in regulating grazing levels and patterns of migration between winter and summer ranges. Access to hunting on a controlled basis, medicinal plants, and fuelwood sources is also permitted. Community forestry plantations are established to take the pressure off of dwindling fuelwood resources that are under heavy pressure due to tourism demands. These community forestry projects also help provide fodder for grazing animals that are important in the local economy and culture. Alternative use of micro-hydropower is also being promoted as a use of a sustainable resource that can help take pressure off of fuelwood exploitation. This case also illustrates very well a model of heavy, local participation and control in designing and administering local resource management systems.

Several of the above case studies illustrate the use of community forestry plantations to compensate local people for closure of fuelwood gathering in core protection zones. To be most effective, these plantations must emphasize fast-growing species, and many fast-growing species used in such plantations are exotics, not native to the regional ecosystems. This raises the potential problem that these exotics might escape into the protected area, negatively impacting nature preservation objectives. Because of this critically important problem we have commissioned a chapter by a forest ecologist, Robert Muller (chapter 15), that discusses the field of "invasion ecology" in relation to this potential problem. While little is known about the escape risks of the many fast-growing exotic species used in community forestry plantations, Professor Muller discusses general factors that may inhibit or promote successful colonization. For instance, exotic tree species are less likely to invade natural ecosystems than exotic herbaceous plants. However, fast-growing tree species such as those promoted in community forestry may have more invasion potential than other slower growing tree species. Several management control implications are also discussed. These key dynamics need to be better understood if we are to manage the critical tension between local resource use by local peoples, and natural ecosystem protection.

7 Continuous Human Use as a Tool for Species Richness in Protected Areas of Israel

Aviva Rabinovitch-Vin

PROTECTED AREA	Goren Park and Gilboa Nature Reserve
CLASSIFICATION	Labeled as: Forest Reserve and Nature Reserve Managed as: Nature Reserve, IUCN Category IV
RESIDENT PEOPLES	Farmers and Other Rural Citizenry (Shepherds and Charcoal Burners)

Israel's Mediterranean area has been affected by man for millennia, through cutting, grazing and cultivation. Humans and nature co-existed in a state of dynamic equilibrium which led to the development of some open, cultivated spaces, grazing areas, and other tracts that were free of the impact of civilization and where there was a natural balance between climate, rock type, soil nutrition, plant communities, and wild animals. The use of firearms caused great changes in the carnivore and herbivore populations.

The introduction in the twentieth century of the bulldozer, the mechanical saw, pesticides, and artificial irrigation has altered the ecosystem and given humans absolute priority over nature.

The first step in nature preservation was a total exclusion of people from nature reserves. Over-exploited areas have turned into dense thickets, particularly on Cenomenian-Turonian rocks and on soils deriving from them. These low-in-phosphorus dolomite and limestone rocks built most of the Galilee region. The Eocenian strata that built the Gilboa Mountains, on the other hand, are rich in phosphorus. A high phosphorus content in rock and soil is essential to herbaceous plants, whereas low-phosphorus soils are dominated by ligneous plants such as bushes and trees (Rabinovitch-Vin 1983).

As a result of accumulated experience and research, there are now two approaches to management: moderate grazing of domestic animals in herbaceous areas, and thinning in addition to moderate grazing and browsing in Maquis vegetation. Having undesirable consequences, fire is not an acceptable management tool in this region.

It would seem that this management system has brought about more stable ecosystems, and has achieved its most important goal: increased diversity of habitat with large numbers of plants and animals.

Problems and Management

Overgrazing, burning or cutting Mediterranean tree species results in exposure of the ground, particularly in steep mountain slopes. The first heavy winter rains cause considerable soil erosion. Having been depleted of their soil, the rough, rocky outcrops invite penetration by invader plants such as *Sarcopterium spinosum* and *Calacotome villosa*—arid-zone batha plants that require full light throughout the day while needing only a minimum of nutrients and water.

Trees and herbaceous plants are unable to compete with the batha covering the land that has been deprived of its nutrients. Erosion results in an expansion of the batha cover which, to get rid of, the shepherds burn down at the end of summer. Fire, not being a natural phenomenon in the landscape, causes a rock desert to be created in the midst of the Mediterranean zone.

Fires, uncontrolled cutting, and/or overgrazing cause se-

vere damage to Mediterranean vegetation, wildlife, and
landscape. The worst of these is fire, because the stump of
each burned (or cut down) tree will grow ten new shoots, resulting in a thicket. In the wake of a fire, all the *Calicotome
villosa* seeds will immediately begin to sprout at once. At the
same time, the seeds will cover the area to such an extent
that even Quercus trees will be unable to survive there. Contrary to what is believed by some, fires will not promote an
increase in plant diversity (Naveh 1973). Under semi-arid
conditions, they will result in a drastic diminution of plant
diversity, leading to a dominance of one batha species (Lahav
1988; Rabinovitch 1982).

Observation of burned areas over the last fifteen years has
established the fact that in this region deciduous trees are
more fire-resistant than evergreen trees: *Pistacia atlantica,
Quercus boissieri, Quercus ithaburensis,* and others.

Evergreen trees, such as *Quercus calliprinos, Arbutus an-
drachne, Laurus nobilis,* and *Olea europea* suffer from fire to
a high degree. *Pinus halepensis* does not recover from the
stump but only from seeds.

Regrowth in evergreen trees starts from the root-neck,
whereas deciduous trees sprout from the branches after the
summer burning. After a sufficiently rainy winter it is virtually impossible to identify an area that was burned down in
the preceding summer. Rehabilitation of a burned-down
Quercus calliprinos association will take at least twelve to
fifteen years. In nature reserves, a dense thicket 3 to 4 meters high will form after human interference has stopped. In
open-site conditions, this community is very rich in annual
species, but herbaceous covering is either sparse or absent in
closed stands.

To cite a management example: the forest of the Goren
Park area in the Galilee has been thinned to a large extent.
After thinning out of trees (which were used for charcoal
burning), cows and goats were introduced to crop the shoots.
As a result of this twofold action—thinning and grazing—
the thicket became a forest. This area is now a well-known
tourist site that attracts many visitors who delight in the
flower carpets in spring and relish the haven of shade in the
long, hot summer.

The work was carried out in several stages. A number of
shoots of *Quercus calliprinos* were thinned out by mechanical

saw, leaving the thickest shoots to serve as the future oak
trunks. Thinning disturbs the equilibrium between root and
apex, causing numerous new shoots to sprout. To prevent a
reappearance of shrubs, domestic animals were introduced to
browse on these sprouting shoots. Simple and easy to implement, animal grazing and browsing are an integral part of
forest management in Israel. Pending full restoration of wild
browsers (Naveh 1973), planned grazing is now being practiced in most Mediterranean reserves. The grazers are cows,
sheep, and even goats, operating in 3- to 4-meter-high Maquis where they open up the thickets, enabling annuals to
grow in semi-shade conditions which prevent the spreading
of batha.

When a thicket becomes a forest as a result of a combined
grazing and tree-thinning program, a rich herbaceous stra-
tum is created. Thinning of trees for the traditional practices
of charcoal-burning and livestock grazing benefits people.
The difference lies in the need of a thinning and grazing program, instead of overgrazing, cutting, or burning. A further
advantage of tree management is the resulting proliferation
of geophytes, such as Orchids, Anemones, Cyclamen, and
Narcissi. Herbivores prefer annuals and, by limiting competition for light and nutrients, promote the growth of
geophytes.

**Conservation
and
Management of
Iris haynei,
Endemic Sp.**

The Iris Uncuciclus section in Israel comprises nine endemic
species. Following a marked decrease in the sixties, the *Iris
haynei* population was reduced to a few groups of plants whose
fruits did not reach maturity. The reason for this, we believed, was the disappearance of the pollinating insect from
the area, possibly as a result of the impact of insecticides. We
concluded that intervention in the fertilization process by
means of artificial pollination would be necessary. After some
trials and errors, this was achieved by the simple method of
pollen being transferred from one flowering Iris group to the
next on the forefinger of our Gilboa Nature Reserve warden.
Many fruits ripened in the following year, and as a result of
six years intervention in the pollinating process, Mount
Gilboa is now once more covered with thousands of trees.

Our success with *Iris haynei* prompted us to adopt a similar procedure with other species of the Uncuciclus section
whose populations had been diminished by uprooting and

picking. Suitable steps were taken to draw the attention of the general public to the Iris problem, and appeals were launched exhorting the public to leave these flowers untouched. As a result, people now come in their thousands just to look at these lovely flowers without touching them.

The expansion of the Iris population has brought back the pollinating insect, and the delicate equilibrium has thus been re-established. *Iris haynei* is a favorite of herbaceous plants. The annuals compete with the geophytes, and without grazing there is not enough light for flowering and ripening. In the fenced-off control plots (where there has been no grazing), there was only scarce flowering of geophytes, and the few that did flower did not fruit. In areas with planned grazing, we have widespread dissemination of rare geophytes in the reserve, and we feel that we have found the right method to preserve the region's diversity within the reserve by maintaining an appropriate equilibrium between vegetation and herbivores.

Conclusions   To achieve a new and better equilibrium between nature conservation and the needs of the public, research is required of every ecosystem, followed by implementation in the field based on that research.

Research of Israel's protected areas has shown that thinning of trees after they have reached a height of 3 to 4 meters, combined with domestic animal grazing and browsing, increases species diversity. Fire decreases diversity, resulting in a dominance of one to three species, severe erosion, and destruction of the population of small animals. Thinning and grazing are also a resource for living. A genuine interest on the part of the inhabitants to live off the protected areas will help to preserve them.

Planning use of open areas, such as nature reserves and forest reserves, is essential to the very existence of an ecosystem. The method suggested for the Maquis regions is an alternative to the wild herbivores that have become extinct in the region. (Deer became extinct in Israel in the nineteenth century as a result of hunting. The Nature Reserves Authority has reintroduced two deer species in an endeavor to solve the problem by restoring the equilibrium between plants and herbivores.)

Moderate grazing creates many niches, even in open areas,

and in virtually every ecosystem: the trodden path and its nearer and farther margins. The tastiness of different species in every season to various grazers and browsers produces changing factors for vegetation growth and for the existence of small animals. Thinning combined with grazing changes shade into semi-shade, up to almost full light. Animals disperse seeds, and some seeds will not sprout unless they have first passed through an animal's digestive tract.

To conclude: animals and plants have always lived together. Grazing—if carried out in the right manner—is an integral part of nature conservation. A nature reserve, if properly managed, can be a source of income from wood, charcoal, and domestic animal pasture, and furthermore can lead us to the goal of biodiversity conservation.

8   Le Parc National des Cévennes

Susan F. Beede

PROTECTED AREA	Le Parc National des Cévennes

CLASSIFICATION	Labeled as: National Park Managed as: Protected Landscape, IUCN Category V

RESIDENT PEOPLES	Farmers and Other Rural Citizenry

This case study will examine the French regional parks system, in particular, the Parc National des Cévennes (PNC) in southeastern France. The PNC and the French regional parks are unusual because, like biosphere reserves and other protected areas in Africa, they are inhabited and utilized by people. In contrast to many African protected areas, however, the PNC and most of the regional parks encompass predominately human-modified landscapes that contain little if any wildland. Describing the PNC, a park publication states:

> Now there is little if any 'virgin nature' in the Cévennes National Park whose features arose from a single natural evolution. The entire area is strongly marked by the imprint of human labor.

The same conditions exist in many of Europe's natural areas where environmental preservation often means protection of a royal forest planted in the seventeenth century, or a grassland kept open by centuries of grazing and deliberate burning. Thus, in order to protect and maintain the unique qualities of areas such as the PNC, traditional land use practices must be continued.

Yet, in the PNC, and some of the regional parks located in depressed rural areas, one of the long-term management challenges facing park administrators is the preservation of dynamic, working human communities to carry on these traditional practices. But how should this be done? What role should the park administration play in the revitalization of old resident communities and the fostering of new ones? Moreover, in these protected areas, how do cultural and natural-resource protection affect the vitality, identity, and autonomy of the resident communities?

Parc National des Cévennes   As early as 1913, Edouard-Albert Martel, a geologist and geographer, recommended that the PNC be made into a system of territorial reserves. For Martel and later park supporters, the area's most valuable attribute was its dramatic and varied scenery. But, when the park was finally established in 1970, its purpose was to protect *human* and *cultural* resources, along with aesthetics and natural resources. The park founders formally recognized the Cévenol and Caussard people, their culture, and interactions with the environment as unique and important features of the area.

Presently, the PNC seeks to revitalize and, where appropriate, to modernize agriculture, animal husbandry, and forestry in the park. However, all development activities are strictly regulated. In addition, the park puts great emphasis on the preservation of the area's cultural sites and resources. In many instances, this requires the restoration of churches, private homes, monuments, and other structures that are characteristic of the region. Among other things, such restoration is intended to improve the living and working conditions of the Cévenol and Caussard people.

Another important goal of the park is to allow for the knowledge and experience of the park's natural and cultural heritage to be made more accessible to visitors. This should be done in a manner that does not jeopardize the dignity of the inhabitants or the integrity of the landscape.

Finally, one of the park's most fundamental concerns is conservation of the natural environment. In an effort to protect and restore some of the park, the administration has restricted hunting (with the killing of certain species prohibited entirely) and reintroduced endangered or extinct bird and animal species. Also, special forest reserves and natural areas, where all human activities are prohibited, have been established.

Beyond the aforementioned park objectives, the administration has set forth broader principles intended to guide the formulation and implementation of park policy. These include:

1. the need to base management decisions on substantive scientific research;
2. the need to provide park residents, the park's peripheral zone, and regional and national political representatives with a permanent basis of association in order to link the park's national significance with local concerns and objectives.

The second principle has been difficult to realize because the area encompassed by the park is poorly developed as compared to the rest of France and has been experiencing economic and demographic decline for more than three decades. For many years most of the farmers in the area have been unable to compete with farmers from other regions in either the national or international market. For a variety of reasons, the agricultural sectors, as well as other dependent ones of the economy, have been struggling. In turn, this has triggered an exodus of residents, particularly young people.

Since the area is a national park, one might assume this phenomenon is not a problem, but rather a potential benefit to wildlife, wildlife habitat, and the character of the landscape. Studies indicate, however, that this is not the case. The park's human dimension, along with the ecological diversity, will be influenced by the future decline or revival of the area's economy.

Thus, one of the park's principal management goals is the revitalization of the local economy, the agricultural sector in particular. Without agriculture, the "living" cultural traditions of the park will continue to die out. At the same time, the park would lose more of its primary "land managers," such as the cultivators and transhumant pastoralists whose activities are essential to the maintenance of the park's outstanding ecological diversity.

Approximately thirty-five different ecological units exist in the park, many of them owing to constant human intervention. The effect of stopping cultivation and pastoral activities would be to increase ecological uniformity. When fields and pastures are abandoned and allowed to "grow wild," hardy plants and shrubs that thrive in disturbed areas take over. Eventually, these fields and pastures become moorlands and forests. For example, if livestock grazing were to cease in the high open meadows of Mt. Lozere, meadows would be invaded, first by *Genista*, a shrubby tree, and followed by the forest. Over time, delicate alpine plant communities would be lost, along with Mt. Lozere's rugged and open landscape.

Another cause of ecological uniformity in PNC is fire, particularly in the moorlands and forests that were once under cultivation. These areas produce a great deal of "fuel," such as brush, shrubs, and trees, which burns easily during dry periods. Over the last ten years, approximately 8,000 hectares below 1,200 meters in altitude burned in the Cévennes and Bouges sectors.

The Causes of Economic Decline in the Parc National des Cévennes

In 1882, there were approximately 35,000 operating farms on Mt. Lozere. By 1970, there remained only 7,000, though during this period the average size of each farm had increased significantly (Bel 1979:144). Between 1963 and 1967, fifteen hundred farms smaller than fifty hectares stopped production and were sold (Bel 1979). As mentioned earlier, most farmers in the PNC are able to compete only in the local markets.

Those who sell their products in the national or EEC markets have farms of more than fifty hectares. At present, 80 percent of the farmers on Mt. Lozere have fewer than twenty hectares. Analysts, such as F. Bel, assert that when their present owners die or retire, traditional farming will disappear, perhaps forever. Bel (1979:146) writes:

> For traditional agriculture the game is over, and given the average age of the remaining farmers, it is possible to determine the date of its disappearance. ("L'interdependance des systemes ecologiques et des systemes d'activites economiques: Essai a propos de la Lozere et des Cévennes.")

At the same time the practice of transhumant pastoralism has decreased dramatically over the years and shows little hope of coming back. Former pasturelands have been enclosed or restricted by hunting associations and owners of second homes. Aside from the lack of adequate pasture, fewer people are willing to tolerate the harsh working conditions that traditional shepherding requires.

These trends and problems are attributable to a number of factors. Since the end of World War II, agriculture in France has benefited from technological innovations and mechanization. But, much of this new technology cannot be used in mountainous zones like the PNC. Another problem is isolation, and another the lack of transportation. Farmers must take their produce long distances over bad roads to reach markets and packaging centers. Farmers also have great difficulty procuring capital. In many instances, high interest rates make it nearly impossible for small farmers to obtain and repay loans. In addition, the area has become more dependent on other regions as a result of crop specialization. Throughout the twentieth century, there has been steady decline of the cereal and chestnut culture. This development has contributed significantly to the loss of the area's traditional economic autonomy.

These problems have prompted many farmers and their children to leave the area. This emigration has caused the closing of schools and a neglect of infrastructure that makes the area even less appealing to those who remain, including the people in service and other agriculture-dependent industries. In addition to the isolation and poor living conditions, many people in the PNC complain that there are few viable alternatives to farm work. The accommodation of tourists and the sale of "wild" products, such as mushrooms and blueberries, provide farmers with some additional income; however, the net result is more work. This in itself has precipitated the departure of young people. Bel explains,

> The consequence of few work alternatives is the augmentation of work time, and the deterioration of the quality of life, which further accelerates the departure of young people. (p. 146)

The Park Administration

Presently, the park and the Ministry of Agriculture provide the resident communities with substantial financial and technical aid, in hope that the economy will be revitalized and young people will stay in the area. In addition to the restoration of buildings and monuments, the park is subsidizing soil rehabilitation projects, irrigation schemes, road maintenance, experiments with rustic cattle breeds, renovation of chestnut groves, fire prevention, and local cultural events. The park has also purchased large tracts of land from residents on Mt. Lozere and in other marginal areas, which the park then rents to those same people for a period of seventy years or more. This is intended to give farmers more security and confidence in their future. Hopefully, this new outlook will encourage farmers to exploit these tracts in a more rational and long-term manner.

Given the amount of aid the park can continue to provide to farmers, it is unlikely that the agricultural sector will collapse or disappear. In recent years the number of big farms has increased due to the purchasing of small farms. Thus, the overall trend is toward a net decrease in the number of working farms and in the amount of arable land under cultivation.

How this trend will affect the park's ecosystems and community is still being investigated. It appears that if the "living" character of the land and its regional culture is to be preserved, farmers, especially small farmers, must be able to make a comfortable income. If park inhabitants live primarily on park subsidies and tourist revenues, the distinctive character and dignity of the area could be lost. In the near future, much will depend on economic policies and development inside and outside the region.

Regarding the future of existing communities in the PNC, a 1980 park publication notes:

But we are well aware that neither good conversation, nor the human warmth of some winter evenings shared among friends, will be enough to strengthen the residents' desire to stay here and work. (Parc National des Cévennes, An X)

NOTES
1. Bel, F. 1979. "L'intérdependance des systemes écologiques et des systemes d'activités économiques: Essai à propos de la Lozère et des Cévennes." *Annales du Parc National des Cévennes* 1:145–147.
2. Ibid.

9   Delimiting Nature: Regulated Area Management in the Coastal Zone of Malesia

N.V.C. Polunin

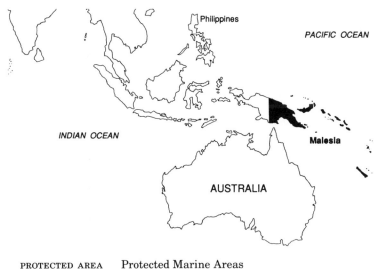

PROTECTED AREA	Protected Marine Areas

RESIDENT PEOPLES	Traditional Peoples

Malesia encompasses that remarkable island-checkered world that stretches between Southeast Asia and Australia, and out into the Melanesian Pacific. This is a region of enormous marine biological wealth, where biota can attain their greatest diversity, while human seafaring and exploitation also exhibit an ancient and unsurpassed variety. However, the region is now subject to rapid economic development and

human population growth, and today there are some star-
tling contrasts to be found. There is, for example, a technological contrast between the canoes of the nomadic hunter-
gathering sea-gypsies and the vast oil tankers that ply the
Malacca Straits to feed hungry developed countries beyond.
There are ecological contrasts such as between the ever-
changing color, shapes, and movements of virgin coral reefs
and the tracts of monotonous rubble that are left when the
explosives-fishermen have gone. There are the millions of
peasant-fishermen struggling for a pittance in areas such as
the northern coast of Java alongside the developing capital-
intensive, export-oriented fisheries for prawns and tuna
(Polunin 1983). Such extremes raise broad questions for the
future as to the whys and wherefores of coastal management. Should some areas be kept "intact," and if so, how can
this be justified and actually done? Do traditional peoples by
virtue of their long-standing association with such areas
have automatic rights to continue their traditional lifestyles?
Can we delimit the "natural" in traditional man from the
modern and "artificial," which is increasingly adopted?

Beyond such questions of preservation lie more practical
ones of how actually to solve ecological problems of development in the coastal zone: do regulated areas in a broader
view have a significant role to play here in a more functional
and immediate sense? Can we restrain human activities by
area to keep them within the limits imposed by nature?

**Traditional
Practices and
Conservation
in Protected
Marine Areas**

Some traditional marine practices with a special bearing on
protected area management have been reviewed previously
for this region (Polunin 1984a, 1984b). In a loose sense,
people in many areas established marine "reserves" long before the idea was reintroduced by modern man. Sites might
be protected from exploitation to honor a deceased individual, for example, in the Sanguine Islands to the north of
Sulawesi (Hickson 1886: 141), or show respect for a deity, as
at Parangtritis in southern Java (Epton 1974:191). However,
most restricted areas have been set up around villages. In
the Kei Islands of eastern Indonesia, the seaward boundary
of the "reserve" apparently lay where the water was about 20
meters deep (Van Hoevell 1890:132). On Tanimbar, access to
marine fishing areas was exclusive to particular lineages,
whose members had nevertheless to ask permission of a per-

son called the "Lord of the Land" (LeBar 1972:113). On the
northern coast of New Guinea, it appears that some areas
were under exclusive control of the chief (Van Der Sande
1907:169). Village-type reserves appear to be more common
in eastern Malesia; regulated areas might never have been
common in the western areas, or they may have died out
long ago. If the former explanation is correct, perhaps village
marine reserves are more common in the eastern parts of the
region because of the peoples' relatively greater marine dependence. In any case, the marine areas most suitable for
preservation are more likely to be found in those areas of
traditional tenure.

What do we know of the origins of traditional marine tenure and its consequences for patterns of resource use? It appears that in some cases, such as the oceanic islands of the
western Pacific Ocean described by Johannes (1978, 1981),
the need for controls in the use of biological resources played
an important role in the establishment of ownership. In
other areas, however, including much of Indonesia and
Melanesia (Polunin 1984a), it would seem that the circumstances surrounding the instigation of marine tenure are
more complex. Most evidence in this second region indicates
an origin in conflict between people, but that in addition, the
issues fought over were not necessarily the marine-biological
resource problems that were overtly focused on. It has been
argued that dispute could lead to some equitable allocation of
areas and their resources to people (Vayda 1976). However,
this has not been demonstrated in any instance. The factors
determining the carrying capacity for people exploiting marine resources but living on the land are difficult to unravel.
Often, it would seem that marine territorial boundaries came
to be established in an ecologically arbitrary fashion (Polunin 1984a). Further, a common characteristic of traditional
tenure seems to have been its susceptibility to change over
time (Crocombe and Hide 1971). For example, it has been
proposed in Papua New Guinea that codification of traditional tenure would be ill-advised because it contradicts the
nature of the system, and it would in any case be very difficult to effect (Anonymous 1973).

As a means of managing resource use, traditional tenure
would also seem to be unreliable in other respects. In many
areas, patterns of marine exploitation have been determined

by opportunism. For example, disputes evolved in northern Papua New Guinea when *Trochus* shell became a valuable commodity and patterns of tenure sometimes changed as a result (Carrier 1981; Johannes 1982). Earlier, but less well documented, cases involving beche-de-mer (trepang) and pearl-shell fisheries in Indonesia also exposed tenure conflicts owing to resource over exploitation (Kolff 1840; Anonymous 1926). In addition, traditional tenure seems poorly equipped, if at all, to cope with the prevalent internal societal problems of immigration and rapid population increase. The overall impression is that in Malesia, marine tenure came about for reasons of economic exploitation, not of restraint (Polunin 1984a).

A conclusion from this is that the sorts of controls that exist in traditional tenure are not always reconcilable with those which are necessary in modern reserves. In modern reserves, specific objectives of management must increasingly be defined, and detailed plans of management drawn up (Polunin, in press). On the broad matter of marine environmental dilemmas, there are further difficulties with the application of traditional tenure to the modern context. Such tenure is largely absent from areas of Indonesia, such as Java, which have some of the greatest problems (Polunin 1984b); tenure may thus be of limited applicability. In addition, the complexities of traditional ownership may deter the development of resources even where this development may be necessary in the face of expanding human population.

Status of Traditional People in the Marine Protected Areas

In many respects, traditional tenure is not directly applicable to modern marine management. It must not be assumed that by somehow promoting or maintaining traditional cultures we are preserving a natural state of affairs. Under these circumstances, it is hard to escape the conclusion that the concern for traditional ownership is a human-rights issue and that the concept of there existing a "traditional conservation ethic" has been commonly a political argument in support of those human cultures. If this is correct, it is still important to examine this conclusion and see how to respond. The ultimate message is perhaps then to consider traditional peoples, where they occur, as a major factor in establishing conservation areas (Polunin 1984a).

There are two kinds of responses to this recognition. The

first is a specialized issue involving protected areas specifically and the roles of traditional peoples in them: given that
reserves will have to be designed more and more with particular objectives in mind, it is perhaps a question of finding
a "niche" for such cultures in these areas. This may be more
effective as a conservation approach than broadly protecting
all that is deemed to be "natural" within an area, as has
typically been the case in the past. The second response is a
more general one, involving questions of how all kinds of
regulated areas can be adapted to real ecological problems of
people and the environment in which they live.

Traditional residents clearly do have many valuable roles
to play in protected areas. Their knowledge of nature is often
unsurpassed (Johannes 1981) and they can thus contribute
enormously in natural historical terms. They can act as
guards, and, more positively, as interpreters of natural phenomena with which only they are often truly familiar.

Their presence also offers an important human historical
perspective on the localities involved. They can demonstrate
their age-old customs, beliefs, and understanding. Their
culture, so frequently under threat, can thus acquire new
significance. It is difficult not to appear patronizing when
speaking in this way, and it is true that we are so commonly
ignorant of their ways and condition in general in making
any pronouncement on the future of such people; we are dealing with sensitive matters from a poorly informed position.
However, it is also certain that the objective of trying to
maintain large patches of wilderness for future generations
can only be accomplished by a system of preserved areas that
have long been the home of others. Ideally, the purpose is to
make traditional residents not only an integral part of such
zones, but further, to persuade them to become active contributors to the growth and development of protected areas
in ways which they can realistically appreciate.

**Broadening
Regulated-
Area
Management**

The second potential response to the human-rights issue is to
appreciate that while cordoning areas off may prevent their
further degradation by people, such protection does not help
to solve the underlying causes of that degradation; nevertheless, such measures may often be equated with "conservation" (e.g., Salvat 1981). Alleviation may come in the long-
term through the benefits of research and education, but in

the meantime advantages to local people may be far from clear (Polunin, et al. 1983). Nevertheless, regulated areas, of which protected sites are one extreme, may be able to help alleviate some of the more fundamental problems of management in the coastal zone (Polunin, in press), as many of these problems arise through competing interests related to the exploitation of common areas. These include the use of the same resources by different techniques (for example, modern trawling versus artisanal fisheries inshore) and the use of quite different but potentially interrelated resources in the same zone (for example, forestry in mangroves versus the peneid fisheries with which they are widely associated). In the former case, the Indonesian government took a lead by restricting, and subsequently prohibiting, trawling in inshore waters. It also set a strong precedent in the latter case by proposing the instigation of mangrove "green" belts in certain parts of the country, areas that were to be exempted from timber extraction (Polunin 1983). The fact that such measures have been suggested does not prove that they will be lastingly successful, but it does indicate that regulated-area techniques are widely considered to be feasible approaches to the solution of fundamental problems.

These and other types of regulated zones, such as replenishment areas for the maintenance of fisheries, will be hampered for some time to come by the lack of extensive information on the many population, ecosystem, and environmental processes involved. Scientists and managers must continue to strive for a better understanding of these critical factors so that the basis and limits of natural productivity can be appreciated. Until man can do better, human activities can thus be kept sustainably within the confines so determined.

Conclusion   In summary, I have argued that the rationale for the inclusion of resident peoples in marine national parks and protected areas should not be based on a romanticized view that traditional tenure systems have a primitive ecological wisdom that regulates resource extraction practices. Rather, it should rest on the fact of this long tenure as a human-rights issue in protected-area management. Because of the negative cultural, social, and economic impacts that could result from fully protected area status, a broader concept of regulated areas designed to protect ecosystems and aquatic species while allowing traditional marine extraction practices involving a system of sustained yield cropping is perhaps more appropriate for these marine island ecosystems.

A greater understanding of traditional maritime peoples in Malesia and their ecology is required before they can be entrusted with marine protected-area management in the region. It is suggested that if there is rather little ecological evidence for the existence of a "traditional marine conservation ethic," then the latter concept becomes largely a matter of the rights of traditional peoples in marine protected areas.

There are at least two ways of responding to these human-ethical considerations. One is to find a niche for traditional owners and to make sure that they are not seriously disadvantaged by protected-area developments. The other response is to appreciate that protected areas are an extreme form of conservation that may help little in solving underlying human problems. Yet we should also consider that other forms of regulated area management may be more appropriate for the management needs of local development, and not be geared primarily toward the preservation of nature. Such approaches avoid the problem of defining the boundaries of the "traditional" for human societies, which, like any other, must be permitted voluntarily to change. Therefore, there may be no need to differentiate between the "natural" and the "unnatural," and thus to delimit "nature."

NOTE

I thank the Governments of Papua New Guinea (through the University of Papua New Guinea) and Indonesia (through the Directorate of Nature Conservation) for helping me to gain a greater appreciation for the coastal zone of Malesia. Bob Johannes and Edvard Hviding kindly commented on my views for which, however, I am still solely responsible.

10   Cahuita National Park, Costa Rica: A Case Study in Living Cultures and National Park Management

Kurt Kutay

PROTECTED AREA	Cahuita National Park
CLASSIFICATION	Labeled as: National Park Managed as: National Park, IUCN Category II
RESIDENT PEOPLES	Peasants, Farmers, and Other Rural Citizenry

Costa Rica possesses a rich natural and cultural heritage within its relatively small territory (50,700 sq. km), providing habitat for both Nearctic and tropical plant and animal species, many of which are endemic. This wealth of biological diversity has drawn worldwide attention for the conservation of Costa Rica's unique natural resources.

Costa Rica currently faces serious socioeconomic consequences from extensive deforestation of more than one-third of its forests (Myers 1979), for cattle ranching, lumbering, and peasant settlements. Deforestation continues at the rate of 60,000 hectares per year on the remaining 1.5 million hectares (Hartshorn, pers. comm.) resulting in decreased rainfall and increased runoff and erosion, leading to downstream flooding.

Additionally, one-third of the Costa Rican population is in poverty, and urban migration has resulted in an overconcentration of population in metropolitan areas and increasing pressure for employment.

As one basis for sustainable economic development, the government of Costa Rica has developed a world-renowned system of conservation areas that cover some 16 percent of the country. National parks are the predominant type of protected area category employed for nature conservation, with 8 percent of the country currently protected in twenty-six national parks and reserves.

There is no explicit policy and, until recently, little direct experience in responding to the large majority of rural peasant cultures living in and around Costa Rican national parks. Where they have fallen within park boundaries, the automatic response has been to relocate them outside. In some cases, this has proven extremely costly and socially disruptive, even though, in the long run, several relocations have been essential to achieve national conservation and development goals. This remains a vital question in park development of Costa Rica, particularly in the case of Cahuita National Park.

Cahuita National Park: Description and Development

Situated along the south Atlantic coast of Costa Rica, Cahuita National Park is a small marine park encompassing 1,100 hectares of land, 600 hectares of coral reef and a twelve-mile offshore marine zone (Kutay 1984: Appendix A). The most prominent feature of the park is a peninsula extending from the coastline, and surrounded by the country's most extensive fringing coral reef formation. The park was established primarily to protect this feature, the only coral reef of great significance in the country, but also to restore marine life of economic importance, to protect the marine resources and the beaches for recreation and enjoyment, and to protect and conserve the biotic diversity of the park's tropical moist forest (Boza, pers. comm.)

Ecological Context

Four major ecological divisions are found within the park: alluvial coastal plain, lowland swamp forest, beach and lagoon, and coral reefs and shallow offshore waters (see Map 10.1). Each has been substantially altered through commercial exploitation and traditional use by the Afro-Caribbean peoples living in the region.

The alluvial plains have been converted primarily to traditional agro-forestry using a combination of cacao, laurel, and

Map 10.1
Vegetative
Communities of
Cahuita National
Park

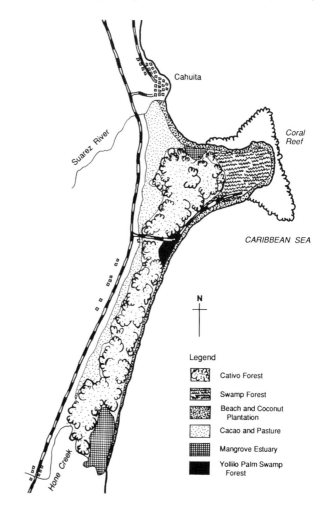

Cahuita

Coral Reef

Suarez River

CARIBBEAN SEA

N

Hone Creek

Legend

Cativo Forest

Swamp Forest

Beach and Coconut Plantation

Cacao and Pasture

Mangrove Estuary

Yolillo Palm Swamp Forest

other common species. The least accessible, but once extensive, swamp forests have also been altered by logging and settlement, with only a small remnant of the cativo forest remaining; these forests provide critical habitat for a variety of bird, mammal, and reptile species.

Beach area vegetation is dominated by coconut stands planted by local residents for commercial purposes. Beaches also provide a critical habitat for seasonal nesting of three endangered sea turtle species. These animals have been exploited for subsistence and commercial consumption to the point that they are endangered, and are now protected by national and international law.

The coral reef and its related marine communities provide food and shelter for an abundance of marine fauna, including the endangered turtle species, and protect the terrestrial environment from excessive shoreline erosion and extreme climatic conditions. Risk, Murillo, and Cortes (1980) note that the ecological condition of the reef is actually declining, with a limited zone of live coral. These scientists agree with Wellington (1974) that turbidity and sedimentation appear to be the most important factors limiting growth and distribution of the corals.

The south Atlantic region of Costa Rica, known as Talamanca, is distinguished from the rest of the country both by its distinct ecology and its socioeconomic conditions. Although the dominant culture of the region is Afro-Caribbean, Mestizo and Indian peoples reside in the area as well, a situation unusual to the rest of the country. Traditionally, the Afro-Caribbeans have remained independent from state control or outside influence, a situation fostered by the continued segregation of blacks from the rest of the Latin society. Priding themselves on having developed a self-sufficient lifestyle based on subsistence fishing and cultivation, the Afro-Caribbeans combine trading and bartering with the sale of turtle and agricultural products to an outside cash economy. Changes in lifestyle and land use in the Talamanca region during the last few years threaten to have serious social and ecological implications on the Afro-Caribbean community and the park environment. Improved transportation links are bringing more tourists in and taking more natives out. Fewer farms are in production and a Monilla fungus infestation wiped out 95 percent of the Talamanca cacao crop with little hope of recovering to previous levels of production (*Tico Times*, April 6, 1983).

Current relations between local residents and the National Park Service are fraught by a history of conflict and controversy. Like most of Costa Rica's first protected areas, Cahuita was established as a National Monument by executive decree (in 1970), with no consultation of local residents. The Park Service initially informed landowners that they would be forced to sell their land. From the outset, residents saw the new conservation area as yet another imposition by outside authority on their lives.

With 87 percent of the park's land currently under private ownership, and 58 percent of the private holdings in five-hectare parcels or less, the issue of land tenure is complex. In 1977, when several public meetings failed to resolve land-tenure disputes, local residents carried their protest to President Daniel Oduber. A commission of government and community leaders was appointed to propose amendments for consideration by the Legislative Assembly, which was reviewing a law to change the National Monument to a National Park. The proposed amendments constituted a compromise by which local residents would be allowed to continue exploiting park resources at current rates, using traditional methods, within regulations established by the Park Service.

However, the subsequent law designating the national monument as a national park in 1977 did not refer to the commission agreement or the unique sociocultural situation (Kutay 1984: Appendix B). Although the Park Service has an administrative agreement with community representatives, neither the commission's recommendations nor the legal rights of local people are guaranteed by law. They are subject instead to resolution in park management planning. To this date, no plan has been approved, and local landowners continue to be restricted in the use and disposition of their property without compensation.

Resident Uses of Park Resources

Local residents continue to use the natural resources of the park and surrounding lands like their forefathers, but within a new set of social, economic, and ecological circumstances. Along the alluvial plain in the arable sections of the park, most farmers have abandoned their diseased cacao plantations, or have begun to harvest selectively the commercially valuable hardwood overstory from their fields. In areas surrounding the park the planting of banana and plantain cash crops is common, as is the clearing of forest for cattle pastures. The increased removal of forest canopy from these activities greatly affects the ecosystem of the area, both within and outside the park's boundaries. Fishing continues from coastal streams in the park for sport, domestic consumption, or occasional sale in local markets (for households and restaurants). Although the exploitation of fishery resources is generally conducted at the local level, subsistence fishermen will exploit the opportunity to sell their extra catch on the regional commercial market. The traditional use of nets to harvest fresh water fish, concentrated at the mouth of the coastal streams, is believed to be depleting the fish populations (Sanchez, pers. comm.); furthermore, declining populations of lobster offshore of the park suggest that site-specific spearfishing is having a substantial impact on population levels (Robinson 1975).

The single most heavily exploited marine resource in the park has been the three species of sea turtle, who use the park environment during their seasonal migration. Despite laws and park regulations to the contrary, the local residents continue to consume and to market turtle meat, eggs, and shells illegally, including sale of the shell of the hawksbill for black market export purposes. Little scientific baseline data exist on the health or relative abundance of specific marine animals in Cahuita National Park; nor is there conclusive evidence documenting the impact of changing patterns of human exploitation. However, it is clear from historical accounts, as well as from observations and complaints by local fishermen, that all marine species that are currently exploited in the park by the local population are in a state of decline.

Management Planning for Conservation and Community Development

Since the establishment of Cahuita National Park in 1970, management and development of natural resources have been minimal. As a result, resource conflicts have intensified to the point that a working relationship between park authorities and local people has completely broken down. Not only is the ecological integrity of the park in jeopardy, but many of the basic needs of local people remain unmet. A management plan for this park must critically analyze and evaluate both ecological factors and cultural characteristics. Consideration of the lifestyle and particular characteristics of the Afro-Caribbean culture surrounding the park will help in assessing its compatibility with management objectives. The local people experience strong and direct links to an urban economy and have become increasingly dependent on outside goods and services. Many families prefer earning a cash income and purchasing their foodstuffs from regional markets rather than cultivation.

Due to the recent destruction of the area's principal cash crop, both commercial and subsistence uses of park resources and those of the surrounding environs have increased. While these resources may provide an important buffer against local economic conditions, they are being exploited beyond sustainable levels.

Cultural change is well advanced in the rural Talamancan community. State intervention and cross-cultural interaction among outside visitors and new residents have accelerated acculturation of the black community into Latin society. As a result, social organization has become more diversified and social stratification has increased. As traditional familial and community ties have broken, community cohesion and cooperation have faded. Instead, residents have formed a centralized, formal political organization to interact with the nation-state government to make decisions in the community interest. Substantial state support is required to fulfill community needs in health care, education, transportation, and agricultural extension.

This analysis of the Afro-Caribbean culture has important implications for how park managers can effectively achieve conservation objectives for the park in its particular sociocultural context. The park could help to control utilization of natural resources for subsistence consumption by promoting integrated regional development on surrounding lands, and by employing and otherwise involving local people in park planning and management. The park might also help reduce social disruption associated with rapid acculturation by offering a place where the Afro-Caribbeans can preserve and promote their traditional values and lifestyle. This may also provide an informative cross-cultural exchange between the Afro-Caribbeans and other Costa Ricans.

**Management
Planning for
Cahuita
National Park**

Zoning is the first detailed level at which management considerations are reflected in planning. Of six zones recommended for Cahuita National Park, one explicitly emphasizes cultural values while the others stress conservation with limited human use (see Map 10.2). Despite substantial alteration of the park environment from past use, none of the zones are designated as off limits to human activity. Nonetheless, most zones impose specific restrictions on the use of park resources by local people.

1. Primitive Zone. The primary objective here is to strictly protect and maintain the natural state of the swamp for-

Map 10.2
Proposed
Management
Zones, Cahuita
National Park

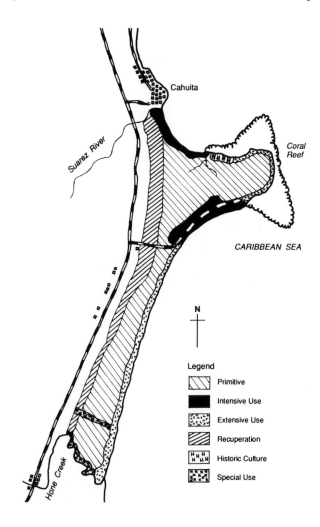

est for scientific research, wildlife habitat, and protection of downstream marine environments. This zone, having not been exploited by local inhabitants, may contain unique ecosystems, individual species of plants or animals, or natural phenomena of scientific value that remain unaltered by human intervention.

2. Extensive Use Zone. This zone consists of natural areas that may have been subjected to limited alteration and resource exploitation. The primary objective is to protect natural resources by minimizing the impact of permitted uses. Recreation, environmental education, and traditional resource use of marine and freshwater environments will be permitted in this zone if further research concludes that it would be compatible with conservation objectives.

3. Cultural History Zone. This zone includes areas of historical, archaeological, and cultural features that deserve preservation and interpretation. Designated an "active" cultural zone, the objectives are to restore and preserve the artifacts and history of the Afro-Caribbean culture, and to promote this cultural heritage for the benefit of local residents and visitors. These areas have been, and continue to be, subject to agriculture, hunting, fishing, or settlement by local inhabitants and consequently show obvious signs of human use and alteration.

4. Intensive Use Zone. Principal uses in this zone include visitor access, snorkeling, visitor transport, and interpretation. Permitted uses would be limited to those that are compatible with the park's conservation objectives and thus subject to its regulations. As three Cahuita Indians currently live in this zone, park authorities and community representatives must establish specific guidelines for site development with regard to the longstanding rights of the three residents; these guidelines must also be compatible with park objectives.

5. Rehabilitation Zone. This zone encompasses areas in which vegetation and soils have been substantially altered, and where exotic plants and animals are to be replaced with local species. Covered in secondary growth, it includes the strip of arable parkland along the western boundary that has been used for many years for homesites, perennial crops, and pasture. Once rehabilitated, this zone will be assigned a more permanent status.

6. Special Use Zone. This zone is generally devoted to ad-

ministration, public works, and other uses that are deemed incompatible with conservation objectives, but are necessary for effective park management. The zone is subdivided into two areas: the one includes two entrance stations, the principal administration center, and a guard station; the other includes traditional use areas, and all of the offshore waters outside the extensive use area beyond the reef.

In terms of traditional use in the park, the objective of this zone is to minimize the impact of certain nonconforming activities on conservation and enjoyment of the park's natural environment, while producing certain socioeconomic benefits for local residents and the nation.

Management Programs

The management of Cahuita National Park involves three major areas: resource management and protection, public use, and general operation of the area. Following Miller (1980), these programs specify activities, norms and requirements to achieve overall objectives. Only those aspects of each management program that pertain directly to issues of resource use by local residents are considered here.

Resource Management and Protection Program

The resource management and protection program attempts to maintain and restore ecological processes, in part to assure a productive natural resource base for sustainable use. The program affects local residents by restricting certain of their uses which conflict with park conservation objectives; however, it does take into account their cultural values and recommends their active participation.

Resource management objectives include the reestablishment and maintenance of natural biological processes, and the conservation of natural and cultural resources. In collaboration with local residents, park administrators are developing two resource use plans that will directly benefit the surrounding communities: the first authorizes the management and subsequent sale of coconuts grown on park land; the second concerns marine resource use and allows subsistence-level fishing only, based on a permit system. Both plans integrate resource management with traditional uses; by effectively monitoring the impact of human use in the park, conservation objectives can be upheld while local residents continue to reap economic benefits.

Resource protection is of equal importance in order both to minimize the deterioration and/or destruction of marine and terrestrial areas, and to ensure park visitor safety. Marine and terrestrial park boundaries are to be clearly designated and marked and a patrol established, particularly for critical areas and time periods such as the turtle nesting season.

By cooperating with surrounding landowners, park managers may forestall further clear-cutting of the forest, promote rehabilitation of cutover lands, and minimize pollution in and around the park. For residents retaining property titles within the park, livestock levels may be maintained at 1977 levels. However, all domestic animals will be eliminated from the park once private lands transfer into park jurisdiction.

In order to develop a knowledgeable information base about the natural and historical-cultural resources of the park, scientific investigation is a necessary and integral activity. In addition to the valuable knowledge that local residents can contribute, in-depth research projects and ongoing inventories can provide detailed data for use in guiding park management and development decisions.

Public Use Program

Public use of the park requires particular management consideration as it encompasses not only recreation and tourism, but environmental education and interpretation, community extension, and public relations. Reflected should be the interests of local residents in terms of their own recreational pursuits—because they also become visitors—as well as economic opportunities through recreation-related concessions.

Recreational activities should offer the visitor diverse opportunities within a margin of safety and without substantially altering the natural environment. Identifying these activities and allowing opportunities for them, establishing entrance fees, and providing facilities for camping, picnicking, diving, and land and sea transport are all management objectives in this area.

Tourism in the park can play a central role in local socioeconomic development as national and foreign tourists are encouraged to visit. Many cases have shown, however, that conventional tourist development, often controlled by a few local entrepreneurs or outside financiers, exploits and de-grades local communities and natural resources (de Kadt 1979; Organization for Economic Cooperation and Development 1980). These problems could be avoided through the promotion of cultural activities by local communities, and integrated regional tourism development for construction of goods and facilities.

Environmental education and interpretive programs provide visitors and the general public with important information about natural resource conservation within the park. With plans to construct two visitor centers, along with development of cultural demonstration sites, local residents are ensured that their historical-cultural values will be acknowledged. Through conservation outreach programs, local residents can be trained as interpreters, and organized groups of the Talamanca Region can utilize the park as an educational resource.

Informing the general public of the objectives, resources, programs, and benefits of the park helps to establish interactive public relations between the park administration and surrounding communities. Efforts should be directed at creating ongoing processes, not only for improving communication, but for easing mediation conflicts between the park administration and local communities. By maintaining regular contact with community leaders, the park administration can keep local residents continually informed of park management and development decisions. In particular, the chief administrator should represent the Park Service in meetings of the municipalities, and in other community and regional development associations.

To promote the park and its role in regional development, park personnel should organize talks and conferences about the natural and cultural features of the park; this role could be expanded to provide introductory courses for travel agents about the resources and benefits of the park.

Operations Program

Operations covers the construction, maintenance, and administration aspects of the park. Indirectly, local people would benefit from improved resource management and increased tourism associated with better facilities. Direct benefits to local residents would be realized through efforts to hire

them for both short-term construction projects and more
long-term construction and maintenance activities. By administering a park management plan that seeks cooperative
involvement of local people, residents could fulfill the role of
consultants in the design, construction and utilization of
park infrastructures. To date, all construction in the park is
to be designed and carried out using traditional methods and
materials wherever practicable.

To reiterate a significant aspect of administrative development and management, communication between park administration and the local community should be an integral
aspect of the park's management style.

The management recommendations for Cahuita National
Park attempt to mediate the ongoing conflict between wildland (including marine) conservation and use of the park and
surrounding lands by local residents.

The question arose during the course planning as to
whether National Park status is the appropriate category
for management of the Cahuita area. It clearly has major
biological limitations including its small size, disturbed
ecological state, and management problems associated with
downstream impacts from outside sources. On the other
hand, Cahuita Point contains unique and outstanding natural values that deserve national and international attention
and adequate public protection.

The implication, as it relates to local residents, is whether
or not human use is considered compatible with overriding
conservation objectives for the ecological integrity of the
park. The currently proposed management plan attempts to
restore and secure protection of the natural values of the
park consistent with national park criteria, while integrating cultural values and accommodating those needs of local
people that are compatible with conservation objectives. This
requires that planners and managers evaluate park management potential on the basis of local circumstances, considering the specific environmental and social impacts of conflicts
between conservation and human use. For example, the plan
calls for elimination of domestic animals from within the
park and enforcement of wildlife protection laws to reduce
poaching.

On the other hand, local subsistence fishing was deemed

important enough that it could continue under strict regulation, as was the coconut farming to be permitted in special use areas. These activities will be monitored by investigative measures to provide data for future decisions on the tradeoff between use and preservation. The sea turtle population cannot withstand further exploitation, as is evidenced by their scarcity. However, benefits from turtle hunting and raiding of their nests is so insignificant that enforcement will have little impact on local people.

Regional Development

The park is clearly linked to its surrounding region both in terms of outside influences upon the ecosystem of the protected area and the current and potential benefits produced for nearby communities. It represents an important opportunity to contribute to sustainable economic development and to improve the welfare of its residents, although the park's growth alone will not necessarily bring locally needed social and economic changes. In fact, past experience has shown that blind faith tourism development can leave local people worse off, by damaging fragile natural environments, disrupting cultural values, altering social class structures, and siphoning away of economic resources by outside entrepreneurs (de Kadt 1979; OECD 1980). An essential recommendation of the plan is to work with community leaders and regional development agencies to prepare an integrated tourism development plan for the region.

MacCannell (1976) suggests that tourism can grow and develop "naturally" within a region if local people develop a regional self-image out of their cultural distinctions and natural environment. Cahuita National Park already plays a very significant role in preserving and defining the unique natural and cultural elements of the Talamanca region. The manner in which it is developed and managed in the future will set important standards for regional tourism development.

Promotion of Local Knowledge, Skills, and Lifestyles

The park is planned as a regional center for promoting and perpetuating local cultural values for the benefit of Talamancans as well as outside visitors. A cultural zone and interpretive program emphasizing past and present lifestyles will promote cultural values of the region. Local residents are encouraged to create programs to pass on traditions among themselves and to share their culture with outside visitors.

Involvement of Local Population in Planning and Management

Involvement of local people in planning and management is perhaps the most important variable determining the outcome of the plan, particularly when most of the land is locally owned. Not involving the community has been the greatest failure of the park staff. There has been little formal opportunity for local communities to make recommendations or comment on the current proposed plan.

While management programs call for cooperation with local residents, cooperation will be very difficult to achieve unless they can become involved in decision making before final approval and implementation. This planning process falls far short of the normative model of planning for eco-development in which local residents would be involved from the outset with an active voice in planning, management, and development. The plan emphasizes the need to develop and implement a structure and process for mediation of conflicts and ongoing, cooperative decision making before implementation.

Conservation and Human Use at Cahuita National Park

The proposed management plan will both produce benefits and have negative consequences for local inhabitants. If present trends were to continue without active management, neither the local people nor the park service would benefit. Natural resources would likely continue to deteriorate and support even less subsistence use, while many potential economic opportunities associated with park development would be foregone.

The final test of this plan is not simply whether it successfully protects the ecological values within the park while permitting human use of its resources. Rather, it is a question of securing national conservation objectives within a management regime that promotes the cultural heritage of the region and the socioeconomic status of its people.

Conclusion

An increasing number of potential conservation areas qualifying for national park designation are faced with issues of human residence and of traditional uses of park resources by local people. Recognizing that management for primary conservation objectives may require restrictions on traditional users of a national park, this author has found many instances in which wildland conservation has unnecessarily and unfairly harmed local people. Not only are the two potentially compatible, they are also sometimes mutually supportive.

This fact, combined with increasing interest in protecting indigenous lifestyles, has made national parks a popular management strategy for nature conservation and for providing for the needs of native cultures. Regrettably, there seems to be a tendency among park planners and managers to maintain the view that human exploitation or residence in national parks is *a priori* incompatible with conservation objectives. On the contrary, national park criteria do permit limited human use of the protected area wherever it has been determined that such uses will not conflict with the essential purpose and objectives of biological conservation. The future challenge is to develop an awareness among park professionals of cultural values and methods for integrating them in planning and management. These include expansion of local park objectives, effective use of zoning, and integration of cultural activities in specific management programs, including resource protection, interpretation, and administration.

From the standpoint of this author, where national priorities for wildland conservation conflict with the needs of local residents, resource protection objectives should predominate. In these cases, however, park service actions should reflect a social policy that protects the legal and moral rights of local people so that they receive just compensation for negative impacts imposed upon them. Special attention should be given to finding alternative ways of providing for their basic needs. Effective communication and conflict management among competing interests is essential.

11 Michiru Mountain Conservation Area: Integrating Conservation with Human Needs

John Hough

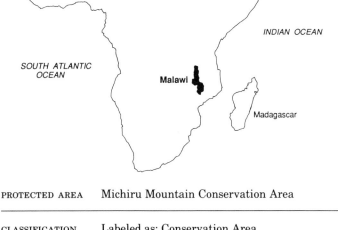

PROTECTED AREA	Michiru Mountain Conservation Area
CLASSIFICATION	Labeled as: Conservation Area Managed as: Multiple Use Area, IUCN Category VIII
RESIDENT PEOPLES	Peasant Peoples, Farmers and other Rural Citizenry

The need to integrate conservation with other forms of land use and the benefits of a multiple use approach to land are slowly becoming more widely recognized. However, there is a reluctance amongst many land users to accept the loss of autonomy and the potential restrictions that such schemes entail. The Michiru Mountain Conservation Area is an experiment in the integration of conservation and multiple land use in Malawi. Productivity has been restored to a much degraded mountain and a variety of other benefits generated. This was achieved by coordinating the efforts of existing land users, both government and private, rather than by establishing a new management agency. Although each party had to make compromises, the final management regime was acceptable to all. The Malawi Department of National Parks and Wildlife played a critical role both by establishing the conservation area and later by maintaining a leadership position in pursuing this integrated approach to management.

Background   The single mass of Michiru Mountain stands on the eastern edge of the African rift valley and ranges in altitude from around 700 meters along its western and northern boundaries to 1,470 meters at the summit. It covers an area of approximately 46 square kilometers. Originally the mountain was covered in a closed canopy of deciduous miombo woodland with evergreen riparian forest along stream lines and a small area of moist sub-montane evergreen forest around the rocky summit. The northern and western sides of the mountain are bordered by rural subsistence farming communities who have traditionally utilized the mountain for forest products such as building poles, firewood, thatching grass, rough grazing, honey, medicinal plants, and meat from hunting. Streams originating on the mountain supply water to these communities. However, the mountain lies immediately northwest of Blantyre, Malawi's largest city (population 250,000 in 1982). During the 1960s and early 1970s high demand for firewood and charcoal from the city's population led to a progressive denudation of much of the mountain, in particular the southern and eastern sections. In addition to reducing the supply of traditional forest products to the subsistence farming communities, the denudation and subsequent grass fires led to major soil erosion and rapid water runoff from the mountain.

During this time, the Forestry Department controlled 82 percent of the mountain area as public forest land while 18 percent belonged to a private European landowner who operated an 840-hectare dairy farm on the northeastern fringe of the mountain. In the early 1970s the private landowner proposed action to prevent further deterioration and to restore and develop the mountain's resources in order to provide sustainable and tangible benefits to the surrounding communities. He offered to give half of his grazing land (240 ha) to the government, in return for government action. This offer was accepted by the Malawi government and a local committee was established to develop a suitable plan of action. This steering committee was chaired by the governmental minister responsible for the region and included representatives from a wide range of government departments, local leaders and politicians, and private organizations with an interest in the mountain area. Under this committee a planning team was established to prepare a scheme for the development of the area. A coordinating officer was appointed to liaise with all interested parties and to draw up a management plan.

Management History: Design

Initial planning work was carried out by staff of the regional office of the Department of Town and Country Planning. However, the primary interest in a multiple-use conservation area came from the Department of National Parks and Wildlife, who appointed a full-time coordinating officer to complete the planning work. This coordinating officer met with all interested parties to draw up a management plan and carried out the initial establishment of the scheme. The support of the Department of National Parks and Wildlife for an integrated approach to management turned out to be critical because the Forestry Department resented the loss of autonomy in decision making that the conservation area would entail and lobbied against it. Action and leadership by the Department of National Parks and Wildlife prevented rejection of the project by the Ministry.

At the same time as the Michiru project was being planned, the Department of National Parks and Wildlife was also establishing a national environmental education program that stressed the more general concepts of conservation of natural resources rather than simply the importance of wildlife. Thus Michiru was seen as an opportunity for the department to demonstrate a broader approach to conservation than its traditional role of managing national parks and game reserves for preservation and limited recreational use.

The planning process itself tried to reconcile local, regional, and national demands with the capability of the land to support the desired uses on a sustainable basis. For management purposes the mountain was divided into three major natural regions: gentle footslopes with colluvial soils and occasional rocky outcrops; steep escarpment slopes with very shallow soils and much exposed rock; and a gently sloping plateau with deeper soils, cooler temperatures, and dry-season moisture from clouds.

The basic land-use pattern to be established on these three regions was: plantations of fast-growing, exotic eucalyptus trees on the footslopes to provide firewood and building poles; initial complete protection of the natural woodlands on the escarpment slopes; clearance and afforestation with pines for timber on the plateau areas. In addition, areas were identified for: dairy agriculture at a preexisting farm on the northern footslopes of the mountain; nature conservation in a large, bowl-shaped valley providing a complete altitudinal cross-section of the mountain; special protection of the remnant of the moist tropical forest that once covered most of the mountain summit; conservation education adjacent to the nature reserve; recreation, including a campsite, information center, view points, picnic sites, and trails; and staff housing.

Within each of these broad areas more detailed management regimes were effected. For example, overall principles applied in the plantation areas for purposes of water-catchment protection and maintaining aesthetic and wildlife values included: eight-meter strips of indigenous vegetation were retained on both sides of all stream lines and plantation roads; all areas unsuitable for plantation due either to rocky outcrops, shallow soils or excessively steep slopes (more than 20 percent for eucalyptus or more than 40 percent for pines) were left uncleared, frequently as isolated pockets within plantations; all planting was fully contoured; and a shelterwood system of management was to be implemented.

To cater to the needs of the local communities, spacing and rotation age of the eucalyptus plantations were reduced to produce a small diameter pole. All removal of poles and firewood was by head-carried loads purchased on-site rather than by vehicle. Clearing for plantations was carefully scheduled to prevent any gap in the supply of firewood from the mountain before the harvesting of the first plantations.

Licensed grazing of the eucalyptus plantations by cattle owners was permitted as soon as the trees were large enough. Once fully recovered, traditional utilization of the natural woodland areas for building poles, firewood, thatching grass, honey, medicinal plants, and meat was permitted under strict license. Coppice management of natural woodland and plantations of slow growing but valuable indigenous hardwoods, in demand for furniture and carving, was also tried on the steep slopes.

Management of the conservation area was placed in the hands of the Departments of Forestry, National Parks and Wildlife, and the private landowner, with consultative input from the Land Husbandry Department. The coordinator, though assigned to the Department of National Parks and Wildlife, reported directly to the permanent secretary of the Ministry of Forestry and Natural Resources. The Department of Forestry dealt principally with all the plantation work, including the establishment of pine plantations (10 percent of the mountain) and eucalyptus plantations for fuelwood (14 percent of the mountain). They also worked jointly with the Department of National Parks and Wildlife in management of the natural wooded areas (50 percent of the mountain), which included administration of harvesting, active fire prevention, early burning and firefighting, and law enforcement, with guard patrols. The Department of National Parks and Wildlife directly managed the nature conservation area (15 percent of the mountain area), the education area (7 percent), and areas zoned for both special protection and intensive recreational facilities. This included trails and view points throughout and educational programs covering the entire mountain. The National Parks Department also dealt with all active research and monitoring. The private landowner maintained ownership of the dairy farm, though it was reduced in size to cover only 9 percent of the mountain area, and was managed in accordance with the conservation area management plan.

The various officers involved in the day-to-day management of the area were brought together for regular management team meetings under the chairmanship of the coordinator, who also reported to a conservation authority. The original steering committee handed over control to this specifically established conservation authority. The latter included local politicians and representatives of the Blantyre City Council in addition to representatives of the government departments concerned with forestry, national parks, agriculture, water resources, and town and country planning. The Authority was responsible to the permanent secretary of the Ministry of Forestry and Natural Resources and was charged with implementing and updating the agreed management plan.

Throughout the development and establishment of the conservation area, the role of the coordinator was critical. Traditional rivalries had to be bridged, particularly those between the Forestry and National Parks departments. The loss of autonomy in decision making, together with compromises and innovations in management practices, were generally resisted. Despite agreement on a detailed management plan there was a general reluctance to diverge from long-practiced methods and principles. Management team meetings were often largely educational exercises. Continuous encouragement, pressure, and vigilance were required. Regular postings of staff to and from the area were a complication, and the extent to which the management plan was followed varied continuously. Such complications were not without their advantages, however. New staff members were often more sympathetic and flexible than their predecessors. A further benefit of such postings was the more enlightened approach adopted by some ex-conservation area staff members after returning to more traditional work within their own disciplines.

Management: Effect on Local Peoples

Acceptance of the conservation area by the local community was reasonably forthcoming. Although local political leaders were represented in the planning process, there was little direct consultation with the local people themselves. However, before strict controls on the exploitation of the mountain area were implemented, a major educational effort was made to inform all the local people of the proposed changes. During a period of one week, public meetings were held at all the primary schools around the mountain. These were arranged through the political party, the district administration, and the schools. Speakers included political, administrative, and governmental officials, and pamphlets designed by the agricultural extension service were distributed to all attenders. Remarkable cooperation was achieved with illegal use of the mountain dropping by around 80 percent almost overnight, followed by a further drop once law enforcement officers appeared on the ground.

Care was taken to ensure that firewood was always available from some locations on the mountain. However, the closure of natural woodland areas to firewood harvesting and the localized nature of plantation work inevitably caused an increase in the distance some people had to walk to collect firewood. The annual clearing and planting were spread over each of the various plantation sites in order to minimize this problem. However, many of those who were affected negatively by this management activity were compensated somewhat by the reduction of the actual time spent collecting fuelwood.

Though a policy of charging for firewood was technically in force prior to establishment of the conservation area, the more rigorous control instituted by the conservation authority clearly affected some of the mountain users. The cost of firewood was set nationally at 5 tambala per headload while the minimum rural wage was 60 tambala and the minimum urban wage was one kwacha (100 tambala = 1 kwacha). The most significant effect was probably on the urban poor who had no alternative sources of free firewood without walking at least 8 kilometers to a wooded area on the hills west of Michiru. This alternative source was a little farther for the rural poor living west of Michiru. Significant deforestation was noted in these woodland areas over the period 1978 to 1984, though the amount caused by users displaced from Michiru is unclear. Professional charcoal burners also moved from Michiru to these western hills.

Active resistance to the control of resource utilization on Michiru was most notable amongst a small group of cattle owners and charcoal burners, though the majority of these shifted their activities to alternative lands nearby. Cattle owners were generally relatively wealthy businessmen while charcoal burners were urban entrepreneurs. Resistance was also significant amongst a few professional firewood gatherers, normally entrepreneurs from urban fringes.

By 1984 the conservation area was receiving favorable comments from members of the local community who could see an improvement in the health of the mountain, and presumably also the rapidly maturing firewood and building pole plantations.

Support from the local leaders steadily improved from a position of apparent neutrality to one of sometimes taking the initiative in assisting the conservation area authority in reducing illegal activity. Perhaps a key feature in this acceptance was the high level of awareness amongst the surrounding communities, noted during planning for the educational effort, that firewood and other natural resource products were becoming significantly harder to find. The distribution of benefits once the firewood plantations mature is likely to be critical to the long-term acceptance of the project.

Conclusion   The integrated approach to land use on which the conservation area was based enabled a degraded mountain to retain its traditional productivity, increase its standing crop, improve the abundance and diversity of its wildlife, and provide an educational and recreational resource. A successful management plan was achieved by combining a variety of demands, both of the local community and of traditionally conflicting agricultural, forestry, wildlife, and watershed interests. Although compromises were necessary on all sides, the end result satisfied the basic requirements of all the parties and is a model which could be profitably repeated in many other parts of Malawi.

NOTE

This chapter is a revised version of an article with a similar title published previously in 1984 in *Parks* 9 (3,4): 1–3 and has been published here with permission of the International Union of Conservation of Nature and Natural Resources, Gland, Switzerland.

12   Lake Malawi National Park: A Case Study in Conservation Planning

Trevor A. Croft

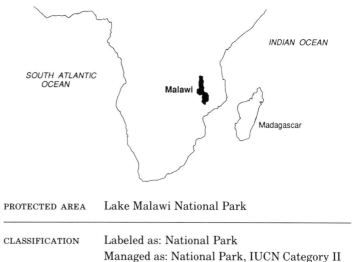

PROTECTED AREA	Lake Malawi National Park

CLASSIFICATION	Labeled as: National Park
	Managed as: National Park, IUCN Category II

RESIDENT PEOPLES	Peasant Peoples (Fishermen-Agriculturalists)

The Malawi government is a signatory to the Organization of African Unity Convention on the Conservation of Nature and Natural Resources. This urges that efforts should be made to preserve, in a national park or equivalent conservation area, a representative section of every distinct biome of Africa, and member countries in particular.

A national park for Lake Malawi was approved in principle by the Malawi government in early 1976. Extensive research work and consultations followed, culminating in the preparation of a comprehensive management plan and gazettement (establishment of the boundaries) of the park under the Malawi National Parks Act in December 1980. It is believed that this is the first time that protection at the national park level had been given to this type of habitat. The designation was in accord with the IUCN World Conservation Strategy which calls for protection of lake systems as an urgent priority.

In this respect, Lake Malawi presented a problem because much of the shoreline is heavily populated and thus precluded from inclusion in a protected area. The important rocky shores are only sparsely populated or uninhabited, but widely separated.

Lake Malawi is of special significance as it has several biotic features of great interest which were, and still are, under increasingly heavy pressure as a source of food, means of transport, and recreational outlet. In establishing the new park, conservation management plans had to take into account a number of conflicting factors, more so than in well-established parks. It is in this respect that the planning of the park is of special interest and provides guidelines of value in considering projects with similar characteristics elsewhere.

Background   Lake Malawi is more of an inland sea than a lake, being 365 miles (587 km) long and up to 50 miles (80 km) wide. Its shoreline ranges from low-lying swamps through sandy beaches to steep hillsides plunging over a thousand feet (305 m) into the lake (see Map 12.1).

The lake's outstanding feature is its fish. The lake contains the largest number of fish species of any lake in the world, with estimates exceeding 450. The lake provides an important fishing industry, and the problem of understanding the evolution and ecological interaction of an exceptionally complex community is of great interest. The interest centers on the family Cichlidae, of which all but four out of an estimated population of over 350 species are endemic to Malawi.

In setting up conservation measures for the lake, the main objective was the protection of a reasonable cross-section of the Cichlid family and particularly the brightly colored "Mbuna" fish. This term is applied by local fishermen to colored rock fish, which provide a remarkable underwater spectacle. There is also a substantial export trade to collectors all over the world, promoting a small but valuable input to the local economy.

An essential feature of any area chosen for a national park is that it be capable of being given adequate protection. Otherwise the main objectives will remain unfulfilled. In practical terms this means that the park should be a reasonably cohesive entity in order to be a workable unit.

The Nankumba Peninsula, with its offshore islands, the Mwenya and Nkhudzi Hills and Nkhudzi Spit, were finally chosen for the park, because they had a number of specific advantages. First, they included about 25 percent of the rocky section of the Malawi shoreline of the lake, giving a good cross-section of the different fish species. Second, the greater part of the area was already forest reserve. Thus there were no permanent residents in the areas to be gazetted (established or drawn) and the problems of physical movement of people did not arise. Third, the area combined landscape types of great interest, ranging from the wooded rocky hills of Cape Maclear to the low-lying marshland and sandy bar of Nkhudzi Spit, together with islands of differing

Map 12.1
Lake Malawi
National Park

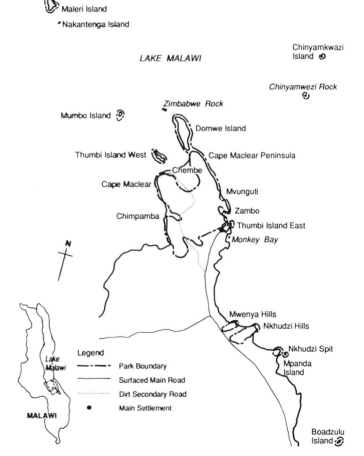

Nankona Island
Maleri Island
Nakantenga Island

LAKE MALAWI

Chinyamkwazi Island

Chinyamwezi Rock

Zimbabwe Rock

Mumbo Island

Domwe Island

Thumbi Island West   Cape Maclear Peninsula

Chembe

Cape Maclear   Mvunguti

Chimpamba   Zambo

Thumbi Island East

Monkey Bay

N

Mwenya Hills
Nkhudzi Hills

Nkhudzi Spit

Legend

Lake
Malawi

--- · --- Park Boundary

——— Surfaced Main Road

············· Dirt Secondary Road

• Main Settlement

MALAWI

Mpanda Island

Boadzulu Island

size and character. Fourth, the whole area is reasonably accessible, facilitating the opening up of specialist tourist trade essential to the overall success of the park. Finally, it has strong historical associations as the site of the first lake-shore mission to be established by the Church of Scotland, designated as a national monument.

Planning

A basic draft plan was prepared in 1976, which identified problems outside the park of fundamental importance to its management.

A particular feature, not found in other Malawian parks, is that the Nankumba Peninsula contains village enclaves cut off between the park and the lake. These villages contained some 5,400 people in October 1977. The villagers depend primarily on fishing for a livelihood, but for their day-to-day requirements of firewood and building poles, as well as fuel for drying and smoking fish, they have traditionally extracted timber from the wooded hillsides of the peninsula and some of the islands. As there was from the outset no intention to move people, these needs had to be met.

Another feature unique to a park within Malawi was the presence of a site used heavily for recreation. This site, adjacent to the old Mission Station at Cape Maclear, was originally developed for a hotel to serve the London—Cape Town flying boat service as an overnight stop. Although the service was short-lived, operating only in 1948 and 1949, the area has had some form of tourist or recreational use ever since. Its use included a rest house and bar with a recreational vehicle and camping site. There was also a substantial number of powerboats based permanently at the site. Such uses were not compatible with the concept of a national park.

It was also clear that the problems affected a number of different disciplines. The Department of National Parks and Wildlife had on its staff planning and research officers experienced in the type of work involved. The Ministry of Agriculture and Natural Resources, of which the Department was then part, had the foresight to set up an expert Ecological Consultative Liaison Group to discuss and coordinate matters of environmental concern.

As a first stage, the senior research officer made a detailed investigation of the park area and the village enclaves. It served as a basic resource survey, and also covered aspects of the daily lives of the people who would affect or be affected by the park. A report was prepared in the form of a summary of the issues—basically an environmental impact statement. This examined the overall ecological balance and was especially valuable in revealing facts about the area that had not previously been appreciated. This was discussed by the liaison group and agreement was reached on the points requiring special attention by the management plan. Further consultations followed during the preparation of the second draft plan by the department's planning officer. This was in turn discussed and approved by the liaison group.

With full agreement within the Ministry and with other interested parties, it was possible to widen the discussion and bring in the Office of the President and Cabinet, the Senior Ministry, which would make the final decision as to whether the park should be recommended to the government. The final stages consisted mainly of the completion of the initial management plan and the commencement of the legal process for gazettement and acquisition once final approval was obtained. Approval for the establishment of the national park was given the government in January 1980, and the final gazettement was completed on 24 November 1980.

Impact

The main area of concern is planning the park centered on the Nankumba Peninsula and its offshore islands, together with the Maleri groups that are nearer to the western shore of Lake Malawi. The park itself is small in area—only about 88 square kilometers—but its component parts are spread out over a much wider geographical area so that potential human impact is much greater than its small area would suggest.

The study concentrated on three main problems:

1. Terrestrial requirements of local residents.
   a. The human population and its increase.
   b. Land for cultivation and agricultural development
   c. The supply of wood for fuel and building poles
   d. Development of amenities, i.e., roads, schools, etc.
2. Exploitation of fish populations
   a. Fishing by local residents
   b. Commercial trawling
   c. Aquarium fish trade for export

3. Tourism development
   a. Construction of a park lodge
   b. Provision of infrastructure

The population directly affected by the park totalled some 5,400 people. There were five villages. Chembe at Cape Maclear was the largest, with a population of some 2,200 in 1977. The rate of population increase in the surrounding area has remained constant since the last available census, 1940. Evidence from District notebooks shows that the rate of increase in the enclave villages had declined, however, from 2.3 percent in 1910 to a very low 0.9 percent in 1977. The evidence suggested that the reason for this was related to a resource shortage in Chembe village because the cultivable land was fully utilized.

Over 90 percent of the land on the peninsula proposed for the park was already under government control as a forest reserve. This land is predominantly steep, rocky, wooded hillsides. The only cultivable land existed in the enclaves themselves, which were outside the boundaries of the park. The largest amount of land available in any enclave was at Chembe and this was a mere 1.2 hectares per household. At the others it is much less, with none at all at Mvunguti.

Resource Utilization

Several factors aggravated this shortage of arable land. The soil was of poor quality and extensive use of fertilizers had been carried out since the 1960s. Average rainfall was about 500 millimeters, but was erratic; crop failure frequency was at least 50 percent. The Land Husbandry Department estimated that in this area a minimum of 1.6 hectares of land was needed to support a household. The only way in which more land could be allocated was by further subdivision. The smaller villages were even more dependent than Chembe on the income from fishing to buy food.

Firewood consumption was studied in detail as denudation of the hillsides had already occurred with subsequent problems of erosion. The main finding was that at the estimated growth rate it was clear that the wooded area—about 6,400 hectares—could not support the present rate of consumption. Air photo interpretation shows a progressive change in vegetation structure, and it was estimated that the woodland would not last for more than thirty years before major denudation and a fuel crisis. The important point is that unless corrected, this would happen irrespective of the establishment of the national park, and would bring with it further destruction of the water catchment and soil erosion problems.

The major area of fishing that concerned the park takes place from the offshore islands that fall within its boundaries. There are three main islands used for this: Mumbo, Maleri, and Nankoma. The latter two form part of the Maleri group near the western shore of the lake.

The study showed that the use of these islands—primarily as overnight bases for fish drying—was much less significant to the overall pattern of fishing than anticipated. The three islands contributed no more than 2 percent of the total catch and gear of the southern part of the lake. The majority of this came from Maleri Island. These bases were, in fact, already illegal, being within forest reserves, and have now been closed down. This did not, however, have a significant effect on the lives of the people in the area.

Of greater concern was whether fish stocks could be sustained at the present level of fishing. The machinery for the sensitive control of village fishing existed through the collection of data on fishing effort and catches, a policy of optimum yield and enforcement of the decisions made. Its effectiveness was limited, however, by the availability of research and management resources. Anecdotal evidence, which could not be considered scientifically reliable, suggested that village catches had declined over the decade to 1978.

Bottom trawling of commercial operators was also an important form of fishing in the area. Government policy had been to allow the fishing effort to approach that calculated to produce the estimated maximum sustainable yield.

The aquarium fish trade has the greatest relevance to the park. Research into this topic was and is being carried out, and provides better evidence for future control.

Social Aspects and Tourism

Other aspects looked at in detail concentrated on physical developments relating to social services and tourism. The provision of social facilities was poor. The villages were served by a low-standard, secondary road that was often impassible during the rainy season. Chembe had a full-intake primary school. None of the villages had a clinic. The general attitude

of the villagers was to welcome any development bringing
them employment and better social facilities.

The development of tourism in Malawi is at a low level
because of the lack of the necessary infrastructure. The development that had taken place on the lake was threatened
by a high rise in lake level since the initial studies were carried out. It is now generally agreed that the type of development appropriate to the lake is a number of small hotels,
sympathetically designed to fit in with the environment.
Small-scale developments also have a minimum of social impact on their surroundings, being much less demanding on
the scale of infrastructure needed to service them. Equally
important is the need to assess park tourist facilities in the
regional context so as to provide a balanced development
overall.

**Planning
Solution**

The impact statement showed a number of serious problems.
It was clear that the park could not stand on its own as the
human pressures on its perimeter were too great. Similarly,
the inhabitants face severe environmental problems relating
to shortages of fuelwood and building poles, agricultural
land, and possibly fish stocks. Any management plan had to
look at the whole area, and not just the park itself, if it was
to have any chance of being implemented successfully.

This view was endorsed by the liaison group. The findings
were accepted and it was agreed that careful management
was needed for the whole area. The management plan which
was then drafted was the first plan for a park in Malawi that
put forward proposals for the management of land areas outside the recorded boundaries. In particular, the point was
made that the warden of the park must be a good manager
and especially be capable of dealing with people. This should
be the situation in any national park, but was all the more
important here in view of the conflicting interests in the
area, and within the park itself. It was envisaged that the
park's warden would be able to call on the service of experts
in forestry, fisheries, agriculture, and recreation development
as an initial starting point. It would be essential for these
people to work together as a team.

The decision was made to extend the park zoning system
into the surrounding area and to apply different management techniques to it. This was a new concept in Malawi at

that time and inevitably, the work would take time. Legislation was being developed to enact a new Conservation Areas Act. This would allow the area surrounding the park to be so designated giving coordinated management and multiple use of the land, with optimum use being applied predominantly in any one area (see Map 12.2). The surrounding of the park by a wider conservation area would allow specific measures to be taken to improve the lives of the people and balance their demands to use resources with those of the park to protect them. The management plan zoning of the park was conventional, ranging from wilderness to intensive use in the tourist lodge area.

Map 12.2

Zoning of National Parks and Proposed Conservation Area at Cape Maclear Peninsula and Nkhudzi Bay

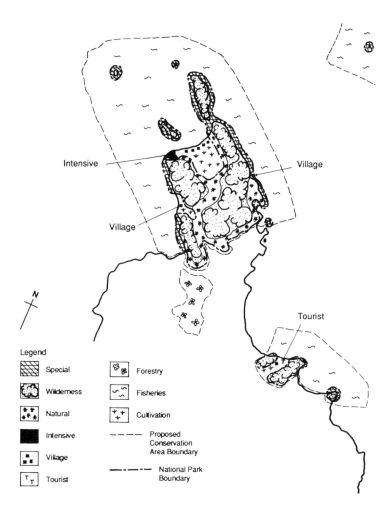

Intensive

Village

Village

N

Tourist

Legend

Special

Wilderness

Natural

Intensive

Village

Tourist

Forestry

Fisheries

Cultivation

– – – – Proposed Conservation Area Boundary

—·—·—· National Park Boundary

The land outside the park, within the future conservation area, was considered under five major areas of interest:

1. The cottage plots. There are ten private cottage plots adjacent to the park at Cape Maclear. Although considered as a site for a possible lodge, the recent rises in lake level have now precluded this. In the long term it is desirable that the area be taken over by the government, possibly as leases expire, for public recreation use.

2. Settlement and cultivation areas. These comprise the enclave villages and their cultivated areas. The anticipation is not that the population will expand significantly. In order to encourage a rising standard of living, it is important to improve agricultural productivity and provide better social amenities, especially health, transport, and education. This will be done by improving agricultural extension services to ensure the best use of available land, and in conjunction with the development of the park, improve social amenities. If, for example, a lodge is developed, better transport and health facilities at Chembe should be brought forward.

3. Forestry. The shortfall in timber stocks means that action must be taken to provide alternatives. Proposals were put forward to plant some 1,200 hectares of land just to the south of the peninsula section of the park, primarily with eucalyptus, to supply fuelwood and poles to the people in the area. This would be carried out as soon as funds could be found for the project. In the short term, until the plantations are established, careful management of the existing woodland was necessary.

4. Fisheries. A managed fishing zone was to be established for two miles off the mainland section of the park and some of the islands. This was designed to cover a sample of the major aquatic ecological zones of the southern part of the lake. Trawling was to be prohibited and careful control made on the use of any bottom dragging gear such as beach seines. Village fishing will be limited to residents and the types of gear now in use. With intensified research and management, it should be possible to build up stocks and maintain a realistic and sensible control system to ensure maximum sustainable yields.

5. Tourist development. It is important that tourist development in the park is related to that of the whole district and through that to national tourist planning. Provision

of a combined land/water access system linked to the main lakeshore hotels, and through them to major tourist circuits taking in areas other than the lake, was envisaged. Special provision was proposed at Cape Maclear for day visitors as well as people staying overnight at the lodge. Emphasis was placed on interpretation related especially to an understanding of tropical fish.

The plan prepared on this basis was approved by the Ecological Consultative Liaison Group. This undoubtedly was helped by extensive prior discussions and consultations. Without these meetings there is no doubt that agreement would have taken much longer.

Conclusion

The major conclusion is that planning a park in a situation as complex as this cannot be carried out in isolation. The maritime aspect made the situation more interesting, and brought in factors that may not have been considered on a largely terrestrial park. It is clear that the aquatic areas are extremely sensitive to damage, not just from over-fishing, but possible pollution from recreational powerboats and siltation from denuded hillsides, as two examples. National parks are as much a form of land use as any other and their existence has to be justified. Consideration of the role they play in the national and regional context makes it easier to appreciate problems within the park.

A multidisciplinary approach is essential to solve problems quickly. This does not mean that the planning team must include experts in every field, but that experts must be consulted at an early stage so problems can then be identified and discussed before plans are formulated. This is more likely to lead to practical solutions than *ad hoc* methods.

The main concerns of this particular park are the water and aquatic life. Nevertheless, the needs of the people have been considered foremost. For the park to work, it is vital that its integrity is safe-guarded. The land/water balance is so delicate that this can only be achieved if people living around the park are informed of developments and see the benefits. If they are to be restricted from certain activities— especially traditional ones—every effort must be made to provide alternatives. The formation of the surrounding conservation area will be a major step forward to implementing the management of these areas outside the park.

Park management must be practical enough to ensure problems can be easily recognized and overcome. Wardens, as well as having technical knowledge, must be able to handle people. Although the lake is being protected, the effort must start on land. This applies to park staff, visitors, local residents, and political leaders. It is essential that there is a will to protect, for without broadly based support—especially in areas of high population pressure—conservation projects, in general, are doomed to failure. This need not be the case with proper planning and management.

The basic principle for success in conservation must be cooperation, and the satisfaction, as far as is possible, of the aspirations of competing groups. It is here that a careful balancing act is required—the demands of national heritage against the needs of a local population with their own lives for which they need to provide.

The developing countries will continue to require aid and assistance from the developed world. The example of Lake Malawi National Park demonstrates the will to succeed. This was emphasized when the Lake Malawi National Park was placed on the list of World Heritage Sites in 1985, because of the international significance of the Mbuna fish. It is important for the world to recognize the importance of this and provide the backing that Malawi needs to support the park. The cooperation shown during the establishment of the park provides a lesson from which many of us can learn.

NOTE

This chapter is a revised version of an article with a similar title published previously in 1981 in *Parks* 6 (2): 1–3, and has been published here with permission of the International Union of Conservation of Nature and Natural Resources, Gland, Switzerland.

13   La Planada: Looking Beyond the Boundaries

Dennis Glick and Jorge Orejuela

PROTECTED AREA	La Planada Nature Reserve
CLASSIFICATION	Labeled as: Nature Reserve Managed as: Nature Reserve, IUCN Category IV
RESIDENT PEOPLES	Peasant People and Farmers Acculturated Tribal People

La Planada, a small nature reserve in Southwest Colombia, is among the handful of new Latin American parks that are reshaping our approach to wildland management. In the past, park administrators and planners have limited their concerns to resource management within park boundaries. It is becoming evident that adjacent land use can and will affect reserve resources, be it through biogeographic isolation, illegal poaching of plants and animals, or other direct and indirect effects from environmentally damaging land uses. This realization has influenced the planning and operation of La Planada, which is becoming both catalyst and facilitator of sustainable development activities in the surrounding region. Although it is far too early to declare the project a success, significant progress has been made, and La Planada has been used already as a prototype for other Latin American conservation units.

Background La Planada was initially identified as an important site for wildland conservation by a Colombian biologist who surveyed the country for areas rich in endemic bird species (Orejuela 1981). It was noted that the La Planada ranch, 1,600 hectares of lush forested plateau and rich in endemics, was threatened by a proposed logging operation. It was also rumored to be up for sale to the highest bidder (see Map 13.1).

To ensure the long-term protection of the area, Mr. Orejuela presented the World Wildlife Fund–US (WWF–US) with a proposal to secure the area as a wildlife refuge. Simul-

Map 13.1
Colombia,
South America,
and the La
Planada Nature
Reserve

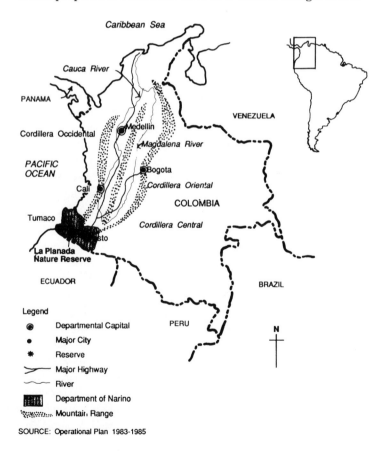

Caribbean Sea

Cauca River

PANAMA

VENEZUELA

Cordillera Occidental

Medellin

Magdalena River

PACIFIC
OCEAN

Bogota

Cali

Cordillera Oriental

COLOMBIA

Tumaco

Cordillera Central

La Planada
Nature Reserve

ECUADOR

BRAZIL

Legend

◉ Departmental Capital   PERU

• Major City

✳ Reserve

⟩— Major Highway

⌒ River

▦ Department of Narino

⌇⌇⌇ Mountain Range

N

SOURCE: Operational Plan 1983-1985

taneously, the Foundation for Higher Education (FES), a Colombian nongovernmental organization, became interested in purchasing and developing the reserve with the assistance of WWF. Until that time in 1982, FES had had little experience in wildland conservation activities. Their primary focus was on the promotion of well-rounded social development through education, scientific, and cultural programs. Their experience in these fields, however, proved invaluable in the later execution of the community-oriented management strategy of the reserve.

Reserve Management

An operational plan was developed soon after the land purchase. The planning team gathered data on the natural and cultural resources of both the reserve and the surrounding region. This information was synthesized into an environmental and cultural profile that has helped to define the orientation and content of the management plan (FES 1983).

The profile underscored the fact that, although the reserve itself was in good condition, the conversion of surrounding forest would soon reduce La Planada to a mere patch of wilderness, ill-suited to the habitat needs of its wide-ranging fauna such as the spectacled bear, *Tremarctos ornatus* (FES 1983). It was agreed that a management plan was needed that would insure that land use in areas adjacent to the reserve created only minimal environmental impact, and was well integrated into the goals of the reserve. It was also obvious that to accomplish this task, reserve managers needed to understand the development characteristics and needs of the neighboring human settlements. Mutual respect and cooperation between the park and the surrounding communities were identified as the best approach to resource vigilance.

The cultural components of these surrounding settlements rival the natural ecosystems in their variety and complexity. North of the reserve, several villages lie in the shadow of La Planada Plateau. These towns are composed of a mix of Latinos from the interior of Colombia, blacks from the Pacific coast, and a scattering of Amerindians from the surrounding mountains. The forested area south of the reserve is inhabited by small groups of Cuayquier Indians that live in rustic, isolated settlements. They have adopted some western clothing and customs, but still demonstrate many traditional land-use practices that seem to have a minimal detrimental impact on forest ecosystems (FES 1983).

The proposed management activities reflect the cultural characteristics and development needs of these various groups, especially as they relate to the natural resources of the reserve. Several facets of the operational plan, such as the objectives, zoning scheme, and the management programs, focus directly on the relationship between the reserve and the surrounding communities. For example, a principal reserve objective, which guides all subsequent park development (Miller 1978), includes as a primary goal: "The implementation of sustainable socioeconomic development projects in communities adjacent to the reserve" (FES 1983).

The zoning scheme for La Planada subdivides the region into distinct management sectors, each with its own development parameters and activities. These sectors include traditional park management zones, such as a "primitive zone" and an "administrative zone," plus additional zones that relate directly to and actually encompass surrounding communities. These include the "manipulative zone," which will be utilized for land-use experimentation and the identification of appropriate forestry, agriculture, and development technologies, and a "zone of influence," which includes all of the surrounding areas that directly affect the reserve—an area of almost 100,000 hectares (see Map 13.2). While La Planada administrators cannot dictate land use in the manipulative zone, they will instead focus intensive efforts in education, forestry, and agricultural extension, community development, and health and welfare projects.

FES, with its many years of experience in community development, has been a great help to the reserve managers in the design of people-oriented activities. An outline of the La Planada's management program is provided in Figure 13.1.

Before the establishment of the reserve, local people harvested firewood, timber, and wildlife from the site. As deforestation increased—especially in the non-Indian lands adjacent to the reserve—firewood-cutting incursions into the wildland area by Latino neighbors rose dramatically. Hunters also utilized the area, and a spectacled bear was shot shortly before the reserve was established. Also, some Cuayquier Indians had established small farming plots in a remote site which eventually became part of the reserve. There was also occasional gold mining by locals in one of the streams which cuts through the area.

With the establishment of the reserve, exploitation of natural resources within the primitive zone was curtailed. However, some Cuayquier Indians were allowed to stay on their plots that fell within the reserve boundaries. Firewood cutting and gold mining within this zone have been eliminated. A tree nursery has been established for the production of seedlings of fast-growing species used for firewood. The trees will be planted in the "influence zone" adjacent to the reserve. Some of the former firewood cutters have been hired by the reserve as workmen and guards. Land-use studies are being undertaken to evaluate the resource utilization characteristics of the surrounding populations in order to better

Map 13.2

La Planada
Nature Reserve:
Management
Zones

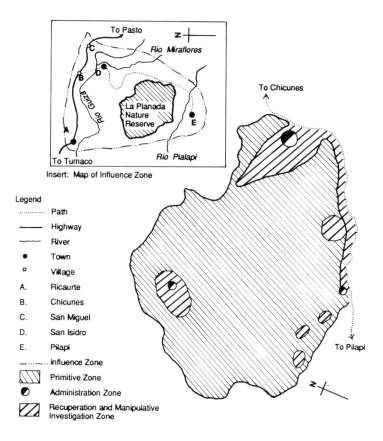

Insert: Map of Influence Zone

Legend
.... Path
——— Highway
—‿— River
● Town
▫ Village
A. Ricaurte
B. Chicunes
C. San Miguel
D. San Isidro
E. Pilapi
—·—·— Influence Zone
▨ Primitive Zone
◑ Administration Zone
▨ Recuperation and Manipulative Investigation Zone

SOURCE: Operational Plan 1983-1985

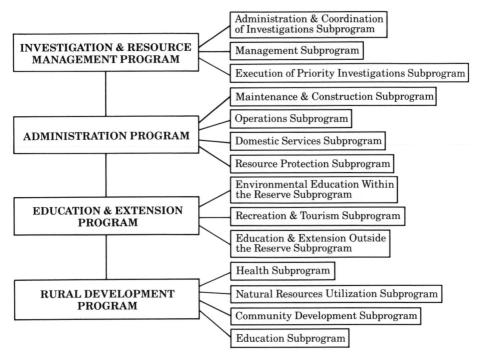

Figure 13.1

La Planada
Nature Reserve
Management
Programs and
Subprograms
(From La
Planada
Operational Plan
1983–1985)

understand their resource needs and to identify viable alternatives to direct harvesting of flora and fauna within the primitive zone of the reserve.

The establishment of the reserve created a controversy related to the Cuayquier agricultural plots that fell within the reserve boundaries. These people have been allowed to continue to farm on these lands. No one in the "influence zone" has been forced to move, nor will they be when the area is formally established as a biosphere reserve. One of the actions being carried out involves helping the Cuayquier to secure title to lands that surround the current La Planada Reserve, and which are scheduled to become part of the proposed biosphere reserve.

**Current
Status of the
Project**

While this plan for integrated development is fairly unique, what is even more significant has been its actual implementation. Unlike many other Latin American parks, reserve administrators at La Planada have been able to carry out nearly all of the activities proposed for the first phase of development (1982–1985). In addition, the Colombian Institute of Natural Renewable Resources and the Environment (INDERENA) has created a forestry reserve adjacent to La Planada, thus placing an additional 2,000 hectares under the protection of Colombia's national system of protected areas.

One program sponsored by FES is Colombia's "Escuela Nueva" (New School), which extends the educational opportunities of rural schoolchildren, trains local teachers, and conducts seminars for all ages on health and nutrition, maintenance of school gardens, and agriculture systems. Through these activities, FES seeks to improve the ability of educators to promote sustainable development practices using local resources in their own villages, and to encourage "cultural recuperation" by fostering pride in local customs, traditions, and community spirit. Since 1985, forty rural schools, mostly in the Cuayquier Indian territory, have benefited from this program introduced in the "zone of influence".

Other people-oriented reserve activities have included: the training of Cuayquier Indians in community leadership, a diagnosis of regional health problems, and a similar profile on the status of agricultural practices. Cooperative work sessions, called "mingas," have been carried out with the Cuayquier Indian communities and have focused upon the improvement of trails and bridges. A joint firewood tree-nursery project between La Planada and the Town of Ricuarte is scheduled to initiate production in late 1986. Plant material from this nursery will be used in the "zone of influence" adjacent to the reserve.

Land-use studies, which are currently being carried out, will help to identify forestry, agriculture, and hunting programs that need to be developed. Eventually, comprehensive extension activities on all three of these land uses will be carried out, and hunting regulations which are supported by local hunters will be initiated.

In 1988, a self-guided "ecodevelopment" trail was completed at the reserve, to be utilized by reserve educators for rural extension programs. This educational trail, which includes an interpretive pamphlet, winds its way past several rural development projects that utilize appropriate technologies. These include demonstrations on the alternative use of sugar cane for forage, biogas generation through the use of animal wastes, mini-hydroelectrical production, agroforestry techniques, and other sustainable land uses.

The community leaders who are trained by FES will provide a direct line of communication between the local populace and the reserve. The reserve, in turn, will be linked to local, national, and international agencies dealing with development issues in the region. The staff of La Planada believe that the surrounding communities must reach an acceptable level of basic well-being before environmental education programs will become an effective tool for changing destructive land-use practices. Even then, these programs must be designed in a manner which relates directly to the developmental needs of the target audience.

In 1986, the La Planada staff submitted a proposal to the government of the Department of Narino (where the reserve is located) that concerned the creation of a biosphere reserve in the adjoining wildlands between La Planada and the border of Ecuador. This region overlaps with the territory of the Cuayquier Indians. Independently, the Cuayquier Indians living across the border in Ecuador have also begun to explore the possibility of managing their lands as a biosphere reserve. Initial bilateral meetings between government and Indian officials of Colombia and Ecuador have been held in the hopes of developing a joint strategy for the creation of an international biosphere reserve. The reserve would straddle the border between both nations and would include the entire region inhabited by these native peoples.

The Phase II La Planada planning workshop was held in early 1987 and focused on the possibility of creating this international reserve. The planning team will work closely with the indigenous inhabitants and relevant government agencies. In addition, international organizations concerned with rural development and indigenous peoples are already expressing their interest in the project. FES is playing an important role in coordinating this inter-institutional, multi-faceted endeavor.

In December of 1988, resource managers representing twenty-two wildland projects in ten different Latin American countries met in La Planada for a two-week workshop focused on "Sustainable Rural Development and Wildland Management." This group analyzed the relationship between natural reserves and surrounding rural development, and explored techniques and strategies for realizing this integration. The La Planada reserve was used as a case study, and workshop participants also related their own experiences.

Funding
Initial funding for the purchase and development of La Planada was shared between World Wildlife Fund (U.S.) and FES. Each of these organizations has invested nearly $250,000 in grants to the reserve. This has resulted in the purchase of the land; the demarcation and planning of the site; the construction of most of the projected infrastructure; four years of active management, investigation, training, and protection; and the initiation of regional ecodevelopment and education programs. The annual operating budget of La Planada is approximately $60,000 (1985). During the second phase of planning several mechanisms will be identified for long-term funding. This may include scientific tourism programs and other money-generating, but environmentally appropriate, activities.

Conclusion
It is far too early to declare the La Planada project a successful integration of conservation and development. Such an ambitious goal will take years of hard work and dedication, and will be measured not so much by what changes occur in the surrounding woodlands as by what does not transpire. Tiny La Planada is, in 1986, contiguous to over 100,000 hectares of intact forest. If it is still adjoining thriving natural ecosystems well into the year 2000, the project will have achieved its objectives. The prognosis is good, and from all indications the project is on the road to success. Some of the key factors that have contributed to this remarkable progress include the following:

1. A well-trained ambitious project staff. The personnel of La Planada have received extensive training and are enthusiastically committed to the project. The three permanent professionals at the reserve have all participated in training exercises related to various aspects of the management strategy. They thoroughly understand the unique orientation of the project and have been successful in communicating this concept to the surrounding communities, to FES, and to international assistance agencies.
2. Solid institutional support. FES has dedicated substantial time, money, and human resources to project development and operation. Their unique skills in community develop-

ment and direct links with numerous governmental and nongovernmental entities have contributed substantially to the project.

3. International assistance. International conservation groups have provided financial and technical assistance. Wildland management, especially when combined with rural development, can be quite costly and demands a long-term obligation of support. The World Wildlife Fund assisted in the purchase and the planning of the site as well as in the operational plan implementation.

4. Solid community support. While public relations between the reserve and surrounding communities have not been without problems, in general the administrators of La Planada have done an outstanding job of communicating the purpose and value of the reserve. This has required a humanitarian approach to wildland conservation that is all too often neglected by resource managers. If La Planada is successful in the long run, it will be because of the cooperative efforts of the reserve staff, FES, the international conservation community, and the active participation of the human populations living near the reserve.

5. An ambitious though pragmatic management strategy. An operational plan that maps out the logical sequence of activities needed to achieve the reserve goals has aided the resource managers in identifying where the project is heading and how it is going to get there. The planning team included the individuals that are charged with its implementation; consequently, they have a stake in carrying the project through to fruition.

The question of replicability of this project in other areas was discussed at length during the aforementioned workshop on sustainable development and rural development. There are several elements in this project that are replicable. It would be a mistake, however, to think that this model could be transferred directly to other areas. The specific conditions and elements important for the success of La Planada or any project vary between each site and community, thus demanding that each conservation project be custom tailored to the national, cultural, economic, natural, and institutional-political idiosyncrasies of its location. What can be transferred, though, is an understanding of the approach and philosophy; the processes, techniques, and materials used; and an understanding of what has worked, what hasn't, and why.

14 Annapurna Conservation Area: Nepal's New Approach to Protected Area Management

Bruce W. Bunting, Mingma Norbu Sherpa, and Michael Wright

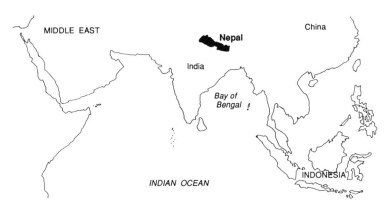

PROTECTED AREA	Annapurna Conservation Area
CLASSIFICATION	Labeled as: Conservation Area Managed as: Protected Landscape, IUCN Category V
RESIDENT PEOPLES	Peasant People, Local Entrepreneurs, and Rural Citizenry

The Kingdom of Nepal is situated among the world's highest mountain peaks, the Himalayas, and between the Palearctic and Oriental zoogeographic realms. The uniqueness of Nepal is exemplified in its varied biogeography, ranging from the subtropical Royal Chitwan National Park and its lush rhododendron forest along the southern slopes of the Annapurna Himal to the sparse alpine desert of the Tibetan plateau.

As in many countries, Nepal's rapid population growth places severe demands on its natural resources, resulting in rapid deforestation, erosion, loss of wildlife, and a decrease in the carrying capacity of the land. In response to these conservation problems, His Majesty's Government of Nepal has established a protected area system covering 9 percent of the Kingdom's total area and representing the ecosystems present in Nepal with four national parks in the mountains, one national park and one hunting reserve in the midlands, and a national park and four wildlife reserves in the lowland terai (see Map 14.1). The addition of the Annapurna Conservation Area strengthens representation of mountain ecosystems by protecting a region of unique diversity as well as the only area of Tibetan steppe open to foreigners. More significantly, it represents a new method in which mountain-protected areas can relate to rural populations in other areas of Nepal and beyond.

**The
Annapurna
Setting**

The region of the Annapurna Himal has long been recognized for its stunning mountain scenery and unique ecology. The area supports an outstanding variety of plants and animals, ranging from dry alpine deserts in the north where some of the last remaining blue sheep and snow leopards reside, to lush subtropical lowlands in the south hosting diverse orchid flora, bamboo jungles, and extensive rhododendron forests.

Map 14.1
National Parks of
Nepal: Protected
Areas and Life
Zones

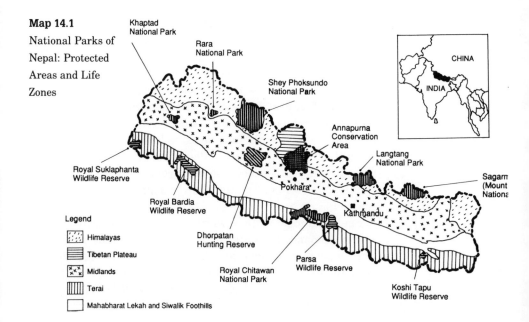

The diverse cultural setting of Annapurna is dominated on the southern slopes by Gurungs and Magar people, both famed internationally as Gurkha soldiers, scattered in small villages. The Manangis have settled along the Marsyangdi River to the east, and on the inhospitable dry steppe behind the Himal, the Manangis, Tibetans, and Thakalis reside in the Kali Gandaki Valley. These people are traditionally dependent upon their natural environment, practicing sheepherding, upland farming, and some hunting. The total population is estimated at about 40,000 within the zone of influence of the conservation area.

Over the last two decades, the phenomenal increase in trekking tourism has upset the delicate ecological balance between land and life in Annapurna. Although trekkers bring needed cash to the local economy, the income generated from this type of tourism is somewhat deceptive. Only twenty cents out of the three dollars spent by the average trekker each day remains in the village. Although tourism is Nepal's leading source of foreign exchange, it has often produced negative effects on the natural environment, village economies, and cultural traditions. The 17 percent average annual increase in trekking tourism has led to the clearing of vast tracts of forested lands to meet the cooking, heating, and lodging needs of international visitors. The social and ecological effects from these visitors are considerable.

The direct impacts of trekking tend to be concentrated seasonally and physically. An early priority in the Annapurna region has been research on existing trekking activities, duration of stay, mapping of tourist movements, analysis of fuelwood purchases, and effects upon local society. Trekking, even at existing levels, may be exceeding the carrying capacity of the fragile Annapurna. Plans for the area focus on ways to increase the local economic contribution at the current levels of visitors, rather than to simply increase visitor numbers.

Fuelwood consumption, which increases significantly from tourist demand, can result in deforestation, soil destabilization, erosion, landslides, and downstream flooding. A typical climbing expedition in Sagarmatha, for example, lasts two months and uses four loads of wood per day for a total of 8,000 kg of firewood. In contrast, an indigenous Sherpa family hearth burns only 5,000 kg of wood per year. One solution mandated by the Department of National Parks and Wildlife Conservation in 1980 requires that trekkers carry kerosene sufficient for the duration of their stay in mountain national parks. A similar approach is now used in the Annapurna Sanctuary, and community-run fuelwood plantations in Annapurna, once mature, will meet both visitor and local firewood use on a sustainable basis.

More difficult to address than the direct fuelwood needs of trekkers are the secondary environmental and social impacts caused by growing recreational use and the resulting disruptions of the local economy. The ripples of impacts are as follows: recreational use converts fuelwood into a cash crop, leading to a change in local lifestyle and an increased desire for high-cost consumption, which in turn leads to increased cutting as one of the only local sources of cash. Increased wealth leads to larger houses and hotels requiring more wood for cooking and heating. Cash also allows lodge owners to hire outsiders who are less sensitive to village restrictions controlling exploitation to cut wood. Wealth is also converted into larger herds of nontraditional species like sheep and goats, which increases overgrazing; in addition to larger herds, more residents have small herds, and as young people pursue trekking rather than herding as their source of income, the stock is less well dispersed, leading to local overgrazing. The increased demand for dairy products by trekkers, and thereafter locals, causes concentration of herds near villages, also resulting in overgrazing. Finally, as a result of tourist demand and high levels of consumption, inflation becomes a new element with which local culture must contend, with few appropriate tools.

A limited conservation consciousness has contributed to and compounded the plight of the mountain natural systems. It is difficult to encourage poor rural farmers to be concerned with nature conservation when they are preoccupied with meeting immediate food needs and fuel and fodder requirements. It is critical to involve the local population in any conservation effort if success is expected. Without direct benefit to an individual family or community, a person is unlikely to alter his traditional behavior. Conservation programs in the Himalayas have often failed because they focused mainly on regulations and external enforcement.

These efforts have not targeted the basic economic and social factors which often result in the villagers illegally collecting products from a protected area. Experience has shown that income-generating alternatives must be provided if villagers are expected to discontinue poor and shortsighted natural resource management. A balance between immediate short-term needs of the local population and sustainable natural resource conservation must and can be achieved. What has been lacking has been the political will of many governments to mobilize the resources—human, financial, cultural and moral—to ensure the integration of ecological principles with economic development.

A New Plan for Protected Areas

Nepal's new approach for joining human values and the conservation of mountain ecosystems in protected areas management, which was formally introduced in 1985, provided the basis for the Annapurna Conservation Area Project. It summarized a series of concepts and approaches developed to protect the mix of human and natural systems in and around the Annapurna Himal. The new approach was inspired by the Nepal Tourism Master Plan of 1972, studies of Nepali conservationists Dr. Hemanta Mishra and Karna Sakya, institutions such as the King Mahendra Trust for Nature Conservation, the Department of National Parks and Wildlife Conservation, the Department of Forests, and other agencies of His Majesty's Government along with international organizations, principally the World Wildlife Fund (WWF). The Annapurna Conservation Area as envisioned was to be a multi-purpose protected area incorporating recreation and tourism along with forestry, agriculture, and the needs of local people as participants in managing the area and the resources it protects.

Although creation and management of national parks have traditionally been the responsibility of government agencies, the Nepali approach is unique in providing a nongovernmental organization with a major role in protected area management. Unencumbered by large bureaucracies, private institutions have the advantage of being able to innovate with new approaches for management and local participation. They can also apply funds generated by a reserve directly into development of the area to establish self-sufficiency. In contrast, most government agencies are required to deposit user fees and other funds into the central treasury, often discouraging entrepreneurial local management. However, even with the advantages of flexibility, private agencies cannot match the security of government establishment and are potentially subject to the government's power of eminent domain.

Nepal's operational design for Annapurna uniquely joins the benefits of both institutions. As with other parks in the Kingdom, the Annapurna Conservation Area meets the International Union for Conservation of Nature (IUCN) international park standards with the government ensuring security. Its administration, however, departs from traditional protected areas with management of the complex being the responsibility of the King Mahendra Trust for Nature Conservation. The Trust was legally established as an autonomous nonprofit institution under the patronage of His Majesty the King in 1982 through KMTNC Act 2039. Despite increasing interest in private approaches to conservation, no such institution has previously undertaken responsibility for an area of such global importance as Annapurna. The King Mahendra Trust, with its close ties to Nepal's political power structure (HRH Prince Gyanendra is the Chairman) and its organizational flexibility, is well-qualified for the task.

History of "Conservation Area" Establishment

In the spring of 1985 His Majesty King Birendra Bir Bikram Shah Dev visited the Annapurna region and issued a directive to improve and manage tourism development by utilizing existing resources to their fullest while safeguarding the environment and natural heritage of the region. Shortly thereafter, a paper summarizing the plan for the Annapurna Area was delivered by the authors of this chapter at an international workshop in Kathmandu, and the King Mahendra Trust endorsed the development of a new concept for the region and its inhabitants. World Wildlife Fund approved a grant for a feasibility study of protected status and community involvement in Annapurna to be undertaken by a team composed of two Nepalis and one American. The team carried out a six-month, in-depth field survey and evaluation of the conservation needs in the area, meeting with local villagers and community leaders. Information was collected on traditional firewood and resource management methods, hunting and wildlife, trends in trekking tourism, local per-

ceptions of development needs and the status of their resources, ongoing government-sponsored development projects, alternative energy potential, conditions of tourist lodges
and hot springs, relationships between villagers and the government administration, examples of locally initiated resource conservation efforts, and attitudes of trekkers and
lodge owners. The resulting report was delivered to WWF
and the Trust in January 1986.

The study team's report contained the essence of the approach and its most encouraging finding:

> Local villagers in principle were found to be remarkably
> aware of problems of environmental degradation, and in gen-
> eral claimed that they would be supportive of corrective
> efforts. Assuming this moral support, and some willingness to
> contribute time and energy, an effective framework must be
> established to allow them to control poaching and random for-
> est cutting, while providing viable, self-sustaining, and eco-
> nomic alternatives. It will be critical that planners, the Trust,
> the regional Conservation Officers and staff consider the in-
> terests of the people in the region first, as true long-term con-
> servation can arise only from a formation of mutual trust
> (Sherpa et al. 1986).

While in many respects expanding upon previously identified
issues, the team made some critical refinements and added a
number of unique concepts.

Out of several proposed options, the final recommendation
of the three member study team provided for the designation
of a "conservation area" to be established in two stages. The
first covers 800 square kilometers of the south slope of the
Himal (mountains), which is mostly within one local political
district, an important practical consideration in an area
where inter-agency coordination can be a problem. Stage one
was targeted for development in the first five years, and an
additional 1,800 square kilometers extension would be developed in the second stage if the unique management approach
proved successful.

Despite the desire for international recognition, easier application of existing legislation, and the possibility of greater
fees being collected, the team felt a national park designation and its associated restrictive management could generate considerable negative local response, as had been the
experience in all mountain parks of Nepal. Instead, the new

custom-tailored concept addressed the specific socioeconomic situation of the region. It allowed for hunting, controlled grazing, collection of medicinal plants and fuel supplies, allocation of user fees to local development, and delegation of management authority to the village level.

On September 11, 1986, His Royal Highness Prince Gyanendra Bir Bikram Shah, in a ceremony to commemorate the Twenty-fifth Anniversary of World Wildlife Fund, announced the formal beginning of the Annapurna Conservation Area Project.

The Nepal Plan in Action

Since official establishment of the Annapurna Conservation Area Project (ACAP), five major tasks have been addressed: production of a management plan consistent with local needs, provision of "park" facilities and infrastructure, training of personnel, initiation of an array of local development projects, and creating a sustainable administrative system.

Management operates from the basic premise that the area should be administered by the community and not for the community. This has ultimately meant that the local people are responsible for decisions relating to conservation area management. Community structure, its social and economic organization, local customs, and the community's perception of their needs differ from one region to another, and there is an ongoing program to collect information on social structure and organization, community perceptions, and resource utilization patterns.

Since the Annapurna Conservation Area utilizes the input of people living in the area for management design and implementation, protected area objectives are met in an appropriate method sensitive to the special needs of the region. The self-identified goals are to consolidate local control over resources, to establish alternative energy sources with less wasteful technologies and to increase local financial benefits from resources used by outsiders and to make this use sustainable. Conservation area staff reside within the local villages, which increases the opportunity for dialogue.

Traditional community organization structures have been identified and strengthened. For example, Forest Management and Lodge Management Committees have been formed along the guidelines of their own "rithi thiti samitee" decentralization act. These committees now see their involvement with the conservation area to be that of a partnership. Committee members have shown themselves to be receptive to new and different ideas and are prepared to try innovations, while the villagers in general have shown a high level of commitment to community projects.

Management Through Zoning

Preparation of a management plan is an essential step in protected area establishment. In the Annapurna region, the critical component has been the integration of management zones and development of an understanding of the local community structure and needs.

The Annapurna study team recommended specific management objectives for the "zone of influence," defined as those areas and communities that exert direct impact on the protected area and vice versa. A series of zones were proposed, including a fully protected wilderness area in the highest elevations, below which lies a protected forest and seasonal grazing zone, and followed by an intensive use zone which encourages a sensible mix of agricultural and tourist use along with community forestry. Most direct management, administration, and conservation education takes place in the final and lowest zone. Several special management zones, such as the Annapurna Sanctuary, where there has been recent disturbance to the environment, also receive particular attention and study, while the Nar Phu Valley and upper Mustang are classified as a biotic/anthropological zone with no access by outsiders.

The *Wilderness Zone* centers on the Annapurna massif and extends to the peak of Dhaulagiri to include the Kali Gandaki River (a major migratory route for birds moving between Tibet and India) to the west, and the Marsyangdi River on the east. The Annapurna Sanctuary is located approximately in the center of the conservation area in a high alpine amphitheater surrounded by seven mountaineering peaks over 6,700 meters (22,000 ft.) and four trekking peaks under 6,000 meters (20,000 ft.). Even excluding other management zones, the core of the Annapurna Conservation Area alone meets international criteria for a national park, including a unique mix of ecosystems, mostly unaltered by human exploitation and occupation. Exploitation and occupation are not permitted in this zone and visitor entrance is managed.

Although a formal agricultural zone is not included in the Conservation Area management plan, the *Protected Forest* and *Seasonal Grazing* zones are important concessions to the traditional income-generating needs of the local population. In a region of limited land resources and where animals are an important symbol of wealth, the challenge is to ensure that grazing use is sustainable, not eliminated.

Community forestry and the establishment of locally operated nurseries represent an important source of fuelwood and fodder. Tourist demand for wood is a serious and immediate issue. Such demand competes with traditional uses of forest products for construction, litter for latrines and animal bedding, medicinal and ritual herbs, fuel for ceremonies and cremations, as well as the major local needs for cooking and heating. Not only must the tourism demand be met, it cannot be allowed to drive fuelwood prices beyond local means.

The key to the Nepal Plan is to buffer the protected core with sustainable human use in a zone of influence. Ringing the Annapurna massif, the *Intensive Use Zone* is being actively developed for tourism. Local lodge owners understand that visitors are attracted to Annapurna for the natural beauty and are supportive of the conservation area. Their Lodge Management Committee, set up under ACAP, attended a training course sponsored by the King Mahendra Trust and developed a standardized menu and room pricing policy. Many lodge owners proudly display the certificates received following completion of the training in much the same manner that lawyers and doctors hang diplomas on the walls of their offices. ACAP also set up check points for trekking permits and monitoring fuel supplies as a way to maintain control and also to assist trekkers with any potential problem.

Near the heart of the Annapurna Sanctuary lies the *Special Management Zone*, and in the upper reaches of the Conservation Area lies the *Biotic/Anthropologic Zone* for scientists focusing on the study of mountain ecosystems. Rehabilitation of the research facility at Kuldi Ghar in the sanctuary provides a base for study of the regions' diverse habitats and the impact in the nearby community forest and seasonal grazing zones. In a very real sense, the research zone and adjacent areas add a biosphere reserve in the heart of the conservation area complex.

Conservation Area Infrastructure

Development of physical "park" infrastructure through visitor centers, trekking "check-in" and information posts, and sanitation services provide an opportunity to educate visitors on natural and cultural issues and to demonstrate sound environmental practices and alternative sources of energy to the local population. Local operation generates local benefit, while oversight by the King Mahendra Trust maximizes educational and interpretive impact.

Use of indigenous construction styles takes advantage of existing experience on climate stability, availability of local materials, and limited skilled labor, and it avoids transportation problems. This appropriately meets the goal of an infrastructure that can be maintained with local human skill and financial resources.

The conservation area significantly uses a broad interpretation of infrastructure development. A major innovation of ACAP is the establishment of Panchayat Nature Conservation Committees, consisting of fifteen villagers selected by consensus for each panchayat (village-level units with a population of 500 to 1,200). These extended "Forest Management Committees" are delegated the authority to select forest guards to oversee enforcement and management of local development projects. Operations and enforcement are funded with fines from illegal hunting, cutting, collecting (divided 50 percent to the panchayat development fund, 25 percent as a bonus to the forest guards, and 25 percent divided between committee members), and from the conservation area entrance fee. The commitment of the villagers and their support for the Forest Management Committee make it one of the most significant achievements of the Conservation Area Project to date.

Personnel and Their Training Needs

The King Mahendra Trust, which is based in Kathmandu, recognizes the importance of remaining in close contact with the conservation area and has consistently emphasized that management of the area be primarily in local hands. Project staff are identified through consensus at community meetings. This utilizes local knowledge in technical and cultural issues while retaining awareness of the pressure that can be exerted upon local protection guards and conservation officers for special favors to friends and relatives.

Realizing that the lack of proper training opportunities for field personnel is one of the major failings of protected areas worldwide, the King Mahendra Trust offers an integrated training package that focuses on developing self-esteem and practical, hands-on skills that enable both staff and villagers to undertake responsibility for the efficient achievement of project activities. Training in appropriate technologies for community-based natural-resource management and technical skills looks specifically at indigenous technological solutions, maximizing sustainability and replicability. The main objective of training in the community is to strengthen the villagers' ability to manage their own development.

Community-Identified Development Projects

Forestry programs receive top priority among all activities identified by the villagers in the conservation area since most families depend solely on the forests for firewood, fodder and timber.

Integrated forest and wildlife management in the conservation area focuses on the supply and demand for forest resources. Activities include plantation forestry on degraded lands, fencing and protecting catchment areas, and providing fuel-efficient technologies such as hydroelectric generators that utilize the fast-flowing mountain streams as an alternative to wasteful use of firewood.

Conservation education and public awareness focus on school children, adult extension, and trekkers. Visitor centers, the Annapurna Museum in Pokhara, booklets and brochures, audio-visual materials, and daily contact through extension activities are the means of sharing the message about the direct benefits from conservation. Significantly, out-of-school youths are an important target group for these outreach programs.

Clean water supplies and sanitary latrines are also greatly appreciated by the local population, and a local community health clinic was established adjacent to the conservation area headquarters in Ghandruk panchayat. The villagers fully utilize the services offered at the clinic and consider it one of the visible achievements of the Conservation Area Project. They willingly provided $5,000 of their own funds as a match to project funds for establishing the clinic and support for continued operations, which is an impressive show of local support in a nation where the per capita income is less than $150.

User Fees and Institutional Sustainability   The Annapurna Entry Fee approved by His Majesty's Government gives the Annapurna Conservation Area Project a unique opportunity to achieve financial self-sufficiency. In a significant and commendable change in government policy, these funds can be used for the direct conservation and development of the region rather than being returned to the central treasury as is done with fees collected for other protected areas. The project has been made a top priority by Nepal, which has committed itself to this policy experiment of putting revenues generated by a trekking entry fee into the local management of biological resources.

Since January 1989, the 200 Nepali Rupee ($8) entry fee has been collected at the Central Immigration Offices in Kathmandu and Pokhara where trekking permits are issued. An unusual secondary benefit of this system is that it cuts out the huge operating costs of putting entrance gates in the protected area for fee collection.

Conclusion   The Annapurna Conservation Area Project is an innovative device directly linking conservation with quality-of-life issues and the basic human needs of the people living in an environmentally sensitive mountainous region of Nepal. Daily needs of the indigenous population are satisfied through the sustainable use of natural resources such as firewood and fodder. It promotes environmentally compatible multiple land use, incorporating traditional methods of resource utilization and animal husbandry.

Administration of the conservation area offers a significant opportunity for the King Mahendra Trust to demonstrate the crucial role of indigenous private institutions in complementing and supporting government efforts for attaining national conservation and development goals. An integrated, "bottom up" approach in resource management distinguishes the Annapurna Conservation Area from most other environmental protection programs. Not only does the Annapurna project provide measurable benefits to Nepal, it also serves as a globally relevant model of ecological restoration, harmonious tourism, and environmental protection.

15 **Exotic Species and the Colonization of New Territory**

Robert N. Muller

Preservation of species diversity has become a watchword in virtually all applications of natural resource management. The focus of much of this concern has been on endeavors that actively remove species or alter habitats. However, passive management poses risks as well. The introduction of highly competitive alien species for agroforestry purposes may lead to an unwanted ecological succession that displaces individual native species or perhaps entire communities of protected native ecosystems. Such invasions are not without precedent and have occurred in the tropics, temperate zones, and even boreal regions of the globe. The potential effects of such invasions are multiple and include: 1) loss of directly competing species; 2) loss of symbionts dependent upon native species that have been extinguished; 3) introduction of nonspecific pathogens that have utilized the invader as a migratory host; 4) ecosystem-level changes in productivity, biomass quality, and nutrient dynamics; and 5) alteration of habitat quality.

Three examples from temperate North America suggest the magnitude of the problem: 1) The accidental introduction of chestnut blight (*Endothea parasitica*) into temperate eastern North America led to the rapid demise of the American chestnut (*Castenea dentata*), which at one time accounted for as much as 40 percent of the overstory in the Eastern Deciduous Forest (McCormick and Platt 1980). The loss of this species has initiated a sequence of processes whose final outcome is unknown. 2) An intentional introduction in temperate eastern North America has had equally long-lasting effects. Kudzu (*Pueraria lobata*) is an aggressive liana that was introduced for erosion control in the 1930s (Mack 1985). When it escapes into natural forests, it climbs into the crowns of established trees and smothers them. Because of its aggressive growth and very effective interception of light, large areas of the southeastern United States have been reduced to monocultures of this vine. 3) The grasslands of California were initially composed of a diverse mixture of perennial grasses. These have mostly been supplanted by European annual grass species, and management appears to offer no means of returning to the original composition (Heady 1988). Many additional examples exist (Mack 1985; M. B. Usher 1986).

This chapter considers the potential for introduced species to successfully escape from agroforestry uses and become pests that threaten the integrity of natural ecosystems. Four points are considered: 1) the characteristics of species that make them successful invaders of natural ecosystems; 2) the characteristics of ecosystems that make them susceptible to invasion by exotic species; 3) optimal strategies for control; and 4) the potential for species described in the preceding chapters to become successful invaders and pests in natural ecosystems. While the emphasis is on agroforestry and the potential for introduced species to become pests in native forests, examples and principles of invasion are drawn from the larger literature dealing with ecological succession.

Character-
istics of
Invading
Species

Most species are not successful invaders and many conditions mediate against successful colonization of new habitats (Crawley 1986). First, the presence of an alien species within an ecosystem provides several opportunities for native organisms. Plants, which form the base of the ecological food chain, supply food for herbivores and are subject to infection by pathogens. Species, which have successfully evolved in the context of a given community, usually exhibit characteristics that minimize the effects of herbivorous and pathogenic attack. However, alien species, which have evolved in the presence of a different array of herbivores and pathogens, may not have the variety of chemical, phenological, and reproductive defenses that would protect them from attack by new herbivores or pathogens. Second, many species depend upon mutualistic relations with beneficial fungi (e.g., mycorrhizal symbionts) or pollinating insects, which may not be present in the new ecosystem. Finally, all species have certain basic physical and chemical requirements for survival. These requirements define a species' niche within a community. In the competitive environment of a closed plant community it appears that most resources, and the possible niches that they represent, are already being utilized, and that successful colonization requires competitive superiority over species that have previously evolved within that community.

Thus, exotic species are frequently at an ecological disadvantage and often do not survive in the new ecosystem. This is readily apparent in the numerous unsuccessful attempts to introduce new cultivars of species into a previously uncolonized region. Unintentional introductions are often equally unsuccessful. For instance, only one out of four alien plant species arriving in imported raw wool in Great Britain achieves a recognizable reproductive size (Crawley 1988).

However, successful colonizations do occur, and the characteristics of successful invaders have been the subject of a considerable body of ecological literature (Baker and Stebbins 1965; Gray et al. 1987; Mooney and Drake 1986). Noble and Slatyer (1980) have identified three attributes of species that contribute to their ability to invade communities in a successful sequence. These have been modified here to consider the special case of invasion in stable ecosystems. One primary attribute of invasion by exotic species is a mechanism of dispersal that allows the propagules of potential invaders to reach suitable sites. In the case of exotics, this requirement is partially met by human intervention, whether accidental or intentional. However, additional mechanisms of dispersal are necessary for invading species to migrate from the initial locale of introduction into native ecosystems. Most frequently, pest status is reached by species that establish a successful colony from which new satellite colonies are derived. As these colonies grow and coalesce, they invade large areas rapidly. Dispersal, both into and within native ecosystems, may come in a variety of forms utilizing wind, animal, or water vectors. However, all mechanisms must provide a reasonable probability that a viable propagule will arrive at a site capable of supporting germination and establishment.

A second attribute of successful invaders is maturation of the new individual, which is dependent upon the physiology of the invading species. Species may be considered to be: (1) tolerant, (2) or intolerant of the conditions of a stable community. Other species may, in fact, require (3) some conditions of the closed community for successful establishment and survival. Tolerant species (1), or those that require environmental conditions of the closed forest (3), may readily establish under a closed canopy. Such a capacity requires a highly competitive photosynthetic mechanism that is tolerant of low light conditions, has the ability to compete effectively for limited soil resources (moisture and nutrients), and has the tolerance of any biotic or abiotic factors of the undisturbed community that may inhibit growth. These species are true invaders of closed communities and pose the greatest threat to maintenance of intact native ecosystems.

Successful establishment of intolerant species (2) involves colonization on sites where environmental influences of the closed forest are minimized. Such conditions frequently result from minor disturbance, which is a natural component of any forested ecosystem. Events associated with the death of a canopy tree, whether by windthrow, pathogenic attack, or simply old age, greatly modify the local environment. Increased light intensity at the forest floor, soil moisture, and nutrient availability create a microcosm of enhanced resources availability where competition is greatly reduced. These naturally occurring disturbances within stable forests provide opportunities for intolerant species to establish colonies. Their continued presence depends upon their capacity to develop viable, self-reproducing populations (Bazzaz 1986).

A third attribute of successful invaders involves demographic features that contribute to the capacity to develop self-maintaining populations. These include the time required for a species to reach reproductive maturity and its overall longevity. Tolerant species and those with specific requirements for closed-forest conditions may be unaffected by longevity consideration. However, for intolerant species, short lifespans may imply reduced seed production and dissemination. These short-lived species may only be able to survive in forests with long disturbance intervals by producing seeds with long viability. These seeds are stored in the forest floor until disturbance conditions occur (P. L. Marks 1974). Long lifespans enable intolerant species to survive as fugitive species in which the population moves about from one disturbance site to another through the production and dissemination of seed. Such life histories are also common among native species that are important in the successful regeneration of natural forests (Buckner and McCracken 1978; Skeen et al. 1980).

The most successful invaders, then, frequently combine rapid and effective dispersal characters with rapid growth to reproductive maturity and large reproductive output. Successful invaders are often intolerant of understory conditions and are successful only by establishing on slightly disturbed sites that allow additional light to reach the forest floor. These are also the characteristics used in selecting highly productive species for agroforestry. This is cause for careful consideration when selecting and introducing species for plantation management.

While successful invasion of stable communities requires life history characteristics that are compatible with the environmental constraints of the ecosystem, it is clear that a significant element of chance exists in the successful establishment of alien species. Colonization is a particularly sensitive phase in the life history of a species, and environmental constraints that may not affect well-established populations may restrict the founding of new ones. Two lines of evidence suggest that successful invasion is a tenuous process at best. First, numerous examples exist in the wildlife literature of species that have required several introductions into obviously suitable habitat prior to successful invasion (Robinson and Bolen 1989). The factors that limit initial establishment may relate to vagaries of the environment during the sensitive period of initial colonization, threshold population requirements for successful breeding, or genetic qualities of the introduced stock. Second, even when viable colonies of invading species are established, range expansion frequently proceeds at a slow pace initially, followed by an exponential increase in the rate of range expansion (Mack 1985; M. B. Usher 1986). This may relate in part to the lag period prior to reproductive maturity of individuals. However, it also occurs for some period of time following reproductive maturity that may reflect in part a period of genetic readjustment of the developing population.

Many of the attributes of successful invaders seem to be found in herbaceous species. It may be of some reassurance to managers of forest preserves that the most successful invading aliens are herbs. For instance, in the highly disrupted flora of California a total of 644 alien species have become naturalized (Raven 1986). Of these, 615 are annual, biennial, or perennial herbs, 28 species are shrubs and vines, and only 1 species (*Ailanthus altissima*) is a tree. The highly complex life history of trees as opposed to shrubs and herbs may limit their success in invading nonnative ecosystems.

Characteristics of Invadable Ecosystems

Successful invasion of ecosystems depends not only upon characteristics of the invading species as described above, but also upon characteristics of the community that may make it more or less invadable. All terrestrial ecosystems of the world have been subject to invasion by exotic species. However, considerable variation exists in the degree of invasion that has occurred among these communities. It has been suggested that this variation may be accounted for by the presence or absence of unfilled niches that contain unutilized resources. Among the numerous alien species introduced to an ecosystem, one or a few may be capable of filling that niche and utilizing the resources it contains. Such a mechanism would suggest that the influence of invading species might be minimal since exploitation of an unutilized niche would have little direct effect on other native species. Ecological niche theory is presently inadequate to directly diagnose the presence or absence of unfilled niches; however, indirect evidence suggests that most invasions of stable communities do not involve the exploitation of previously unutilized resources. Analyses of mature ecosystems indicate little variation in net primary productivity beyond that predicted by regional differences in climate. This similarity of production suggests that utilization of resources by plants is limited by availability, and not by the absence of species (Vitousek 1986). Direct measurement of major limiting resources (i.e., light, moisture, nutrients) further suggests that each is utilized completely, and that in mature communities there are no niches of unutilized resources that might be exploited by invading species.

Several regional analyses show that the success of invasion by alien species is greatest on disturbed sites. These are also sites where competition is less intense. The flora of Great Britain, which has a well-documented history of invasion by alien species, varies from 78 percent to 0 percent alien in composition. The single best predictor of this variation in alien composition of communities is the average degree of plant cover (Crawley 1986). In temperate North America two common examples of highly invasive communities are the successful communities occurring on abandoned agricultural lands and the open native grasslands of California. As a generalization, communities with the greatest alien composition are those with low plant cover. This implies that competition for resources plays a critical role in determining the invadability of ecosystems. Ecosystems in which competition is particularly stringent (i.e., stable forests) should have increased resistance to invasion by alien species. Further, this suggests that the ecosystems that are in greatest need of agroforestry for land stabilization and maintenance of productivity are also the ones that are most susceptible to invasion by alien species.

Control Measures

These observations concerning the characteristics of invadable ecosystems should mollify some (but by no means all) concerns pertaining to invasion of native forests by introduced alien species. Certainly, invasion of undisturbed forests does occur, as earlier examples attest. While perhaps relaxed vigilance is warranted, vigilance is nonetheless necessary to avoid losses of diversity in established preserves.

The control of alien pests has been the subject of considerable agronomic and ecological study. While specific measures of control are beyond the scope of this review, it is perhaps worthwhile to consider the philosophy of control and overall control strategies. Along with the low rate of success of introduced species, a significant feature in the life history of invading species is the lag period in rate of spread, followed by exponential expansion through new terrain. Clearly, control measures will be most effective when range expansion is limited. However, rarity of occurrence during the lag phase of expansion may limit the success of finding newly established populations.

Once populations are well-established, effective application of control measures is constrained by another dimension. Usually, resources for control are limited and control efforts must be applied in a manner that will achieve optimal results. Simulation models of simplified systems of invasion have indicated that best results can be achieved by directing control efforts toward satellite colonies emanating from the original invasion focus (Moody and Mack 1988). Effective control of population spread can be achieved by the elimination of 30 percent or more of the satellite foci of invasion. However, direct attacks on the expanding front of the original population will have little effect.

These observations suggest that effective protection of native forests might be best achieved through vigilant surveillance and rapid elimination of outlying colonization foci.

Finally, it is worth considering the methods of management in the practice of agroforestry. Certainly the process of dissemination is the critical link in the escape of introduced species and their invasion in native ecosystems. Any cultural activities that might limit the effectiveness of dissemination would contribute to the control of potential invaders. Thus, initial selection of species with low dissemination potential would significantly reduce the possibility of escape. Management programs that include harvest before trees reach reproductive maturity would also limit dissemination. This latter approach depends upon detailed and effective management schedules and may not be practically reliable.

In the final analysis, however, use of native species as urged by S. Raval (chapter 6) and cessation of human disturbance in native forests may provide the most effective protection against alien invaders. Native species have known responses to the environment in which they are utilized, and protection against disturbance minimizes the opportunity for invasion of protected ecosystems.

Practical Considerations for Management of National Parks in Developing Regions

The chapters of this volume describe a variety of case studies that integrate the preservation of natural diversity of species and habitats with the economic development of indigenous peoples. Achievement of these goals necessitates redirection of human activities from preserved forests to plantations that may provide firewood and housing materials. In an ideal formulation the principles of agroforestry would prescribe utilization of the native diversity of species for all plantings. Several conditions dictate against application of these principles, including availability of economically suitable species, resistance of local cultures to use of native species that have been supplanted by introductions, and biological suitability of native species to the uses that are being introduced. Consequently, several of the studies of this book describe use of nonnative species for plantations for firewood, lumber, and other economic uses. The genera described in the preceding chapters belong to two of the most widely planted tree genera of the world: *Eucalyptus* and *Pinus.*

Eucalypts are widely valued for their ease of establishment, rapid growth, and quality of products. Although they are native only to Australia, eastern Indonesia, and the Philippines, species of *Eucalyptus* are preadapted to a variety of climates and soils. Today they are planted globally throughout the tropical and temperate zones. Although there is considerable variation within the genus, eucalypts in general exhibit many of the characteristics colonists have in common, including rapid growth, early reproductive maturity, large seed output, and winged seed in some species (Penfold and Willis 1961). Such characteristics raise concerns about the possibility of permanent establishment of the genus in the floras of new regions. An additional character that might ensure its establishment is a well-developed coppicing capacity. Vegetative reproduction from stumps would ensure long-term establishment on a site. However, two characters limit the rate of spread of *Eucalyptus* species (Cremer et al. 1978). Because of a general dependence upon insect pollinators, viability of seed is low. Frequently, less than 10 percent of the total seed production is capable of germination. Seedlings and saplings are intolerant of shaded conditions and thus must depend upon disturbance in order to establish. In native forests in Australia, eucalypt seedlings regularly establish in naturally occurring gaps or after fire. Because of a high production of essential oils eucalypt forests are highly flammable and are reasonably considered to be a fire cycle vegetation type.

Pines are also characterized by ecological life histories that favor colonization. In addition to the above features, pines are uniformly wind-pollinated, meaning that they have little dependence upon biotic vectors for effective pollination. Pines are also intolerant of shade. However, *Pinus radiata* has demonstrated the capacity to invade native eucalypt forests in Australia from nearby plantations (Burdon and Chilvers 1977).

Species of *Eucalyptus* and *Pinus* have been selected for

their ecological characters that ensure rapid economic returns. Unfortunately, these are precisely the characters that may enable invasion of native forests. While it is impossible to predict which species have the potential to become invaders, close attention to details of ecological life histories may allow land managers to make intelligent decisions regarding the protection of native forest ecosystems.

Part Five NATURE PRESERVATION AND
ECODEVELOPMENT: TOURISM

Traditional use
lands *(above)*,
Grand Canyon,
Arizona. Boat
repairs *(center)*
before opening
of Bacalau fish-
ing season in
the Galapagos
Islands. An
example of
intensive use
area *(below)* in
Fuki-Hakone-
izu Park, Japan.

Introduction   In addition to the environmentally sustainable use of protected area resources, local ecodevelopment can also result from the preservation of protected area resources. The primary documented cases of local ecodevelopment involve tourism which depends on the protection and integrity of park resources that tourist visitors come to see. While tourism development can have negative environmental impacts, protection of the integrity of ecosystems is essential to the successful sustainable economic benefits of tourism. Our main hypothesis (mentioned in chapter 1 and elaborated upon in the comparative conclusion) is that the capture of tourism benefits for local people depends in large measure on the political economy of the tourism sector. The chapters by Bailey and Woo demonstrate that large-scale, highly capitalized tourism, which is frequently controlled by outside economic interests, contributes little to local people and can have a variety of other negative economic, social, and cultural impacts on local people. The chapters by Weber and Hough illustrate that smaller-scale, locally controlled tourism can be a viable means of local ecodevelopment.

In chapter 16 Bailey analyzes the political economy of the tourism sector involved in the Galapagos Islands National Park (off the coast of Ecuador). General impressionistic writings in the conservation literature (Villa and Ponce 1984) claim that tourism in the Galapagos Islands is a compatible form of ecodevelopment benefiting local people. However, Bailey's careful analysis of the tourism sector clearly demonstrates how the political economy of highly centralized tourism fails to adequately benefit local people. It clearly demonstrates how the interests of the park administration and conservation scientists stationed there also play into the hands of the powerful, concentrated tourism industry based on the mainland.

Bailey's chapter also illustrates local ecodevelopment based on local people's sustained use of fishery resources. If the boundaries of the national park had simply been extended to the marine environment, fishing would have been eliminated because of the automatic exclusionary policies in Ecuador's National Parks Act, modeled after the United States park system. Instead, a special marine reserve designation was established that allowed for sustained-yield fishing without damaging the park's protection objectives.

Woo's chapter on tourism in Korean parks echoes Bailey's theme that highly capitalized, large-scale tourism dominated by nonlocal economic interests benefits local people very little. He argues that such large-scale, externally controlled tourism corporations can drive out smaller-scale, local tourism enterprises, leading to economic concentration and external monopolization of the tourism economy. In addition, this form of tourism can have negative cultural and economic impacts on local people, including inflation in the local economy.

In chapter 18, Weber analyzes the tourism sector for Sagarmatha National Park in Nepal. In sharp contrast to Galapagos and Korea, local Sherpas are able to monopolize trekking guide services through multiple local, small-scale operations. The case of tourism at Sagarmatha Park presents one of the best examples documented in the literature on ecotourism of the potential capture of tourism benefits by resident peoples. As we will see in the comparative conclusion to this volume, there may be particular structural conditions that have made this possible here, but which may not come so easily elsewhere.

Chapter 19 by Hough on the Grand Canyon and the adjacent Havasupai Reservation illustrates how local peoples next to protected areas can benefit from tourism. The Havasupai's control over the nature and pace of tourism development on the reservation has ensured that the tribe controls the economic benefits of tourism development by not relying on external capital investors. It has also helped to mitigate negative social and cultural impacts on the tribe. Hough documents various conflicts with the Park Service over issues related to tourism that continue to cause strain between the Havasupai and the Park Service. But on the whole, this case is a positive example of tourism-based local ecodevelopment stimulated by the presence of a major national park with a heavy draw of national and international tourists.

16   Conservation and Development in the Galapagos Islands

Conner Bailey

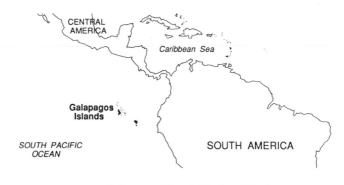

PROTECTED AREA	Galapagos Islands National Park
CLASSIFICATION	Labeled as: National Park Managed as: National Park, IUCN Category II
RESIDENT PEOPLES	Peasant Peoples, Farmers and Rural Citizenry, and Local Entrepreneurs

Since publication of Charles Darwin's *Origin of Species* in 1857, the Galapagos Islands of Ecuador have been recognized to be of unique scientific importance. To have reached these islands, living organisms either traveled along one of several converging oceanic currents, were carried through the air by wind or birds, or were recently introduced by human visitors. In this isolated setting, the processes of adaptation and natural selection produced an unusually large variety of floral and faunal species found nowhere else in the world.

As a living laboratory, the Galapagos Islands continue to attract scientists from around the world. Because of isolation and limited human contact, many bird and reptile species have little or no fear of people. This not only facilitates the work of scientists, but is a major attraction for tourists. Tourism to the Galapagos Islands is a major economic activity and a significant source of Ecuador's foreign exchange earnings.

Both the international scientific establishment and the tourism industry of Ecuador are interested in protecting the Galapagos Islands from human disruption. Effective measures have been taken through the creation of a national park, including allowing tourists to enter only in the presence of a trained and licensed tour guide.

This chapter examines the powerful interests that support policies restricting human access to most natural resources within the Galapagos Islands. These include the National Park Service of Ecuador, the international scientific establishment, and Ecuador's tourism industry. The combined influences of these three interest groups are substantial in shaping national policies that affect the Galapagos Islands. These three groups are interested in effective protection of the marine and land developments and have supported policies that restrict human access to most of the natural resources on the islands. Local development is therefore strictly limited.

These groups, however, believe that sustainable local development depends on tourism (Villa and Ponce 1984) and not on agriculture or fishing, which until recently served as the twin bases for the local economy. Though tourists are attracted to the Galapagos Islands, relatively few local residents have benefited from tourism. The primary beneficiaries of the restrictive conservation policies have been large tour companies from the mainland.

History of the Park

Compared to most other islands of the Pacific, the Galapagos Islands have been relatively undisturbed by human activity. Nonetheless, by the time of Darwin's investigations, human intervention had already begun to disrupt the balance of fragile local ecosystems. The continued impact of human disruption of local ecosystems provides the necessary rationale for strong conservationist policies in the Galapagos Islands. This conservationist philosophy is embodied in three major institutions that have come to dominate life in these Islands: Darwin Station, representing the interests of the international scientific community; the National Park Service, representing the government of Ecuador; and the tourism industry, representing the private sector of the national economy.

Darwin Station

The Charles Darwin Research Station was established in 1964 by agreement between the Charles Darwin Foundation and the Government of Ecuador. The foundation is a non-governmental international scientific association, devoted to conservation and scientific study of the Galapagos Islands. It has a small permanent international staff that organizes and supports research of visiting scientists from around the world. Scientists at the station are frequently requested to assist and advise government agencies, including the National Park Service. Specifically, the Darwin Station has been asked to help delineate nature reserves, to identify species with special conservation needs, and to recommend means of control or extermination of exotic feral species that endanger local ecosystems and endemic species. Darwin Station scientists were actively involved in demarcation of park boundaries and the establishment of the Park Service's regulatory system.

The National Park Service

The National Park of the Galapagos Islands was created in 1959, but it was only in 1973 that regulations for park administration came into effect and not until 1979 that boundaries of the park were established. The park is controlled by the National Park Service, an administrative division of the Forestry Service within the Ministry of Agriculture. The Park Service effectively controls access to over 90 percent of the land area of the archipelago. The only areas lying outside park boundaries are the small coastal communities on each of the four inhabited islands, an agricultural zone in the interior of these four islands, and Baltra Island (a military reservation and location of the primary airport used by tourists [see Map 16.1]).

Access to the Park is restricted to scientists and visitors in the company of trained guides who are licensed by the Park Service. Tourist visits are limited to forty-three approved sites. Each site has clearly marked paths and the guides ensure that visitors keep on the trails. Only authorized scientists and park staff are permitted elsewhere in the park.

The Tourism Industry

Tourism in the Galapagos Islands has expanded rapidly since 1970. Most visitors arrive by plane on Baltra and tour the islands on one of four large tour ships (Garces and Ortiz 1983). These ships are owned and operated by tour com-

panies from the mainland and are designed to accommodate
relatively wealthy travelers. About one-third of all visitors
travel through the islands on smaller boats owned by local
residents. This portion of the tourist trade, not controlled by
large tour companies, consists of low-budget travelers whose
needs are met by simple accommodations and services (e.g.,
day trips to nearby sites by small boats). For the most part,
these boats are based at the small port town of Puerto Ayora
on Santa Cruz Island, which has become the center of the
local tourist industry.

The tourism boom has led to the construction of several
small hotels and provides an international clientele for local
restaurants in Puerto Ayora, but has had relatively little
impact on the other three inhabited islands. Once aboard the
tour ships, all meals and accommodations are provided; visitors have little or no contact with local residents. Supplies
are obtained from the mainland, crews are hired from the

Map 16.1
The Galapagos
Islands: Dock,
Port, and Airport
Facilities

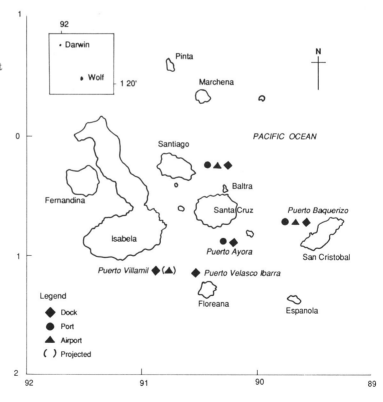

mainland, and the profits accrue to owners who live on the mainland.

Those who operate the major tour companies realize that tourists attracted to the Galapagos Islands are interested in natural history and the unique flora and fauna of the archipelago. It follows that acts that are detrimental to the environment would lessen the attraction. It is not surprising, then, to find that the tour companies are among the strongest supporters of conservation in the Galapagos Islands.

In sum, these institutional sources of support for conservation in the Galapagos Islands agree that there is a need to limit and control all forms of human activity that may affect the local environment. The combination of the National Park Service's legal authority, the tourist industry's economic clout, and the international scientific community's professional influence makes a powerful alliance.

Establishment of Human Communities

The first recorded human sighting of the Galapagos Islands occurred in 1535. Over the next three hundred years pirates, whalers, and naturalists visited the islands, but it was not until 1832, the year Ecuador proclaimed sovereignty, that the first settlement was established. For the next hundred-plus years, the national government officially encouraged migration from the mainland to buttress Ecuador's claim to the islands.

During the first one hundred years of settlement, agriculture and fishing provided the twin bases of material existence. Throughout the nineteenth century the archipelago remained sparsely populated. The total population of the Archipelago in 1935 is estimated to have been only 320 (Direccion de Turismo del Litoral 1980:46). In recent years, however, the population has dramatically increased. The 1980 census reported a population of just under 5,600, with 89 percent living on either Santa Cruz or San Cristobal. Since 1980, the flow of migration appears to have increased substantially; by 1986 the population may have approached 10,000 (J. M. Broadus per. comm. 1986).

Population growth during the 1980s has centered on Santa Cruz. This increased population, specifically that in Puerto Ayora, is linked to opportunities in tourism, employment in government service (including the National Park Service), and government-sponsored development projects.

The Instituto Nacional Galapagos (INGALA) is the government agency with primary responsibility for development in the Islands. Created in 1980, INGALA has adopted an engineer's approach to development by emphasizing the use of heavy-duty construction equipment for building physical infrastructures. In 1983, INGALA's budget totaled approximately U.S. $8.9 million (INGALA 1982). Assuming a population of 8,000 in that year, per capita development expenditures would have exceeded U.S. $840, more than three times the national average in 1983 (U.S. Department of Commerce 1983:2).

The flow of development funds into the Islands has drawn migrants to the archipelago, and especially to Puerto Ayora where INGALA's impact has been most obvious. INGALA construction projects also have created employment opportunities on San Cristobal and Isabela, though relatively few resources have been expended for development on Floreana, which had a population of sixty-two in 1983. On Isabela, the flow of resources from government development projects has been sufficient to cause people living in the agricultural zone of the interior to move to the coastal community of Puerto Villamil, where most construction activity is taking place. As a result, several hundred hectares of land have gone out of production on Isabela and the degree of dependency on agriculture has declined. Nonetheless, agriculture remains an important occupation among Isabela residents, as indicated in Table 16.1.

Table 16.1   Distribution by Island of Primary Occupations in the Galapagos Islands, 1980

Island	Gov't.	Agric.	Tourism	Commerce	Fisheries	Total
San Cristobal	223	129	6	39	64	461
Santa Cruz	167	115	283	81	34	680
Isabela	40	123	9	12	16	200
Floreana	8	9	2	3	3	25
TOTAL	438	376	300	135	117	1,366
PERCENT	32.1	27.5	22.0	9.9	8.6	100.1*

*Total does not equal 100% due to rounding.
(From Loza 1981)

That many individuals have secondary occupations should be kept in mind when interpreting these figures. On Isabela, for example, 68 percent of all resident households own agricultural land, yet farming is a secondary economic activity for a majority of these owners (Consultora de Investigaciones para el Desarrollo Urbano Regional 1983).

This pattern of occupational multiplicity occurs throughout the Galapagos Islands. From the perspective of the individual, this strategy serves to increase income and reduce risk associated with dependence on a single activity. More broadly, the ability of individuals to engage in two or more occupations serves to allocate scarce labor resources to match seasonal opportunities and needs.

This second factor is of particular importance for seasonal activities in agriculture and fishing. Although farming and fishing have declined in relative importance compared with tourism and governmental services, they remain important economic activities within the overall economy and are of special importance to long-established residents whose ties to the Galapagos Islands extend over decades or, in some cases, generations.

The Agricultural Sector

On each of the four inhabited islands, the land most suited for agricultural production is located in the interior. Like many other small oceanic islands of volcanic origin, rainfall tends to be abundant at high elevations but relatively sparse along the coast. In the foothills of volcanic mountains, adequate rainfall and fertile soils provide an environment favoring a wide range of agricultural activities. In contrast, the coastal environment is arid, rocky, and rather inhospitable.

Until recent years, agriculture was the dominant sector of the local economy. Within the agricultural sector a dualistic pattern of agricultural development is apparent wherein a few individuals with larger farms control a high proportion of available land; most are engaged in cattle ranching for mainland markets. The more numerous small farms, in contrast, produce a diversity of crops primarily for household consumption. Local market demand for food crops is weak due to small population size and the high proportion of local residents who are engaged in farming. Marketing local products to the mainland is economically feasible only for relatively high-value commodities such as beef and coffee. The

Table 16.2 Distribution of Landownership on San Cristobal Island, 1981

Hectares	Owners			Area		
	No.	%	Cum. %	Ha.	%	Cum. %
0.1–4.0	34	24.6	24.6	120.8	1.8	1.8
4.1–10.0	57	25.8	50.4	374.4	5.5	7.3
10.1–25.0	47	21.5	71.9	835.0	12.4	19.7
25.1–100.0	41	18.7	90.6	2,005.0	29.7	49.4
100.1–250.0	18	8.1	98.7	2,526.5	37.4	86.8
>250.1	3	1.3	100.0	887.9	13.2	100.0

(From INGALA 1981)

Table 16.3 Distribution of Landownership on Isabel Island, 1978

Hectares	Owners			Area		
	No.	%	Cum. %	Ha.	%	Cum. %
0.1–4.0	22	20.0	20.0	44.7	1.4	1.4
4.1–10.0	24	21.7	41.7	157.3	5.2	6.6
10.1–25.0	23	20.4	62.1	397.0	13.27	19.8
25.1–100.0	36	32.4	94.5	1,607.1	25.81	72.9
100.1–250.0	6	5.5	100.0	815.1	27.13	100.0

(From Consultura de Investigaciones para el Desarrollo Urbano Regional 1983)

Table 16.4 Distribution of Landownership on Santa Cruz Island, 1980

Hectares	Owners			Area		
	No.	%	Cum. %	Ha.	%	Cum. %
0.1–4.0	9	5.0	5.0	7.1	.1	.1
4.1–10.0	4	2.3	7.3	28.2	.2	.3
10.1–25.0	21	11.8	19.1	379.4	3.4	3.7
25.1–100.0	109	61.7	80.8	5,965.3	52.8	56.5
100.1–250.0	33	18.6	99.4	4,534.1	40.1	96.7
>250.1	1	.6	100.0	373.8	3.2	100.0

(From INGALA 1981)

latter is an important cash crop for small farmers throughout the islands.

The distribution of farmland ownership differs from island to island. On San Cristobal, half of all farms are ten hectares or less, but these account for only 7 percent of all agricultural land (see Table 16.2). A similar pattern is found on Isabela (Table 16.3). Data describing farm structure on Floreana are not available. There are far fewer small farms on Santa Cruz. Only 7 percent are less than ten hectares (see Table 16.4). Given the extremely small population, there is little need to expand production beyond relatively small "enclaves" in an otherwise wild environment. These agricultural enclaves continue to exist in the form of specified "zones" created when the national park was established. Even though current agricultural practices may be regarded as ecologically benign (Broadus et al. 1984), the cumulative impact of human intervention has been significant both within and beyond established agricultural zones. The introduction of exotic plant and animal species has had a major impact on local ecosystems. Farmers on Santa Cruz have introduced exotic trees and pasture grasses. On Isabela, several hundred hectares of farm land have been overgrown by kudzu, a creeping vine introduced as a ground cover. On San Cristobal, some farmers allow their cattle to roam within the national park, while on Isabela and Floreana herds of wild cattle have become established. Observing the impact of these intrusions, conservationists have argued successfully that farming in the Galapagos Islands should be restricted to existing enclaves. Demarcation of park boundaries effectively foreclosed opportunities for new residents to open virgin land and made it impossible for established residents to expand their holdings. Regulations prohibiting cultivation of land within park boundaries mean most local farmers will continue to be small-scale operators. Furthermore, this means that opportunities for their descendants will also be constrained, particularly should existing plots be subdivided.

The Local Fisheries Sector

Establishment of a national park in the Galapagos Islands has placed very real limitations on local farmers. In contrast, virtually no restrictions limit operations of local fishermen because no marine areas are included in the park. Over the past decade, however, consideration has been given to restricting access to the marine environment surrounding the islands, including fisheries resources that generations of local fishermen have harvested.

The primary impetus for extending control to the surrounding seas has come from scientists at the Darwin Station who argue that the marine environment deserves as much protection as the terrestrial portion of the archipelago. The marine environment shares many of the characteristics that make the terrestrial environment of the Galapagos Islands of great scientific importance. There is a wide range of habitats and highly complex marine communities that, compared to most marine areas of the world, have been relatively undisturbed (Wellington 1976). The marine environment is characterized by a high degree of endemism, offering opportunities for basic biological studies comparable to those available on land (Wellington 1976).

Initially, consideration was given simply to extending the national park. However, Ecuador's National Parks and Reserves Law of 1971 clearly prohibits removal of any organism from a national park (Ley de Parques 1971). Extension of the national park to coastal waters would have eliminated the local fishing industry. However, imposition of a policy

Table 16.5 The Bacalao Fishery: Fleet Size, Fishing Trips, and Landings Per Trip, 1973/74 to 1980/81

Fishing Effort	1973–74	1974–75	1975–76	1976–77	1977–78	1978–79	1979–80	1980–81
Number of Fishing Trips	17	16	12	12	16	14	11	10
Total Fishing Trips	94	94	76	64	90	84	67	66
Average Trips Per Boat	5.5	5.9	6.3	5.4	5.6	6.0	6.1	6.6
Total Landing (metric tonne)	191.0	196.4	159.4	168.6	198.0	183.0	158.0	169.7
Average Landings Per Boat (mt)	2.0	2.1	2.1	2.6	2.2	2.1	2.4	2.6

Note: These weights are for dried salted fish (seco salado). Rodriquez uses a factor of 1.83 to convert dry weight to fresh fish (e.g., for 1978/79 198 mt of dried fish equals 362 mt live weight).

having this effect appears unlikely. The existing fishery poses no threat to endemic species or coastal ecosystems in general. Recognizing this, Darwin Station scientists appear willing to accept the claim that local fishermen have traditional resource-use rights (Reck 1983; G. Robinson 1983).

While this chapter was in preparation, and after considerable debate, the Ecuadorian government established a marine reserve extending fifteen miles from a baseline drawn around the islands (J. M. Broadus per. comm. 1986). It was stipulated that local fishermen would be permitted access to their traditional fishing grounds. These areas contain 90 percent of the marine biota and are therefore of considerable importance to scientists and others concerned with protecting the unique flora and fauna of the Galapagos Islands (Wellington 1984).

However, the small number of fishermen and the simple technologies they employ suggest little reason to be concerned that resource depletion will occur (Reck and Rodriguez 1978). Finally, available data show that the size of the fishing fleet and levels of fishing effort have declined steadily since 1973 (see Table 16.5).

The key factor leading to decline in the level of fishing effort has been development of the tourist industry. In response to growing demand for interisland travel by tourists, some boats have been built with this purpose in mind. However, the National Park Service has banned any further conversion of fishing boats for tourist use. At present, most tourists come to the Galapagos Islands on package tours arranged by major tour companies from continental Ecuador.

From the Park Service's perspective, limiting tourist travel through the islands to the ships of these companies greatly facilitates their job. Ensuring the presence of trained guides on numerous small fishing boats would make the job of the Park Service far more difficult.

Conclusion   The Galapagos Islands are of unique scientific importance. Large numbers of tourists from around the world come to these islands to see a range of remarkably unspoiled ecosystems containing floral and faunal species found nowhere else on earth. Tourists come away with a greater appreciation of natural history and leave behind hard currencies for

Ecuador's exchequer. The international scientific community and Ecuador's tourism industry work closely with the National Park Service. Together, these three groups dominate conservation and development policies affecting the islands.

Establishment of park boundaries has imposed clear limits on the further development of established human communities on the Galapagos Islands. Opportunities for expanding land under agricultural production have been removed. Fishermen also may find limits placed on their operations or on their ability to introduce new technologies, though for the present their traditional resource-use rights appear to be protected.

One may argue that imposition of such limits is a small price to pay for protection of floral and faunal resources that are of unique scientific importance, but this would not be without significant socioeconomic impacts on local people. Properly managed, tourism may be the most appropriate form of economic development, given the importance of protecting the unique floral and faunal resources of the Galapagos Islands. At present, approximately 20,000 visitors per year come to the islands and there has been no observable negative impact on local ecosystems.

To date, the local population has been largely excluded from gaining any significant benefit from a tourism industry dominated by a few large companies on continental Ecuador. Most tourists never come into contact with local residents, patronize local businesses, or purchase local products. Isolation of most residents from development opportunities based on tourism stems from the congruence of interests between science and the established tourism industry, and the enforcement of this interest by the government's Park Service.

Regarding development, a fundamental question needs to be addressed: "Development for whom?" If the goals simply are to earn the most foreign exchange with the least negative impact on local ecosystems, current policies are appropriate. However, if a broader set of policy goals is adopted that include increasing economic opportunities for local residents, then a new approach is needed. There is considerable interest among residents in taking part in tourism development by providing local services. Small hotels and restaurants exist and several of these could be upgraded to accommodate a wider range of tastes than the simple fare currently available.

A critical constraint to this expansion of local involvement is the ability to meet transportation needs. Unless tourists are able to hire local boats to transport them to sites approved by the Park Service—and these can only be reached by boat—there will be little demand for onshore accommodations and other services. Local fishing boats and other craft could provide the needed transportation and should be encouraged to do so. It still would be necessary for each boat to carry a licensed guide, and the importance of protecting the quality of visitation sites would have to be emphasized to those local residents who may become involved in this portion of the industry. Assuming reasonable care in issuing licenses to residents who are aware that the sustainability of tourism development depends on preserving local ecosystems, the added risk of environmental damage and increased management burden on the Park Service would be small when balanced against the potential benefits of increased local employment and more equitable distribution of income.

NOTE

Preparation of this chapter was supported by the Alabama Agricultural Experiment Station, Auburn University. I gratefully acknowledge the financial assistance of the Donner Foundation and the Pew Memorial Trust, which supported field investigations in the Galapagos Islands as a member of a four person team from Woods Hole Oceanographic Institution. My thanks to Jim Broadus, Howard Clonts, John Dunkelberger, and Glenn Howze for their constructively critical comments.

17   An Assessment of Tourism Development in the National Parks of South Korea

Hyung Taek Woo

ASIA

PROTECTED AREA	National Parks of Korea
CLASSIFICATION	Labeled as: National Park Managed as: Protected Landscapes, IUCN Category V
RESIDENT PEOPLES	Peasant Peoples, Farmers and Rural Citizenry, and Local Entrepreneurs

Tourism has often been one of the major incentives to the designation of national parks in many countries where national or local economic resources are limited, or public land scarce. National governments in such countries have seen the creation of national parks as one of the major opportunities for generating new sources of national revenue by attracting foreign visitors to them. In addition, many local governments of such countries have supported this national tourism policy because they anticipate development will bring new jobs and income to economically depressed local areas. Powerfully concerted tourism policy has often produced the massive scale and urban leisure type of tourism development found in many national parks that has been promoted under the guise of providing recreational uses for the public. Consequently, large-scale tourism development has not only caused the immense destruction of nationally important natural and cultural resources, but has destroyed local life, culture, and economic structure.

Tourism development in Korea has often followed the examples found in other nations. It has been one of the principal objectives for designating national parks and one of the major, influential factors that shape planning and management decisions in the national parks of Korea (Woo 1980). Tourism interests and related development strongly supported by governmental and nongovernmental sectors will have long- and short-term impacts on resident peoples. This chapter discusses a number of the important sociological considerations and major impacts of tourism development that might apply to national parks in Korea and other countries.

Economic Impacts

Tourism is basically the business of making a profit out of the demand for leisure and recreation, and by encouraging visitors to spend money. If the tourist industry is seen as one of the major answers to the national or local economy, tourism policies tend to be: (1) the intensive development of attractive areas; (2) the construction of a well-developed transportation network to facilitate easy access; (3) the attraction of more visitors and wealthier tourists; (4) the provision of more convenient and luxurious facilities and services; and (5) the encouragement of visitor spending. The implementation of these policies requires large capital investment, goods, and services from outside organizations with the support of government subsidies, loans, and grants.

Such tourism development has also occurred in the national parks of Japan and Korea. The central governments in both nations have promoted the tourist industry with money and incentives, and their national parks have been central areas in designing and implementing tourism policies and plans (Prime Minister's Office 1980; Woo 1980). The development process has enormously changed the physical, social, and economic environments of local communities in the areas of national parks that are valued by resident peoples as well as the general public.

Large-scale tourism development has inevitably caused the immense destruction of important natural and cultural resources of the park, since it is accompanied by extensive and intensive development including: new roads; a variety of hotels and leisure homes; new attractions and service facilities; increased visitor use; and consequent waste and trash. The destructive impacts of such development on the park ecosystem have been well known in different parts of the world. Throughout the history of Japan's national park system, many areas have been destroyed by extensive and intensive tourism development (Nature Conservation Bureau 1981). This has also been occurring in many areas of Korea's national parks. A major consequence has been the destruction of the nationally significant natural and cultural resources that tourism, as well as traditional rural cultures and lifestyles, depends upon. These catastrophic environmental effects also result in a loss of public image, recreational opportunities, and the educational experience that can only be obtained in Korea's national park system.

There are both positive and negative economic impacts associated with tourism development. It can improve the economies of rural communities through new tourist-related jobs, extra income, expenditures by developers and visitors, and increased tax revenues that can be made in local areas. However, negative economic impacts usually far exceed such local economic benefits.

Most of the local jobs created by tourism development offer low wages, are seasonal, and mainly suited for women. The few well-paid jobs available are taken by qualified outsiders because of the inexperience of the local people. Although extra income can be generated, local people incur the higher cost of living in communities with increased tourist consumption, higher prices of goods and services, and mounting housing and land values. Visitor spending helps to maintain marginal local shops and services, but it usually stimulates them to change from local convenience to tourist specialty. It generally benefits only a few merchants since most goods, supplies, and services depend on the external area. Large-scale tourist accommodations and residential establishments, such as hotels and leisure home complexes owned and operated by big businesses from urban centers, make locally based small-scale accommodations less economical and competitive (Hakone Accommodation Association 1986; MacCannell 1976; Machlis and Burch 1983). This often forces small local accommodation owners to sell their properties to new investors, abandon their business, or expand accommodation capacity and facilities. A study done in Britain concludes that small local accommodations such as bed and breakfasts, farms, and cottages generate considerably more local income, based on the same amount of tourist spending, than large hotels and guest houses that are not owned by local people and depend on outside supplies and labor (Wales Tourist Board 1974). Tourism development projects can increase local tax revenues, but they increase public service demands and related expenditures. These projects can cause negative fiscal impacts on local government over a period of time, if the public services and expenditures necessary for developing and maintaining such projects exceed the new tax revenues that they generate (Zinser 1980). This, in turn, will impose an additional tax burden on local residents. In sum, urban-based, large-scale tourism development can generate some benefits to the local economy, but a large share of tourist income is passed on to others outside local areas.

Social Impacts

The final important effects of tourism development on local communities in national parks are the social impacts. As the tourist industry is introduced, it changes traditional rural cultures and lifestyles (MacCannell 1976; Machlis and Burch 1983; Zinser 1980). These social changes in local communities will be considerable mainly due to the close exposure to tourists from urban centers with attitudes, values, and lifestyles in marked contrast with those of most local people. In addition to these influences, locally held traditional festivals and religious events turn into tourist-oriented functions to satisfy visitors rather than local residents. Local responses to these social pressures vary widely. Thus, long-held, rural community identity and cohesion are damaged. Local governments also face the dilemma of not being capable of properly providing increased public services and expenditures resulting from the large influx of tourist facilities, traffic and visitors, and waste and trash into their areas. They usually do not have adequate money, time, experience, and skilled personnel to deal with such problems.

Those who can benefit most from large-scale tourism development are not local people, but big development companies, private investors, merchants, and newcomers from outside local rural communities. Such large development has often caused not only immense damage to the park environment, but had serious negative social and economic impacts on local communities. Small-scale tourism projects can create more local jobs and income, enhance recreational experience, and accommodate park landscapes (MacEwen and MacEwen, 1982). Tourism development must create a direct link between revenues generated by tourism and the economies of local communities (MacCannell 1976). Thus, tourism in national parks must be small-scale and suitable to local environmental, social, and economic structures.

With the careful consideration of the impact of tourism, policies and plans of the Korean government involving national parks must be reassessed and changed, not only to protect the physical, social, and economic environments, but wisely and constructively to use the important resources on which both tourism and rural communities depend. National parks in Korea have been used by public and private tourism development projects and designated as key tourism development areas by the Ministry of Transportation, which is charged with the tourism administration but not with the national park administration (Woo 1980). This development will cause both serious environmental damages to park landscapes and significant socioeconomic impacts on local people.

Conclusion

Tourism is important to the economies of national parks in many countries, but it is not the answer to building up the national or local economy. Urban-based, large-scale tourism neither benefits the local economy of rural communities, nor protects important natural, scenic, and cultural resources of the park. In addition, it has significant social influence on traditional rural cultures and lifestyles. Tourism development in national parks must be small-scale and adapted to the local community so that it can create more local jobs and income, maintain rural cultures and lifestyles, enhance public recreational opportunities, and protect park ecosystems.

To guide tourism development in national parks, principles, which are also applicable to Korea and other countries with similar problems of tourism, are needed. Major principles that need to be considered are: (1) Tourism should value the character of important natural and cultural landscapes rather than cater to business and the urban visitor; (2) it should benefit both conservation and recreation, the two main purposes of a national park; (3) the development of tourism policies and plans should not only take into account social and economic conditions of local communities, but involve local participation; (4) the scale and type of tourism development should reflect local socioeconomic structures and institutional capability; (5) tourist revenues should improve the local economy and return dollars to local people as broadly as possible; and (6) the tourism administration and industry should make public the mutual relationship between tourism, park protection, recreation, and local community. Tourism in national parks planned and developed by these principles will demonstrate new creative and constructive paradigms that significantly benefit conservation, recreation, tourism, and local people.

18

Enduring Peaks and Changing Cultures: The Sherpas and Sagarmatha (Mount Everest) National Park

Will Weber

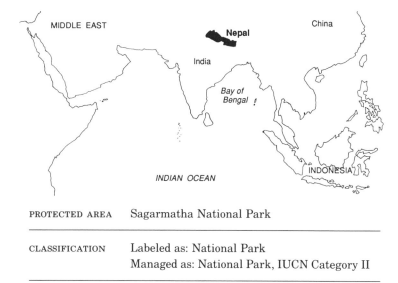

PROTECTED AREA	Sagarmatha National Park
CLASSIFICATION	Labeled as: National Park Managed as: National Park, IUCN Category II
RESIDENT PEOPLES	Peasant Peoples and Local Entrepreneurs

The area surrounding Mount Everest in the Himalayas of northeast Nepal was established as Sagarmatha National Park in July 1976. Since then, efforts have been made to manage the area that contains about 2,500 Sherpa people. This local population is benefiting substantially from the tourism which Everest attracts, but conflicts between local people and park authorities are numerous. The park management plan recognizes Sherpas and their culture as important elements of the national park, but evident opportunities for individual economic progress in the short term have often obscured the desirability of preserving and managing community resources on a sustained basis.

The Creation of Sagarmatha National Park

Sagarmatha National Park consists of 1,113 square kilometers ranging in elevation from valley bottoms at about 3,000 meters to the highest mountains on earth over 8,800 meters. The most spectacular resource of the area is the highest portion of the Himalayan Range itself. While Mount Everest is a focal attraction, the park and surrounding region are in many ways geologically unique. High, broad glacial valleys, sheer peaks that can be closely approached on foot, high lakes, trails, and passes offer a unique recreational context which is enhanced by the lore of mountaineering. In recent years, about 6,000 foreign tourists have visited the park annually (Bezruchka 1985).

Virtually all arable land is cultivated for barley and potatoes, but this is a small percentage of the total area. Lands accessible to yak or yak/cattle hybrids below 6,000 meters are extensively grazed. The naturally occurring, large mammals of this area of the Himalayas—such as blue sheep, Himalayan tahr, snow leopard, wolf, and Tibetan sheep—have been greatly reduced or eliminated as a direct or indirect result of competition for limited food and human activities. Slow growing juniper, rhododendron, birch, and blue pine forests have been severely depleted through fuel wood-cutting. Certain forests are traditionally protected as sacred sanctuaries associated with monasteries, but even these have suffered encroachment related to tourism and mountaineering in recent years.

Suggestions and proposals that the Everest region be made into a national park long preceded its actual creation. An environmentally conscious king assumed leadership in the early 1970s. He placed a high priority on creation of Sagarmatha and other national parks and wildlife reserves. The Sherpas saw the national park concept as a government land-grab and a way to introduce unacceptable controls on their culture and activity: they had long argued that creation of a national park was not necessary to preserve their rugged towering peaks that are the primary attraction of international interest. The Sherpas had administered their own society and resources successfully for centuries and seldom resorted to the national or regional government for aid, justice, or political assistance. Public works projects were typically accomplished by local people themselves, and civil

disputes were usually settled by traditional forms of recon-
ciliation rather than courts.

Through the urging and persuasion of Sir Edmund Hillary,
local Sherpas tentatively accepted the principles of resource
management that a park could accomplish. Hillary, along
with Sherpa Tenzing Norgay, was the first person to climb
Mount Everest in 1953. Hillary is much venerated in this
area of Nepal because of his singular devotion to improving
the lives of local people through schools, hospitals, bridges,
and other projects. While it may have been beyond the power
of the local population to prevent creation of the park, Hillary's support of the idea had the effect of converting outright
opposition to lingering skepticism and suspicious acceptance.
Hillary followed through on assurances to the Sherpas that
preserving the culture of the Sherpas would be a high priority in the park management plan.

The Sherpas   The Sherpas are the guides, innkeepers, interpreters, and organizers who make it possible for mountaineers, tourists,
hikers, and naturalists to make extended explorations of this
high area. Sherpas have occupied the Everest area and other
regions of the east Nepal Himalayas for about four hundred
years. Traditionally, they have been pastoralists, farmers,
and traders. Sherpas are Buddhist highlanders with ancestral, cultural, and linguistic affinities to Tibet, and all
Sherpas are now citizens of Nepal. Their economic success is
envied by many other Nepalese. While not frequently involved in executive or management aspects of tourism, they
are widely acknowledged as the best guides and organizers of
trekking trips into all of Nepal's vast roadless areas.

Many important religious institutions and communities of
the Sherpas are within the areas designated as Sagarmatha
National Park, such as Tengboche Monastery, the residence
of the most venerated local spiritual leader of the Sherpas.

In the decade prior to park implementation and since park
creation, Sherpas have flourished economically as a result of
tourism to the area that the park was created to protect.
Prior to the advent of Himalayan mountain tourism in the
1960s, the Solu Khumbu region, where the park is located,
was among the poorest regions of Nepal. Now, most Sherpas
earn much more in private tourism than they can make

through any sort of government employment through the park (Jeffries 1982). Many tourists return from the area with as many positive memories of the Sherpas as of the high mountains.

Significantly, both the Sherpas and the national park officials recognize that the current prosperity enjoyed by local people is not because the national park was created. If anything, local people tend to feel the park is limiting their economic success with management restrictions on new buildings, sale of firewood, and the charging of park admission fees (N. W. Sherpa 1979).

The Social Challenge of Management

With economic prosperity and exposure to Western ideas the Sherpa culture has changed. Park managers, guided by a management plan that does not attempt to prevent cultural change, are challenged not to preserve indigenous cultures as much as accommodate traditional uses in a context of changing traditions. The "Preamble" to the management objectives of the park management plan includes the following statement:

> The major problem of the park is one of reconciling the requirements of the resident population with those of conservation objectives. In the long term, the protection of the natural values of the area is also in the Sherpas' best social and economic interest.

The importance of local people to the park management plan is formalized in Policy 1.1 and 1.2 of the plan providing for consultation and "close formal and informal relationships" with the local population. Other policies recognize the preeminence of the lama of Tengboche and the importance of preserving traditional religious architecture.

The conflict anticipated in the management plan does, indeed, exist. While income of Sherpas has risen, so have local prices. Basic commodities are more expensive in the park area than in any other area of Nepal. Sherpas wishing to pursue a nontourism, traditional lifestyle have great difficulty competing economically. They may be forced into selling wood or opening an inn to pay rising prices for kerosene, rice, and flour. Human behavioral patterns detrimental to local natural ecology in the park areas have become well established in response to the demands of tourism. There has been great resistance to changing these patterns in the absence of alternative supplies for fuel, fodder, and construction materials.

Park–Local Population Conflicts

Management problems involving park regulations and local people can be divided into several categories: cultural preservation, deforestation, uncoordinated development, and overgrazing and soil erosion.

Cultural Preservation

Prior to the popularity of mountain tourism, very few non-Sherpas ever visited the Everest area. Certain traditions of personal, social, and ecological behavior were culturally shared and observed. With the establishment of the national park infrastructure, many non-Sherpa Nepalese are now either residents or frequent visitors to the Sherpa homeland. This has produced resentments and prejudice that have impaired park administration. The stationing of non-Sherpa regulars of the Nepalese army in the park as guards has angered many people. The army has been notorious for destroying the forests they have been sent to guard. Lowland Nepalese have difficulty thriving in the high-altitude cold of the Everest area and often desert their posts for reasons of health or cultural frustration.

Another major trend that seems independent of the park is the increasing wealth and mobility of the local population. While some people seem willing and destined to occupy ancestral lands within the park as long as they live, many younger Sherpas have also established permanent family homes in Kathmandu. This trend has favorable implications for the natural ecology of the park but complicates park regulations that distinguish between residents and visitors. It appears some Sherpas occupy park areas for the economic advantages of tourism rather than in pursuit of more traditional lifestyles. The park must define its position on such opportunistic residents.

Deforestation

Regeneration of natural forest cover is extremely slow in the high, dry climate of the Himalayas. In light of this problem, park authorities have had to face the challenge of restricting wood harvesting. At the same time, the park staff and associated personnel have, at times, been forced to utilize wood resources for certain cooking and construction requirements. Contractors and laborers hired by the park have also either violated wood cutting agreements, or have been forced to use wood for fuel in the absence of alternatives.

Deforestation leads directly to soil erosion and landslides. In the intermediate term, however, areas that are deforested do not lose all economic utility. Former forests become grazing lands. In fact, the number of livestock a family holds is a cultural measure of wealth and prestige. The influx of tourists eager to buy wood and dairy products enables people to buy more yaks, which in turn require more grazing area. In part, this is created by cutting more forest. Breaking this destructive, culturally reinforced cycle is probably the greatest challenge of the park managers.

In years just preceding establishment of the park, local people and outsiders associated with trekking and mountaineering groups were exploiting their common property forests and rangeland without regulation to the detriment of the resource base (Garratt 1981). The scale of unregulated exploitation gained momentum because the large numbers of foreign visitors were willing to pay a lot of money for fuel and food. Sherpas have traditionally been merchants and traders: when the region was opened to foreign visitors in the 1950s, the commerce came to them, and many families evolved from farmers and herdsman to trekking or mountaineering guides. Wood had always been the preferred construction material as well as cooking and heating fuel. It had also been a measure of conspicuous wealth to have a large pile of firewood in front of one's house. With the coming of the mountain expeditions and trekkers, wood became a source of great income. By the time the park was established, a large number of people were economically dependent on the sale of wood as a means of livelihood. It has become a primary task of the park management to separate the legitimate use of wood for personal consumption from the now illegal cutting and sale of wood for trekking and mountaineering.

Uncoordinated Development   Prior to creation of the park and the influx of tourist money in the 1970s, there was little money for new construction and no purpose for new buildings for tourists or local people. Satisfying demand for lodging, meals, and services was seen as a way to make relatively large amounts of money quickly. Specific conflicts concern plans for new hotels near religious sites and in very fragile high-altitude areas.

Overgrazing and Soil Erosion

The grazing of animals is a full-time occupation for many Sherpas: about 3,000 head of livestock regularly graze in the park (Bjorness in Garratt 1981). Many hillsides have been severely eroded due to overgrazing. Yak and various hybrids of yak with lowland cattle continue to cause extensive damage, especially with their sharp hooves. Bovine paths crisscross most slopes of the Khumbu. As Sherpas embrace more Western symbols of wealth, there is some prospect of livestock grazing becoming less important. On the other hand, with a shortage of human porters to handle the great transport requirements of trekking groups, yaks have proven a lucrative and readily available substitute. Also, some people are increasing their yak herds to supply trekking needs.

Owing to the relative prosperity of the local Sherpa population from income earned through trekking and tourism, the park has not been able to offer attractive employment options to the local people. Government wage scales are far lower than available earnings through tourism. Local Sherpas have not been eager to accept employment from an agency often viewed as making policies contrary to the interests of local people. The few dedicated Sherpa park employees face bureaucratic problems associated with distant separation from national park executive and policy-making authorities in Kathmandu, in addition to charges from lifelong friends and neighbors who claim that they are not sympathetic to the needs of their own people.

The genesis of these conflicts predates the creation of the park. The traditional means of settling disputes in Sherpa culture are very different from the adjudication system of government agencies, but the traditional elder councils that made resource management decisions for Sherpa lands are no longer the legitimate authority in resource management issues. Prior to the 1950s, these elder councils made direct, specific decisions about where wood could be cut, yaks grazed, or settlements established. The national government established in the 1950s voided the authority of these councils and established general forest and range-use laws. These laws, however, are not effectively enforced.

Conclusion

Whatever might be said about the failures of Sagarmatha National Park in preserving the resources of indigenous people and protecting their rights, the current situation is an improvement over the escalating destruction of natural and cultural resources that was underway before creation of the park. While clear solutions have not emerged, the problems are being confronted in a context of management that does recognize the rights of the Sherpas. Policy decisions and administrative action have been guided by a sincere effort to acknowledge the importance Sherpa people play in the ecosystem of the park. Reflecting this philosophy, some Sherpas are employed in administrative park positions.

The National Park has established tree nurseries and reforestation projects that are recognized as beneficial by the local population. Through the influence of the park, an experimental micro-hydroelectric project has been built to determine the feasibility of substituting electricity for wood as a fuel; however, its performance has been erratic. The national park has tangibly established its intent to preserve traditional architecture of the region through the creation of a museum that includes displays of Sherpa cultures and tradition.

Alternative energy sources, such as kerosene depots, have all been attempted but not delivered at a level to have significant ecological impact. To date, these innovations have had negligible collective impact on escalating wood consumption. Imposition of a park infrastructure, which itself places large economic and ecological demands on limited and fragile environments, has led to charges tantamount to ecological hypocrisy. Staff, quartering of army troops as forest guards, research teams, and park-management visitors require cooked food, housing, transportation, and services of local people that result in increased use of local wood, animals, housing, and other scarce resources. Even where wood may be brought in from outside the park, its collection has an ecological impact on nonpark natural ecosystems and is contrary to watershed protection objectives of the management plan.

The park bureaucracy has succeeded in establishing an authority from which to attack the fundamental environmental and management problems of the area. It now must convince local people that cooperation to achieve environmental objectives is in their own long-term interest.

There are evident shortcomings that need to be addressed if the relationship with the Sherpas is to improve. There has been a failure of the Park to deliver the ecologically sound alternatives necessary to justify environmental restrictions. In addition, park personnel tend to feel local people do not appreciate the long-term prospect of environmental destruction and the need for regulation now to insure long-term economic and environmental health. Local people, many confronting short-term survival concerns, still see the park as a scheme of outsiders for controlling and limiting the economic success of local people. Cooperative action is absolutely necessary because the local people are, in a very significant measure, the park. Practical alternatives to abusive environmental practices are the only equitable solution to fulfilling both cultural and nature conservation objectives. Reasoning based on a global view of environmental imperatives tends to guide Western-trained park managers while the personal and family survival imperatives tend to guide the woodcutters and pastoralists. The challenge to resource managers in Nepal is in creating alternatives to destructive short-term human survival strategies. These alternatives must be affordable in both economic and cultural terms.

19

The Grand Canyon National Park and the Havasupai People: Cooperation and Conflict

John Hough

PROTECTED AREA	Grand Canyon National Park
CLASSIFICATION	Labeled as: National Park Managed as: National Park, IUCN Category II
RESIDENT PEOPLE	Acculturated Tribal Peoples

The Havasupai are the major extant people, around 520 in number, who previously utilized the central part of the present-day Grand Canyon National Park, Arizona, in the United States. They arrived in the area sometime before the twelfth century and spent the winters roaming the Coconino Plateau, immediately south of the canyon itself, as hunters and gatherers. In the summer months they descended into the canyon and tended irrigated crops where springs brought water into the otherwise desertlike area. However, following the arrival of European explorers and settlers, they were largely confined to living in a small reservation, established in 1882, in Havasu Canyon along Havasu Creek, one of the larger springs in a side canyon south of the main Grand Canyon.

In 1975 the Havasupai reservation was expanded by 185,000 acres to include a large area of land on the plateau around Havasu Canyon. In addition 95,300 acres of national park land between the new reservation and the river were designated as Havasupai Use Lands, to be used by the Havasupai under the jurisdiction of the National Park Service (see Map 19.1). Although some temporary and seasonal residences have been established on the plateau, the village of Supai in Havasu Canyon remains the only area of year-round occupancy for the Havasupai, with the exception of five wooden cabins in an area known as Supai Camp, immediately to the west of Grand Canyon Village.

Between twenty-five and thirty thousand tourists visit Havasu Canyon each year. The Havasupai economy is dependent primarily on income from these tourists and federal government funding. Other commercial enterprises are limited by the remote nature of Havasu Canyon, though the Havasupai are starting to establish a ranching business on the plateau.

Map 19.1
Traditional
Range of the
Havasupai
and Present
Reservation
Boundaries

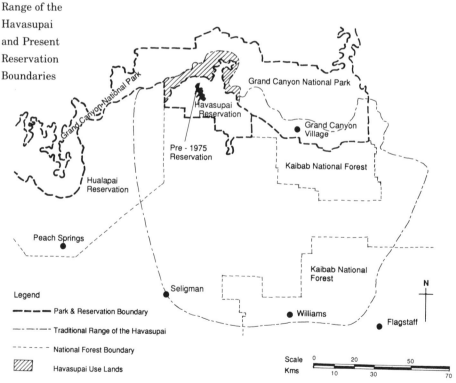

Legend

──── Park & Reservation Boundary

─·─·─ Traditional Range of the Havasupai

────── National Forest Boundary

▨ Havasupai Use Lands

Parts of the Grand Canyon were first protected as a national monument in 1908. The national park was established in 1919 and significantly expanded in 1975 under the Grand Canyon National Park Enlargement Act. The park and the Havasupai have had an ongoing relationship since 1919 but this was altered significantly by the 1975 act. Since 1975 the Havasupai have been able to control and develop tourist access to Havasu Canyon instead of being largely dependent on the park. The expansion of the reservation also means that access to certain parts of the park is now through the reservation and in order to protect the resources of the entire Grand Canyon area the park has to be concerned about Havasupai activities on the reservation. The Havasupai also continue to claim much of the national park land south of the Colorado River as rightfully theirs. The combination of these factors, and the communication required over the management and use of the Havasupai Use Lands, generates a special relationship between the park and the Havasupai.

This chapter examines this relationship, first from the perspective of its history, and then in terms of the existing cooperation and conflict between the park and the Havasupai. Obstacles to further cooperation and some of the benefits that overcoming them might bring are also considered.

History of the Relationship Between the National Park and the Havasupai

The Havasupai, or their direct ancestors, have lived in the Grand Canyon area since at least the twelfth century (Dobyns and Euler 1971). Their traditional way of life, which continued up until the mid-nineteenth century, included the cultivation of crops on the more moist areas of the plateau, and the growing of irrigated crops in Havasu Canyon. Winter months were spent hunting and gathering on the plateau (Spier 1928).

The Havasupai continued this seasonal migration through to the 1870s when the increasing numbers of settlers moving into the plateau area started to disrupt the traditional Havasupai hunting and gathering patterns (Euler 1979; Martin 1987). By fencing the range and water holes of the plateau, the settlers limited the grazing available to the Havasupai horses. In addition to the miners who started staking claims on Havasupai lands, the arrival of the Atlantic-Pacific railroad in 1881 brought in increasing numbers of settlers and introduced the Havasupai to trading and a cash economy (Dobyns and Euler 1971; Martin 1987).

In 1880 a presidential executive order designated sixty square miles as an Indian reservation for the Havasupai around Havasu Canyon. Two years later, the reservation was reduced in size to 518 acres, consisting primarily of intensively cultivated land in the bottom of Havasu Canyon, because of problems with mining claims and the difficulty the army had surveying outside the walls of the canyon (Dobyns and Euler 1971; Hirst 1985). This gave no protection to plateau land used by the Havasupai for hunting, grazing, and gathering wild plant foods and firewood.

In 1893 much of the plateau area immediately south of the Grand Canyon itself was set aside as the Grand Canyon Forest Reserve, which further restricted the Havasupai use of the area, though 10,000 acres were later designated as horse-grazing land for the Havasupai. When the Grand Canyon National Park was established in 1919, the area available to Havasupai grazing was increased to 150,000 acres. At the same time grazing permits were also given to white ranchers to graze in the Pasture Wash area, the most valuable of the traditional Havasupai grazing areas on the plateau (Hirst 1985).

During the 1920s and 1930s the Havasupai started raising cattle to replace meat no longer available due to hunting restrictions (Dobyns and Euler 1971). The park also provided wage employment for thirty to forty young Havasupai men in activities such as road and trail building (Dobyns and Euler 1971; Martin 1987). These men were housed in camps on a surveyed 160-acre piece of land, now known as Supai Camp, immediately to the west of Grand Canyon Village.

In 1957, the Park Service opened a public campground adjacent to the Havasupai Reservation. This facilitated a dramatic increase in the number of visitors to the Havasupai reservation during the 1960s, which enabled the Havasupai to establish a restaurant and tourist lodge and generated tourist-related employment within the tribe.

During the 1950s and 1960s the Havasupai were also actively involved in presenting their case to the Indian Claims Commission, which in 1969 finally decided that the federal government had wrongfully seized over 3,500 square miles of aboriginal Havasupai lands. Although they would have preferred the return of all land still in government control

(Dobyns and Euler 1971; Hirst 1985) the Havasupai finally accepted $1,240,000 as compensation for these lands.

During the early 1970s, the Park Service started developing a master plan that included provisions for expanding the park to incorporate some of the national forest lands around the Havasupai Reservation. A Havasupai proposal to use some of the compensation awarded by the Indian Claims Commission to improve their permit grazing lands on the plateau was firmly rejected by the Park Service (Hirst 1985). The Havasupai interpreted these actions as an attempt to dislodge them from their plateau grazing areas, which they had actually been able to continue using despite the non-inclusion of any plateau lands in the reservations of 1880 and 1882. The Havasupai opposition to the proposed park master plan, in the context of park proposals to reorganize land holdings between the National Park Service and the National Forest Service, eventually led to the passage of the Grand Canyon National Park Enlargement Act (GCNPEA) in 1975.

The significant aspects of this act for the relationship between the National Park Service and the Havasupai include the following:

1. The enlargement of the Grand Canyon National Park by incorporating into it the Grand Canyon National Monument and part of the Coconino National Forest.
2. The return of 185,000 acres of government land, much of it on the plateau and previously designated as national park, national monument and national forest land, to the Havasupai. This also included the return of the Park Service campground in Havasu Canyon. A variety of conditions was also attached to this return including prohibitions on commercial timber production, mineral extraction, and the requirement that a Land Use Plan be prepared for these areas.
3. Designation of 93,500 acres within the Grand Canyon National Park as "Havasupai Use Lands" which the Havasupai could use for "grazing and other traditional purposes," though under regulations established by the government.
4. The extinguishment of all other Havasupai land claims including the 160-acre Supai Camp adjacent to Grand Canyon Village.

Conflict Between the Park and the Havasupai

Although the GCNPEA removed many of the causes of antagonism between the national park and the Havasupai, and cooperation between them now exists at a variety of different levels, a number of areas of dispute and conflict still remain. These include visitor access to the park across the Havasupai reservation, management and use of the Havasupai Use Lands, and Supai Camp.

Visitor Access Across the Reservation

Section 10.b.6 of the Grand Canyon National Park Enlargement Act requires the tribe to allow access across the reservation for visitors to the park, at locations agreed upon by the Tribal Council (see Map 19.2). A few of these are at remote locations where patrolling entry is impractical for the tribe. The Havasupai have asked that the park collect the reservation entry fees from the visitors at the park's back-country office, and forward them to the tribe. The park refuses to do this because of the costs of administering such a scheme. The park does have a policy of notifying such visitors of the reservation entry fee and encourages the visitors to telephone the Havasupai reservation. However, unless obtained by mail in advance, to obtain a permit would require a 400-mile round trip drive, plus 16 miles of walking.

Havasupai Use Lands

Section 10.e of the act designates 93,500 acres of the canyon area of the national park as "Havasupai Use Lands." The act permits the Havasupai use of the area for "grazing and other traditional purposes" subject to "reasonable regulations . . . to protect the scenic, natural and wildlife values thereof."

The National Park Service is particularly concerned about the presence of horses in the Havasupai Use Lands (HUL). A 1982 Memorandum of Understanding between the tribe and the Park Service allowed for the grazing of horses and cattle in the area, but not sheep, as "consistent with acceptable range management practices." The latter was to be determined by an "outside agency," in practice the U.S. Forest Service. Their scientific study of the range capacity of the Havasupai Use Lands set the carrying capacity for horses at zero (USDA 1982). The Havasupai countered this on the basis of their long association with and knowledge of the land (Sinyella, pers. com. 1987). By 1986, only seven horses were counted on the HUL (D. Brown, per. com. 1987). Though it is known that in the areas accessible to them, horses reduce the abundance of certain species of grass, the magnitude of this change and the implications for other species of plants and animals, in particular the bighorn sheep, have not actually been quantified (S. Hodapp, per. comm. 1987).

Though the Park Service is concerned about the ecological impact of the horse grazing in the HUL, the Havasupai seem less concerned about the horses than about the "ownership" of the land. The Havasupai claim ownership of this land on the basis of traditional use. They feel that they should be free to use the area as they wish, including grazing horses, developing springs and water tanks, and developing visitor use. These lands comprise virtually all the land between the Havasupai reservation and the Colorado River. Apart from Havasu Canyon these are the only areas where the Havasupai have access to land below the plateau. It is in this "inner canyon" area that many of the springs and seepages traditionally used by the Havasupai occur.

The park does permit limited hunting, gathering of plants, and other traditional activities, including the "minimal" improvement of springs, by the Havasupai in the HUL. The park controls visitor use of, and access to, the HUL in accordance with its backcountry management plan (USDI 1983)

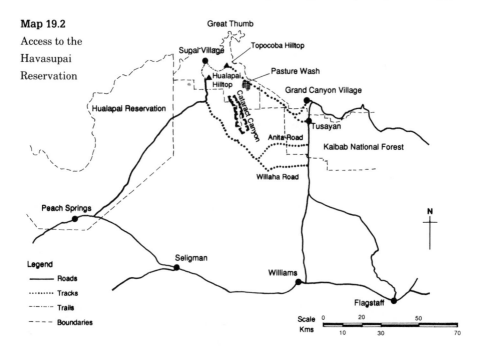

Map 19.2
Access to the
Havasupai
Reservation

which incorporates many Havasupai concerns as laid out in a Memorandum of Understanding.

Supai Camp   Section 10.f of the Grand Canyon National Park Enlargement Act states that by passing this act Congress recognizes that all other Havasupai claims to rights, title, or interest in any other lands are extinguished. The implication of this is that Havasupai claims on Supai Camp at Grand Canyon Village are void. This is of particular concern to the Havasupai for a variety of reasons.

Cultural Identity. Not only are the Havasupai concerned about their loss of identity as a distinct ethnic group (USDI 1982), but they also have a marked individual preference for living among their own people. Many young people return to, or do not leave, the canyon because they want to live amongst their own people. Some of the Havasupai working for the park or the concession live in institutional housing in Grand Canyon Village, but Supai Camp, despite its poorer quality of houses and services as compared to those of institutional housing, provides an opportunity for the Havasupai to live together. It should also be noted that rents at Supai Camp, paid to the park, are considerably lower than those for institutional housing.

Ownership. The Havasupai continue to claim ownership of land traditionally used by them. They see giving up occupancy as reducing their claim to ownership of the Grand Canyon Village area and the adjacent parts of the canyon itself (see Map 19.3).

Access to Opportunity. The remote location of Havasu Canyon, eight miles from the road and then sixty miles to the nearest town and through road, prevents its occupants from seeking out employment, recreational, educational, and business opportunities. The establishment of a settlement on the plateau where the young people, in particular, would have access to such opportunities, both on and off the reservation, is a stated priority of the Havasupai (USDI 1982). Until this is achieved and road access improved, Supai Camp is the only location "belonging" to the Havasupai that provides access to Grand Canyon Village and the nearby settlement of Tusayan, the sites of such opportunities.

Temporary Accommodation in Grand Canyon Village. Havasupai from the reservation visit Grand Canyon Village to utilize services such as the large grocery store, the bank, and the clinic. In addition, since the reservation has a ban on alcohol, Supai Camp is a convenient location for tribal members wishing to temporarily escape this ban.

The National Park Service objects to the presence of the camp on two grounds. First, the camp is used by some Havasupai for occasional drinking sessions that last a number of days. During this time these people often disturb other camp residents and visitors to Grand Canyon Village. Secondly, employees of both the national park and the concession are entitled to institutional housing; therefore, technically, the Park Service feels this camp is unnecessary.

Although 160 acres were surveyed for Supai Camp in the 1920s, the 1975 act extinguished all Havasupai claims to land outside the reservation. Despite threats in the past to bulldoze the camp (Hirst 1985), present park policy is to allow it to remain under a five-year renewable Special Use Permit, issued most recently in 1989 (D. Brown, per. com. 1990).

The terms of the 1989 permit are essentially the same as the 1982 permit, with one notable exception. As part of a

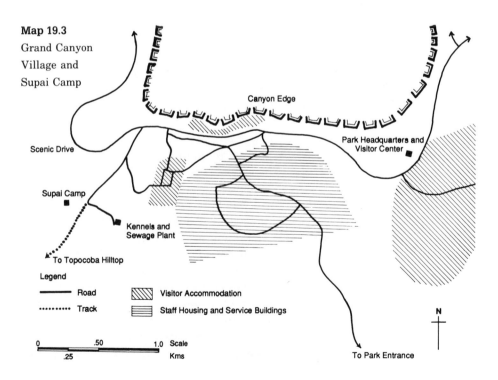

Map 19.3
Grand Canyon
Village and
Supai Camp

Canyon Edge

Scenic Drive

Park Headquarters and
Visitor Center

Supai Camp

Kennels and
Sewage Plant

To Topocoba Hilltop

Legend

——— Road   ▨ Visitor Accommodation

·········· Track   ▤ Staff Housing and Service Buildings

0   .50   1.0 Scale
   .25   Kms

N

To Park Entrance

general park renovation program, the Havasupai Tribe is entitled to renovate or replace the five existing log cabins currently used for lodging. The tribe is permitted to replace each cabin with a duplex unit, effectively doubling the potential occupancy of the camp. A renovation or replacement of cabins is contingent upon the tribe's obtaining needed funds and to date, no construction has been installed.

In 1989 the Havasupai petitioned Congress for funds to remedy imminent problems related to water and sewage service for the camp. Funds were allocated through the Bureau of Indian Affairs; Indian Health Service and an alternate septic system were installed. In the fall of 1989 the Supai Camp was connected to the park water system. Now Supai Camp meets the requirements of the Arizona Department of Public Health and has a permit to continue to operate and possibly expand.

Cooperation Between the Park and the Havasupai

By permitting the Havasupai the use of the Havasupai Use Lands within the park, the Grand Canyon Enlargement Act of 1975 requires a formal relationship between the park and the Havasupai. While the secretary for the interior is entitled to prescribe "reasonable regulations" for the Havasupai use of this area, the Park Service proceeded with a series of meetings that led to the joint signing of a Memorandum of Understanding (MOU) over these lands. This cooperation was probably facilitated by the presence on the park staff of a sympathetic anthropologist who had done a considerable amount of work with the Havasupai. The initial MOU over the Havasupai Use Lands was renewable on an annual basis and actually specified an annual meeting between the park and the Havasupai. This memorandum has been allowed to lapse. A revised version sent out by the park in 1985, following a meeting in which new arrangements were discussed, has not been signed by the Havasupai. In the opinion of one Park Service official, communication with the Havasupai deteriorated following the departure from the park staff of the sympathetic anthropologist.

The special relationship between the Havasupai and the park is also furthered by the presence of Supai Camp within Grand Canyon Village; the requirements of access for park staff across Havasupai lands and the Havasupai across national park lands; and their sharing of the tourist visitors to the Grand Canyon Area. This special relationship is explicitly recognized in the Grand Canyon Natural and Cultural Resources Management Plan of 1984 (USDI 1984).

The park and the Havasupai have an agreement whereby people on Havasupai tribal business are not charged an entry fee for entering the park and likewise people on National Park Service business are not charged an entry fee for entering the reservation. Though longstanding in practice, this agreement was formalized in writing in 1987.

Though the memorandum specifying annual meetings has lapsed, there continue to be two or three meetings per year initiated by either the park or the Havasupai. Neither party sees value in having regular meetings for the sake of contact, yet both seem ready to meet over issues of concern. For example, in 1986 the Havasupai requested a meeting with the park so that they could have some input into the discussions on aircraft overflight policies and regulations.

Both the Havasupai and the park wish to maintain direct communication with each other, and the present park superintendent has met with the tribal chairman on a number of occasions. He was instrumental in arranging for the manager of the Havasupai tourist lodge to spend time with the park concession in order to gain experience in managing such an enterprise. The national park continues to employ an anthropologist in the position of "cultural resources management specialist," who is the primary official point of contact with the Havasupai.

Obstacles to Increased Cooperation Between the Park and the Havasupai

The existing cooperation between the Havasupai and the national park provides a basis for both expanding this cooperation and addressing some of the areas of conflict. However, three key obstacles are apparent.

Trust. Given the history of the relationships between the Havasupai and white Americans, the United States government as a whole, the Forest Service, and the National Park Service, it is not surprising that there is a high level of distrust. Recent developments, as outlined above, indicate that greater levels of trust and cooperation can be achieved over time. Though individuals can play a key role in trust building, as suggested by the perceptions of deteriorating communications following the departure of a sympathetic anthropologist from the park staff, the policies and attitudes of both the Park Service and the Havasupai are a result of a mixture of individual and corporate personalities thus compounding the process.

The Institutional Environment. The Havasupai and the National Park Service have rather different objectives that affect their interest in addressing the other's concerns. The Havasupai are interested in maintaining their cultural, social, and political integrity, and in developing economic independence. Their main objective is to retain their own sovereignty.

By contrast the Park Service objective is to maintain the natural resource values of the Grand Canyon as a whole, and, in particular, the scenic and wilderness values of the inner canyon. They are concerned that intensive grazing by the Havasupai, both in the Traditional Use Area and, to a lesser extent, on the plateau, will endanger indigenous plants and animals and, through erosion, cause severe damage to the natural environment. They are also concerned about Havasupai activities restricting visitor access or diminishing the quality of the visitor experience.

Legislation also plays a key role in that the Park Service is bound by its congressional mandate. Thus, Havasupai sovereignty over the TUL is a concern for Congress, not for the Park Service, and there are legal issues surrounding the preferential employment of Havasupai in the park.

Cross-Cultural Aspects. The national park concept is based in the Western scientific culture, but the Havasupai are not. An illustration of the potential difficulties this causes is the disagreement over the carrying capacity of the TUL for horse grazing. The Park Service cites "scientific" studies while the Havasupai cite "traditional" knowledge. In light of this difference in view, discussion and agreement on the meaning of data are likely to be very difficult.

Basis for Increased Cooperation Between the Park and the Havasupai

Despite the obstacles described above, the cooperation already established between the national park and the Havasupai provides a basis for further cooperation on a number of issues. This could produce benefits for both. The following areas of cooperation appear significant.

Tourism. The Park and the Havasupai have a converging interest in the visitors to the canyon area. The Park's interest is in providing visitors with a quality experience while preventing them from damaging the environment. The additional cultural dimension provided by the Havasupai could be an asset from their perspective. The Park also has to consider the economic interests of its concessioner. The Havasupai have an internal dilemma; on the one hand they are economically dependent on tourists, while on the other the tourists are an intrusion into their life and lifestyle.

Since the Havasupai now control access to the reservation they can control the number of visitors and avoid the "human zoo" aspects of being under Park Service control (Hirst 1985). However, they consider the present use of Havasu Canyon as "somewhat intense under present conditions" and would prefer to spread the load to other parts of the reservation on the plateau, with the exception of the Great Thumb Mesa (USDI 1982). By constructing a tourist lodge, Supai Lodge, in 1982 and by limiting helicopter flights into the canyon, the Havasupai have the potential to increase the economic benefits of tourism without necessarily bringing in more visitors. Although developing tourist facilities on the plateau might increase tourist revenues by increasing the number visiting the reservation, this is not necessarily desirable from the perspective of maintaining the Havasupai culture.

Neither the park nor its concessioner promotes the existence of the Havasupai waterfalls, canyon, lodge, or campsite. This corresponds to the wishes of the Havasupai not to advertise, though it is unclear whether this is a deliberate arrangement between the Havasupai and the park. However, in view of the congestion at the South Rim in summer, it would appear that the Park Service has an incentive to disperse some of the visitors. Hence, cooperation between the park and the Havasupai would appear to be beneficial in both planning and managing tourism.

Some such cooperation has already taken place with the park superintendent arranging for the Supai Lodge manager to undergo a period of training with the park concessioner. The Havasupai could draw on the Park Service expertise in other aspects of tourism management while continuing its own unique approach to tourist services. The Park Service is well aware of the potential attractions of the Havasupai reservation to tourists (USDI 1984).

Interpretation. Section 6 of the Grand Canyon Enlargement Act encourages the Park Service to cooperate with other interests around the canyon, including "interested Indian tribes," for the "unified interpretation of the entire Grand Canyon." Park interpretation of the human ecology and culture of the area is largely restricted to the Tusayan Museum twenty-five miles east of Grand Canyon Village. There is very little information on the Havasupai and no evidence that their assistance was sought in preparing it. Cooperation in this area could benefit both the park, by expanding their interpretation of the local culture, and the Havasupai, by increasing visitor understanding of their contemporary situation.

Havasupai Isolation and Cultural Identity. The maintenance of the Havasupai culture is of primary importance to the Havasupai and is of significance to the park as part of the canyon's cultural resources. Although the park already restricts visitor access to sites deemed important by both the Havasupai and other Indian tribes, it does little to assist in maintaining the living culture.

The Havasupai recognize that maintenance of their culture is dependent on the presence of sufficient local economic opportunity, particularly for the young people, to support the population of the reservation without them having to leave it. In view of the remoteness of Havasu Canyon and the Havasupai desire to preserve its nature by limiting access primarily to foot and horseback, increasing the economic opportunities within the reservation is dependent on establishing settlements on the plateau. A number of locations for such settlements have been identified with the principal location being Pasture Wash (USDI 1982). The latter is only twenty miles from Grand Canyon and Tusayan villages and would provide the opportunity for employment while living on the reservation. This would increase the interaction between the Havasupai and the park through Havasupai use of park facilities such as the clinic, store, and bank, and might increase the number of Havasupai employed within the park. An additional aspect to this might be the preferential recruiting of Havasupai to work within the park. In addition to the potential economic benefits to the Havasupai and the potential benefits to the park in terms of cultural interpretation, such an approach might begin to address the concern of Havasupai sovereignty, provided the Havasupai were employed in positions of real responsibility and not just in menial positions. Clearly, the latter is dependent on the willingness of some Havasupai to undertake the appropriate training.

Resource Protection. Both the Havasupai and the Park Service are concerned about maintaining the resources of the Grand Canyon Area. But their values, and therefore their perceptions of what is needed and what constitutes a problem, differ. The main obstacle to increasing cooperation in resource protection is the issue of horses and carrying capacity.

There is opportunity for exchange of skills. The Park Service has technical skills in resource management that could be of use to the Havasupai, and Whiting (1985) documents a wealth of Havasupai cultural knowledge of resources that might be of use to the Park. Though the differences in the cultural basis for technical and traditional knowledge could generate problems, as noted earlier, they could also complement each other.

Recent evidence from conservation biology indicates that many existing protected areas are too small to maintain viable populations of certain species in the long term (Frankel and Soule 1981). Thus, cooperation over resource protection may become crucial to the national park if the Havasupai reservation could provide critical habitat for species such as the mountain lion for which the existing national park is too small (Newmark 1985).

Conclusion

Historically, the relationship between the National Park Service and the Havasupai has been one of distrust and enmity. This has improved considerably in recent years. There have been a number of instances of active cooperation, and communication between the two is now quite open. However, there is still a certain level of distrust and, consequently, misperception of the other's intent.

The Havasupai, in particular, have benefited from the new relationship ushered in by the Grand Canyon Enlargement Act that returned a significant amount of their traditional lands to them. The development of Grand Canyon Village and the park headquarters has brought them a considerable amount of tourism; a limited amount of employment; access to a major store, a clinic, the opportunity to limit aircraft overflight of Havasu Canyon; resources such as training for their lodge manager; and, recently, official "friends" who can assist in times of need and keep the Havasupai informed of external issues that might affect them. The benefits of this improved relationship for the park seem, so far, to be very few, though hostility from the Havasupai is clearly much reduced.

This neighborliness does open the way for increased cooperation and communication which could be of great significance to the park. If the resource values of the entire Grand Canyon are to be effectively protected and made available to the large number of tourists visiting the area each year, then cooperation is required with both the Havasupai and other tribes whose reservations include significant parts of the Grand Canyon ecosystem. There may also be benefits to the park of increased protection and interpretation of cultural resources, and the opportunity to draw on indigenous knowledge of the canyon in management.

For the Havasupai, the benefits of increased cooperation could include utilization of the Park Service expertise in recreational management, the capture of increasing amounts of tourist revenue without the associated cultural disruption of this occurring within Havasu Canyon, and increased employment opportunities within the park. There are reciprocal benefits for both in keeping the other party informed of events or issues that might affect both.

Further cooperation must take place within the context of Havasupai concerns for maintaining their own cultural identity, and with it their sovereignty. Any actions by the park that are seen as undermining rather than facilitating this are likely to increase conflict and distrust. Similarly, the Havasupai will need to recognize that concerns of the Park Service about overgrazing and resource protection, both inside and outside the official park area, are legitimate. Although restrictions on Havasupai sovereignty are imposed by the Grand Canyon National Park Enlargement Act, it should not restrict their access to positions of responsibility and influence within the Grand Canyon National Park.

NOTE

This chapter is largely based on a study prepared for the 21st International Park Seminar with funding provided by the Wildland Management Center of the University of Michigan. Its revision for this book was facilitated by a University of Michigan Research Partnership Award and discussions with Patrick West. The author would like to thank the Havasupai Tribal Council, the Grand Canyon National Park, and the various individuals and officials of both the park and the Havasupai whose cooperation and assistance made this study possible.

Part Six   **PLANNING AND DECISION PROCESSES IN SOCIAL CHANGE**

Schoolchildren in educational program *(above)* in Kinabalu Park, Sabah Malesia. Toby Gangale *(center)* and Bill Neijie explaining the meaning of Aboriginal rock art *(below)* are two of the cultural advisers and Aboriginal owners of Kakadu National Park, Australia.

Introduction   In part 6 we present a set of thematic essays that collectively address key aspects of planned social change necessary for a more sensitive treatment both of resident peoples in national parks and of protected-area policy, planning, and management. Topics include processes for public participation, social impact analysis, land-use zoning, conflict management, and co-management.

In Chapter 20, Hales presents a case study in the use of public participation by local residents of the Pinelands National Reserve in New Jersey. Originally declared by the United States Congress as a national reserve and eventually included as part of the South Atlantic Coastal Plain Biosphere Reserve, its management is geared to protect traditional local uses such as agriculture, forestry, and cranberry bog farming while preserving a resource of national importance. The Pinelands is administered by an agency that crosscuts normal governmental boundaries and includes representatives from state, federal, and local interests. It presents a good example of how public participation can be constructively utilized to deal with issues of local ecodevelopment in protected areas. However, we should keep in mind that while public participation may be relatively easy to implement in democratic societies, it may be more threatening to administrative bureaucracies in more authoritarian developing societies.

The use of systematic social surveys of local residents in and around protected areas can be another form of public input into protected area planning and management. Jacobson illustrates this potential in her chapter on Kinabalu National Park in Malaysia. She conducted her survey among communities surrounding the park and found a remarkable degree of acceptance of the park and its management policies. While acknowledging that certain biases in the survey—such as sampling communities that have benefited more from tourism, and people in those communities that are literate—the degree of acceptance is still striking.

In chapter 22, Woo analyzes the land-use zoning system in Korean national parks from the perspective of social impact. Other chapters in this volume have illustrated the use of zoning as a planning tool, but Woo's analysis is particularly significant in its attempt to examine how size, the relationship among different land-use zones and placement of each zone in relation to the other can affect the nature and extent of social impacts. This type of analysis is badly needed as a key analytical tool in attempting to balance local residence and resource use by resident peoples and protected area objectives.

The chapter by Hough discusses more general considerations in social impact analysis (SIA) as a planning process that can help planners understand, anticipate, and mitigate likely social change impacts of protected area establishment and management on resident peoples living in and around these reserves. Hough emphasizes the importance of SIA both in doing better planning to avoid or mitigate social impacts, and as a basis for conflict management between protected areas and local people. This important link with conflict management has been emphasized in a recent paper by Manring et al. (1990), and is echoed again in the chapter by Bidol and Crowfoot on integrative planning processes and conflict management strategies.

The chapter by Bidol and Crowfoot addresses the critical importance of interactive, participatory, and culturally sensitive planning processes in the determination of the siting and management policies of protected areas. Deliberate and appropriate methods of managing and resolving conflicts among local people and protected areas are stressed within this interactive planning process model. The authors emphasize that specific planning processes need to be adapted to the social and cultural context in which they are developed and utilized, so no hard and fast rules can be rigidly specified. However, they argue along with most authors in this volume that careful participation and involvement by local peoples are essential. They also argue, based on comparative research in the anthropology of law, that conflict management techniques involving mediation and negotiation are preferable to approaches that rely heavily on judicial mechanisms, denial, or power plays by dominant institutional actors. At the same time, participation in such mediative alternatives carries with it risks for low-power parties such as resident peoples. This emphasizes the need for building stronger coalitions between conservationists and resident peoples in areas where their interests converge to increase the power of resident peoples to determine their own fate and protect their legitimate concerns.

The following three chapters seek to go beyond participatory planning processes in which local people may participate in planning but not share in ultimate decision authority. They argue for the need for true co-management in which resident people share decision-making power.

The chapter by Goodland on "Prerequisites for Ethnic Identity and Survival" focuses more specifically on the special social and cultural considerations related to cultural preservation for more isolated tribal societies. While written originally as a primer for broader economic development projects, its message applies equally to protected area planning and rural development components of protected area functions. His strong emphasis on local control of land tenure and self determination underscores the critical importance of alternatives for protected-area management involving local tribal controls, and true power-sharing co-management. These same prerequisites, as emphasized earlier, are also critical to the success of ecodevelopment functions of protected areas for local rural development following the bottom-up model of rural development.

In chapter 26, Weaver evaluates programs of co-management for Kakadu and Cobourg national parks in Australia involving Australian aborigines. Her careful research is particularly important in identifying disparities between the conception of co-management at Kakadu in the mainstream conservation literature and her empirical findings from field research. For instance, Hill (1983:166) cites Kakadu as a prime example of local aboriginal participation and control over park management and policy—"Aborigines are involved in planning for and managing the Park at both the consultive and employment levels. Aboriginal agreement is required before any development or management action affecting them may proceed." Other advocates of aboriginal co-management such as Lawson (1985) echo this image of power sharing co-management at Kakadu. However, from Weaver's research we can see that this simply is not the case and that, in practice, very little involvement and control have been granted to the aboriginal residents of Kakadu. Only Fox's (1983) essay in the wider conservation literature begins to acknowledge some of the differences between pronounced involvement policy and the realities of implementation documented more fully by Weaver. We begin to see the

Centuries old
Buddhist Tem-
ple in harmony
with natural
setting *(above)*,
Kayasan Na-
tional Park,
South Korea.
One of the many
trappers' cabins
in Wood Buffalo
National Park.

importance of looking carefully at the differences between the rhetoric and reality of co-management of protected areas by resident peoples.

Conflicting images over the degree of actual co-management have spilled over into debates about the efficacy of co-management systems in Canadian national parks. Lawson (1985) is critical of the effort to date, but in chapter 27, East takes issue with this claim. The difference in their perceptions of the success of co-management concept may be based, in part, on the fact that Lawson is an external critic while East is an internal member and defender of Parks Canada. Although it would not be unusual for one's perspective to be shaped by one's affiliation, the debate appears to be rooted in issues that are a bit more complex.

Although the native populations are formally guaranteed their traditional access to the resources, Lawson (1985) argues that the government has failed to live up to its agreement to share with the Inuit in the full management of Canadian national parks:

> No joint management regimes presently exist in the national park system; however, Parks Canada has continued to work on a suitable model for the future. At present, aspirations for joint management regimes by native groups may be too optimistic.

East argues that Lawson's assessment is out of date and that true co-management is now functioning, based on recent agreements, for several northern parks, including Wood Buffalo National Park where he is the superintendent. However, the debate is clouded by a lack of clear consensus over what constitutes true co-management. Natives and advocates may feel there is no true co-management unless they have full control over policy and management. East, however, argues that joint management was never intended to be equal, let alone a self-management regime. The role of advisory councils certainly raises the specter of formal responsibility without power. Is this debate, then, an issue of simple cooptation? East clearly thinks not. He agrees the native people do not have full control over the management of their lands, but they are not without substantial influence. His chapter contains several more recent case examples where he argues that native populations have exerted important influences in the decision-making processes; and future agreements look even more promising for greater Inuit control of management agendas. However, these experiments in co-management are quite new and there has been little systematic evaluation research on these attempts similar to Weaver's research on co-management in Australian national parks. Until we have such a systematic analysis, the debate over co-management may be swirling around conflicting perceptions that the co-management glass is either half-full or half-empty.

In our final chapter in part 6 we have asked Stuart Marks, an anthropologist who has been involved in the resident peoples and national parks issue in Central Africa, to comment on the planning and decision-making processes in part 6. Marks emphasizes that many of the techniques and analytical tools are creatures of Western society and culture and there is a danger that simply transplanting them to other cultures in developing societies may be, at best, ineffective, and at worst, counter-productive. Using ethnographic data from Zambia's Central Luangwa Valley, he cautions, for instance, that greater local participation and co-management must take account of past patterns of entrenched privilege and vested interests among both local leaders and local representatives of external government authorities. He argues that careful ethnographic social analysis must be done before general ideals of greater participation and co-management can be adapted to local social and cultural realities. The use of social impact analysis advocated by Hough (Chapter 23) can be an important tool in this adjustment process.

20   ## The Pinelands National Reserve:
An Approach to Cooperative
Conservation

David F. Hales

PROTECTED AREA	Pinelands National Reserve
CLASSIFICATION	Labeled as: National Reserve Managed as: Biosphere Reserve
RESIDENT PEOPLES	Farmers and Rural Citizenry

The Pinelands is a 1.2 million acre (480,000 hectare) mosaic
of low, dense forest of pine and oak, pitch pine lowlands,
cedar and hardwood swamps, and bogs and marshes covering
more than 20 percent of the most industrialized state in the
United States. It provides the setting for an ongoing experiment relevant to the protection of natural resources throughout the world.

Born of fire and water, and sculpted by interaction with
human activities, this area was designated by the U.S. Congress as the Pinelands National Reserve, and subsequently

as a part of the South Atlantic Coastal Plain Biosphere Reserve. It is representative both of the challenges of sustainable use of land and water resources, and the potential to meet such challenges inherent in the biosphere reserve concept. As a case study, it provides insights into methods for developing positive relationships between local citizens and the management of conservation areas.

The Pinelands: Background and Characteristics

The maintenance of the Pinelands as a stable, self-regulating ecosystem is dependent on several key factors, including the Cohansey aquifer, extremely porous and acidic soils, and the presence of fire as an essential ecosystem process.

The Cohansey Aquifer, which underlies the reserve, is one of the primary determinants of the nature of the Pinelands. Containing some 17 trillion U.S. gallons of fresh water (65 trillion liters), its water table is rarely more than seven meters, and quite characteristically less than one meter from the surface, which is generally comprised of chemically inert soils through which both rainfall and pollutants pass equally unfiltered. The aquifer is characterized by a remarkably stable water regime, and this stability and close relationship to the surface make the aquifer an extremely important factor in the total Pinelands ecology. Both the quality of surface and sub-surface water and the quantity of water held in the Cohansey aquifer must remain relatively unchanged if the Pinelands is to retain its present characteristics (Rhodehamel 1973; Rutgers 1978).

The soils in the Pinelands are sandy and acidic. They have little ability to retain moisture or nutrients, or to filter organics, nitrates, or pathogenic viruses. Although fertility varies throughout the reserve, the majority of the soils will not support field or vegetable crops or orchards, although the area is naturally well suited for blueberry and cranberry cultivation (United States Department of Interior 1980).

Fire is the third dominant factor in the maintenance of the unique characteristics of the Pinelands. For at least 10,000 years fire has occurred frequently throughout the Pinelands area, and the fire history of the Pinelands determines its forest composition to a great extent. The plant species that tend to predominate in the reserve—scrub oaks (*Quercus marilandica, Q. ilicifolia*) and pitch and short leaf pine (*Pinus rigida; P. echinata*)—are resistant to fire damage, though highly flammable. Other plant species found in the Pinelands tend to share these characteristics.

There is substantial evidence that, in the absence of fire, the pines that currently dominate the Pinelands would eventually be replaced by oaks and other hardwoods, substantially modifying vegetation communities and eventually modifying the ecological characteristics of the Pinelands (Pinelands Commission 1980).

The complex interplay of earth, water, and fire has created a diverse habitat, which includes seventy-one rare plant species, and seven threatened or endangered species of reptiles that are endemic to this area. The uniqueness of the Pinelands is further demonstrated by the fact that more than one hundred southern species of plants reach the northernmost edge of their range in the Pinelands, while fourteen species of plants reach their southernmost extent in the Pinelands.

When one considers the diversity of habitats available in the Pinelands, the image of a wildland area far removed from civilization is likely created. Yet the Pinelands Reserve is within 160 kilometers (100 miles) of the major urban centers of New York City, New York, Philadelphia, Pennsylvania, and the Baltimore/Washington complex. It is bordered on the northwest by the Philadelphia–Trenton, New Jersey, industrial complex, and traversed by major North and South highways and rail lines linking the Baltimore and Washington area with New York and New England.

During the past three hundred years the landscape has been impacted by extensive timbering; mining of iron, sand, and gravel; agricultural practices; hunting; and residential development. In the past, other areas with richer soils, better access to power sources and transportation, and more valuable mineral deposits have been more attractive for human development. As a result, the human use patterns that have endured have been those most dependent on, and most complementary to, the unique characteristics of the Pinelands. In the past thirty years, however, increasing population pressures, housing costs, and transportation efficiencies have resulted in expanding residential development within the Pinelands, which is characteristic of suburbanization patterns elsewhere in the United States. In addition, the establishment of retirement communities and vacation homes has increased the number of housing units constructed.

The relative emptiness of the Pinelands also led to its being considered an attractive repository for solid waste generated by the surrounding areas. The relative wilderness characteristics of the Pinelands made the region a likely destination for many who would dispose of waste illegally. The permeability of soils in the Pinelands area meant that any liquids that were dumped would percolate rapidly with direct, immediate, negative impacts on ground and surface water quality. As the federal government and the states surrounding the Pinelands increased their regulatory control on the deposition of solid waste, and particularly as controls and costs associated with the deposition of toxic waste increased, so did the use of the Pinelands as an illegal dumping ground.

As a result of these pressures, residents of the area, particularly those engaged in agricultural and forestry enterprises, conservationists, and various governmental agencies charged with protecting the ecological and environmental resources of the area, found themselves with a common interest.

The Area of National Concern Approach: A Cooperative Tool

Local residents and their governments, the government of the state of New Jersey, and the federal government, all interested in preserving the unique characteristics of the Pinelands, found their authorities and capacities limited in some essential way. The fragmentary nature of local jurisdictions meant that those who did adopt strong environmental safeguards imposed costs on themselves, often without any real hope of recognizing large-scale benefits. Meanwhile, those who did not adopt strong environmental safeguards were able to realize immediate economic benefits, often turning the costs into externalities to be paid by adjoining jurisdictions.

While state government authorities were broader and more comprehensive than those of local jurisdictions, it was apparent that the state's financial, technical, and legal resources needed augmentation in order to address fully the challenge of protection. Commitment of the federal government to support the state in areas such as the protection of navigable waters—where the federal government has pre-eminence—was necessary.

The authority of the federal government to address resource protection issues was not well adapted to the Pinelands situation. An acquisition and management approach—the method by which most of the United States national parks, refuges, and forests have been protected—was seen to be unrealistic when confronting the need to protect an ecosystem covering more than 20 percent of the State of New Jersey (1.2 million acres; 480,000 hectares). Even if money were available for acquisition, a range of private activities that are appropriate to the resource would be prohibited if the area were to be included in any federal system. It was also clear that the purchase of small enclaves of representative ecological niches within the area would not provide for the sustainability even of those enclaves, much less protect the ecosystem as a whole.

Recognizing these limitations, Congress established the Pinelands as the first national reserve, and in so doing, established an approach to preservation that relies on a mixture of state and local land-use planning and regulation, coupled with federal participation in the form of financial and technical assistance. The program encouraged the maximum use of state and local government planning and regulation procedures; mandated measures to ensure the involvement of local populations; included a federal guarantee of overall consistency for governmental policies affecting the area; and made available the technical and financial expertise of the federal government necessary to develop and enact a plan for the Pinelands (Hales 1978).

The federal statute required the creation of a planning commission representing local, state, and federal interests, which was charged with developing a Comprehensive Management Plan (CMP) for the Pinelands. The law, augmented by actions of the New Jersey state legislature, specifically required the planning commission to provide for "maximum feasible local government and public participation in the management of the Pinelands" (Hales 1978).

The commission, comprised of individuals appointed by local county governments (seven people), the governor of New Jersey (seven), and the United States secretary of interior (one), developed a CMP that was approved in 1981, and which is conceptually similar to the model for biosphere reserves designed by Eidsvik for IUCN in 1979. The CMP divides the Pinelands into two generic areas, a 148,000-hectare preservation area that is generally managed for minimum human interference, and a 290,000-hectare protection area within which an array of more intensive activities is allowed depending on the carrying capacity of the resource (see Map 20.1).

Within the preservation area—60 percent of which is publicly owned—human activities are limited to those directly related to and compatible with the natural regime. Berry agriculture, a traditional use, is encouraged, and horticulture of native plants, along with low-intensity recreation, is permitted. Residency is limited to people who have family ties or a cultural, social, or economic link to the Pinelands, in-

Map 20.1
Pineland
National Reserve

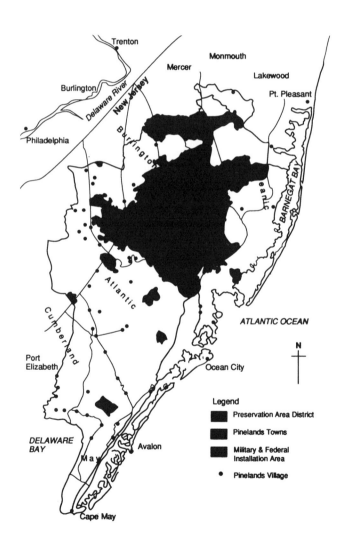

cluding primary employment in the Pinelands and land tenure prior to 1979. Population density is also regulated. The results of these measures include a decrease in the market value of some properties, as well as increased incentive and protection for traditional economic endeavors and lifestyles. Of particular importance in this regard is the establishment in both generic areas of Agricultural Production Districts (APD), covering traditional and potential farmland, where farming is mandated as the major activity, and where stringent regulations protect the soil and water quality essential to traditional agriculture. Approximately 32,000 hectares outside of the preservation areas are in APD's.

Although the protection area generally is not regulated as strictly as the preservation area, some 156,000 hectares are designated as Forest Districts (FD). Areas in which human influence remains minimal and critical ecological values are present, FD's are regulated to promote forestry, horticulture, and recreational use. These areas also protect watersheds that are in active berry agriculture and subwatersheds, which support threatened plant or animal species. The FD designation is also used to establish a corridor linking environmentally sensitive areas to the preservation area. Defined by the CMP as an "ecological imperative," the corridor is intended to provide a protected natural passage for the dispersal and migration of native plants and animals. Residential development in FD's is stringently limited (17 units per square mile over current usage).

Other segments of the protection area are the CMP-designated Regional Growth Districts (RGD) (i.e., 48,000 hectares or 10 percent of the Pinelands) to "encourage appropriate patterns of compatible . . . development . . . in order to accommodate regional growth influences in an orderly way while protecting the Pinelands." The purpose of RGD's is to direct new development into environmentally suitable areas within, or adjacent to, existing developed areas, and, by so doing, reduce pressures for use conversion on more environmentally sensitive areas and areas dominated by traditional use patterns.

Surrounding the RGD's, the CMP designates Rural Development Districts (RDD) (58,000 hectares). Based partially on existing use patterns, RDD's allow controlled resource extraction activities and intensive recreational development, landfill establishment, and limited residential development, as well as activities permitted in more restrictive districts. As a general rule, RDD's serve as transition zones and buffers between more intensive and less intensive uses throughout the Pinelands Reserve.

In addition to the major classification, the outright purchase by governmental agencies of approximately 30,000 hectares was recommended, and special land use categories were developed for existing villages and towns as well as existing subdivisions and recreational communities. Further, general environmental standards and several specific resource management programs that focus on crosscutting issues such as solid waste management or protection of cultural resources were adopted as part of the comprehensive planning process.

The zoning patterns and programmatic aspects of the CMP are complemented by the employment of a relatively unique conservation tool. In an attempt to equalize the effects of differing regulatory standards on individual landowners, and enhance protection of more sensitive areas, the CMP mandates a device by which development rights can be transferred from more environmentally sensitive areas with stringent regulations to less sensitive areas with fewer development restrictions. The mechanism allocates Pineland Development Credits (PDC) to various unusable development rights pertaining to private property in the preservation area, Forest Districts, and the Agricultural Production Districts. Owners of credits may sell them on the open market to landowners in less restrictive areas who can then develop at a greater density than would otherwise be allowed. (For extensive discussion of transferable development rights see Randle 1982; Greenbaum 1982). This mechanism allows landowners in restricted areas to share in the increased value of more suitable land for development resulting from the restrictions. In addition, it further encourages the clustering of development activities in areas most capable of carrying them without widespread negative environmental impacts.

An additional distinctive feature of the Pinelands Reserve is the relationship between its planning commission and county and local governments throughout the reserve. The combination of federal and state legislation resulted in clear authority for the commission to regulate land use and growth.

County and local ordinances and plans must comply with the Pinelands CMP, and each locality must engage in a master planning process coordinated by the commission. Further, although primary jurisdiction for land use decisions remains with local planning units, the commission retains the authority to review any decision. If local governments do not meet CMP guidelines and performance standards the commission has the authority to preempt local land use decisions. In short, the Pinelands approach created a new level of government charged with resource protection throughout the entire reserve, and endowed with the necessary authorities to regulate land use activities to accomplish that goal.

Impacts on Pinelands Residents

Any protection approach that is effective will have impacts—positive and negative—on local residents. It is apparent that this is true of the Pinelands Reserve. One clear result of the establishment of the reserve and the enactment of the CMP is to limit future uses of land within the reserve and, concomitantly, opportunities for economic gain from those prohibited uses. Because traditional land uses and related livelihoods are actually promoted by the CMP, the activities and lifestyles of most natives are unlikely to be disrupted. For many, the values that led them to choose homes in the Pinelands will be enhanced and their way of life reinforced.

Farmers, for example, will find that land values in agricultural areas will be determined by productivity, and pressure to convert agricultural land to more intense use will be reduced. In addition, and of particular relevance to berry agriculture, protection measures will ensure necessary water quality and availability. Other resource values including forestry, wildlife, recreation, and aesthetics will also be sustained and enhanced. Perhaps most importantly, the ability of natives to participate in determining the future of the Pinelands appears to be enhanced. Although the Commission is not elected, fourteen of its fifteen members are appointed by elected officials. The legal framework for the reserve is amenable to legislative action. Interpretations of the Plan are subject to judicial review. Finally, the CMP itself provides for periodic reconsideration of issues in response to changing demands.

Conclusion

The U.S. Congress has declared the protection of Pineland resources to be a matter of national interest, and, in cooperation with state and local governments, has devised an approach to resource protection that emphasizes local determination of means to achieve nationally recognized goals; relies on rational regulation rather than large-scale acquisition; and promotes coordinated, scientific management on the basis of an ecosystem. This approach will continue to be challenged by speculators who are denied short-term profit at long-term public expense. Furthermore, the details of the plan will be continually challenged by environmentalists who find its restrictions too lax, and by honest developers and other residents who find its controls to be unnecessarily restrictive. It is, nevertheless, a working experiment grappling with the complexities of meeting human needs on a sustainable basis that may lend itself to adaptation in other areas. It is also an effort that depends for its success on the continuing support and involvement of those who live in the Pinelands.

Consideration of the Pinelands experience leads to the identification of several principles for local participation in protected area management that seem to have been successful, and which may be useful considerations elsewhere.

First, constraints on human activities should be determined by the ability of biophysical systems to maintain the values for which the area is recognized. Limitations should be determined by the best "science" available, but these scientific data must include, and be seen to include, local knowledge and wisdom. Natives must be recognized as essential and sophisticated information sources, while teams developing management regimes should have the capacity to appreciate and access this information. One cannot learn from natives if one condescendingly believes that they have nothing to teach.

As a corollary to this principle, management programs must provide for ongoing monitoring and *resource-based evaluation* to provide feedback on the accuracy of planning assumptions. One of the most important contributions of an effective participation effort is that it provides a means for identifying unresolvable conflicts between local needs and aspirations, and the sustainability of important resource values and characteristics. These conflicts must be recognized, and conscious choices made, perhaps in favor of the resource, perhaps not. The key is to avoid conflict "resolution" techniques, or propaganda campaigns, which obscure the basic nature of the conflict and lead to "compromises," the resource-related consequences of which are unclear.

Second, effective and sustainable protection is dependent on a strong public-involvement campaign that begins very early in the planning process. In its early stages, the campaign should inform natives about how to participate and about sources of substantive and procedural information, as well as transmit substantive resource data. The campaign must be based on a real commitment to involve the natives and not be just a public relations or sales campaign to persuade locals to give in to experts. Real commitment, at a minimum, entails being able to demonstrate the impact of local input and being willing to share decision-making authority with locals. In addition, the campaign should be based on traditional local forms of communication and decision making, although the use of other media may be appropriate.

Third, local participation should be a continuing element of the management regime. This means that any plan produced should be clearly an ongoing process, not something written in stone and imposed on the future. A clear role for locals should be structurally built into the governing process, and some authority must be granted to locals; a purely advisory role is not sufficient. It is critical that the governing structure be familiar, comfortable, and customary to the locals.

Provision must be made for the continuous sharing of scientific information in a form that has meaning to natives. "Meaning to natives," in this context, does not mean the condescending translation of scientific findings into "words they can understand." In this sense, it includes being understood, but more importantly, it means "having value" to locals. If management or scientific activity has no "meaning," no value, to local populations, the fault lies with the scientist, not with the citizen.

Fourth, the definition or concept of "local" must distinguish between individuals who are local residents, but do not share local interests, and those who are and do. The most effective guide in dealing with this complex issue will derive from broad local involvement itself and from the continual recruitment of natives into an open process. The last, and perhaps most important, principle derived from the Pinelands experience is not to underestimate the local commitment to sustainable use, as well as to preservation of less tangible values, including beauty. The manager who does so gives away one of the most effective elements of a strategy for sustainability. There is no conclusive evidence that democratic processes lead inevitably to good resource decisions, nor is the argument that local people have a greater right to unilaterally determine the use of resources than those in distant places uniformly persuasive. Yet the experience of the Pinelands is additional evidence that the self-interest of natives will tend to promote sustainable use, rather than exploitative use, of resources if the information necessary for decisions is made available to them.

21   Resident Attitudes About a National Park in Sabah, Malaysia

Susan Kay Jacobson

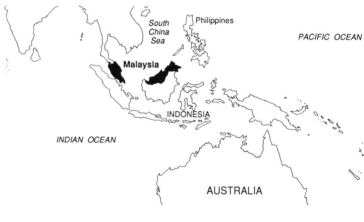

PROTECTED AREA	Kinabalu Park
CLASSIFICATION	Labeled as: National Park Managed as: National Park, IUCN Category II
RESIDENT PEOPLES	Peasant Peoples and Local Entrepreneurs

Preserved as Sabah, Malaysia's first national park, Mt. Kinabalu dominates the Bornean landscape. Its eminence is reflected by its prominence in the religious beliefs of the indigenous people and by the park's profound effect on the economic development and infrastructural changes that have occurred in the area.

In 1985, a survey was conducted to assess the attitudes of the local people about Kinabalu Park. Data were collected through questionnaires designed to obtain information on their perceptions of the value of the park, and their utilization of natural resources. Although the survey was implemented as part of an evaluation of a program developed by the park for local villages (Jacobson 1987), the results are presented here to illuminate the sociodemographic background of the indigenous people and their relationship with the park.

The Park

Gazetted in 1964, Kinabalu Park encompasses an area of 754 square kilometers on the northern tip of Borneo. The park stretches from an altitude of 300 meters to 4,101 meters at the peak of Mt. Kinabalu, Southeast Asia's tallest mountain. Famous for its rich diversity of plant and animal life, over half the world's families of flowering plants are represented in the park. These include endangered species of orchids, insectivorous pitcher plants, and *Rafflesia*, the world's largest flower. Over three hundred species of birds and one hundred species of mammals have been recorded in the park; some are found nowhere else (Jacobson 1985).

When the National Parks Ordinance No. 5 was passed in 1962, it gave His Excellency the Yang Dipertua Negara the right to constitute a national park on any state land and to appoint a board of trustees to control it. Parks in Sabah were to be established for the "conservation of the scenic, scientific, and historical heritage of Sabah for the benefit and enjoyment of its people" (Jenkins et al. 1976). However, the ordinance did not provide any guidance about environmental or administrative policies to be followed.

The park system in Sabah is a statutory body subsidized by the state government, under the jurisdiction of the Ministry of Manpower and Environmental Development. In the 1970s, the need for a national park policy was recognized. A policy based on the Canadian National Park System was drafted in 1976 (Jenkins et al. 1976). This was presented to the Sabah National Parks Board of Trustees who then submitted it for ratification to the state cabinet. Chapter 2, Section 5 pertains directly to human activity inside the park, and it states that "the following activities are detrimental to natural history values and should not be permitted in national park: (1) grazing of domestic stock; (2) pollution of air, soil or water; (3) harvesting of forest produce for commercial gain; (4) harvesting of animals and their products; (5) the construction and operation of hydroelectric power installations and other water diversions or impoundments for industrial purposes and the exploitation of ore bodies."

However, these caveats are followed by the qualifier that "Sabah is a developing country and the exploitation of these resources of land and water may be necessary for the well being of the State. Where no alternative resources are available, then impairment may be accepted if these resources are of such national importance that the sacrifice of park values can be justified" (Jenkins et al. 1976). Based on this clause, land has been excised from Kinabalu Park several times for various government projects. In the 1970s, 2,512 hectares of park land were leased to a joint Japanese-Sabahan mining company. In full operation, about 6,800 kilograms of ore are mined daily, and about six hundred people are employed. In 1982, 1,822 hectares were excised for a golf course, cattle farm, agricultural station, and farming schemes. In 1984, an additional 1,620 hectares were taken out.

For the most part, the park has enjoyed a good relationship with the neighboring people. Much of the park is above 1,200 meters, and because of its basic soil and steep slopes, it is unsuitable for agriculture. When it became a park in 1964, it was virtually uninhabited (Burrough 1978). Local people were not displaced.

The park's relationship with the local people is a symbiotic one. It permanently employs more than one hundred workers, mostly from the neighboring area. More than one hundred more work on a temporary basis or are self-employed guides and porters. The influx of visitors to the park has created a market for local produce and goods, both at the park where employees have established a cooperative, and in the surrounding towns. The growth of the park was concomitant with infrastructural improvements such as road construction and availability of public transportation. The synergistic effect of these changes, together with the effect of the park's school programs and recreational activities, has directly influenced the lives of the local people.

Antagonisms between the park and the local villagers have been minimal since its establishment (McCredie 1973). Threats to the inviolate nature of Kinabalu Park, such as illegal plant collecting or hunting, have been relatively few. Kinabalu's rare pitcher plants and orchids fetch as much as $1,000 per plant in international markets. But illegal collection is thought to be carried out mainly by foreigners. Though the park is not well patrolled, animal poaching by local people does not appear to be a serious problem; few arrests have been made. The recent land excisions may have instigated the most serious illegal threats to the park. Parts of the boundary remain unsurveyed or unmarked, and there has been an increase in illegal felling of trees and crop cultivation in these areas.

The People

Most (95 percent) of the population living near the park are Kadazan (Dusun), Sabah's largest indigenous group (26 percent of Sabah's population in the 1975 census). They live in villages scattered on Mt. Kinabalu's flanks and on the Ranau plain. The largest town bordering the park is Ranau, with a population in 1980 of 27,307 Pribumis (classification designating Kadazans and other natives), 624 Chinese and 14 Indians (Sabah State Government 1983).

Traditionally, Kadazans are shifting cultivators. They burn a plot in the forest and plant rice with other crops like corn, tapioca, sweet potatoes, and tobacco. After a year or two, heavy weed infestation and leached soils force them to move, leaving the plot to lie fallow for six years or more. The biggest change in the local economy occurred in the 1950s with the cultivation of temperate vegetables, a project sponsored by the government and a Roman Catholic mission.

The planting of temperate vegetables has been absorbed into the system of shifting cultivation. Since the 1960s the Department of Agriculture has been trying to persuade the farmers to grow vegetables on permanent, terraced fields. The department has done so by providing grants for terracing land, subsidizing fertilizers and insecticides, and establishing the Kundasang Farmers' Association to assist with marketing (Burrough 1978). Nowadays, many farmers have abandoned shifting cultivation altogether and sedentary agriculture is becoming more predominant. This, in turn, lessens local pressure for the development of additional park land for agriculture.

Long before Mt. Kinabalu was established as a park, it was a place of cultural significance for Kadazans. The mountain's name is derived from the Kadazan "Aki Nabalu" meaning "the revered place of the dead"; the summit of Kinabalu and a neighboring peak were believed to be the resting place of deceased ancestors. European explorers who climbed Mt. Kinabalu in the nineteenth century reported ceremonies held by their Kadazan guides to appease the spirits of the mountain (e.g., St. John 1862). Though many Kadazans have now joined formal religions, legends and stories about Mt. Kinabalu are still popular. Kadazan guides who work at the park perform an annual ceremony at the summit honoring the spirit world.

Kinabalu Park serves as a recreational resource for the resident population. Many villagers have visited the park with their school or church groups and some have scaled Mt. Kinabalu. The park provides special education programs for school children and has developed a mobile unit program that visits local villages with slide and film shows.

It is evident that some villagers enjoy an intimate relationship with the park through employment or leisure use. Indirectly, villagers experience increased market sales and infrastructural benefits, and in some cases, a spiritual communion with the mountain. The social survey conducted in 1985 examined some of these perceptions about the value of the park.

Methods

In March 1985 a villager survey instrument was developed to collect information on the attitudes about Kinabalu Park and natural resources held by local villagers. Information on their sociodemographic background was also obtained to explore its influence on their perceptions. The villages to be surveyed were small, rural settlements, with populations ranging from one hundred to one thousand people. They were located on the southern boundary of the park, within an hour's drive from park headquarters.

The original pilot questionnaire was an oral interview conducted by five Sabah Park staff workers. The workers went from door to door at Kinasaraban Village asking an individual from each household to respond to twelve attitude statements based on a Likert scale, and six background information questions. The interviews lasted from five to fifteen minutes, and only ten questionnaires were completed in two hours. Some questions had to be repeated in Malay as well as Kadazan to help clarify their meaning. Some villagers wanted to discuss each answer and were reluctant to give their opinions. Other villagers hesitated to give answers to questions they thought may have political overtones; they may have said "no opinion" to avoid imagined problems. For example, after the interviewer made the statement "Kinabalu Park is too large" a villager responded, "If the government says it should be large, then it should be large."

Due to the difficulty in obtaining accurate opinions, the small sample size obtained, and the limitations of personnel and time, the survey was modified, eliminating four confusing statements from the original, and adding directions for the villagers. The resulting questionnaire consisted of seven attitude statements which the respondents checked depending on whether they agreed, disagreed, or had no opinion about the statement. The questionnaire also asked six background questions to determine their age, sex, and occupation, and whether they still hunted, used forest products, or had ever visited the park.

These questionnaires were distributed to from fifteen to thirty households in each of eleven villages on the southern boundary of Kinabalu Park (see Map 21.1). Villages were chosen that had never been visited by the park's mobile unit program and that were located within an hour's drive from park headquarters. It should be noted that the surveys were conducted along Kinabalu's southern border, an area which has benefited from the park's growth as a recreational and tourist facility. About 90 percent of the park lies north of the mountain and remains inaccessible. Villages along these boundaries were not surveyed. The written questionnaires also discriminated against illiterate villagers. Therefore, older members of the population with more traditional views may be underrepresented. At each village, of the 30 to 60 questionnaires distributed, between 30 to 70 percent were returned to park personnel, totaling 249 questionnaires.

Villagers with more negative attitudes toward the park may have been less inclined to return their questionnaires, and again would be underrepresented.

For analysis, the questionnaire response scores were converted to reflect the negative ($=1$) or positive ($=3$) attitude to each statement. No opinion responses were scored as 2. The scores of the seven attitude statements were summed for each individual, giving a possible score from seven to twenty-one, and then compared using ANOVA procedures to determine the effects of age, sex, occupation, hunter, and forest product user classes. Village differences were also analyzed for the three villages with the greatest sample sizes. Chi-squared tests were used to determine if there were differences among villages' scores, as well as among individual attitude scores for the classes listed above. The results should reveal the overall perceptions of the villagers and

Map 21.1
Kinabalu Park:
Villages
Surveyed

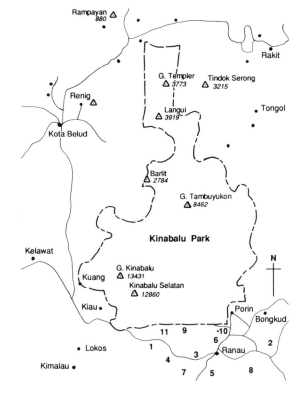

Legend

1. Dumpiring Jaya
2. Kalingan
3. Ruhukan
4. Kaparingan
5. Minisalu
6. Kasiladan
7. Tambiau
8. Silou
9. Lipasu Baru
10. Tagudan Baru
11. Cinta Mata

how specific sociodemographic variables influence their
ideas.

Results

As shown in Table 21.1, the results reflected a favorable attitude toward the park. An overwhelmingly positive attitude
was expressed to the statement: "It is good that Mt. Kinabalu is being preserved as a park," with 88 percent of the
respondents agreeing. A high percentage of people (77 percent) also believed that parks were not just for wealthy
people. Most (82 percent) believed that permanent agriculture was better than shifting cultivation. For two other statements about half the respondents gave positive responses:
56 percent thought there was a need to preserve natural
areas and 52 percent thought Kinabalu should not be developed for agriculture. Two statements elicited negative attitude responses: only 16 percent of the respondents disagreed
with the statements that Kinabalu Park is too large and that
there is still plenty of natural forest in Sabah.

The results of the summed attitude scores ranged from 10
to 21 for the 249 questionnaires, with a median score of 16.
The responses were analyzed on the basis of the respondent's
background. The results of the differences in attitude scores
for the independent variables (village, occupation, age, sex,
forest product user, hunter, and park visitor) are presented
below.

The total attitude scores of the three villages (numbers 1,
6, and 7) with the highest sample sizes did not differ ($F_{2,89}=$
0.34, $p > 0.05$). However, village 6 was substantially different
in that fewer people still utilized natural forest products
($\chi^2 = 7.75$, $p < 0.05$) and only 47 percent of the respondents
were farmers, compared to 81 percent in village 1 and 76 percent in village 7. Village 6 also reported 17 percent of the
population in business, while villages 1 and 7 had none
($\chi^2 = 18.09$, $p < 0.05$).

Comparing differences in attitude scores among different
occupational groups showed some significant differences.
Government servants had higher total attitude scores than
farmers ($F_{1,241} = 3.69$, $p < 0.01$). Both government servants and
students scored significantly higher than farmers on the
statement declaring a need to preserve natural areas.

There was no difference in total attitude scores among
the four age categories ($F_{4,231} = 1.25$, $p > 0.05$), between sexes

Table 21.1 Results of the Mobile Unit Questionnaire Showing Aggregate Attitude Scores from 11 Villages Bordering Kinabalu Park (N = 249)

Information Requested	Least Favorable	No Opinion	Most Favorable
A. *Questionnaire Statements*			
1. There is no need to keep areas of natural forest.	28	16	5
2. National Parks are mostly for wealthy people.	11	12	77
3. It is better to have permanent agriculture than shifting cultivation.	12	6	82
4. Kinabalu park is too large.	52	32	16
5. Kinabalu Park should be developed for agricultural use.	31	17	52
6. There is still plenty of natural forest in Sabah.	53	31	16
7. It is good that Mt. Kinabalu is being preserved as a Park.	6	6	88
B. *Background Information*	*% Yes*	*% No*	
8. Hunting is important to my way of life.	20	80	
9. Wild forest products are still useful to me.	67	32	
10. Have you ever been to Kinabalu Park?	63	37	
11. How old are you?			
10–19 years 32			
20–29 years 33			
30–39 years 18			
40+ years 17			
12. What is your occupation?			
farmer 64			
business 3			
housekeeper 9			
gov't. servant 7			
student 17			
13. Sex?			
male 35			
female 65			

($F_{1,244}=0.11$, $p>0.05$), or between individuals who still found forest products useful and those who did not ($F_{1,247}= 0.35$, $p>0.05$). However, there were differences in responses to some of the individual attitude statements. Forest product users showed a more favorable score to the statements about not developing Kinabalu Park for agriculture ($\chi^2=10.21$, $p<0.01$) with forest product users responding favorably 58 percent of the time and nonusers only responding favorably 38 percent of the time. Forest product users also scored higher for the statement that it is good Mt. Kinabalu is being preserved as a Park ($\chi^2=10.21$, $p<0.01$). In contrast, the forest product users scored less favorably than nonusers, agreeing with the statement that there is still plenty of natural forest left in Sabah ($\chi^2=22.56$, $p<0.0001$).

The total attitude scores did not vary between hunters and nonhunters ($F_{1,247}=2.62$, $p>0.05$). Significantly more of the hunters were also forest product users than were the non-hunters ($F_{1,247}=13.85$, $p<0.001$): 90 percent of the hunters used forest products, but only 62 percent of the nonhunters did. There was no difference in total attitude scores between the hunters and nonusers. However, the hunters did respond less favorably to the statement that the park was mainly for wealthy people ($\chi^2=12.72$, $p<0.01$).

Finally, there was no difference in total attitude scores between those who had previously visited Kinabalu Park and those who had not ($F_{1,241}= 1.22$, $p>0.05$). The only individual statement on which these two groups differed concerned the amount of natural forest still left in Sabah. Previous park visitors had more favorable responses ($\chi^2=9.42$, $p<0.01$).

Discussion   Different sociodemographic backgrounds among the villagers accounted for some of the variations in attitudes that emerged from the results of this study. All eleven villages appeared to be fairly homogeneous, agrarian settlements except for village 6 which was located near a copper mine. When compared with two other villages with large sample sizes, village 6 had fewer farmers and more business-oriented occupations, yet their attitude scores did not differ.

Other independent variables, such as whether the villager had ever visited the park, used forest products, or hunted, showed no differences in total attitude scores but did reveal response differences for individual statements. Villagers who had visited the park previously showed an increased awareness that natural forests in Sabah are dwindling. In fact, Sabah's habitat has changed extensively in recent years, primarily due to timber extraction. In 1971, 61 percent of Sabah was primary forest. By 1980, only 27 percent of the forest remained, and it is disappearing at a rapid rate (Davies and Payne 1982). Visitors to Kinabalu Park may experience various interpretive programs which highlight the value of natural areas, or they may be exposed firsthand to the differences between primary and secondary forests.

Total attitude scores between hunters and nonhunters did not differ. However, the hunters agreed more with the statement that national parks are mainly for wealthy people. It is not known if the hunters are in a different income bracket than nonhunters. The hunters were also associated with a greater use of forest products. This is not surprising as these activities, such as gathering medicinal plants or rattan, and hunting can be done concurrently.

Villagers who claimed to use forest products showed no difference in total attitude scores from those who did not, although they responded more favorably to the statements about preserving rather than developing Kinabalu Park. At the same time, forest users believed plenty of natural forest still existed in Sabah. This could be because their utilization of forest products may be met by both primary and secondary forest types.

Other sociodemographic characteristics, such as gender and age, revealed no differences in attitude scores. Occupation was one of the few variables that affected the total attitude scores. Government servants scored more favorably than farmers for total attitude responses. Both government servants and students were more aware of a need to preserve natural areas than the farming group. This may reflect higher education levels attained by government servants and students, with an increased understanding of the scientific or economic value of a park system. The farmers also compete more directly with the park for land, and may have less free time to take advantage of the park's services.

Although the great majority of villagers were satisfied that Kinabalu was preserved as a park, many thought it was too large; self-interest in obtaining additional farmland may foster this attitude. In 1983, 3,034 applications for state land were dealt with by the Sabah government, and a further 22,436 were still outstanding at the end of the year (Sabah State Government, 1983).

Because of the poor agricultural potential of most of the park land, and Sabah's low population density (thirteen people per square kilometer; Sabah State Government, 1980), there has historically been minimal conflict over land with the local villagers, but with the government's recent land excisions, conflicts have increased. Several villagers have voiced dissatisfaction with the policy, stating, "If the land is going to be excised, it should go to the villagers, not to a golf course." New boundaries remain unmarked and incursions into the park by shifting cultivators seem to be increasing.

Overall, the villagers' favorable responses to the park indicate their perception that some cultural, ecological, or economic benefits accrue from the park. Mt. Kinabalu has long been an important religious symbol to the Kadazans as the homeland of their spirit world, and it has always been treated with veneration. Also, the concept of conservation is not foreign to the Kadazans. At the turn of the century, Rutter (1922) reported that the Tambunan Kadazans established reserves ("tegah") along the river where fish were abundant. Human disturbances to these areas were carefully controlled to help ensure a sustained yield of food. Kinabalu Park protects the headwaters of eight rivers in Sabah which are vital for irrigation and fishing in the area.

The favorable attitude of the villagers toward the park may also stem from the economic development that has occurred in the area, directly from employment opportunities and indirectly from infrastructural changes related to the park. The majority of the 115 park staff hail from the neighboring area and over a hundred of the temporary laborers and guides come from the local villages.

In the past few decades, the area bordering Mt. Kinabalu has changed dramatically with the establishment of the park, the road improvements between Ranau and the capital, the introduction of temperate vegetable production, and other development projects. The advent of the good road connection between the park and the capital had wide-ranging repercussions on the local villages. Mohamad (1983) found that there was an increase in ownership of televisions and radios, an increase in knowledge about "family planning," a change from farming to other occupations in service and labor fields, and a movement from shifting cultivation to sedentary farming. Concomitant with these changes, the Ranau area has greatly expanded, schools and clinics have increased, and the Ministry of Industrial Development has completed a new township with filling stations, restaurants, hotels, shops, and a marketplace, creating a closer market for local farmers' produce.

Kinabalu has become the most popular park in Malaysia, and the tremendous influx of people visiting the park has provided another market for local products. From 879 visitors in 1965, visitation rates have grown two hundred times, to 163,337 visitors in 1985. About 64 percent of these visitors are local Sabahans (Jacobson 1987). On some weekends and public holidays, hundreds of visitors often drive to the park from the capital city. They provide a ready market for the farmers selling vegetables and seasonal fruits in the area. In many cases this has lessened the necessity of transporting the crops to the coast or selling them to middlemen. Additionally, because most of the visitors to the park are Sabahans, many of the negative cultural effects associated with tourist centers are minimized at Kinabalu.

Conclusion

In spite of difficulties in sampling, the villagers' responses show strong support for the preservation of Mt. Kinabalu as a park. In large part this is probably because the establishment of the park was concomitant with transportation improvements and new development schemes. The park created an influx of consumers for local markets, and provided employment, education, and recreation facilities. The park also preserved a significant area of cultural heritage for the Kadazans and all Malaysians, as Mt. Kinabalu continues to dominate the Bornean landscape.

NOTE

I thank Sabah Parks for making the study possible. F. Liew, A. Phillipps, G. Sinit, F. L. Tan, H. Peter, M. Zaini, A. Gunsalam, and T. Yussop provided valuable assistance. I am grateful to L. Maguire and M. Meade for reviewing this manuscript. The Shell Foundation and Duke University's Asia/Pacific Studies Institute provided funding for my research.

22 The Social Impacts of Land Use Zoning in the National Parks of South Korea

Hyung Taek Woo

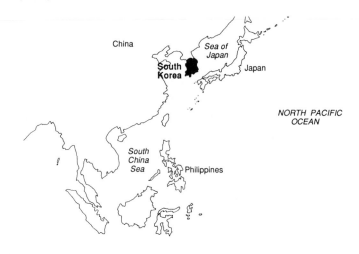

PROTECTED AREA	National Parks of S. Korea
CLASSIFICATION	Labeled as: National Park Managed as: Protected Landscapes, IUCN Category V
RESIDENT PEOPLES	Peasant Peoples, Farmers and Rural Citizenry, and Local Entrepreneurs

The traditional idea of national parks in the United States—the preservation of natural landscapes in an undisturbed state and their use for public and recreational purposes—has spread to many developing countries in recent years. The export of this concept to developing countries has often caused the displacement of resident peoples from national parks, based on the conviction that they destroy important natural landscapes by exploiting natural resources. This displacement policy has caused a number of social and economic dilemmas and there has been considerable controversy over the pros and cons of relocating residents.

Korea imported the traditional idea of national parks, but management policies were adapted to the socioeconomic and cultural context unique to Korea. The management decision was made to leave existing local communities inside the parks to avoid significant social impacts on traditional cultures and impoverished rural people. The reasons for this management policy are complex and varied: (1) Korea lacks alternative land for resident displacement due to the country's small land area, high ratio of population to land, and highly intensive land use; (2) there exists a long history of private landownership; (3) the resources necessary for displacement compensation are extremely limited; (4) agriculture has been long recognized as an important traditional economic activity. Finally, it was felt that traditional rural communities in Korean national parks have not destroyed the important natural and cultural landscapes, but have learned to live in harmony with them over centuries of coexistence and adaption.

Although resident peoples are allowed to live in national parks, other management decisions to achieve different objectives can have direct or indirect negative social impact on residents. One fundamental element in the management of Korea's national parks that may significantly affect local populations is the land use plan that divides the park area into five different districts and regulates the land use types and activities according to the importance of each district.

This chapter presents some important sociological considerations and social impacts that should be weighed in the land use decision-making process by drawing on the strategy of land use zoning found in Korea's national parks.

Background

The first Korean national park, Mt. Jiri, was designated in 1967 by the Parks Law. The Ministry of Construction has been responsible for the administration of national parks in Korea. The actual management of the park is shared between central, state, and local governments. In 1980, the more comprehensive Natural Parks Law replaced the 1967 Parks Law to create the natural park system that includes national, state, and county parks. As of 1987, there are seventeen national parks designated fairly evenly across the country, covering a total of 5,578 square kilometers of land and sea area.

The national parks of Korea are characterized, not by wilderness, but by nationally important natural and cultural landscapes that are the results of interaction between man and nature. They are listed under Category V, Protected Landscapes, of the IUCN classification system (IUCN 1985).

Much like the British and Japanese system, the Korean national park administration has found it difficult to set aside large, undisturbed natural areas exclusively for the purpose of preservation, and to protect them under public ownership. The Korean park system must deal with the un-availability of such areas resulting from: a small land area; a high density of population; the intensive utilization of land resources; the established private landownership; and a long history of human influence in most areas of the country. Therefore, Korean national parks have had to accommodate a variety of land uses such as agriculture, forestry, fisheries, and other development activities for national and regional economy, in addition to tourism. Most national parks also in-clude many historical and culturally important features and sites, such as Buddhist temples, shrines, historical monu-ments, and human settlements.

Korean national parks encompass both public and private land. About 68 percent of the total land area is under public ownership while private land occupies about 32 percent. Most public land belongs to the Forest Agency. About 36 per-cent of private land is temple land. Buddhist temples have played a significant role in protecting unique and important natural and cultural resources because of the Buddhist reli-gious tradition of respect for harmony with nature (Woo 1980).

Thus, a variety of socioeconomic, cultural, and physical conditions have affected the management policy of national parks in Korea. These conditions mandate a management policy more in tune with "multiple use" philosophies, than the "preservation" philosophies that guide national park pol-icy and management in the United States.

The Land Use Plan

The land use plan is the major framework for the multiple use management of national parks in Korea. The land use plan depends on the typical zoning technique combining both land use districts and regulatory systems. The land use plan divides the national park into five different districts, regulates the types of land use allowed in each district, and the types of land use required for permission in all districts. The five land use districts are: (1) the Natural Protection District; (2) the Natural Environment District; (3) the Agricultural and Fishing Village District; (4) the Intensive Use District; and (5) the Park Protection District.

The Natural Protection District represents the core area of the national park that includes the naturally, culturally, or aesthetically most unique and important features. The Natural Environment District is defined as all the remaining area exclusive of the Natural Protection, Agricultural and Fishing Village, and Intensive Use Districts. Although the character and policy of this district are unclear and ambiguous in the Natural Parks Law, it may be intended to accommodate a great deal of development activities within national parks. The Agricultural and Fishing Village District provides the minimum area necessary for farming, fishing, and the housing needs of local people. The purpose of this district is to provide local farming or fishing communities with the ability to maintain their traditional lifestyle and continue their economic activities. It includes existing villages and areas where farming or fishing activities are based. The Intensive Use District is an area that integrates and concentrates park facilities for the comfort of park users. This district provides accommodation facilities such as hotels, motels, inns, and other commercial and public facilities necessary for park users. The Park Protection District is designated around the park boundary and along the approach road to the park for the protection of the national park. It is designed to control undesirable development from spreading outside the park area.

With this system of land use districts, a regulatory program has been designed to guide the development and use of park resources. This system specifies the types of land use to be allowed, requires the permission for development to be regulated, and provides minimum specified permission criteria applicable to each district and all districts. These basic provisions and regulations are summarized in Table 22.1. The different intensity of regulations and permission criteria are based on the values and importance of natural and cultural resources and the needs for resource utilization in each district.

Social Impacts of the Land Use Plan

Three important aspects of the land use plan seem to significantly affect the resident peoples in national parks. The first is the spatial relationships between different land use districts that have different characteristics and purposes. The second is the area of agricultural and fishing villages created for maintaining resident activities and providing for their needs. The third is a regulatory program that may restrict the activities of villagers and limit their access to the resources necessary for maintaining their livelihoods.

The direct and indirect consequences of the land use plan affecting resident peoples should be carefully considered and reflected upon during the land use planning process for each national park (see Table 22.1).

In delineating land use districts, special attention should be given to the spatial relationships between the Agricultural and Fishing Village District and other districts. Spatial relationships between different land use districts may affect resident peoples differently, for each land use district has its own characteristics and purposes that make it unique. The location and size factors of land use districts incompatible with the Agricultural and Fishing Village District may cause negative social impacts on local populations. First, there is a tendency to locate the Intensive Use District within, between, or near local communities in most national parks since these sites may provide the most economical and physically feasible location for the purpose of constructing various park facilities. However, this practice may have negative impacts upon local communities.

Although it is very difficult to pinpoint specific social impacts resulting from this spatial relationship (due to the lack of research in this area), typical social impacts may include: a higher cost of living; a higher tax; decreasing labor available in farming and fishing; changes in employment structure; negative impacts on local community identity and cohesion; and changes in the lifestyle, attitudes, and values of resident peoples. The final result of these impacts would be an uneven and unfair distribution of social and economic costs and benefits among members of the local community. Such negative impacts will be more severe in cases of the location of Intensive Use Districts between or within the Agricultural and Fishing Village Districts rather than away from them because of close access and high visibility. The effects of this spatial relationship may also differ in terms of

Table 22.1 Land Use Districts in Korean National Parks

Land Use Districts	Uses Allowed	Uses Regulated	Permission Criteria
Natural Protection District	Scientific research. Minimal park facilities. Facilities necessary for military missions, communications and airline signaling.	*The following development activities require permission criteria. Activities are regulated within all land use districts except for the Park Protection District.	No timber cutting—except public and military purposes. No mining—except public and military purposes.
Natural Environment District	Uses allowed in the Natural Protection District, plus: Primary Industry. Grassland development. Park facilities. Forestry activities. Plantations. Public projects.	Construction, reconstruction and extension of buildings and structures. Changes of colors to building and structure. Mining and resource extraction. Land excavation or reclamation. Water reclamation.	Selected & clear cuttings are allowed but subject to limitations. Mining is allowed subject to its type and estimated amount of deposits.

District	Allowed uses	Prohibited activities	Specifications
Agriculture and Fishing Village Districts	Allowed uses in the Natural Protection, and Homes, buildings and structures necessary for farmers and fishermen, for their usual operations and functions. Non-polluting domestic industry.	Activities that cause changes in water levels or water quality. Removing/picking plants or cutting trees. Hunting. Grazing. Land filling and storage of goods and collectibles.	Identical to permission criteria in the Natural Environmental District.
Intensive Use District	Appropriate Facilities for public outdoor recreation.	*As above.	Maximum building coverage area ratio: (i) 50% for commerce, (ii) 40% for accommodations, (iii) 30% for public facilities and (iv) 20% for other.
Park Protection District	*No specifications.	*Activities 1 to 6 above.	

NOTE: The following general permission criteria apply to all districts. All activities should:
1. be compatible with the land uses allowed in each land district,
2. not have an adverse impact on natural landscapes that need protection,
3. not interrupt public recreational use,
4. not interrupt enforcement of the management plan,
5. not impair park aesthetics and benefits.

SOURCE: Korean Government Documents, 1980. *The Natural Parks Law*, Ministry of Construction. 1977. *Plan for the Protection and Facility Regulations of National Parks*, Ministry of Construction. 1977. *Notice No. 113*, Ministry of Construction. 1977. *Forestry Guidelines in National Parks*, Ministry of Construction, and 1977. *Mining Regulation in National Parks*, Ministry of Regulation.

the type and capacity of local communities involved. In general, small, remote communities tend to be more vulnerable to the pressures of tourism development than larger communities.

The second important spatial consideration is the proportion of land area allocated between the Agricultural and Fishing Village District and the Intensive Use District when both areas adjoin one another. A proposed Intensive Use District in Naejangsan National Park is a case in point. It is located between three surrounding local villages (see Map 22.1). This area is quite large compared to the total area of three local communities. Its large size and location change the entire character of the local farming society mainly due to the dominance of a large number of tourist facilities and users to be accommodated.

Whenever possible, the location of Intensive Use Districts should be away from existing local communities to minimize negative social and economic costs. A good example is the proposed land use plan of Mt. Jiri National Park (see Map 22.2). If no alternative sites suitable for the Intensive Use District exist away from local village areas, its size should be carefully considered in relation to the existing character and size of local communities.

Map 22.1
Land Use Plan
in Naejangsan
National Park

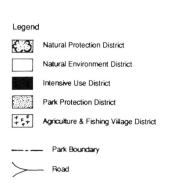

Legend

Natural Protection District	
Natural Environment District	
Intensive Use District	
Park Protection District	
Agriculture & Fishing Village District	

— · — Park Boundary

Road

The larger the Intensive Use District, the greater the impact will be on local culture, lifestyle, and resource use by resident peoples. This, in turn, will have both direct social and economic impacts on the local people and their communities, decreasing the availability of resources necessary for their traditional lifestyle and increasing the negative impacts of tourism as discussed above.

Another spatial relationship that may affect local residents is the relationship between the Agricultural and Fishing Village District and the Natural Protection District. In a few cases, the Agricultural and Fishing Village District is enclosed entirely or in part by the Natural Protection District. This situation may restrict the activities of local people and their access to natural resources if the village areas do not provide enough resources to maintain their basic needs because of strict regulations imposed on the Natural Protection District. This may also force local people to exploit natural resources in other, less strict areas inside or outside a park to satisfy their living requirements. The entire enclosure of the Agricultural and Fishing Village District by the Natural Protection District will have greater impacts

Map 22.2
Land Use Plan in
Jirisan National
Park

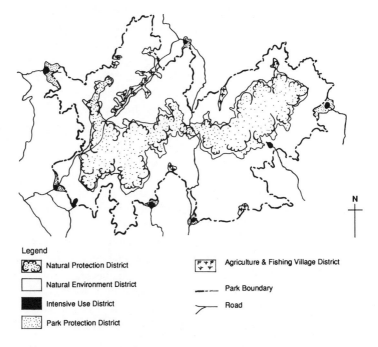

Legend

Natural Protection District

Natural Environment District

Intensive Use District

Park Protection District

Agriculture & Fishing Village District

Park Boundary

Road

than a partial enclosure. Small communities at the margins
of survival will be affected more significantly than larger,
more affluent peasant communities where, for example, wood
is used less often for energy needs.

The size of Agricultural and Fishing Village Districts
should be carefully considered in planning and determining
areas for villagers. It is important to determine how large an
area is required for maintaining traditional subsistence activities of the local people. From the standpoint of the important needs for human living and maintaining local culture,
the determination of village area should not be based simply
on local housing and farming needs, but rather on the area
required for the actual subsistence-level, resource-utilization
activities. If the area does not properly provide local requirements, villagers will be forced to exploit other areas, inside
or outside the park, to meet their needs. Unfortunately, the
continued exploitation of other areas not only degrades the
affected areas, but also contributes to an overall decline of
the park environment.

A third important sociological consideration of the land
use plan is the regulatory system imposed on the park area.
The regulatory system can directly and indirectly restrict the
activities and resource use of local people. This system is
usually developed from the broad perspective of conservation
and development needs rather than from the particular perspective of resident peoples. The process of regulation development must incorporate the perspective and needs of local
people, and must provide necessary provisions to ensure traditional cultures and lifestyle will be maintained.

As shown in Table 22.1, Korea has at least a minimum of
provisions to help maintain and protect local communities in
their ways of life. However, these measures must also take
into account that a resident culture values not only their
living space but the activities and resource utilization that
take place beyond these boundaries. The overly strict regulations limiting local activities and resource use may entice
involved local people to exploit natural resources in other
areas. Resident people will experience more difficulties and
resentment as regulations become more strict. In this case,
loose enforcement may help lessen this tension. However, the
better option is to design a practical and flexible regulatory
system that properly reflects local needs.

One major potential problem in Korea is the uniform application of the regulations shown in Table 22.1 to all national parks without regard to the socioeconomic differences in local communities. Local people in areas where poverty is high and the land is managed by tenant farmers may experience more difficulties than those in areas maintained by free peasants. The way to correct this potential problem is to develop a regulatory system suitable for solving specific local problems and to provide technical and financial assistance programs for improving the local socioeconomic conditions of each park.

Conclusion

This chapter has focused on how the land use districting process can resolve conflicting interests between conservation, development, and the needs of local people and how it can minimize negative socioeconomic impacts of the land use plan in the national parks of South Korea.

In general, land use districts that differ in purpose and policy from the Agricultural and Fishing Village District should not be located in or near areas where local living, culture, and resource use are based in order to protect the park environment and minimize social and economic costs to local populations. The spatial relationships between the Agricultural and Fishing Village District and other districts have been examined to illustrate this particular point.

If districts such as the Intensive Use District cannot be located away from areas of local communities, then the size of incompatible land use districts should be determined in relation to both areas of existing local communities and their socioeconomic conditions. In addition, consideration should be given to the question of whether a buffer zone might lessen negative impacts.

It is also very important to provide the appropriate areas necessary to maintain local culture and traditional ways of life based on living space, activities, and resource use requirements. The overly strict land use regulations affecting local people may cause significant difficulties and resentment, and may eventually force them to exploit natural resources in other areas where regulations are less rigorous. In this regard, the management of Korean national parks attempts to provide a minimum of provisions for local populations by allowing their living and related resource use in designated areas. However, the design of the regulatory system must carefully consider the activities and resource utilization occurring beyond their residential territory and the socioeconomic conditions unique to each community.

In summary, a well-designed land use plan can adequately accommodate the needs of both park protection and local populations, and minimize conflicts between the two. The land use plan should be developed by including the local perspective and reflecting the specific needs and the different socioeconomic conditions of local communities. This development process should introduce local involvement and communication strategies for working effectively with resident populations. These measures not only provide a way of obtaining the support of local people, but eventually lead to better protection of the park environment and the improvement of the social and economic well-being of local communities.

23   Social Impact Assessment: Its Role in Protected Area Planning and Management

John Hough

Though protected area authorities have traditionally focused on biological issues, the growing realization that conservation and development are inseparable and that protected areas cannot continue to exist as islands surrounded by hostile land uses indicates a need for protected area planners and managers to become familiar with the potential and practice of Social Impact Assessment (SIA). SIA is a tool that, through the systematic gathering and analysis of social data, can be used to assist in predicting the impacts of alternative courses of action on human societies. This chapter examines some of the undesirable impacts of protected areas on local human populations and discusses the potential role of SIA in predicting and mitigating these, in identifying new options, providing feedback, building trust, and facilitating institutional learning.

Impacts of Protected Areas on Human Societies

Protected areas are often justified on the basis of their importance in conserving resources for humankind as a whole (Munro 1984) rather than the benefits they generate for local human communities. This approach is exemplified by the World Heritage Convention where sites of "outstanding universal importance" are held in trust by each nation "for the rest of mankind" (Hales 1984). However, as many of the case studies in this volume describe, these same protected areas are often important to local humans for different reasons. Protecting values for humankind as a whole often interferes with the realization of those local values. Consequently, local people tend to resist the imposition of protected areas.

There appear to be much-lauded exceptions to this model, such as Kakadu National Park in Australia where Hill (1983) suggests that the local people themselves proposed the establishment of a protected area, though he goes on to note that this was actually in order to protect themselves and their land from other powerful interests. Weaver (chapter 26, this volume) considers that, in practice, the "non-park" option would not exist if the Aboriginals were to gain title to their claimed lands.

Whether the protected area is imposed on or requested by local people, the requirements of a protected area generate a variety of social impacts. The internationally recognized definition of a national park actually requires the central government to prevent and eliminate human exploitation or occupation (Miller 1982; IUCN-CNPPA 1984). These requirements generate a series of possible outcomes for the resident human population when a national park is imposed on them:

1. Relocation: where people are physically removed to another location. This may be either voluntary or forced.
2. Restricted access to resources: where people are barred from access to resources such as firewood or grazing land by nature of zoning or total exclusion from the protected area.
3. Alienation: where people continue to reside within the protected area but are strictly controlled.
4. Cooptation: where local people are coopted as managers of the protected area.

Adverse social impacts have been recorded for each of these outcomes:

1. Economic: All or a significant proportion of people's economic base is removed (for example S. A. Marks 1976; Croft, chapter 12, this volume). In addition, their crops and livestock are subject to the depredations of wild animals, which the local people have little power to control (see Mishra 1982) or are afraid of controlling for fear of breaking the law. Tourist demand may force the price of certain goods beyond the reach of local people (Mishra 1982) or may deplete traditional resources, such as firewood along popular expedition routes in the Himalayas (McNeely 1985; Weber, chapter 18, this volume).

2. Cultural: Traditional ways of life and relationships with the land, such as ancestral burial grounds, are lost (see Calhoun, chapter 4, this volume).

3. Social: Traditional patterns of authority, reciprocity, and social bonds break down (Calhoun, chapter 4, this volume). Socioeconomic relationships may be affected by increased inequities (see Deihl 1985).

4. Ecological: People are removed into an environment for which they are not well adapted ecologically. A largely undocumented example of this occurred with the establishment of the Myika National Park in Malawi where the Phoka people were relocated from high altitudes to lower altitudes where malaria was prevalent. Their lack of acquired resistance led to many deaths. McNeely (1985) notes the pollution of drinking water supplies resulting from increased visitor use in the high Himalayas.

5. Technological: Traditional tools and techniques are not suited to the new environment to which people are located. In the case of the Ik in Uganda their traditional skills of hunting and gathering were of little use in farming the steep dry slopes to which they were relocated (Calhoun, chapter 4, this volume).

In addition, these adverse impacts can generate hostility on the part of the affected people, which is dysfunctional to the protected area itself. Local resentment can easily be manifested in poaching and acts of vandalism, such as the deliberate setting of fires. Under increasing population pressures, local political support will be essential to the maintenance of protected areas established by the central government. Local support will also be needed in order to establish sympathetic land uses around protected areas, which conservation biology is now demonstrating are vital if viable populations of large mammals are to be maintained. Hence, understanding, avoiding, and mitigating adverse social impacts are clearly in the interest of both the affected people and protected area planners and managers. Social Impact Analysis (SIA) could play a major role both in offering a solution to traditional conflicts between local people and protected areas and assisting in the implementation of more cooperative forms of management, such as biosphere reserves.

Social Impact Assessment

SIA is primarily regarded as a tool for predicting the human consequences of a particular project or activity in the same way that an environmental impact assessment (EIA) tries to predict environmental consequences. Like EIA, SIA has grown out of the recognition that many development projects have unintended consequences, both for the environment and for human societies. It represents the application of social science to policy making in the same way that EIA represents the application of the biological sciences to policy making.

SIA involves the systematic gathering and analysis of social data through techniques such as direct observation, interviewing local residents and leaders, surveys and questionnaires, and collecting demographic and economic statistics. The likely social consequences of protected area policies and management activities can then be predicted.

Though SIA is primarily used proactively to predict and allow modification of plans to minimize adverse effects (Finsterbusch et al. 1983), it can also be used retrospectively to identify and mitigate adverse effects in ongoing projects. SIA differs from evaluation in that it focuses on unintended consequences rather than on effectiveness.

Freudenburg (1986) provides a clear summary of the history and development of SIA and identifies four key developments:

1. Although SIA has often used "laundry lists" of potential impacts in assessing outcomes, there is a need to focus more on sociological variables. In the case of the Ik (Calhoun, chapter 4, this volume) this would involve identifying the structures and linkages that maintained society

and modifying the project to maintain these, rather than focusing on the outcomes or symptoms of their breakdown, which Calhoun describes but which cannot be remedied without addressing their roots in the social structure.

2. SIA should address the problem of "the quality of life," including sociocultural aspects, in addition to traditional socioeconomic indicators. Much of this data will be qualitative rather than quantitative. Efforts to reduce it to the latter are dangerous. For example, even if tourist demand was forcing the prices of some local foodstuffs out of the range of the local people (see Mishra 1982), it might not significantly affect their quality of life.

3. SIA should focus on distributional impacts. For example, among the Masai in Kenya a few individuals who were able to capitalize on the tourist trade became very wealthy, while others gained few benefits (Deihl 1985).

4. Sufficient SIA work has now been done in some instances to allow the generalization or abstraction of conclusions from one situation to another. This also aids in focusing on critical variables that might be, for example, the strength of existing community organizations.

Uses of SIA in Protected Area Planning and Management

Prediction of Adverse Impacts

When a new protected area or any modification or change in the management of an existing protected area is being planned, SIA can be used to predict the effects of alternative courses of action on the resident peoples. Mitigating measures can then be incorporated into the plan to minimize adverse impacts. For example, in the planning of Lake Malawi National Park a simplified form of SIA, concentrating primarily on demographic and biophysical measurements but including a survey of firewood consumption patterns, was used and adverse impacts on local fishermen due to loss of fuelwood resources were predicted. A survey of attitudes toward tourism was also conducted. The plan was subsequently modified to include the provision of replacement firewood resources through the establishment of fuelwood plantations, and to promote tourist development (Croft, chapter 12, this volume).

When Kakadu National Park was being established in Australia, the issue of protecting Aboriginal ceremonial life surfaced as a result of a social assessment. The park plan was subsequently modified to institute a zoning system whereby park visitors were excluded from important ceremonial areas (Fox 1983).

Identification of Unanticipated Options

Two notable cases of conducting some sort of social assessment in the planning stages of protected area design are the Annapurna Conservation Area in Nepal (Bunting et al., chapter 14, this volume) and the Mount Kulal Biosphere Reserve in Kenya (Lusigi 1984). Both involved discussion and study with local people from the early stages of project design and continuing into implementation. In both cases new alternatives were discovered that theoretically facilitated an outcome beneficial to both sides. Convergent interests might also be identified, as, for example, in the miombo woodlands of southern Africa where traditional spiritual beliefs have already led to the protection of certain natural features (Hough 1986).

Mitigation of Adverse Impacts

Where protected areas already exist there may be ongoing conflict and resentment caused by continuing adverse impacts. This might manifest itself as poaching, the setting of fires, or in extreme cases physical hostility towards protected area personnel. SIA can assist in understanding the impacts of management activities on resident peoples and in designing strategies to minimize adverse effects.

Mishra (1982) records two cases of effective mitigation. In the first, the Royal Chitwan National Park was opened to the collection of thatching grass in response to a shortage of grass outside of the park. In the second, the discovery by park authorities of a locally circulating rumor that the park had deliberately released a man-eating tiger in order to keep people out of the park, enabled them to shoot the tiger in the presence of up to 300 villagers, demonstrating that the park was concerned about human life and not just animals.

In addition to the need for SIA to determine possible mitigation measures during ongoing implementation of the project, there is a similar need for SIA monitoring of the mitigation itself. Promoting the adoption of social forestry projects, for example, is one strategy for mitigating the impact of loss of fuelwood resources when a protected area is established. However, certain wood species might impart unpleasant tastes to food cooked over them and be unacceptable. If women collect the firewood then fuelwood projects might need to be addressed to women. In Kenya dual gate fees were instituted for national parks in an effort to encourage native Kenyans to visit them while still maintaining significant income from foreign tourists by charging them a higher fee. However, ongoing SIA would have demonstrated that it was not gate fees but the traditional family structure that discouraged native Kenyans from visiting the parks (Lusigi 1984).

Monitoring and Feedback

Ongoing monitoring of effects through an SIA framework can provide feedback for changing or "fine tuning" project design. A variety of questions can be answered.

Is the project doing what it said it would? At Lake Malawi National Park, park planners designed fuelwood plantations to replace the original source of firewood (see Croft, chapter 12, this volume). These plantations were to be established by another department, but in fact never were (Nzima 1986). This only came to light when people were arrested.

Are the provisions of the project having the intended effect? The case of tourism and the Maasai noted above is a good example. The intention was for tourism to benefit the Maasai. In practice it only benefited a few of them (see Deihl 1985). Modification of the project to address this concern might be possible.

Are there secondary unanticipated effects? Although some of the effects of establishing protected areas can be predicted in advance, such as loss of grazing and firewood resources, others cannot. For example, although tourism was expected to generate some economic benefits to the Maasai an unexpected effect was that the people themselves became tourist attractions (Deihl 1985).

Do changes in the external environment suggest changes in park policy? The collection of thatching grass in the Royal Chitwan National Park in Nepal was permitted in response to a shortage of grass outside the park caused by increasing human densities (see Mishra 1982).

How do the resident people view the park? Again Mishra records a variety of views of the local people toward the park, including a perception that the park was more concerned about animals than humans.

Building Trust

A vital prerequisite to reducing conflict is to build trust between the disputing parties. Many disputes can be resolved simply by getting each party to understand the positions of the others (see for example Bacow and Wheeler 1984). In addition to assisting protected area authorities in understanding the position of the resident peoples, SIA might start a process of building mutual trust since an essential part of SIA is to discuss and agree upon the findings with the people concerned. Provided the people concerned approve the content of the SIA study, it would seem likely that they would be happy to have information about the harm a protected area is causing them passed on to the protected area authority by a neutral party.

However, this initial distrust poses one of the greatest obstacles to SIA. Conducting an effective SIA relies on establishing sufficient target population trust in the investigators to undertake the SIA in the first place. Berreman (1972) and Dandekar (1986), for example, both note the difficulty of building such trust. In a situation of conflict with a protected area authority, it may be essential that the investigator is not associated with the protected area. Bell (1986), for example, observes that Stuart Marks had a villager accompany him at all times when he left the village he was studying in the Luangwa Valley so that the villagers could be assured that he was not talking to the national park authorities.

Institutional Learning

In view of the wide range of possible social impacts, a predictive SIA study to examine the full range of possible impacts of a protected area proposal would be prohibitively large and time consuming. The normal practice in SIA is to study what is known about the people concerned, to examine the known effects of similar projects elsewhere, and to then design the study to include likely effects. However, impacts may not manifest themselves until many months or years later, or they may only occur at particular times of the year. Postproject monitoring within an SIA framework can reveal delayed or unanticipated impacts, knowledge of which can then be used to improve both protected area planning and other SIA studies elsewhere.

Discussion

SIA is not a solution to the problem of conflicts between protected areas and their resident peoples. It is simply a tool which may be useful in predicting and mitigating undesirable social impacts, discovering new alternatives and possibilities, improving protected area planning and possibly starting to build trust.

Most of the impacts noted above are major, and it can be

argued that they are "obvious" without the need for ongoing SIA studies. However, if "obvious" effects such as these do occur, then there are also likely to be less obvious effects. Unless SIA studies are done, these will not be discovered and documented arguments will be difficult.

Apart from the problem of ensuring accurate predictions, the major difficulty with SIA is deciding whether the predicted impacts are desirable or undesirable. The protected area authority cannot play the role of God and decide what is best for the affected people, nor are the affected people necessarily the best judges of what is best for themselves. However, by offering some alternative future scenarios, SIA can assist in making explicit some of the choices and tradeoffs involved.

In a case where close cooperation already exists between a protected area and the affected human communities, such as it should in a Biosphere Reserve (Eidsvik 1985), the full participation of local people in the project should ensure the inclusion of their views on how proposed actions might affect them. However, there is still a role for SIA in ensuring that all interests are accommodated, not just those of the participating representatives, and in providing an external neutral observer who may be better able to predict likely consequences than the involved people themselves.

One interesting issue SIA raises is the definition of "resident people" who might be affected by a protected area development. Olwig (1980) demonstrates, for example, potential impacts on absentee landowners in the USA arising from the policies and management of the Virgin Islands National Park in the Caribbean. From a pragmatic perspective, since protected areas are dependent on political support for their survival, influential, remote urban populations who have spiritual, cultural or economic ties back to their rural origins may be important.

Conclusion   SIA appears to offer significant potential for mitigating some of the adverse effects of protected areas on resident peoples. It can offer an external perspective and assist in identifying adverse impacts that even the local people themselves cannot predict. Hence, even extensive local participation is not likely to remove the need for SIA, though this participation is still also essential. SIA must be ongoing as human and ecological conditions are not static and even mitigating measures themselves can have unexpected social impacts. In view of the number of cases of adverse social impact cited here, even without applied SIA studies of protected areas, it is likely that such studies will generate large amounts of useful information. Ongoing SIA might assist protected area planners and managers in steering a more desirable course for both conservation and local resident people.

24 Toward an Interactive Process for Siting National Parks in Developing Nations

Patricia Bidol and James E. Crowfoot

The Western world's practices of siting and managing national parks have been implemented by developing nations throughout the world. This tradition of national parks usually does not allow the local resident peoples to live within the boundaries of the park or to use and extract the park's resources. However, there are other established classifications for natural and cultural conservation areas that differ in the allowable levels of direct use of natural resources by the local, traditional peoples and the degree to which the natural environment can be altered (Miller 1980).

The primary purpose of national parks is to conserve natural resources by selective protection of ecosystems, maintenance of ecological diversity, and conservation of genetic resources (Miller 1978), while providing opportunities for recreation, tourism, education and research. The protection of ecosystems by means of national parks can result in additional benefits such as the use of marginal lands, watershed protection, soil conservation, preservation of cultural heritage, and limited rural development. Multipurpose management of national parks for nature conservation and nonexploitive human use can occur through management of designated zones for specific purposes, creating a situation in which conservation of natural resources and cultural purposes can be mutually supportive (Bright 1982).

Impacts of Natural Parks on Local Peoples

Historically, local areas have been unilaterally designated as national parks or other conservation categories by governmental agencies. These mandated decisions have often caused social and economic hardships on the resident peoples (Kutay 1984; Calhoun 1972). When actions are not taken to achieve settlements that satisfy the interests of all the affected parties and promote effective ongoing relationships between these parties, then there will be chronic, ongoing and rancorous conflicts that impede the park's mission and management, and interfere with the meeting of local needs.

Traditional cultures often depend upon social, economic, political and environmental processes and outcomes that are severely affected by the siting and use of their immediate geographic base as a natural park (Kutay 1984). Social conflict may also occur when the establishment of a park causes a change in the behavior and values of nonlocal populations.

The specific nature and the degree of past uses by local people and other human populations for physical and cultural needs affect and are affected by the siting and management of the park. If the food-producing practices of local populations are not provided for, the immediate population may not be able to feed itself. In addition to local use, the agricultural practices of the regional area can affect the conservation goals of the park. When adjacent areas are used for high yield cash crops with concomitant irrigation, pesticide application, and landscape alteration, natural resources can be adversely affected. Additionally, more distant human populations and organizations are sometimes affected by new parks which alter the symbolic meaning of regions and distinctive natural features, and at times their past patterns of use of the area are altered.

The government agencies who select a site for a park often do not acknowledge that the traditional land management practices of the local people can be supportive of the natural resource management goals of a park in that area (Glick 1981). In some situations the traditional human use of an area is essential to the preservation of given species of flora or fauna. On the other hand, the extreme economic poverty of most traditional rural peoples sometimes causes them to inflict extensive damage on the natural environment. When authorities force the displacement of populations to site a park, the new location of settlement often does not provide the population with the potential for improving their financial conditions. In addition, displacement often causes a severe loss of the cultural integrity and political autonomy of the displaced group.

Recommendations for Park Siting and Management

While there is no simple formula or model for siting and management processes that will be effective in every local situation, there are important concepts and guidelines that can be adapted to specific situations that will improve the process and outcomes of park siting and management. The foundation of the processes and practices we recommend is an *interactive planning system* that focuses on and accommodates needed processes of complex information gathering, multi-group communication, and joint decision making. The information gathering should incorporate both broad-based values and political considerations as well as specialized scientific and technical information. We recommend *holistic, social impact assessment* as a viable approach to supplying the information needed for park siting and management that are responsive to the needs of local populations and other impacted social groups.

Multiple groups with different values, life experiences, and cultures are usually involved with parks; almost always both traditional indigenous cultures and modernized outside cultures are involved. Thus, we recommend *synergistic, multicultural interactions* as a means of communication and interaction for mutual problem solving. The fact that siting and management of parks includes change as a major component, and the fact that the people affected and involved have different values and needs can give rise to conflicts. Ideally, during the planning stages of siting a park, the process will support the settling of key disputes, formation of mutually supportive relationships, and the establishment of effective management. This requires that special attention be given to the management of conflict in ways that ensure that the needs of local groups are met. We recommend *mediation, negotiation, and joint problem solving* designed for a particular potential park.

In each of the sections that follow we briefly describe recommended approaches to planning, impact assessment, multicultural collaboration, and conflict management.

Interactive Planning Systems

The dysfunctional conflicts, such as those that were described in the first part, usually emerge when parks are unilaterally sited. These dysfunctional conflicts are usually reduced when a planning system is developed as an interactive process, which assumes that local populations must participate in the planning and implementation of the national park or preserve. The planning system would include governmental representatives of all levels, natural resource scientists and managers, and local residents and other impacted groups working together to design a siting and management process. The goal of this planning is to protect the ecosystems and special natural and cultural features, while also meeting the core interests of all who are impacted by the park or preserve.

An interactive planning system is based on the following principles:

1. The planning is a deliberate problem solving and educational process for all involved groups and is understood to require the values, ideas, and expertise of local peoples, scientists, professionals, and government representatives.
2. The developmental perspectives would include consideration of the geographical region's needs for natural resources, economic development, political involvement, social community, and cultural identity and integrity.
3. The processes of developing social and environmental impact statements must include the participation of local residents, experts, governmental representatives, and representatives of other impacted groups.
4. The planning and dispute settlement processes must be multiculturally designed so that they are compatible with the local decision making and planning systems as well as those of natural resource professionals.
5. The resulting siting and management process must both support and enhance the biosphere, the local human culture(s), and broader societal needs.

Such an approach to planning is very demanding and requires time and other resources. However, because of the long time horizons for the life of a park and the survival needs of local populations, such a process and its costs are justifiable.

Interactive planning systems are being used in the siting and management of some parks. An example of an interactive system is the management of the Cahuita National Park in Costa Rica (see Kutay, chapter 10, this volume) using an ecodevelopment planning methodology developed by Miller (1980). All successful interactive planning systems include holistic social impact assessments, synergistic multicultural interactions, and effective dispute settlement procedures.

Holistic Social Impact Assessments

Social impact assessments, SIAs, are components of environmental impact evaluations that can either have technical or sociopolitical orientations (Finsterbusch 1977). The purpose of purely technically oriented SIAs is to improve a government agency's decision making by the gathering and analyzing of social impact data. The technical perspective is based on a scientific model of inquiry that uses explicit theories and concepts along with systematically gathered data and quantitatively based decision-making methods. The purpose of sociopolitically orientated SIAs is to improve joint decision making (by experts, residents, and other impacted parties) through the study of probable political and socioeconomic changes that would differentially impact multiple societal groups as a result of the proposed siting and subsequent park management.

The data-gathering procedures for technical SIAs include the quantifiable measures of explicit concepts of life quality or social well-being that require the use of specialized techniques like surveys, economic ratings, and computer simulation modeling scenarios (Naik 1981). The data-gathering procedures for sociopolitical SIA's emphasize alternative value choices that require the use of techniques like community needs assessment, regional leadership analysis, participant-observation, and action research (Lang and Armour 1981).

Holistic SIAs incorporate the methods of technical and sociopolitical SIAs. Subjective input from the potentially impacted parties is a key aspect of the assessment process. The affected parties not only participate in the data gathering but work with the experts and government representatives to analyze information and discover the impacts. Holistic

SIAs can identify multiple and often opposing trends that are present in a given situation (Seley 1983). The proposed siting can be carefully examined to determine the extent to which it is a threat to the local community's integrity as well as its effect on the regional and national economy. An effective holistic SIA can determine whether a proposed park siting reflects an incremental planning process or an explicit, systematic proposal that has carefully considered both regional and local natural system processes and constraints, as well as the needs of multiple social groups and the criteria of distributive justice.

The siting of a given park can cause injustice to the local residents, particularly if the traditionally powerful groups and organizations in the country control the park siting and management systems so that their needs are met without regard for meeting the needs of local peoples. A frequent factor in the siting of parks at local levels is a strong emphasis on market forces as the determinant of maximum economic gain, and the requirement that such gain must be achieved from the area. These constraints are more likely to be equitably managed by a SIA that is linked to a national-level planning process that is designed to provide locally acceptable incentives for siting projects.

A given siting also can be promoted or opposed for ideological reasons that reflect the values of any of the impacted parties. A holistic SIA can help identify and legitimate these other perspectives. Often agency experts have difficulty in accepting the ideas of those who do not have technical expertise or vast political power. Many experts believe that facts must be rigorously separated from values. They often do not believe that people can understand complex technical issues if they are presented in nontechnical language. When experts also believe that their agency has a narrowly focused mission, such as creating a certain type of national park, they may have difficulties in developing and fairly evaluating other alternatives. The development of only a single "solution" increases the conflict among the involved parties and stiffens the resistances of local groups whose needs are not adequately met by the proposed "solution." The implementation of a holistic SIA can be hindered by the inability of the involved governmental agencies to assess adaptively and plan with the citizens. If the involved agencies refuse to consider options favored by other parties, they will not be able to work collaboratively in an interactive process.

If all parties work to develop and use a comprehensive view that considers and respects local interests, the environment, and the greater societal good, new multifaceted options will emerge during the assessment and planning stages. The inclusion of purely technical data along with the sociopolitical values and goals in a joint decision-making process can result in a SIA process that is credible and comprehensible to all concerned. Such a process of information gathering and analysis enables the representatives involved in the joint decision-making process to design equitable and effective siting and management plans that are supported by both parties and that effectively help to resolve or manage conflicts (Manring et al., 1990). The SIA process lays the foundation for an interactive management process that includes adaptive provisions for monitoring the effects of management, and the development, where necessary, of mitigation measures. The implementation of an effective holistic SIA in the siting of national parks where local resident peoples will be impacted also requires the use of synergistic multicultural interactions and supportive dispute settlement procedures.

Synergistic Multicultural Interactions

The basic question is whether or not it is possible to transport a specific management practice like Western national parks from one culture to another. Can people from one culture or subculture (such as urban-rural and Canadian-Thai) plan and manage projects so that cultural support and equitable arrangements are developed? The reality is that one culture cannot effectively use the innovations and other practices of another culture without modifying the innovation to meet the local situation (Nevis 1983). The contrasts that arise when multicultural assessment and planning teams work together can be used to devise new options that support the mission of an innovation (such as national parks that protect ecosystems), and maintain the core values and practices of the culture that is directly affected by the innovation (for example, letting Nepal Royal Chitwan villagers harvest the park's grasses).

In synergistic multicultural interactions all of the parties value the perspectives and knowledge of one another.[1] They are able to create innovatively something that satisfies their multiple interests and solves their joint problems. They use decision-making processes, communication patterns, and dispute-settlement approaches that are acceptable to all parties and include methods from all of the represented cultures. The positive inclusion of the mores and methods of all parties supports the creation of a temporary multicultural interaction system that can empower all participants.

International and national technical experts and other governmental representatives who wish to interact synergistically with resident traditional peoples need carefully and mutually to enter into the joint assessment and planning activities. Such experts and representatives need to have studied the topic of "differences" (Geartz 1986). They also need to have had experiences of being taught by someone from a different culture, and of discovering the points of blindness in their own culture's values, language, and technology. They need to face the challenges of making contacts with relevant groups, being introduced, observing protocol, and building rapport with each other and with the local residents. It is particularly important that representatives of advanced technological cultures who are interacting with more traditional cultures remember that:

1. They can easily exhibit impressions of superiority as if only they can create the best solutions and as if their own culture is without weaknesses.
2. Outside experts often do not understand, use, and respect local customs and procedures.
3. Outside experts often come with a predetermined solution that they do not intend to change, and in fact expect to manipulate the locals into accepting.
4. Outside experts and officials often will not consider traditional natural resource management practices of local groups as possible solutions in the siting and management of a proposed park.
5. Outside experts often fail to develop creative and innovative solutions that meet local needs, and fail to design assessments that adequately include local factors.
6. Outside experts and officials often refuse to respect the local leadership and their relationships with their constituents, as well as the administrative channels that are already in place for dealing with the government.

7. Experts often forget to share credit for joint efforts with citizens and other governmental representatives.

As already stated, when national parks are being sited in developing nations, the governmental representatives, the outside experts, and the local, traditional peoples represent many cultural backgrounds. The resulting multicultural communications will be improved if cross-cultural communication premises are understood by all parties. The principles of effective multicultural communication need to be shared with all participants, in a manner which is compatible with the cultural preferences of all parties.

The core premise is that the effectiveness of cross-cultural communications is enhanced when the participants are explicitly aware of how they are influenced by their cultural conditioning. For example, whenever we listen to someone, we usually use our internal, implicit cultural assumptions to interpret the overt message. If the sender and the listener are not aware of this phenomenon in general, or are not knowledgeable about the particular cultures represented, and are not careful about cultural differences, they can misinterpret each others' messages and responses.

The syllogistic meaning of the communications (overt message and covert assumptions) need to be shared by the sender and the listener to avoid distortion of meanings and misunderstandings. For example, a United States scientist might be describing his belief that the individual can change and improve the environment and his Bolivian listener might be translating those words into his belief system that individuals must adjust to the physical environment as it is. The situation-associated assumptions might cause the communicators to assign different meanings to the same word. The concept of family in most Pan American cultures differs from that in the United States. Assumed similarities often cause difficulties in cross-cultural planning teams. For example, is a leader supported because of his title or because of his family connections? Must one defer to the leader, or can each team member respond to all statements? In cross-cultural dialogues, all must attend to the large and small aspects of protocol. For example, is time a scarce resource measured by the clock, or is it relative and measured by the mood of the group?

Planning with local traditional peoples will be enhanced if the above principles are applied to the given situation. The location of the meetings, the use of time, the choice of participants, the leadership styles, the decision-making methods, and the food served can all be selected so that the local participants perceive that they are respected and accepted as co-planners with the outside experts and governmental representatives. The choices should also reflect the traditions of the experts and other representatives so that the resulting climate supports the creation of synergistic innovations that reflect the core interests and values of all the participants. Since differences and inevitable conflicts are viewed as opportunities for the creation of synergistic solutions and development of ongoing relationships, the assessment and planning processes in creative multicultural planning teams require the skillful use of conflict-management procedures.

Mediation, Negotiation and Joint Problem Solving for Dispute Settlement

As stated earlier the siting and management of parks often create conflict among social groups. Interactive planning systems, holistic social impact assessments, and synergistic, multicultural interactions are based on this reality, but further attention needs to be given to means of settling conflicts. Conflict itself is a social process, and ways of responding are culturally rooted. It is essential to understand the overall commonalities among means of settling disputes before giving attention to typical cultural differences in selection and use of these means. Work done in the field of anthropology of law has concluded that the following procedures are used worldwide in attempts to deal with grievances, conflict, or disputes (Nader and Todd 1978):

1. adjudication
2. arbitration
3. mediation
4. negotiation
5. coercion
6. avoidance
7. lumping it

The first two procedures, adjudication and arbitration, involve a party outside of the dispute at hand (generally referred to as a "third party") whose judgment the disputants must accept as the settlement. Adjudication and arbitration are most often rooted in law. Mediation utilizes a third party who aids the principles in achieving an agreement; generally the disputants must agree to the activity of the mediator. In negotiation the principal parties are the decision makers, and they reach a settlement without a third party. Coercion refers to one party unilaterally imposing a particular outcome on the other party. Avoidance refers to one party withdrawing from a situation, or reducing or terminating a relationship by leaving it. Where lumping it occurs, a party ignores the issue in dispute because of feelings of powerlessness, or the economic, social, or psychological costs of seeking a solution; here the relationship between the parties continues.

In smaller, homogeneous societies, including the local, traditional peoples discussed in this paper, the boundaries between formal and informal systems of settling disputes are often blurred (Nader and Todd 1978). Generally, law plays a less important role in dispute settlement in these societies than it does in industrialized societies. In traditional societies people know each other personally, are directly interdependent in terms of their social welfare, share multiple interpersonal relationships, and share a greater level of consensus about values and power relations. In larger, more diverse, industrialized societies, people are more likely to be strangers, are less immediately and directly dependent on each other, and in the face of disputes, utilize laws with their mechanisms for adjudication. Also, in these latter societies unequal power and lack of agreement tend to become more pronounced among groups concerning important values.

Groups involved with the siting and management of national parks need to understand their own cultures' means of dispute settlement, and the commonalities and differences between their experiences and those of the other involved cultural groups. Decision making on the park itself will require development and use of mutually acceptable means of dispute settlement.

It is important that park planning and decision making not rely on coercion, avoidance, and lumping it as dispute settlement procedures. These approaches will prevent local groups' needs from being met and will prevent development and destroy effective working relationships. Local peoples in particular will have day-to-day contact with the park, its staff, and the park's policy makers. The maintenance and effectiveness of these relationships will be of critical importance to both the well-being of the park, and to the ongoing satisfaction of the needs of the local peoples.

Decision making on siting and management that relies exclusively on law-based adjudication and arbitration also has serious drawbacks. Based on their extensive cross-cultural investigations of legal systems, Nader and Todd (1978:30) have concluded:

> The law at points of intersection between national and local systems is not one that often serves the interest of local peoples. In many of the developing countries the least qualified legal personnel are sent to the hinterlands. In many, national law runs roughshod over customary law and even worse, uses national law to legitimate acts of conquest and imperialism.

Thus, the use of law-based adjudication and arbitration must be approached with extreme caution in the development of means of dispute settlement for park siting and management. It is imperative that the customs and needs of local peoples be explicitly included in the process and outcomes of siting and management, and that truly joint decisions be developed.

To maintain effective relationships between local people and the park, and to ensure that local peoples' needs and those of the park are met, requires the use of mediation and negotiation along with joint problem solving. Problem solving is needed to develop the information and understandings required for the complex decisions involved in park siting and management. These procedures taken together ensure direct, face-to-face interaction in pursuit of agreements that satisfy the needs of each of the involved parties. Developing such mutual agreements requires understanding the interests of each party and crafting alternative siting and management plans that meet these interests. Creative and joint problem solving that allows for negotiation is required. Sometimes this work will require a third party who is acceptable to the involved parties and who has specialized skills in facilitating problem solving and advancing negotiations.

In recommending the use of these means it must be remembered that: "As a tool for achieving change, mediation has both advantages and disadvantages. Negotiations convert power and potential power into a settlement that reflects the relative strength of the parties . . . groups choose to negotiate when they wish to solidify the gains that they have made so far, or when they want to buy some time to reorganize, develop new strategies or further develop their power base" (Laue and Cormick 1978: 217). So even with the preferred means of dispute settlement—mediation, negotiation, and collaborative problem solving—the power of local people must be developed and respected. This will require that local people be organized, have effective leadership who can advocate their concerns and needs, and be able to access and use outside resources for needed information and additional advocacy.

Design of an Alternative Conflict-Management Process

The exact nature of each alternative conflict-management process (ACMP) for park siting and management will be different, and needs to be designed for each interactive planning process and its multicultural team. These differences are nested in the cultures of the involved groups and other characteristics of the specific situation. However, certain guidelines can help the participants to develop a structure and to design procedures for their situation. The use of ACMP is based on premises that are compatible with those used to select and develop multicultural planning teams. The following premises were developed by one of the authors (Bidol 1987):

1. The parties to the ACMP are many and represent the proponents, outside experts, and locally impacted residents.
2. Fair ACMP solutions occur when all the parties have the power, skills, and information needed to pursue their interests during the meetings. If any of the parties are not able to freely interact, the ACMP needs to be redesigned, outside intervention needs to be used, or other methods need to be selected. Whenever the ACMP is used in inequitable situations it causes the less-powerful parties to feel more dissatisfied and can increase the short- or long-range conflict and resistance.
3. The disputed issues are complex and include data about biophysical and sociopolitical systems. The proposed solutions often include aspects which are risky and uncertain as to their long- or short-range impacts.

4. Most ACMPs are used in disputes where the solutions
   need to be designed by a blending of already established
   and newly agreed upon alternative decision-making and
   dispute-management approaches.

The use of ACMPs offers ways of understanding and using
the complexity of the biophysical and sociopolitical situation
as an opportunity to produce satisfactory and creative solutions. ACMPs are not always helpful. They can result in
unacceptable settlements if there is a lack of thorough understanding of the issues, if the interacting parties take
unyielding stances, or if some of the parties use their
established power and other resources to oppress the less-
privileged participants. When parties are sincerely willing to
engage in collaborative problem-solving, along with negotiations and mediation where necessary, ACMP techniques designed for the given situation will minimize the chance that
these problems will occur.

The ACMP structure and techniques are selected after
studying the *key antecedent variables* for the given situation.
The antecedent variables are: nature of the disputed issues,
situational influences, characteristics of the parties, and degree of interdependency between the stakeholders. The *nature of the disputed issues* is assessed by diagnostic questions
such as: How broad is the issue (is it only related to siting
the park or does it include other regional considerations)?
Can the issue(s) be clearly defined? Is the issue of such
importance that failure to solve it will have serious consequences? Are the biophysical and sociopolitical conditions re-
versible? The *situational influences* are identified and
evaluated by diagnostic questions such as: What are the history, traditional cultural values, and international pressures
related to the issues and parties in this dispute? What are
the government's laws, regulations, and legal precedents on
the federal, provincial, and local levels that are related to
this dispute? What is the political climate surrounding the
issues and the parties? What other pressures are there?

The *characteristics of the parties* are discovered through
answering diagnostic questions such as: What are the mission, goals, values of each party? What are each party's
personal and organizational orientations to the planning
process? How much power and influence does each party
possess? How do the informal and formal policies, proce-

dures, and values of each party's organization or reference group affect his/her participation in the planning process? The *degree of interdependence between the parties* is assessed through diagnostic questions like: What kind of long- and short-term relationships exist between the parties? How does the power, influence, expertise, or membership in reference groups affect their relationships with each other? Do any of the legal, regulatory, or private sector policies related to this dispute affect their relationships?

The four antecedent variables are the cornerstones for creating an effective *intervention process* to manage the conflicts present within the planning situation, with the goal of achieving mutual processes and joint decisions. The purpose of the intervention process is to support the creation of a synergistic solution that protects the ecosystem without harming the cultures or physical well-being of the local, traditional peoples. The intervention process consists of social, process, and physical components. The *social components* are designed by considering: For each participant, who are his/her constituents? How do the parties interact with each other, the outside world, and other networks? What is the influence of the media on the planning process? What is the influence of the general public and peripheral parties on the conflict?

The *process components* are designed by considering: What alternatives and/or traditional processes are applicable for use in solving this problem? Can a planning process be developed to create a temporary system in which the parties can jointly interact to create mutually acceptable solutions? What needs to be done to use the problem-solving, leadership styles, and communication patterns of the different cultures represented by the participants? How can complex technical data be shared with all participants (including representatives of the local peoples) so that they can understand its implications for their interests as they jointly work on the siting and management of a national park? Is a third party intervener needed to facilitate the participants' interactions with each other? If so, what should be the role, behavior, and power of the intervener? The *physical components* are selected by considering: How will the physical setting and surroundings impact the participants' interactions? What are the symbols and artifacts that can support the participants' interactions?

The outcomes of the planning process can be assessed to determine whether the use of a collaborative process with negotiation and mediation involving local peoples, outside experts, and governmental representatives produced a solution that protects the environment and the impacted peoples. The *output components* include: issue resolution, equity factors, parties' relationships, power levels, and resource levels. The outcomes related to *issue resolution* can be determined by diagnostic questions such as: What are the tangible and intangible decisions and agreements present in the solution settlement? Are the ecosystems and the impacted human systems positively affected by the solution? What implementation, mitigation, and monitoring processes are present? The outcomes related to *equity factors* can be assessed by answering the question: How equitable is the agreement for the involved parties and the general public (i.e., what are the costs and benefits for each party in both the short and long term)?

The *parties' relationships* as an outcome can be assessed by answering the following questions: As a result of the conflict-management process, what are the short- and long-range relationships and cultural arrangements between the parties, within the parties' networks, and with the general public? Will the park managers be able to interact peacefully with the local peoples as the park's management goals are implemented? The *power levels* can be determined by describing factors such as: How did the process and agreement affect the power and influence of each party? What effect, if any, did it have on established decision-making processes? Has it supported the cultural integrity and power of the local residents? What is the precedent, if any, established for the use of temporary planning systems like this to jointly conduct SIA's, use ACMP's, and develop management solutions? The *resource levels* can be determined by describing factors such as: What gain or loss of resources did the parties or general public experience as a result of the agreement? Did the gains outweigh the losses?

The temporary planning system for information gathering, development of alternatives, and dispute settlement can be designed so that the parties can work in a total plenary group and in a variety of subgroups to examine the biophysical and sociopolitical aspects of siting and managing the proposed natural park. The participants can use a variety of decision-making and idea-generating techniques. These can include procedures like the delphi and nominal group methods that can be modified by the decision-making practices of the local traditional peoples. The use of these processes usually enables the participants to design siting and management options that will support public ownership of the land, provide just compensation of the owners at fair market value, allow for involvement of local residents in park development and management, support appropriate local park use, support the ecological and economic development of the region, and protect the cultural integrity and political autonomy of the local residents. They allow for the development of different management strategies that are appropriate for the ecosystem, human cultures, and their interfaces. The processes called for in this chapter increase the probability that local people can maintain a compatible and beneficial relationship with the natural environment of the national park.

Conclusion
The siting and management of national parks call for special attention to the needs of impacted local peoples; the development of working relationships that will further the park's mission; and the well-being of involved groups, particularly traditional peoples, and the region in which the park is located. Achieving such outcomes requires creative and proactive action to utilize the conflicts that will occur when such an important set of changes is sought. Multiple groups will always be involved, and they will require an effective interactive system of planning to achieve the joint communication, problem solving, and decision making that will be required.

The changes being sought are complex ones involving biophysical and sociobehavioral systems and multiple cultures. Holistic social impact assessment processes are needed to develop the information required for effective problem solving. For such problem solving actually to occur, synergistic, multicultural communication is needed. At the foundation of these planning processes, information-gathering techniques and communication methods are processes for managing conflicts, particularly the techniques of negotiation, mediation, and collaborative problem solving. These are essential, deliberately pursued methods of responding to the inevitable conflicts of park siting and management.

There is no simple formula or set of rules that can be used in all situations to develop the processes that we have described. A specific conflict intervention needs to be designed based on the special characteristics of a specific proposed park. Developing such an intervention requires a design that draws on the special characteristics of the situation.

NOTE

1. It should be noted that this is not always possible precisely because of cultural systems, such as the caste system in India.

25 Prerequisites for Ethnic Identity and Survival

Robert Goodland

Certain basic needs must be acknowledged and accommodated if tribal groups are to benefit from—rather than be harmed by—development projects. These fundamental needs are equally important, and each must be met for continued physical, socioeconomic, and cultural survival in the face of development.

Fundamental Needs

The four fundamental needs of tribal societies relate to autonomy and participation, and to conditions that will maintain their culture and their ethnic identity to the extent they desire: (1) recognition of territorial rights; (2) protection from introduced diseases; (3) time to adapt to the national society; and (4) self-determination. Clearly, freedom of choice is worthless without understanding the implications of the given alternatives. Thus, tribal people must be allowed time to make their own adjustments at their own pace and must be given the opportunity to learn about the wider society to gain a place within it.

The needs of tribal groups outlined in this chapter differ critically from those of other rural and urban populations for whom World Bank–assisted projects and most other development projects are usually designed. Also, social needs differ among tribal groups themselves. Hence, each project affecting such peoples must be designed to meet the specific needs of the tribal groups within or near the project area.

Effects of Contact

Particular problems and needs are evident in cases of uncontacted tribal groups. While there are only a few such groups remaining in the world today, special action is necessary if they are in the area of influence of any project considered by the bank. Contact with certain tribes could have adverse affects on the members themselves, such as stress, starvation, and disease. A number of precautions are necessary to prevent this from occurring.

Territorial Rights

The first and most fundamental need for tribal survival and cultural viability is continued habitation and use of the traditional land areas. Each tribe's economic resource management, sociopolitical organization, and belief systems are tightly woven into the particular land areas. Maintaining the traditional land-based patterns of environmental adaptation is essential to the perpetuation of most aspects of the tribal way of life.

Tribal lands include not only areas that are obviously inhabited at a given time, but others that may be used or occupied only intermittently in supra-annual cycles. Hunter-gatherers, pastoralists, and shifting agriculturists are groups requiring large tracts of land for subsistence.

To the extent that tribal groups inhabit marginal areas, much larger land areas may be required to support the population than would be the case in more fertile regions. When common shifting-agriculture methods are used, new areas are needed for clearance every two to five years when weeds encroach and yields decline. This method of tropical forest land use does not damage the environment when practiced by an appropriate number of people, since exhausted soils have time to recuperate while other tracts are planted. The isolation and small size of the cleared areas avoid excessive erosion and accelerate regrowth of the forest. Tribal people have the knowledge to select more fertile areas and avoid less productive soils. Nontribal settlers without sophisticated agricultural extension lack such selective ability. Tribal societies practicing such systems have traditionally developed population control, which enables the society to stay within the technoenvironmental carrying capacity of the land.

The extent and boundaries of tribal lands are also important for intertribal exchanges. Tribal people may travel weeks or even months on hunting or trading expeditions. Limitations on such routes used for such necessary travel and for transhumanance will damage tribal viability.

Modern legal concepts of "private" property are inapplicable to tribal land-use patterns, since land is owned in common and parcels of land are used intermittently. The solution of corporate ownership is outlined later in this chapter. Governments have often acquired lands used by tribal people on the assumption that they were uninhabited wasteland. In the process, the larger human-land equilibrium systems evolved by the tribal cultures have often been disrupted (Bodley 1982). When land-use patterns are radically altered, traditional tribal economic and social organizations, authority, and belief systems are inevitably impaired.

Along with economic significance, the traditional land base holds important symbolic and emotional meaning for tribal people. It is the repository for ancestral remains, group origin sites, and other sacred features closely linked to tribal economic systems.

In Brazil, attempts by the National Indian Foundation (FUNAI) to transfer the Nambiquari out of the Guapore Valley into an inappropriate reserve generally resulted in failure. The Nambiquara's refusal to move involved not only the natural resource scarcity in the new area, which was savanna rather than forest, but also the fact that they would lose touch with the land where their dead had been buried (Price 1977a, b).

Legalization of Tribal Land Rights

Land rights, access to traditional lands, and maintenance of transhumanant routes are vital to the economic, social, and psychological well-being of individual tribal members, as well as for the maintenance of the group's cultural stability. Those national governments that are signatory to the United Nations charter and require World Bank assistance can be guided by the UN Declaration of Human Rights, 1948, on tribal issues and land title. Legalization of tribal land rights is often difficult to accomplish because most tribal peoples hold land in common, demarcated only in the perception of their members. Land is regarded as a common good, to which individuals have rights of use, but from which there cannot be exclusion. The tenure is in the nature of a trust in which all members—dead, living, and unborn—are co-sharers. Communal title, or group tenure, may need legislative innovation on the part of a nation; such innovations are neither unknown nor especially difficult. The bank can discuss tribal policies with governments, which would then act to implement agreed upon policies.

Many transhumanant migrations are regular; their routes are well-defined and can be demarcated. It should not, therefore, be difficult to grant those tribal people rights of way or easements recognized by law. In most countries, rights of way resulting from continuous use are part of the general law available to all persons. These rights cover both private and public use of lands.

Creation of Reserves

In some cases, the creation of a tribal reserve may be the most feasible means of protecting a tribal group whose culture is endangered by national intrusion, or by a development project. The creation of a reserve mainly provides the time necessary for adaptation. Such a reserve should function as a secure base, providing the tribe time and space to make its own adaptations, not as a prison in which the tribe is confined. In many cases land held in reserve status could quite simply be transformed into title held communally by the tribe or, in the early stages of contact, in trust by the national government. Most countries lack such legislative mechanisms, although they are not difficult to draw up. This is the spirit of the Peruvian Law of Native Peoples of 1974. If lands are protected as reserves, recently contacted tribal groups can receive some medical attention for introduced diseases and some protection against encroachment from outsiders. In Brazil, the living conditions of tribal people on reserves are better, in general, than among those who have lost their lands. Health benefits, however meager, derived from the establishment of reserves are critical to the well-being of tribal groups (Ramos and Taylor 1976). Although the reserve becomes less necessary as the tribal society is able to tolerate the pressures of the national society, title to their lands remains fundamental.

A major drawback to the establishment of reserves is tribal exposure to the national authorities who often encourage or enforce possibly well-intentioned, though often detrimental, modifications of traditional tribal practices. Disruption occurs when a government removes a tribe from its tribal area for resettlement in a reserve administered by that government. The ecological setting is usually quite different on the reservation, movement is usually restricted, and nomadic groups suddenly are forced to become sedentary. Religious and cultural practices are usually modified. Even the type of crops planted may be determined beforehand by government representatives. The procedures for involuntary settlement formulated by the bank will alleviate these problems.[1]

Enforced "primitivism" is also a disruptive policy occasionally practiced on a reservation. This policy is often implemented to promote tourism—since "primitive" costumes, houses, and crafts are tourist attractions—or it is defended as a means of preserving the tribe's cultural identity. Although enforced "primitivism" is always damaging, elective "primitivism" can be beneficial as in the case of the Cunas of Panama. Minority culture never has been a static entity that must be preserved exactly as it is found, or as it is believed to have been. Rather it is a dynamic reality that should be allowed to develop in a natural and progressive manner. Cultural continuity should be encouraged in all spheres, but the choice to continue modifying old ways should be left to the tribal people themselves, and not imposed upon them.

The reservation system easily accommodates these practices and systems of exploited labor, as the reservation is usually located in a remote area and its inhabitants have little legal recourse or representation at higher political levels. The administration of the reservation represents the government and may not be inclined, or even able, to respond to the interests of the inhabitants. If the tribal group has no channel through which to articulate its rights and needs, abuses are likely to occur. The major problem with reserves is that, as currently practiced, control of the tribe and its lands is transferred to outsiders—such as government administrators or a specially appointed group. The role these administrators generally play is one of pacification, the resolution of disputes within the tribe, and the partial prevention of contact with the national society. Few administrators have readily moved from a traditional "law and order" concept of their role to one that is more development oriented. In these circumstances, the socioeconomic gap widens between the tribe and the nationals. The bank's emphasis on strengthening the tribal agency and the role of tribal administrators in member governments is more appropriate than for the bank to assume a leading role in tribal affairs.

A reservation could form the basis of tribal development if first the governance of the tribe and its resources were left to the tribe, much as it was before the reserve was created. Second, administrators should act as facilitators, bringing to the tribe the protection, benefits, or specially designed education and health programs it may request. Third, the administrators and eventually the tribal leaders should have the power to defend tribal lands against incursions by outsiders. Only when tribal people are accorded equality under the law,[2] and are allowed to choose their own destiny, can they contribute fully to the national society. This will be difficult, time consuming, and not amenable to acceleration. Tribal representatives capable of dealing with administrators, nationals, and the government, as well as with communal title, are crucial to tribal survival. Though examples are few, it can be done. The Gavioes in Amazonia, Brazil, requested the tribal agent to operate outside the reservation gates, then bought and managed their own truck the next year, and finally started hiring nontribal day laborers the third year.

Health Effects   After recognition of title to land, the maintenance and protection of health standards are the second[3] fundamental prerequisite to the tribe's survival. Indigenous medicine in tribal areas has usually controlled endemic diseases and met the needs of the tribal society in its traditional habitat. Therefore, the objective of health measures within the context of development is to foster existing therapies, to introduce appropriate new repertoires, and to avoid the introduction of unfamiliar diseases and conditions. The literature on tribal groups is filled with accounts of contracted illnesses and frequent deaths due to contact with outsiders. Since disease can be transferred to the tribal group by any interchange with outsiders, protection or isolation is essential until a massive vaccination campaign can be implemented. Medical screening of project workers is imperative. In addition, health is affected by diet and, particularly, by sudden changes in it. Frequently, tribal peoples are compelled to adjust to sharp dietary changes, for many reasons. Also, sudden changes in lifestyles due to relocation or willing adoption are usually detrimental to health.

The diet and health aspects of relocation have been recognized by the bank, although until recently this was limited to involuntary relocation. These principles are now applied whenever tribal peoples are affected, whether or not there is relocation involved.

Social Change   While all change involves some degree of social disruption, rapid change increases social tension and can ultimately lead to vulnerability to disease, as well as emotional disorders, antisocial behavior, and alcoholism. While societies are dynamic, the capacity to adapt to change is not infinite, especially in the case of tribal populations. The social resources that help tribal members manage and cope with change are limited. Unfamiliar concepts, values, and roles impose additional demands on the coping process of the tribal society. Sudden demands decrease the capacity to adapt successfully. Major and rapid social changes are associated with: 1) a loss of self-esteem; 2) an increase in actual and perceived role conflict and ambiguity; and 3) an increase in the perceived gap between aspiration and achievement. A tribal population confronted with development or modernization often experiences loss of self-esteem, and its members feel a deprivation of their sense of personal worth and a devaluation of their social identity. Rapid social change introduces new individual or group roles and modifies old ones. These modifications increase role conflict and ambiguity, which further erode the self-esteem and social identity of an individual or group. For example, people in a hunting and gathering society are trained to be independent and opportunistic, and to use initiative. These qualities become disadvantages when such people are forced to offer themselves as dependent and obedient wage- or debt-bondage laborers. Rapid social change widens the gap between the aspirations of an individual or group and the ability to achieve new goals, often because traditional methods are disrupted.

Cultural Autonomy   The prerequisite to successful survival of a tribal group as an ethnic minority is the retention of cultural, social, and economic autonomy. This freedom of choice involves continued control by the tribal people over their own institutions, including tribal customs, beliefs, language, and means of subsistence or production (Goodland 1985).

Economic development has often been promoted at the expense of tribal institutions. Development strategies often tacitly assumed that there were no viable institutions or practices existing in the tribal culture that could be used to foster development. This "vacuum ideology" has led to the large-scale transfer of national structures or practices to tribal cultures where they are little understood (Colletta 1975, 1977). A primary example of this is the spread of Western technology and schooling throughout the non-Western world by colonial wardens. While contact with nationals will inevitably bring change in tribal practices and attitudes, prevailing basic customs and traditions need not be altered or eliminated. Furthermore, the tribe alone should choose which traditions should be altered. Retention of tribal customs enhances the maintenance of ethnic identity, stability as a productive unit, and, more importantly, adaption to new circumstances. For instance, the reason the Balinese have been relatively impervious to outside influence is that they have maintained their cultural integrity, will not admit non-Balinese as members of their communities, and have adopted changes that reinforce their culture.

Policy of Cultural Autonomy

Many policies concerning the degree of social change within tribal groups vary widely. The two extremes are: total enforced isolation of the tribal groups allowing no change; and rapid and complete assimilation resulting in the loss of tribal identity. Isolation in a zoolike arrangement of an enforced primitive state should be rejected. Conversely, complete assimilation into the national society denies, then extinguishes, ethnic diversity. Furthermore, as noted earlier, rapid change can separate tribal people from their cultural identity, thus causing extinction.

The intermediate policy adopted by the World Bank finances more humane, prudent, and productive projects. This allows the retention of a large measure of tribal autonomy and cultural choice. Such a policy of self-determination emphasizes the tribal groups' own choice of their way of life. The imposition of different social or economic systems is minimized until the tribal society is resilient enough to tolerate the effects of change. This policy provides safeguards for tribal people so that they themselves can dictate the pace and style of their own involvement with the national society. The following conditions are essential if this intermediate policy is to succeed:

1. National governments and international organizations must support rights to land used or occupied by tribal people, to their ethnic identity, and to cultural autonomy.
2. The tribe must be provided with interim safeguards to deal with unwelcome outside influences on its own land until the tribe adapts sufficiently.
3. Neither the nation nor the nontribal neighbors should compete for resources with the tribal society on its own lands.

The bank adopts this intermediate policy, where appropriate, in order to assist these beleaguered societies. When these conditions are observed, not only does tribal culture survive, but the tribe becomes a productive contributor to the nation, rather than a ward of the state.

Cultural autonomy differs from the integrationist approach in several respects. First, cultural autonomy stresses the value of the tribal culture and the desire to maintain it rather than replace the culture as quickly as possible with the customs and values of the dominant society. Second, cultural autonomy recognizes the harmful effects of unrestrained contact between dominant culture and tribal culture, and seeks to moderate them. Third, cultural autonomy creates conditions under which the tribal members themselves control the pace and manner of their adjustment to national society and culture. Finally, cultural autonomy does not preclude the training of selected tribal representatives in the dominant culture and their role as mediators. The tribe must design controls to prevent abuse of authority by the dominant society.

Recommendations

Action to guarantee the physical survival of tribal populations and encourage freedom of cultural choice is directed towards the following outcome:

1. A tribal population that forms a recognized and accepted ethnic minority—one component of an ethnically pluralistic national society.
2. As such, this ethnic minority must maintain its traditional way of life, modified in accordance with the preferences of the tribal population itself.
3. The tribal economic system progressively evolves from "precontact" subsistence to a sustained yield, agro-ecosystem with the production of a surplus.

Immediate integration of tribal populations typically swells the numbers of rural and urban poor. Developing countries already face enormous problems in their attempts to eliminate poverty, and adding to the numbers of the poor by dispossessing tribal societies only worsens their situation. This is ameliorated by maintaining ethnic minorities as viable and productive societies, and by retaining their cultural autonomy. This policy will be facilitated by recognizing the need for a pluralistic view of national identity and by understanding the importance of cultural or ethnic diversity. Through these efforts, tribal peoples will be fully participatory and productive members of society.

Given the importance of economic patterns in all cultures, and the extreme contrasts between tribal and national economies, interaction between the two economies is critical. A tribal culture may surrender part of its political autonomy, yet still continue to be ethnically distinct if it is allowed to retain its economy unexploited by outsiders (Bodley 1975).

NOTES

This chapter is a portion of a document published previously by the World Bank in 1982 entitled: "Tribal Peoples and Economic Development: Human Ecological Considerations." It has been reprinted here with permission.

1. The bank tries to avoid involuntary resettlement whenever feasible. Where relocation is unavoidable (for instance, in the case of large construction projects, such as dams, irrigation schemes, ports and airports, and new towns and highways), a well-prepared resettlement plan should allow for flexibility in the solutions and implementation that are most suitable for a particular case. When only a few people are to be relocated, appropriate compensation for assets, coupled with arrangements for removal and a relocation grant, may suffice. In the case of large numbers of people, or whole communities, the resettlement plan could include compensation as one principle element, as well as relocation and establishment in a new area, or integration with existing communities in an already settled area. The major objective is to ensure that settlers are afforded opportunities to become established and economically self-sustaining in the shortest possible time period at living standards that match those before resettlement; that the settlers' social and cultural institutions are supported and their own initiative is encouraged; and that the new area should be one in which the skills and aptitudes of the involuntary settlers can be readily employed. Important considerations include access to land, markets, employment, the provision of needed services and infrastructure in the new area. Careful preparatory work with the involuntary settlers, the host community, and respective leaders prior to the move is of primary importance.

2. Legal recognition of "pastoralist groups" was deemed an essential precondition to implementation of bank-assisted livestock projects in Chad and Niger.

3. The exception is in the rare cases of "first contact," in which health measures are initially most urgent.

26   The Role of Aboriginals in the Management of Australia's Coburg (Gurig) and Kakadu National Parks

Sally M. Weaver

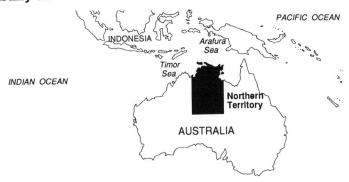

PROTECTED AREA	Cobourg (Gurig) National Park Kakadu National Park
CLASSIFICATION	Labeled as: National Parks Managed as: Anthropological Reserve, IUCN Category VII
RESIDENT PEOPLE	Acculturated Tribal Peoples

The ways in which indigenous minorities participate in the management of national parks, whether these parks are on or near Aboriginal land, are essentially uncharted in the literature of any discipline. Systematic studies are exceedingly few, and I found many of the papers at the IUCN conference in Bali (October 1983) unsatisfactory because they tended to be prescriptive and they failed to tell me what was actually happening on the ground from empirical observation and study. In this chapter, I present the findings of my investigation of Aboriginal participation in two Australian parks based on anthropological field research evaluating the status of joint management of these parks after nearly five years of implementation.

The first park, Cobourg or Gurig National Park, lies northeast of Darwin, Australia (see Map 26.1). It is operated by the Northern Territory government through its Darwin-based Conservation Commission of the Northern Territory (CCNT). The second studied is Kakadu, due east of Darwin. It is managed by the federal park agency, the Canberra-based Australian National Parks and Wildlife Service (ANPWS).

Analytically, the terms I use in this study can be briefly defined. By "policy" I mean the selection and allocation of "values" which guide the future actions of park agencies and governments. Policy is generated at the apex of park-government systems, and it may or may not be publicly stated. Policy also may be nonexistent. The values guiding behavior will include, among others, political survival of the park agencies, centralized versus decentralized authority in the park agencies, and the role assigned Aboriginal owners and the Northern Land Council (NLC)[1]—their representatives—in policy, planning, management of the parks, in addition to the more conventional parks-related values of conservation, public enjoyment, etc.

By "planning" I mean the political-instrumental activity in which the policy-values are rationalized and translated into more specific objectives, priorities, and guidelines. This is a bridging process in which the general policies become more explicit and specific in relation to a particular park through the more conventional means of the plans of management. But planning also occurs in an equally significant, although much less visible way, within governments in the form of corporate planning in the annual budget preparation, the establishment of staff, and program development.

By "management" I mean the day-to-day operations of the park estate in which personnel, finance, knowledge, and attitudes are assigned to administer the natural and cultural resources of the parks. The management level is important because it is there that the most continuous, face-to-face interaction occurs between Aboriginal residents and park personnel.

By "joint-mechanisms" for policy, planning and management, I mean "formal power sharing" between government agencies and Aboriginal people or their representatives in such a way that the Aboriginal people owning the land have an equal chance to determine decisions, on an ongoing basis, as the park agencies. This implies that Aboriginals have the resources (knowledge, skills, time, authority, etc.) to bring to the decision-making process and the capacity to use these resources. Successful joint mechanisms produce mutually agreeable decisions and require clear and honest communication by both parties as well as compromises by both sides over time. Essential to this relationship is the evolution of mutual trust based on the "empirical behavior" of both parties, not simply on verbal assertions of trust.

Map 26.1

Nature Conservation Areas Near Kakadu National Park

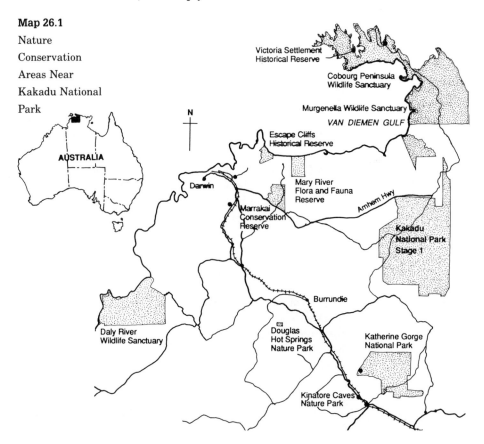

I believe joint mechanisms will become an increasingly common form of political relationship between indigenous minorities and the nation-state, especially where Aboriginal organizations become sophisticated about the impotence of purely advisory powers in influencing governments, and where, as in these two cases, independent action by government agencies or Aboriginals was not possible in the judgment of the day. The study of Cobourg and Kakadu provides us with local-level examples of these relations, not as they are often idealized in the parks' literature, but as they have been practiced empirically.

General Observations

My general observations on the state of Aboriginal participation and the two parks' establishments were as follows:

1. In neither park did joint management systems, as defined above, exist in practice.
2. Neither park agency had an overall policy on the role of Aboriginal landowners in the policy, planning, management spectrum of parks operations.
3. I found no evidence to suggest that Aboriginal owners of the park land in fact wanted joint management, meaning the coresponsibility of actually running the parks on a day-to-day basis, although this will undoubtedly come in the future. Rather the Aboriginal owners sought a joint policy and planning role in order that the parks be run in accordance with their wishes and concerns. They also wished to have Aboriginal people employed as rangers in the day-to-day operations, and to have their rangers' ideas about park management be respected and considered seriously.
4. Both governments and park agencies were "expansionist," meaning they sought to extend their political-bureaucratic power base by increasing their park estate through long-term agreements with Aboriginals in the land claims process. The "nonpark" option was in fact a nonoption for the Aboriginal landowners because they would not have been granted title to their traditional land if they had not first agreed to its use as a park. In essence, Aboriginals were granted "parklands" and by this fact lost significant control over the use of the land and its resources. To regain control, they must realize an authoritative role in the policy-planning-and-management spectrum of the parks' operations. This point makes the distinction be-

tween landownership and land control, and emphasizes the latter as the more significant factor in the Aboriginal-park relationship.

5. Both park agencies, although very different in their knowledge of the Aboriginal cultural traditions, had personnel and procedures which were sensitive to Aboriginal owners as individuals and collectives. The most impressive group of park personnel in this regard were the European rangers. They were generally young (in their twenties and early thirties), had the most extensive face-to-face contact with Aboriginal residents, were enthusiastic about working in the parks with Aboriginal people, and took the time and personal interest in getting to know Aboriginal people in their districts. This time and interest were recognized by the Aboriginal residents who, although having no clear concept of the role of rangers, viewed them positively, as friendly and helpful.

6. Because of the constructive European ranger–Aboriginal interaction on the ground, but also because key officials in both park agencies sought to maintain smooth relations with Aboriginal owners and to try to communicate openly across cultural boundaries, both parks had generally workable relations with Aboriginal residents.

7. Both parks were "experimental," meaning that they were "innovative" in their efforts in their separate institutional courses in which no established blueprints existed to guide either the governments or the Aboriginal owners. Consequently, the parks were "fluid" in almost every aspect of their operation. This unsettled condition also reflected the fact that both parks were "young," less than five years old, and that conventional park development, as well as ways and means of involving Aboriginal residents, was still evolving.

8. Although both parks had experienced a highly political birth in the land claims process, both had seen the land transfer legally to Aboriginal claimants, and both had witnessed the resettlement of the Aboriginal claimants as resident peoples within the new parks, the two parks were at "different points in their life histories." Cobourg was the younger park, with its first draft plan of management completed (CCNT 1984), whereas Kakadu was entering its second cycle and was preparing its second plan of management[2]. Local Aboriginal participation in the planning stage was nearing completion in Cobourg, while in Kakadu it had just begun.

9. The two parks differed significantly in the official style of the joint management relationship between Aboriginal owners and park agencies. Generally, the Cobourg relationship was formal and legally structured in that the collective Aboriginal interests were, ideally, to be represented by four Aboriginals on the eight-member Board of Management whose chairman was Aboriginal and had the decisive vote to break a split decision—in short a veto power. In Kakadu the relationship was informal, characterized by a system of ANPWS consultation with three Aboriginals employed by ANPWS as cultural advisers,[3] with individual landowners, and with the Gagudju Association composed of the Aboriginal landowners. Unlike most consultative relationships, the one prevailing in Kakadu since its inception in 1979 was ongoing, open, highly sensitive to and often responsive to Aboriginal wishes, especially in regard to sacred-significant sites.

Before identifying the factors that influenced Aboriginal participation in the policy-planning-management spectrum of the park operations, it is useful to sketch briefly the nature of the parks, and the Aboriginal presence and participation in their management.

Cobourg

Briefly, Cobourg was a newer (1981), smaller (2,207 sq. km), and more isolated park than Kakadu. Occupying a peninsula, its most outstanding features were (and still are) its beautifully scenic coastline of sandy beaches and dunes, and its relatively "pristine" condition, undisturbed by European settlement or mining. It was essentially an undeveloped park with limited visitor use (621 permits issued in 1982). Access, made difficult by a poor road from Darwin and by the need to secure an NLC permit to drive through Arnhemland, was mainly by air.

The Aboriginal population was small (43 in 1984), with members living in one of three outstations in the park—Araru Point, Reef Point–Gumuragi, and Danger Point–Gul Gul, only one of which is located near park headquarters at Black Point.

The park was managed by a small staff of eight: the Chief Ranger, three European rangers, three Aboriginal rangers, and an Aboriginal laborer. Most of their time was devoted to "keeping the place running" (i.e., repairing generators, maintaining the physical plant, and arranging transportation, including that for VIPs). Little activity was devoted to conservation of the natural resources, but a considerable amount of time was given to Aboriginal residents in the form of physical maintenance of the outstations, running the Gurig (Aboriginally owned) store, and handling correspondence and communications for social-welfare benefits and medical emergencies.

In terms of social organization, the European and Aboriginal families in the park resembled an "enclave society," a small-scale, isolated population living with little privacy from one another and at times feeling the strain of continuous interaction. Relations between the young European rangers and Aboriginal families were very good.

The unique feature about Cobourg's operations was the existence of its Board of Management which had, in fact, a policy function. Under the Cobourg Act of 1981, an eight-member Board of Management was created.[4] Four members were Aboriginal residents, including the chairman, and four members were CCNT officials representing the interests of the CCNT which managed the park on a day-to-day basis and provided the overall policy framework and the planning resources.[5] Issues to be settled at the board could be discussed on several occasions at the supervisors' meetings prior to board meetings. NLC representatives attended both meetings to discuss and clarify issues with and for the Aboriginal board members and to attempt to ensure that Aboriginal interests were represented.

To date, however, Aboriginal residents had not been able to use the formal legal power which the Cobourg Act gave them for cultural, educational, and political reasons. Only some of the younger generation (teenagers and those in their twenties) had English literacy and numerics skills, and none had political or bureaucratic skills that would enable them to play a role equal to the CCNT members on the board. European board members, NLC representatives, and CCNT planners attempted to explain the meaning of European concepts such as park, conservation, and tourism, but understandably encountered severe communication problems because equivalent concepts were absent in Aboriginal experience and culture. Unlike Kakadu, there was no Aboriginal organization to collectively shape, express, and press for Aboriginal interests in the park operations or in the wider field of federal and Northern Territory government services. Also, unlike Kakadu, the Aboriginal residents had no independent countervailing advice on park or other issues since they lacked their own environmental advisers. Their main source of advice on parks matters was the CCNT and secondarily the NLC. The CCNT had certain key officials who were determined to make Cobourg a success, thus demonstrating that the Northern Territory could run a park on Aboriginal land and work in harmony with the Aboriginal residents.

The role of the NLC in the Cobourg operations had varied over time. In the history of Cobourg, the NLC negotiated the (verbal) resettlement agreement and the Cobourg Act, and thereafter provided field officers to advise the Aboriginal board members on agenda items and at meetings. In total, the NLC monitoring had been neither sustained nor consistent. The NLC was not created or staffed with the purpose of providing local-level advisory services of the order from which the Cobourg Aboriginal community could have benefited. However, the NLC's legal and field staff were conscientiously attempting to familiarize themselves with Cobourg, and to seek park planning experts to assist in reviewing the draft plan of management. Relations between the CCNT and the NLC (as between the ANPWS and the NLC) could be tense due to anticipation of adversarial behavior from the NLC, but generally communications between individuals in the NLC and park agencies proceeded informally and in a style of equanimity.

In summary, Cobourg was a small, isolated, and undeveloped park whose Aboriginal owners were dependent on the park agency for income, for linkages to social welfare benefits and government programs, and for advice on park-related issues. The formal legal powers provided in the Cobourg Act of 1981 were unusable directly by Aboriginal owners, but the potential of the act ensured them a significant future authoritative role in the policy, as well as the planning and management of the park.

Kakadu

Kakadu was a different order of national park than Cobourg, and it provided us with a very different model of Aboriginal participation and of park management.

Kakadu was a larger (Stage I, 6,144 sq. km), older (1979), more accessible, and more developed park with World Heritage Listing (1981). The recent declaration of Stage II and intent to declare Stage III will triple its size and compound the management challenges for both the ANPWS and the Aboriginal owners. Its major features were its sandstone escarpment with numerous Aboriginal Rock Art sites[6], and its wetlands teeming with bird life.

Geopolitically, it emerged from the nationally controversial confrontation between uranium mining interests and Aboriginal land rights interests in the Alligator Rivers Region in the late 1970s (Fox et al. 1977), and its brief history had been characterized by constitutional conflict between the federal and Northern Territory governments. Established and managed by the ANPWS as its first major park, Kakadu's first plan of management (ANPWS 1980) was nearing the end of its enforcement period (1980–1985), and its second plan (1985–1990) would incorporate Stage I and Stage II (see ANPWS 1986). The federal government's announcement of Stages II and III included a massive tourist development scheme over a five-year period, so like Cobourg, but on a larger scale, Kakadu would shortly experience the pressures of establishing tourist facilities to cope with its visitors (150,000 visitor days in 1983) who were increasing at a rate of 20 percent annually.

Like Cobourg, Kakadu had a history of a wildlife sanctuary in a part of its territory, but public use prior to its establishment was much greater. Unlike Cobourg, it was readily accessible by road from Darwin (225 km to the west) and tourist companies operated regular excursions to the park with no permit required by visitors.

The Aboriginal residents, including owners, numbered 273 (1983). They lived in twenty scattered locations throughout the park in outstations, camps, and small family groupings separate from the park staff. One exception to this residential pattern was Nourlangie Ranger Station where park personnel and Aboriginal families lived in close proximity and experienced some of the "enclave society" characteristics found at Black Point on Cobourg.

Generally, Aboriginal participation in the management of the park took the form of advising and of employment. Since the establishment of Kakadu the ANPWS had employed three Aboriginal cultural advisers, which the park staff consulted individually on a wide range of issues (e.g., location of roads, proposed tourist facilities, etc.). The ANPWS had trained a dozen Aboriginal rangers, eight of whom it employed[7]; it also employed, on a temporary basis, Aboriginal residents in a variety of other jobs. Finally, it consulted informally, and less frequently on a formal basis, with the Gagudju Association, created in 1979 to distribute the uranium royalties to the traditional owners under the 1978 Ranger Uranium agreement. There was no formal role for the Gagudju Association and, unlike Cobourg, there was no formal authority for Aboriginal owners in the policy, planning, or management of the park, a condition that the Gagudju Association and NLC desired to change in the forthcoming planning process. Generally, however, relations between park staff and the Aboriginal residents were exceedingly positive. Consultation occurred on a daily, informal basis, and the park staff did accede to the wishes of the owners. Relations between the Gagudju Association spokesmen, including its environmental adviser, and the mid-management of ANPWS contained an element of strain over differing views of how the park should be run, but despite the tensions at times, interpersonal relationships were workable and issues were talked out if not resolved.

The administrative style, scale, and complexity of Kakadu contrasted sharply with Cobourg. In the ANPWS, power was concentrated in the director of the service in Canberra and there was very little delegation of financial or decision-making authority to the park staff. The ANPWS was a highly centralist agency; it is not inaccurate to say that the park was superintended from Canberra and to a lesser extent from the mid-management office in Darwin. Reluctance to delegate authority made the jobs of the park superintendent, deputy superintendent, and the five district supervisors extremely difficult. It also limited the contributions (including innovations) that the highly professional and dedicated personnel of the ANPWS could make to the Kakadu experiment, and to the smooth running of the park on a daily basis. Although tensions exist in most bureaucracies between ground-based staff and those at headquarters, those in Kakadu were very pronounced and in this regard contrasted markedly with the decentralist style of the CCNT.

Finally, the presence of specialists based in the park, including a recently appointed interpretation officer, was unusual in Australia and it gave the local management a depth

of expertise not available on site in Cobourg. More research
on the management of cultural sites (rock art, archaeological
sites) had occurred than on biological management, although
the hiring of a new officer in this field would soon redress the
imbalance. Thus Kakadu, in the size of its staff establishment (twenty-nine in total: superintendent, deputy superintendent, four specialists, five district supervisors, eighteen
rangers [ten European and eight Aboriginal]), its hierarchi-
cal structure, its degree of specialization, and its educational
level, contrasted with the smaller, less specialized, and edu-
cated staff in Cobourg. It also gave greater priority to the
selection of staff for the park to ensure that personnel were
sympathetic to and could work with Aboriginal people.

Overall, Kakadu had an Aboriginal orientation in its on-
ground management, not because of its origins in the land-
claims process or the Fox Inquiry, but because the key mid-
management personnel who were selected to establish the
park had an ideological commitment to Aboriginal people. At
the apex of the ANPWS the motivations were as political as
those of the CCNT in regard to Cobourg: both park agencies
and governments wished to demonstrate that they could operate successful parks on Aboriginal land with Aboriginal
people; both park agencies needed land to expand their park
estates; and both agencies and governments had used parks
in their constitutional battles for power.

**Aboriginal
Participation
in Parks
Management**

I will now identify what I believe were major factors influencing Aboriginal participation in the operations of the two
parks. The factors identified are not exhaustive nor were
they assigned priorities.

**The Evolution-
ary Nature of
the Park
Administrations**

Neither park could be described as having a settled administrative system. Although Kakadu was a more developed park
than Cobourg, both were still evolving. One consequence of
this evolutionary nature of the parks for Aboriginal participation was that Aboriginal people were not dealing with
static institutions about which they could have accumulated
knowledge and reasonably predictable modes of relationship.
Rather, they were expected to adapt to "a moving target," so
to speak—to a changing administrative milieu around them
whose direction and motivation for change were not clearly
understood.

**Political-
Bureaucratic
Responsibility
for
Administration**

This factor applies to Kakadu where the difficulty of Aboriginal participation was compounded by the unclear political-
bureaucratic responsibility for the park. By this I mean that
although there was no question that ANPWS was the bureaucratic agency responsible for managing Kakadu, its minister played a secondary role to the Minister of Aboriginal
Affairs who took a very strong personal interest in the park
but whose bureaucracy, the Department of Aboriginal Affairs
(DAA), had not maintained close local or regional contact
with the Aboriginal owners and was therefore not fully informed of the issues. This "skewed" institutional arrangement had already raised some concern in both Gagudju
Association and the NLC in respect to their lobbying activities, and they had asked both federal departments to clarify
the lines of responsibility.

**The Role of
Management**

Departmental responsibility raised a related issue. It seemed
to me that park agencies were expected by Aboriginal owners and some critics to be "total institutions" responsible for
providing a wide variety of services to the Aboriginal residents. At Cobourg, Aboriginal needs of a social welfare and
development nature were brought to the CCNT, in part because of the isolation of the park and Aboriginal community,
and in part because the CCNT had in fact responded to some
of the Aboriginal needs in this regard. At Kakadu, some senior Aboriginal owners and some critics had argued that the
ANPWS should take action to preserve some of the Aboriginal languages spoken by only a few persons, to which the
park service did respond positively. These examples raised
the broader question of what role park services, in these circumstances, should or could play in regard to these expectations and demands. If they took on the functions of "total
institutions" they would become even more "patron" institutions on which Aboriginal dependency would increase. On
the other hand, the presence of the park agencies in Cobourg
and Kakadu seemed to have diminished the interest and involvement of other government agencies with the Aboriginal
residents, leaving the residents with little recourse but to direct their demands to the park services. The answer to this
difficulty may have rested with the need of the park agencies
to develop a more active referral and liaison function if they

wished to ensure that Aboriginal residents were properly served by governments.

The Role of Aboriginals in Fundamental Policy Decisions

Fundamental, far-reaching policy decisions that were to have a significant effect on the daily lives of Aboriginal owners were made by both governments in the two parks *without* Aboriginal input. Both decisions were political-partisan initiatives taken by cabinets in election posturing (November 1983) and, although the issues were generally known to Aboriginals involved in park management, Aboriginal owners were not consulted. I am referring here to the Northern Territory announcement of the creation of a marine park at Cobourg, and to the federal announcement of Stages II and III of Kakadu with its unexpected $70 million tourist development scheme. This type of policy making can be expected to continue given the behavior of political parties and cabinets at election time. In such instances Aboriginal participation in fundamental decisions will be relegated to *post facto* consultation at best.

Political Significance of Park Issues

"Parks" have not been on the political agenda as items in their own right. Rather, parks have been "masked invariably" in the media and in government attention by other issues assigned greater significance, namely: land rights, uranium, and most recently tourism. One consequence of this is that the public has not been informed about the issues facing park managers or Aboriginal residents in the two parks. Furthermore, plans of management, despite the rhetoric surrounding them, were not designed to spark public involvement, to crisply identify issues, or to inform in an open and clear fashion. Thus, neither the public at large nor Aboriginal owners have experienced an informed public debate on the parks.

Public Support for Aboriginal Participation

Public support for Aboriginal participation in the operations of the two parks had been minimal. One exception to this was the Canberra-based Australian Institute of Aboriginal Studies (AIAS), which was highly critical of the ANPWS failure to give the Gagudju Association a decisive and formal role in the management of Kakadu when the first plan of management was being prepared.[8] There was no conservation lobby in the Northern Territory that was highly active and effective in monitoring conservation issues. Such groups could support Aboriginal interests, but no such support had been forthcoming. Ministerial encouragement of Aboriginal participation had been limited as well; park affairs remained "private" business between Aboriginal owners and their representatives on the one hand and the government agencies on the other, and they lacked the critical scrutiny of informed public monitoring.

Differing Concepts of "Park"

In the context of uranium mining, Kakadu was especially seen as a nonthreatening, supportive "buffer." Consequently, a discerning or critical view of the impact of park interests on Aboriginal owners had not been forthcoming.

One example is tourism. Parks attract tourists, indeed "public enjoyment" is an integral part of their raison d'etre, and parks with World Heritage Listing status, like Kakadu, have even greater public appeal. Yet no tourist impact studies had been done in either of the two parks, and some observers and participants seemed surprised that tourism could become an issue. A second example of the uncritical view of parks was the inherent conflict between use versus conservation of natural resources in the parks. This type of issue had yet to be engaged in both parks (e.g., dugong and turtle in Cobourg, and a domesticated buffalo herd to replace the feral buffalo in Kakadu). Aboriginal interests were in competition with larger interests such as commercial tourism, and conservation on both a national and international level. To compete with any degree of effectiveness, the Aborigines needed to be politically organized to ensure that the information base on which decisions were being made was accurate (e.g., are Aboriginals in Cobourg overhunting dugong and turtle?).

I had no evidence to suggest that Aboriginal owners of either park, with certain notable exceptions, understood the park concept. This then begged the question of how Aboriginal people could participate effectively in an institution which they did not understand. It also begged the question of how accurate the putative statements were that Aboriginals voluntarily offered their land for park use. Nor was the role of park ranger clearly understood, in part because in practice the role was not dissimilar to components in early white roles (e.g., boss, helpful Balanda). Also, the role itself was not easily defined nor homogeneous in practice.

Still, I anticipated that the CCNT would promote the ethic of "development on the basis of sustained yield" more forcefully as it pursued according to its policy, innovative joint management and development systems with Aboriginals (e.g., Tiwi) and pastoralists, among others. I also believed that some Aboriginal owners would themselves begin to promote the development of their natural resources (e.g., for tourism) in parks for much the same economic motivation that exists in the Third World nations. If Aboriginal tourist development occurred in this way, park agencies might well experience Aboriginal "participation" of an unwelcome nature, and Aboriginal owners might be viewed as a "fifth column," an internal force endangering the conservation values and/or the anti-tourist attitudes held by some staff and officials in both parks.

Homeland vs. Park

Although the land was viewed as park land in the conservation idiom, in the Aboriginal idiom it was a homeland ("our country") to which the Aboriginal owners returned following the land claim—park creation process. Even though the clan territory boundaries were not precisely demarcated in Aboriginal knowledge, interest in and affinity with the land were strong and clan identity and membership well known. Homeland was a concept that embodied the notion of clan territory, the desire for privacy to live their own lives in their outstations and camps in the park, the desire for freedom from white intrusion, as well as the more conventional spiritual notions of the man-land relationship. Thus, although Aboriginals did not yet share the concept of park, which has a territorial basis like "country," they seemed to view the activities of park management through their homeland concept. Hence they were, and continue to be, selective about the aspects of park policy, planning, and management in which they wished to participate. For example, there seemed to be a generous willingness among Aboriginal owners in both parks to share their country with tourists so long as the visitors were kept away from their outstations, sacred-significant sites, and areas used for food sources (e.g., hunting, fishing). There was also the desire on the part of Aboriginal rangers in both parks to participate primarily in the patrolling activities of the role, and less interest in dealing with the tourists and the rubbish runs, preferences not dissimilar to those of European rangers.

In Kakadu, there was the desire among some senior Aboriginal spokesmen that European rangers be kept in the park because it was believed they could control the tourists who did not readily take advice from Aboriginal residents or rangers. Although there was no denying that some Aboriginal owners were dissatisfied with certain aspects of management in both parks and that others were disinterested, it seemed that so long as the essential elements of homeland were honored by the park managers, the Aboriginal owners were reasonably content with the operations of the parks on their land.

Aboriginal Cultural Advisers

In the early days of the park, current mid-management personnel at Kakadu spent an extensive amount of time walking with the senior Aboriginal owners over the land to identify its sacred-significant sites for the purpose of ensuring that park developments (e.g., roads, walking trails, buildings) did not encroach on them. These park officials (who had previous knowledge and working experience with Aboriginal people in the territory) not only learned the landscape from the Aboriginal and physical perspectives, but developed excellent rapport with the owners and demonstrated a respect for and a compliance with Aboriginal wishes. Thus Aboriginal–park relations were launched on an extremely positive footing, which continues today.

In a more formal relationship, ANPWS employed three aboriginal owners as cultural advisers who were consulted on an as-needed basis by park staff. Over time, however, there seemed to have developed an overdependency by the ANPWS on the older, more traditional persons (advisers and others); such a bias excluded women and the younger generation who in some instances had a more practical conservation interest, and an equally strong commitment and association with their land. This same observation applied to the CCNT's reliance on the opinions of the senior board members; in both instances it raised the question of how extensively, if at all, these advisers reflected and represented the views of their fellow residents.

**Aboriginal
Participation as
Rangers**

In both parks neither the park staff nor the Aboriginal own-ers involved in management were satisfied with the Ab-original ranger training schemes or employment programs. Kakadu personnel had made a dedicated effort to mount an Aboriginal ranger training program before the park was offi-cially declared in compliance with its 1978 agreement with the NLC. But its subsequent failure to establish a career structure for Aboriginal rangers had been a source of sharp criticism from some Aboriginal rangers. The CCNT effort to train Aboriginal rangers had been ad hoc, less dedicated and uncoordinated. At Cobourg, its selection of three rangers for permanent employment had left strained relations with Ab-originals. Both park agencies, however, were reassessing their experiences.

The CCNT had led this intiative by hiring an officer to ex-amine the needs of the CCNT in Aboriginal communities throughout the Northern Territory, not simply those in parks. This resulted in proposals for the CCNT's considera-tion in which Aboriginals would receive not only a new type of ranger training, but instead would be trained in a new type of role (community ranger) in the conservation field to serve the needs of Aboriginal communities. Despite very dif-ferent beginnings, there was a convergence of concerns in the two parks about the effectiveness of the Aboriginal training program and about the reliability and job satisfaction of the Aboriginal rangers. Ironically, neither park had made an effort to obtain systematically the views of Aboriginal rangers on their own roles and experiences. Aboriginal rangers obviously had as valid an input into the reorganiza-tion of the training programs and role changes as park staff; Aboriginal participation was essential if the problems of role definition were to be sorted out, and if the genuine desire of European rangers to enhance the Aboriginal rangers' contri-bution and job satisfaction was to be achieved.

**Aboriginal
Knowledge as
Participation**

In both park agencies certain persons had expressed the de-sire for greater use of Aboriginal traditional knowledge of the environment in the management of the park and in the interpretation of its features to the public. Although this de-sire was much stronger in Kakadu than in Cobourg, as with the parks officials' knowledge of Aboriginal traditions, the Cobourg park planners had made a genuine effort to incorporate Aboriginal views and concepts into the planning process and throughout the plan of management document.

The desire to incorporate Aboriginal traditional knowledge is commendable and genuine, but I believe that it occurs, in principle, more readily in the interpretation than in the resource management area of the park operations. I say this because the basic problem continues to be the epistemology of Aboriginal knowledge—the system of how you know what you know—and I believe that Aboriginal knowledge may not be readily acceptable to Europeans with a scientific system of justifying knowledge. Fire management of the land was a partial incorporation of Aboriginal knowledge, but it was rationalized and validated by the scientific approach and therefore vulnerable to new research discoveries that might contradict present knowlege.[9] Ironically, the use of Aboriginal knowledge in Kakadu's interpretation for the public had been minimal, not because the park staff lacked the knowledge—in fact they had a high degree of expertise—but because of the centralist powers of ANPWS in Canberra, which, in practice, discouraged interpretation and consequently under-utilized the expertise based in the park.

Participation of Local Aboriginal Organizations

I have already discussed briefly the presence of a local Aboriginal organization in Kakadu (Gagudju Association) and the absence of one in Cobourg. I might have argued that the existence of a local organization was a significant advantage to Aboriginal owners if it identified and advocated Aboriginal interest in the park policy, planning, and management activities; its existence might have benefited the NLC, which could not play a daily role in the park nor have the knowledge of the operations of a specific park yet must, under existing legislation, represent the interests of aboriginal owners to the ANPWS. Finally, it could have been a positive resource to the ANPWS if the association ever developed a capacity to represent local Aboriginal views on the park. "Representivity" was a problem in the consultation process because there was no certainty or ability to demonstrate that the advice received was representative of Aboriginal views. Furthermore, the informal consultative process placed conscientious park staff in a very difficult position. They could not be sure that they received representative advice, and when controversy arose they had little to fall back on except their personal judgments based on experience.

The Gagudju Association's executive members and environmental adviser already held an important informal advising and cooperative working role in the management of the park and had initiated some of the land management activities (e.g., levee building to stop salt water intrusion). Tensions between the association and the ANPWS arose not in the park, where relations with the superintendent and staff were good, but at the mid-management and headquarters level of the ANPWS where the control of power and policy was concentrated. Through its environmental adviser, a former ranger-officer in the CCNT with longstanding personal ties to Aboriginal people in Kakadu, and through a few key members (rangers and cultural advisers), the association had the capacity to provide informed countervailing advice to the ANPWS. Generally, it had been critical of many aspects of park management, especially the ANPWS refusal to discipline Aboriginal rangers in their job performance. It had also criticized the antitourist sentiments at mid-management level, and its environmental adviser had been outspoken about the reluctance of the ANPWS to open more of the park to responsible public use. ANPWS officials tended to question the representivity of the association and the wisdom of its proposals, and the association found the ANPWS unresponsive to its demands, including its request in 1983 for a formal board of management like the Cobourg model. The association was expected to make stronger demands for power sharing in the forthcoming planning process, and the NLC was pursuing negotiations with ANPWS over possible new mechanisms for joint planning.

Who Participates? The Nature of Aboriginality

I will overdraw this point by saying that Cobourg and Kakadu were at opposite ends of the continuum on this issue: the issue being the construct of reality, in the minds of park personnel, of the nature of Aboriginality. Specifically, personnel in both agencies had expressed a concern whether the Aboriginal owners of the parks were "traditional" Aboriginals or, phrased otherwise, whether there was a traditional culture remaining in the minds and daily behavior of the Aboriginal owners. In the CCNT and at Cobourg the factor of traditionality was generally deemphasized and, because of the limited knowledge about Aboriginal traditions, traditional aspects of behavior were often not recognized and Aboriginal sensibilities had been affronted. In Kakadu, most park personnel had an ideological commitment to Aboriginals and the interest in traditionality predominated. Consequently, the construct of Aboriginality was that of "the traditional culture," and the realities of cultural change among Aboriginals were often disregarded.[10] In general, the park agencies' constructs of Aboriginality denied legitimacy to the Aboriginal reinterpretation process, reflecting, as in the broader societal treatment of Aboriginals (and Canadian Indians, Metis, and Inuit) a double standard: Australians and Canadians could reinterpret their own past, but Aboriginals (and Indians) could not with legitimacy. Thus, although the two park agencies did not differ from other white institutions in this regard, their constructs of Aboriginality significantly influenced Aboriginal participation in the parks because their notions shaped how Aboriginal people per se were perceived, how programs should be developed and interpreted, how demands from Aboriginal owners should be received, and how relations with Aboriginals should be managed.

The Parks Agencies

Any inquiry into the nature of Aboriginal participation in the park policy, planning, and management cycle begs the question of the willingness and the capacity of park agencies to share power with Aboriginal owners and to select and support personnel who can work with the Aboriginal people. Cobourg and Kakadu provided different models in this respect. Briefly, the CCNT and the Northern Territory government initially, in the Cobourg Act of 1981, had indicated a formal willingness to share power with the Aboriginal owners through the board of management, but the CCNT as an agency was uneven in its commitment to the Cobourg experiment. In contrast, the ANPWS and the federal government had a more homogeneous commitment of their personnel to the Kakadu experiment, but had not been willing to share formal power with the Aboriginal owners. Their highly centralist nature may have been a positive force in the formation of the park, but it was an undeniable obstacle to Aboriginal participation, as it was to the initiatives of Kakadu park staff in many aspects of daily management.

However, some evidence from both park agencies did suggest that the contrastive picture above was changing gradually. In the CCNT new personnel were not only bringing a high caliber of expertise to the agency, they were also committed to developing the CCNT's capacity to work with Aboriginal communities in the territory. And the NLC had received indications that the ANPWS would be willing to support a "joint planning approach" in the preparation of the new plan of management for Kakadu.

Concluding Observations

Empirically based studies of joint management systems involving indigenous minorities with national parks are exceedingly rare. Existing studies are often prescriptive, and ignore the inherently political nature of the relationship between parks and indigenous peoples. This chapter presented findings from a field-based research project that sought to determine the extent to which Aboriginals participated in the joint management systems of Cobourg and Kakadu national parks.

It was found that in neither park did joint management systems operate as defined above in terms of the formal sharing of day-to-day authority in administering the parks. There was no evidence that Aboriginal owners wanted the coresponsibility of daily management. Rather, the Aboriginal owners sought a joint policy and planning role, one in which they could coshape the key values (policy) guiding the parks' operations and development, and influence the steps (planning) by which these values would be interpreted and implemented. However, the Aboriginal owners in neither park had, in any de facto sense, a joint policy and planning role, a role that gave them the same opportunities as the park agencies to make decisions on the park's activities. The findings indicate that there was much less power sharing between park agencies and Aboriginal owners than government rhetoric and legislation suggested and that the process of Aboriginal involvement at all levels—policy, planning, and management—in both parks had essentially just begun.

However, learning from Cobourg and Kakadu had already begun in Australia. It was possible to discern an evolutionary trend toward joint mechanisms from Kakadu, the first experiment, to Cobourg, to the Jawoyn-Katherine Gorge proposals, and to Uluru or Ayers Rock (see Uluru 1986). The trend appeared to have moved from informal (Kakadu) to formal (Cobourg) mechanisms for Aboriginal participation, from advisory to authoritative powers for Aboriginal owners, from a management focus to a policy and planning focus for Aboriginal input, and from the absence of formal boards to boards composed of Aboriginals and non-Aboriginals with policy as well as planning functions. Although Cobourg set the legal precedent for joint policy structures in its Act, in practice it had not yet achieved a joint operational status. Its legal precedent, however, became the basis for the NLC's draft Jawoyn Act, which proposed a board with central policy and planning functions, a reality achieved in large measure in the case of Uluru. Such overall trends suggested that Aboriginal demands for real authority in park operations would continue and would intensify in the future.

NOTES

Data for this paper derive from fieldwork in Australia for a total of eight months in 1984–85 (April to August of each year). The data consist of field observations in the two parks; of in-depth interviews with most of the key Aboriginal and parks personnel (at the local, regional [Darwin] and national [Canberra] levels), and relevant academics; and of relevant documentation provided by the parks agencies and the NLC. I wish to thank the Social Sciences and Humanities Research Council of Canada for funding this research, the NLC and the Aboriginal people in both parks for permission to undertake the work, the CCNT and ANPWS for their generous assistance, and the Australian National University's North Australia Research Unit in Darwin for logistical support in fieldwork.

1. The NLC is the federally created statutory body responsible for representing, in land claims negotiations, the interests of Aboriginal communities in the northern half of the Northern Territory (including Aboriginal residents of Cobourg and Kakadu). The NLC is based in Darwin whereas the Central Land Council (CLC), which represents the interests of Aboriginals in the southern half of the Northern Territory (including Uluru National Park), is based in Alice Springs.

2. The planning process to the point of formal completion, including NLC approval in both cases, took one year longer than anticipated. Cobourg's first plan was officially approved in mid-1986 and Kakadu's second plan was finally approved in late 1986 (ANPWS 1986).

3. See Neidjie, Davis and Fox (1985) for an interesting account of Aboriginal culture by one of the Aboriginal cultural advisers, Bill Neidjie.

4. The Cobourg Act of 1981, the Northern Territory statute specifying the conditions of joint management of the park, was negotiated by the NLC and the CCNT in lieu of a more conventional land-claim settlement under the federal Aboriginal Land Rights (Northern Territory) Act 1976.

5. The Board meets quarterly, but discussion of park matters occurs more frequently and informally in the monthly supervisors meetings on Cobourg attended by the four Aboriginal board members and CCNT officers from Darwin as well as the chief ranger (park superintendent).

6. See Gillespie (1983) and Sullivan (1984) for very useful discussions of rock art management issues.

7. See Smyth, Taylor, and Willis (1986) for a very useful report on Aboriginal ranger training.

8. Australian Institute of Aboriginal Studies, "Comments and Recommendations on the Kakadu National Park Plan of Management," May 30, 1980, Canberra.

9. For an excellent analysis of the fire management issue in regard to Aboriginal knowledge, see Lewis (1989).

10. See Levitus (1982) for a social history of Aborigines in the Kakadu (Alligator Rivers) Region.

27   Joint Management of Canada's Northern National Parks

Ken M. East

| PROTECTED AREA | 1. The Western Arctic Claim |
| | 2. Wood Buffalo National Park |

| CLASSIFICATION | Labeled as: National Park |
| | Managed as: Resident Peoples Multiple Use Management Area, Category IX |

| RESIDENT PEOPLES | Acculturated Tribal Peoples |

Willie Courtoreille and Jackson Whiteknife are the native trappers in Wood Buffalo National Park. Normally, they spend three or four months a year on the land pursuing an

occupation that has been in their families for over two hundred years. For another three or four months each year, they
are fire fighters, helping to protect the land that they rely on
for furs in the winter. Jackson and Willie are also involved in
joint management. As representatives on a wildlife advisory
board, they have a considerable role to play in determining
how a portion of Canada's largest national park will be managed. They believe that their relationship to the land entitles
them to input. They believe their knowledge of the land is
reason enough that they be involved in the resource management decisions affecting that land.

This chapter is not about political self-determination for
native people in Canada's north. It is not about how the native organizations that represent Willie and Jackson are attempting to define a new political future for Canada's native
people. Rather, it is about efforts to provide native people
who live in and around some of Canada's northern national
parks with an opportunity to influence and determine how
those parks are to be managed.

This chapter will attempt to describe the dynamic political
environment in which northern joint management strategies
are evolving and will describe two joint management regimes that have been established and protected by law.
Finally, some of the opportunities and constraints of joint
management will be identified.

Why joint management? Why is the concept being specifically applied to Canada's native people—particularly in the
north? The answer to these questions is rooted in the unique
relationship of native people to the land. Whittington
(1985:65) advised a Royal Commission on Canada's Economic Prospects that, to the Dene and Inuit, "the land and
its resources are held in reverence for it is the fruits of the
land upon which the community must depend for survival."
The aspirations are simple enough. Native people want to decide what is going to happen on land they regard as theirs.

The case for increased native control over decisions affecting northern lands is compelling. Feit (1983) argues that
there is a tradition of management amongst northern natives: that the literature strongly supports the existence of
native wildlife management systems in the pre-government
period and probably in the pre-European contact period.

Usher (1983), in the same publication, describes the management systems that existed in earlier times. The description establishes clear and predictable territorial usage: a local system that accorded "certain pre-eminent rights of use and occupancy" to households or other subunits; and "a set of customs and rules that regulated . . . foraging behavior so as to ensure the survival and harmony of the group." Usher concludes that "the native peoples who now live in arctic and sub-arctic Canada not only occupied distinct territories according to systematic patterns since aboriginal times, but also had relatively stable systems of political authority, land tenure, and rules for resource harvesting, and if their continued existence over generations is anything to go by, these systems worked." The tradition of organized wildlife management regimes amongst native people in Canada's North has been further documented by Gunn et al. (1988) and Feit (1988).

Despite Weaver's (1984:64) contention that "the system of financing, rather than the needs of people, has become the driving force in [government] policy formulation" and her conclusion by extension that government is unlikely to be receptive to the notion of native self-government, there are indications that the situation is changing.

The Constitution Act of 1982 confirms the special status of native people in Canada by affirming the "aboriginal, treaty or other rights or freedoms that pertain to the aboriginal peoples of Canada." The Act further offers protection for these "rights or freedoms" against infringement by other legislation including the Charter of Rights incorporated elsewhere in the Act. This protection will take many years, if not generations, and many legal interpretations to find tangible expression.

Cumming (1985:732) argues that "the special hunting and fishing rights extended by land cession treaties" are examples of rights protected by Section 25 of the Act. It may be further argued that the broader protection of aboriginal hunting and fishing rights on lands not covered by treaty is provided by Section 35. Merritt (1983:75), in turn, suggests that these sections demand "meaningful and influential Native involvement in land management and planning and decisions on Crown lands." Merritt interprets this to mean "guaranteed representation" on management committees and boards. Attempts by the federal government to settle outstanding aboriginal claims have provided the mechanism for implementing this representation. *Calder et al.* v. *Attorney General of British Columbia* in 1973 established clearly the principle of aboriginal land title. This effectively forced the federal government to introduce a policy statement later that year committing itself to move toward the resolution of claims.

Precedent was established by the James Bay and Northern Quebec Agreement and the Northeastern Quebec Agreement. These 1975 settlements provided the Inuit with a form of public regional government and the Cree with an alternative form of Indian Government "based on existing Band Council Structures" (Canada 1985b:24; Moss 1985). These structures were then responsible for evolving the resource management mechanisms to be used in conjunction with the provincial government to ensure management of the land in the interest of both parties.

The Report of the Task Force to Review Comprehensive Claims Policy, *Living Treaties: Lasting Agreements* (Canada 1985a:55), advised the government on the importance of the land and control over the land to aboriginal people.

> Many of the objectives of claims policy cannot be achieved unless aboriginals play an active role in decisions concerning lands and resources within their traditional areas. Because their culture is deeply rooted in the land, it cannot be protected and enhanced if the land and resources are managed unwisely. . . . Moreover, we believe that, as a matter of principle, aboriginal people should be able to participate in the decisions which affect them.

The federal government in *The Comprehensive Claims Policy* (Canada 1987:14) accepted the involvement principles espoused by the task force and incorporated them into the official policy governing the negotiation of comprehensive claims.

Settlements are expected to recognize particular aboriginal interests in relation to environmental concerns, particularly as these concerns relate to wildlife management and the use of water and land. Provision for the exercise of such interests may be afforded through membership on advisory committees, boards, and similar bodies that have decision-making powers.

Although the policy supports aboriginal involvement in land and resource management decisions, the policy stops short of accepting George Erasmus' objective, "We want to be our own boss." The task force observes that "governments have an overriding obligation to protect rights of all users and manage resources within their particular jurisdictions. Thus governments cannot abdicate their functions through a wholesale delegation of decision-making powers." This caution is reflected in the claims policy.

The National Parks Experience

Many natives contend that this constraint on the limits of their effective authority over land and resource management makes the whole involvement process meaningless. Support of this position is provided by observers like Lawson (1985:54), who argues that local advisory committees at Auyittuq National Park "advise the Superintendent, but make no decisions on issues affecting the Inuit." Lawson contends that this is "inadequate" participation in park planning and management.

Is Lawson correct or is he simply articulating a somewhat idealistic objective that is inappropriate for the management of Crown land or for application to an agency with a national mandate? It may be argued that Lawson and others who espouse this position, do so without real understanding of decision making in the public sector, without a balanced perspective of the motives of public servants, and without a practical appreciation of the demands of resource management at the field level.

Above all, Lawson might be simply out of date in a field that is evolving faster than the literature can keep pace. Since 1985, one major comprehensive claim (Western Arctic) and several specific claims have been finalized and implemented. Two claims particularly—Western Arctic and Fort Chipewyan Cree—will affect existing or proposed national parks in the north and provide formalized joint management regimes that are constitutionally ingrained. Three similar agreements are at or near the agreement-principle state. These agreements define a new style for the management of national parks in the north—a style that has evolved solely for the purpose of providing native people with a profound influence over park management.

Progress toward the development of joint park management regimes in Canada has largely been restricted to the north. One explanation for this is the existence of national park policy that promotes joint management specifically for the north. Section 1.3.13 of Parks Canada Policy, 1978, states:

> Where now national parks are established in conjunction with the settlement of land claims of native people, an agreement will be negotiated between Parks Canada and representatives of local native communities prior to formal establishment of the national park creating a joint management regime for the planning and management of the national park. (Canada 1978)

Another explanation for the emergence of joint management regimes in the north relates to a set of unique geopolitical realities that make it an ideal host environment. First, the north has been the target of most of the comprehensive land claims in Canada under active negotiation. Settlements to date have included provisions to ensure protection of the land and of the hunting and trapping traditionally carried out on those lands. According of "park" status is one of these mechanisms. Either the land in the north was never ceded by formal treaty or government has recognized that the basis of at least one treaty is somewhat uncertain.

An important element of claim settlements to date has been their inclusion of provisions to ensure protection of the land and protection of the hunting and trapping traditionally carried out on those lands. Several mechanisms have been developed through the claims process to ensure protection of the lands.

Native negotiators see park lands as an opportunity to protect these areas and significantly influence their management without selecting them as part of their final land allocation. Park officials, on the other hand, see the claims process as an alternative approach to adding areas of importance to the park system. Both parties accept that some form of joint management regime is a prerequisite to accord.

Secondly, new northern parks offer opportunities to pioneer alternative management regimes unhindered by history. They are often unhindered by influential nonnative interests or constituencies with conflicting objectives. The efficacy of other interests is often marginal.

Thirdly, neither the Yukon nor the Northwest Territories

is fully self-governing. They are federally administered territories with elected legislatures that have many, but not all, provincial powers. The Provinces, for example, have jurisdiction over land while the Territories have influence but not absolute jurisdiction. This permits the federal government to negotiate almost directly with native representatives for the establishment of new parks.

Finally, discussions are underway, particularly in the Northwest Territories, to define a system of government(s) to replace the status quo. These discussions are evolving a unique, locally based and consensual style of government clearly resembling traditional native government. This style seems likely to be more consistent with the notion and objectives of joint management than does the European style of timed debate and decision.

The Western Arctic

These considerations provided the backdrop for settlement of the Western Arctic Claim, the most recent, large, comprehensive claim settled by the federal government. The claim covered 435,000 square kilometers of traditionally used and occupied Inuvialuit land in the Mackenzie Delta–Western Arctic Islands region.

In the settlement, which draws its authority from constitutionally protected federal legislation passed in 1984, the Inuvialuit received title to approximately 91,000 square kilometers—including 11,000 square kilometers with full surface and subsurface rights. Considerable financial compensation was provided for as well as a series of economic and employment measures designed to provide for the economic self-sufficiency of the Inuvialuit and the region.

In the area of environmental management, the Final Agreement provides the Inuvialuit with guaranteed representation in structures, functions, and decisions involving wildlife management. The "goal," according to the *The Guide to the Final Agreement,* is to apply "the knowledge and experience of both Inuvialuit and the scientific community to the task of conserving the wildlife resource" (Canada 1985b).

An Inuvialuit Game Council will be responsible for appointing Inuvialuit members to the various other joint bodies with an interest in wildlife; advising governments in wildlife management matters; assigning hunting and trapping areas, determining quotas and generally overseeing wildlife-related matters. Numerous other committees and councils are established by the settlement legislation to provide for formal consideration of a multitude of environmental management matters.

Of special interest to this chapter is the designation of the Yukon North Slope as a special management zone and the establishment by settlement legislation of a national park in that zone. The legislation requires that the park be zoned and managed as a wilderness. The legislation also requires that any change in the "character" of the park be with the consent of the Inuvialuit.

Ongoing involvement for Inuvialuit in park planning and management is provided for through another Wildlife Management Advisory Council (North Slope) with equal native and government representation. Indeed, the structure of this committee is such that the park is not guaranteed representation or even observer status with the committee. Although the name of the committee implies that it is "advisory," the legislation requires that the committee *recommend* the management plan. This could have the legal effect that the Inuvialuit must approve the proposed Management Plan before it is submitted to the minister. Given the role of the management plan to establish the nature of any activities permitted within the park and to define the fundamental management perspective toward the park, it is influential indeed.

Finally, the legislation is insistent that the Inuvialuit will be the principle beneficiaries of any economic benefits associated with the park. The "predominant number of persons employed in the operation and management of the (national park) . . . should be Inuvialuit." In addition, any other economic activities arising out of the existence of the park are to be "provided to the Inuvialuit on a preferred basis."

Implementation of the parks-related provisions of the settlement has been slow. The Wildlife Advisory Council (North Slope) did not meet until May 1988 due to a variety of difficulties experienced in organizing and staffing all the boards and other structures provided for in the claim.

Initial Parks Service concern that the overall consultative–joint management structure might be too large and complex given the area and number of beneficiaries involved appears more recently to have been overstated. Although both parties experienced early difficulties in staffing all the

Boards, this problem has been overcome. All boards appear to be functioning and gradually defining a clearer role for themselves.

Parks Service staff have been surprised at the degree of involvement sought by the Inuvialuit in daily operational decision making and are concerned that the technical and administrative time required to interact with the various boards was underestimated. On the other hand, they feel that the Inuvialuit "can play a strong role in the conservation of park resources" and that the Agreement "add[s] another layer of protection" to the National Parks Act (Dolan per. com.).

The Cree Band Settlement

The second example of a formally established joint management regime affecting a national park is the Fort Chipewyan Cree Band Settlement involving Wood Buffalo National Park signed in December 1986. This settlement is the resolution of a long-standing specific claim to ensure final satisfaction of government obligations arising out of the signing of Treaty No. 8 in 1899.

If one were to search for a park to be a target for joint management experimentation, it is unlikely that one would find a better candidate than Wood Buffalo. It is a long-established park with an equally long tradition of native resource harvesting. Indeed, much of its early management under the Northern Affairs Branch was predicated more on an objective of maximizing native economic return from the park than on the accomplishment of more conventional park goals such as tourism and resource protection.

This area is a giant (44,000 sq. km) and inaccessible wilderness that receives very little use by other than native hunters and trappers. In other words, there are very few non-native interests that are likely to feel actively alienated by establishment of a bipartite regime.

There is, however, a recent and modest history of hunter-trapper involvement in resource management decisions. Much of the early management of the park differed little from the government's arbitrary and paternalistic approach to native people elsewhere. In recent years, however, efforts have been made to create consultative structures through the establishment of the Wood Buffalo Park Hunters and Trappers Association (HTA) and through management of trapping using the Group Area system. This system provides for considerable effective control over trapping in specific areas by the actual trappers who have formal membership in that area.

The Cree Band Settlement has been extensively described in Waquin (1986) and East (1986). They list the major provisions as follows:

Guarantees of perpetual hunting, fishing and trapping rights for Cree Band members in a three million acre parcel known as the "tradition area."

Establishment of a Wildlife Advisory Board to advise the Minister on many aspects of the management of the traditional area of interest. The Cree Band will have the majority of voting members on the Board.

Authority given to the above Board to determine who amongst Cree Band members will receive hunting and trapping permits for the "traditional area" in any given year and, by implication, to determine how many permits will be issued.

"Rights of first refusal" on economic activities which might be developed in the traditional area of interest.

Preferential access to training and employment opportunities in the park, particularly the southern end.

The board has now been established. On the Cree Band side, most of its representatives are active hunters and trappers. The government, for its part, has used its representation to ensure that nonbeneficiary Metis interests are represented in the discussions. Initial discussions have indicated that the board will wish to be involved in the full range of park management matters from long-term strategic planning to daily operational response.

It is already clear that considerable benefit will accrue to park management from the existence of the board. The board, as a formal and funded entity, has taken over the consultative duties of the former Wood Buffalo Park HTA. It has accepted its responsibility to consult native park users and represent their interests on the board. Indeed, as mentioned in earlier comments (East 1986:92), "no longer will park management face the uncertainty of trying to determine who they ought to consult with on what issues."

Other benefits will include the existence of a widely recognized forum for conflict resolution and formal access to a significant body of knowledge on park resources. Finally, the existence of this structure formalizes the "vested" interest of the Cree people in the park and provides decision-making access to people with a greater stake in the future of the land than perhaps is the stake held by transitory government officials.

The Outstanding Issues of Joint Management

Structures are now being put in place that will provide for the active involvement of native people in the management of Canada's northern national parks. The provisions described are the only ones formally "on the books" to date; however, negotiations are underway to provide essentially the same structures for all other northern parks including the northern sector of Wood Buffalo.

Existence of the structures will not be a guarantee of their success. The question of "advice versus authority" raised by Lawson (1985) and East (1986) will continue to stimulate comment. In according powers to the various boards and committees, the government has stopped short of giving outright authority beyond a narrowly defined range of considerations. Is this an expression of a legitimate government obligation to protect the broader interest? Or is it a statement that the government is not really interested in according real power to native people?

Although there is no absolute answer to that question, those who consider it should do so with an understanding of the real dynamics of decision making in the public service. Ministers do not make all the decisions regarding park management; in fact, they make very few of them. Invoking of ministerial involvement in a decision is generally a reflection that the matter has some major political implications. The majority of decisions regarding the management of a park are made at the park level. The actual dynamics of park-level "advisory" boards will be based in a mutual desire to ensure that as few issues as possible are directed to the minister or up through more senior levels of the bureaucracy. This will effectively create a consensual park-board relationship.

"Mutuality of Objective" will continue to be a thorny issue in the functioning of joint management regimes. The objectives of the national parks program are not always the same as those of the native people who live in and around the parks. Park policy has made some considerable concessions in recognition of native aspirations and traditional use, and indeed there are those who contend that the emerging northern park model is incompatible with conventional park standards because of those concessions.

This recognition should also include agreement that other interests in the park must be accommodated. The Metis people, for example, have a long tradition of use of the southern area of Wood Buffalo. Their interests must be protected as must the interests of nonparticipants who wish to use the park for nonconsumptive recreation and the concerns of scientists and researchers who use parks for study.

Despite clauses providing for preferential access to employment and economic benefits, all parties must be cognizant of the existence of substantial numbers of nonparticipants in the affected area, which are, in fact, a majority in some cases. Outright denial of opportunities to these groups will not be well received.

Existing regulatory styles and mechanisms will not be conducive to effective joint management. Regulatory change is a ponderously slow process and at the present time is not able to respond to suggestions to alter management regimes to accommodate often rapidly changing natural conditions. Those involved in joint management will wish to see evidence that their input is regarded as meaningful and has impact. There is a considerable danger of frustration developing amongst the parties if responsiveness is not evident.

On the other hand, some aspects of park management demand the capacity to respond quickly to deal with immediate resource concerns or park user needs. Expeditious response to urgent problems may not be possible if consultation is demanded on every issue. Some adaptation of the process will be required to ensure that capacity for rapid response when required still exists.

Finally, there is the danger that joint management, particularly when conferred via the comprehensive claim route, could lead to the creation of parallel bureaucracies that are every bit as cumbersome as those that existed in pre-agreement days. The Western Arctic Claim, with its numerous levels of consultative committees, might be a case in point. The potential of such a structure to react expeditiously to "grass roots" needs is questionable. Indeed, the capability of both the government and native organizations to provide members for all the boards and committees remains to be seen over the longer term.

Conclusion   The foregoing chapter has attempted to describe the evolution and structure of Canadian efforts to provide for the meaningful involvement of aboriginal people in the management of some national parks. It has briefly traced the legal recognition of aboriginal title to national policy statements which commit the government to negotiating outstanding claims and also to providing for the membership of aboriginal representatives on decision-making bodies.

Joint management structures have been established to provide significant aboriginal involvement in the operation of two national parks in the north and there are relatively immediate prospects for others to follow.

Whether the structures provide for meaningful deviation from the centralized planning–decision-making models conventionally applied in Western democracies is in some dispute. Final authority for all decisions continues to rest legally with the minister, and thus, no real power has been transferred. On the other hand, alternative models have been effectively unable to guarantee adequate accountability to the full range of stakeholders in a very heterogeneous population.

Many issues have yet to be addressed. Can there be mutuality of objective? Can some form of joint accountability be attached to joint management? How can nonparticipant interests be protected? The answers to these questions and many others are obscured for the moment in the haze of the future. There is no tested and true formula for joint management. Adaptation to newly learned realities will be the prerequisite for ultimate success.

COMMENT

28   Some Reflections on Participation and Co-management from Zambia's Central Luangwa Valley

Stuart A. Marks

I have returned to Zambia's central Luangwa Valley nearly a quarter century after doing my initial ecological and social research here. The central valley is still spatially remote, especially during the rainy season. To reach my present location, one travels four days by foot with carriers, east from the administrative post atop the Muchinga escarpment. This year will be spent much as on the previous occasion: on surveying household activities and decision making; on making observations on resource uses and their current levels; on participating in rituals and seasonal rounds of work, always asking questions while struggling to answer those asked; and on attempting to describe the many dimensions of cultural, social, economic, and environmental changes brought by time.

My current surroundings are bereft of the accessories normally associated with scholarly writing. Most of my goods were brought in on the heads and shoulders of others. For reflecting on what might be going on in their heads while peering over their shoulders to interpret their behavior, perhaps this isolated place is better than most for considering the agendas for national park and wildlife management in central Africa. Local participation, co-management, and social impact assessments are concepts and tactics forged in the struggle between Western ideas and institutions and the realities and concerns of other cultures. For these ideals to become effective in development, they must be matched by actions stimulated by new ways of perceiving and behaving in a more inclusive world. Since the book's introduction has a precautionary tale written in the 1970s and attributed to me, I use this occasion to review the more obvious continuities and changes observed in the central Luangwa Valley and to examine the broader prospects for wider participation in wildlife management there and for co-management.

The Place

The spatial isolation of the central Luangwa Valley has been asserted above. In most directions, the Munyamadzi Corridor, some 30 to 50 kilometers in width, follows the Munyamadzi River eastward from its tumble over the abrupt Muchinga escarpment and is surrounded on three sides by national parks. The North Luangwa and South Luangwa national parks form its longest borders. The eastern boundary, some 60 kilometers from the escarpment, is the Luangwa River. This river is also a provincial boundary within Zambia and is the western boundary of yet another national park, Luambe. The vast wildlife estate of the valley was demarcated during the late 1930s as game reserves. In common with most wildlife sanctuaries in this part of the world, these decisions were made without local consultation. The lines were drawn initially by colonial fiat and reflected outsider perceptions and political concerns over the declines in African wildlife. In the process of boundary marking, the colonial officers shifted a few villages and their residents to make their lines coincide with important topographic features. These game reserves became national parks during the early 1970s (Chapter 316, Laws of Zambia).

Stocks of elephant and other larger mammals have been the magnets attracting outsiders to the valley for several centuries. Even the valley's present inhabitants are probably no more than a few centuries in residence. Wildlife is still found in the valley. Outside interests and influences are here as well, more visible and entrenched than before.

People are also residents in this valley in increasing numbers. In some places their habitations and fields abut the boundaries of the national parks. In the late 1930s the Munyamadzi Corridor and its several thousand inhabitants were left alone as an expedient. The colonial government of Northern Rhodesia hoped eventually to induce its inhabitants to shift by promising them amenities elsewhere. This plan to shift the corridor's inhabitants, the Valley Bisa, was never realized and, with the achievement of Zambian independence in 1964, forced resettlement became politically unacceptable.

The Valley Bisa today number some eight to nine thousand people who live in scattered settlements along the Munyamadzi and Mupamadzi rivers and their tributaries. In fertile pockets along these rivers, the Valley Bisa grow varieties of sorghums, maize, millet, pumpkins, and a few other crops mainly for subsistence. The abundant tsetse flies, carriers of the blood parasite Trypanosoma, precludes the keeping of domestic livestock. Tobacco, chickens, and smoked fish are the main exports for cash. Wild game meat is also a commodity that figures in both subsistence and commercial exchanges.

In the following sections I sketch the more prominent continuities and changes for the corridor within the past twenty-five years. I use these circumstances to sketch an agenda that features local participation and co-management with outside authorities.

Some Continuities

Outsiders and their interests in the valley's wild mammals have been a source of contention with residents for many decades. In these contentious encounters, outsiders have often seemed to hold the upper hand, for their orientations have become sanctioned in national laws and enforced, often with "negotiated modifications," by resident officials. On the surface, the issue is that of access and at what price. At deeper levels are the personal issues of cultural identity, livelihood, and ways of coping in a rapidly changing world.

Within the corridor, conflict occurs not so much between utilitarian and aesthetic values as the forms utilitarianism takes. The controversies have become more pronounced and bitter as wildlife has grown scarcer throughout rural Zambia. For government, wildlife in the corridor provides an important source of foreign exchange through the yearly sales of licenses and safari concessions during the dry seasons. For safari hunters, these fees are quoted in U.S. dollars and the hunters expect record-bearing trophies and vistas populated by abundant game. For some outsiders living on the adjacent western plateau, wildlife within the corridor has become a legal way of generating species for investments elsewhere. A

Kwacha 150 investment in a buffalo license can return over
Kwacha 4000 if the meat from the dead animal is dried,
smoked, and sold on the plateau where animal proteins are
scarce. For still other outsiders, some with rapid-fire weapons
and friends in high places as well as others without such con-
ventions, the elephant, rhino, hippo, and buffalo in the valley
provide an even higher rate of return. Both run a small risk
of capture by the game scouts and, once caught, of nominal
fines. For the resident valley Bisa, wildlife is for consumption
within the household and for earning some income from the
sale of meat or from collusion with outsiders, given appropriate conditions and circumstances. Locals feel that they pay
yearly and dearly in terms of lives, limbs, and agricultural
production for keeping the wildlife around.

Outsiders blame the locals for the reduction of wildlife.
Locals place the blame on some corrupt officials and on outsider poaching with modern weapons and machines. If the
truth were known, both groups have made considerable in-
roads into the valley's wildlife. Yet it is locals who face the
constant threat of harassment and illicit dealing with the
resident game scouts for their utilitarian impulses. Scout
raids, accompanied by military and paramilitary forces,
oftentimes feature abusive use of force and needless im-
proprieties. Whereas these raids may pick up a few un-
registered muzzleloading guns and wire snares, they also
keep alive local memories of injustices and disillusionment
with government-sponsored programs. So far, the raids have
done little to dissuade the commercial scale of outside poaching. And local gossip and knowledge of the illegal activities
of civil servants, especially by those who are the supposedly
legal guardians of the wildlife, make a mockery of any local
compliance with proclaimed laws.

Outsiders have been long on promises, short on delivery.
Rarely have those things discussed with monetary enthusiasm materialized in delivering the benefits promised. Early
in 1988, representatives from an international donor agency
with a reputation for preserving nature appeared within the
corridor. They came to launch a new initiative: local people
would henceforth benefit from wildlife. The unspoken bottom
line was that these benefits would be on outsider terms and
ideas. The external donor was to provide much of the initial
funding for vehicles and for operating expenses. After a few

years the project was expected to generate its own recurrent expenses and thereby become self-sustaining. District and local wildlife management authorities and their committees were to be established. Funds for local discretion were set at 35 percent of safari concession fees. The majority of the remaining funds would support the village scout and management programs and be for use by the national tourist board. The district warden was to implement the plans, to inform everyone of the new rules, and to place the committees.

Since this initiative occurred the momentum to implement the program has built. The warden held one organizational meeting during which those attending were told what persons would constitute the local committee—the majority were civil servants. His lack of motivation was locally interpreted in terms of his reputation for profiting from the previous arrangements. He held the meeting just before being transferred to another district and while under investigation for illegal collusion with poachers in which a machine gun was implicated. Fresh from training for his new position, the unit commander spent much of his time running errands on the plateau in the new Toyota. While still under his control, the payroll for local workers was stolen. A personality clash between him and the warden resulted in the unit commander's dismissal, leaving the local authority in leaderless limbo for most of the year. And the new Toyota truck, which local people believed was to help their development efforts, was rarely seen. When seen in the corridor, it was rarely without a heavy load of buffalo meat. To learn that some of this meat was taken as allocation rations for the scouts was to miss the local perspective.

My motive in mentioning these moves, countermoves, decisions, and interpretations is that behind each is found powerful entrenched interests. Outsiders have profited most from the past system of license allocation, repressive measures, and protocols and conveniences for legally taking wildlife. New organizations and initiatives confront and must supplant these interests if they are to have impact on the flow of events.

Spatial isolation and government reluctance to consider major capital improvements within the valley have contributed to entrenchment of these attitudes and behaviors. Despite these barriers, changes in local behavior and actions are noticeable. They also reflect vested interests.

Some Changes

Under the tenure of the chief who reigned from 1934 to 1984, Bisa lands were alienated for national parks. This chief was a firm believer in witchcraft as the reason for human malaise and was one of its major practitioners. A local palliative for witchcraft is social and spatial distance between kin. By the time of his death in 1984, the structure of the village life had changed. Lineage members were no longer living together in definable villages. They were scattered, instead, in settlements of one or few households, with each homestead protecting its crops and belongings from real and supposed calamities. The "traditional" norms of community living under the leadership of an elder, always exaggerated by memories, are eclipsed currently by rough individualism, mutual suspicion, and opportunism. Concurrently, most of the reciprocal relations among lineage members have been monetized with tangible difference appearing between haves and have nots. Most material possessions today belong in a few hands.

After the new chief assumed leadership in 1984, it took him four years to rally his lineage segment against contenders. One contender, not in the "normal" line of succession but with powerful outside allies, obtained temporary ascendancy. There may be some truth in the gossip that these allies were heavily into poaching elephants and rhinos. The new chief was affirmed in August 1988 prior to the national elections. His demeanor is that of a civil servant and he has spent much of his adult life as an entrepreneur on the Copperbelt. He professes not to believe in witchcraft and is desperately pushing economic developments in the corridor. During his first tour as chief he reiterated his goals. Among them are a return to "normal" village settlement, the completion of an airstrip enabling the flying doctors access in cases of medical emergencies, the manufacture and burning of bricks to build a local secondary school, and the formation of cooperative societies to bring in basic commodities. He is a staunch supporter and beneficiary of the current wildlife initiatives.

Most of the proposed projects are self-help with the funds derived from the wildlife authority designated for purchases of nonlocal materials and for maintaining the road. It will be a long struggle building local support for these projects. Within the corridor, the chief is assisted by a few others, who, having spent much of their working lives elsewhere, have returned to the valley. They bring their skills and a different perspective from those who have long lived there. Keeping development dreams alive while making viable alliances within and without the valley remains the leadership challenge.

As young men and women mature in an increasingly materialistic world, they see little in their elders' lives worth emulating. Many have refused the discipline of communal living and opt for personal gain at community expense. The decade of the 1980s saw several famines produced by poor and widely distributed rainfall. These ecological strains encouraged people, especially the young, to cope in unprecedented ways.

The lower primary school, established in 1957, now includes seven grades with four teachers in residence. One former student has graduated from a university, five from secondary schools. Even these meager results provide an alternative to the local webs of lineage and poverty that ensnare most people. Besides the civil service, seasonal employment within the safari camps, and the new village scout program, there are few job opportunities within the valley. For most men, options remain subsistence farming and opportunistic windfalls of gain or migrant marginal labor. Women remain the backbone of household subsistence, spending much of each day providing essentials for themselves and their dependents. And with increases in population they must increase their times for firewood and water collection.

What this patchwork of continuities and changes has to do with wildlife and national park management is the subject for the next section. I argue that the connections between perceptions and behaviors are pervasive, that what one proposes to do about wildlife concerns values and ideas about how the world and society work. Ideas about society and wildlife are separated only within a truncated epistemology that within the western world has become part of the professional mantle in an age of specialization.

Some Ideas   The ways in which the word "participation" is often used in discourse and documents suggest that increased participation inevitably produces a more democratic and equitable society. In many ways, participation in development accentuates inequality with influence and resources going to those who are already influential and powerful while those with less benefit little or not at all. The tendency of local leaders and elites to capture projects and programs to use for their own benefits must be recognized. The aims of good leadership and management on the one hand and distribution and equity on the other hand are likely to remain persistent and difficult features of any development project striving toward increased participation.

Local participation may be analyzed in terms of who participates, what institutions are involved, and what functions and objectives these institutions have (Chambers 1974). Those from the "top-down" originate with government or external donors and the benefits supposedly percolate outwards into rural areas through specific projects. Often these projects are conceived without sufficient grounding in cultural and social research. Projects originating among rural people are directed upwards to the government hierarchies for assistance and support. The essence of a "bottom-up" project based on self-help is that people themselves identify their needs and try to satisfy them. Self-help projects can increase local people's confidence and competence in handling their own affairs and may generate a sustained commitment and a greater capacity and creativity for overcoming unforeseen problems.

The history of the central Luangwa shows that current initiatives are imminently top-down with resources and decisions made by outsiders. Given the trend toward the concentration of political power and decision making begun before Zambian independence, leadership and institutions at the local level are mostly lacking or underdeveloped. Given this situation, the current decisions by government toward decentralization and diversification should be applauded and encouraged. Yet the current program assumes that rural people will preserve and protect wildlife simply because government asks them to do so and because they will derive discretionary benefits by going along.

A dilemma of participatory projects is one of achieving the appropriate balances between initiatives of outsiders and insiders, between the flows of money and efforts between those involved, between the level at which devolution takes place and the capacity of decision making at that level. Too much assistance and interference from above can kill sustainability and self-reliance; too little may mean participation in a project is never undertaken and incorporated or, if undertaken, never completed.

Wildlife protection is often a means through which poorer rural people have been denied access and other entitlements to important life-sustaining resources without any, or fair, compensation (S. A. Marks 1984, 1990). National parks and wildlife management areas have been created through the political power of urban dwellers with little consideration for the traumas caused to the welfare of others. John Hough (chapter 19, this volume) proposes social impact assessments as a tool for realizing the adverse conditions such unilateral acts have for rural life and livelihoods. Adverse impacts may take many dimensions—economic, social, cultural, ecological, and technical. In many cases, it may be too late to redress past grievances, yet SIA may be an important method for calling attention to the "quality of life" in rural areas caused by such interventions.

As a resource, wildlife can be managed and owned by a variety of social groupings. These groups range on the one hand from the state and corporations to kin groups and individuals on the other hand. Resource tenure is an important and evolving component of all resource planning, for rights in resources affect their uses in general and the distribution of benefits in particular. Wildlife policies, programs, and projects require a sound tenurial strategy that not only identifies the rules about who can use what, when, and where, but also identifies the institutions that enforce and mediate those rules. Such strategies must be compatible with the capacities of the institutions responsible for implementing and for enforcing those rules. Groups and individuals may have different proprietary attitudes about resources that may not receive formal recognition but which nonetheless affect behavior. Investments of local people in resource-related projects may be conditioned to a large extent by such issues as exclusivity of use and security of tenure. Any prevailing system of tenure, policies, and projects sets the framework for conflicts over benefits.

With the tenure and management of wildlife legally invested in the nation-state in central Africa, there is precious little information of the workings and effectiveness of other systems of tenure. Since most ecologists and biologists are employed by the state and international agencies, there has been little incentive for them to investigate or acknowledge the rights or competence of other types of tenure or regimes. Common property regimes involving wildlife and other resources existed in the central Luangwa Valley and elsewhere until the late 1960s. Thereafter their efficacy was progressively undercut by state power (S. A. Marks 1988). The assumption that the state is the best wildlife manager within unencumbered domains such as within central Luangwa should be evaluated in light of the deteriorating cultural and environmental conditions. Investigations of local systems of tenure and rights with the view of incorporating some of these ideas into a different scheme might provide incentives for motivating toward the conservation of wildlife. Practical questions are how other management schemes arose and worked, under what conditions they persisted, and what makes them locally effective (National Research Council 1986).

Interests in wildlife incorporate both tangible and intangible forms. There are many cultural ways of expressing an interest and concern for wild animals. The existence of the animals themselves is a tangible expression of an interest. Stories, folklore, rites of passage, knowledge of ecological processes, beliefs, and languages are intangible expressions of an interest in wildlife. Local interests in wildlife may take forms other than those with which outsiders are most aware and comfortable. As yet, few resources and little intellectual space have been expended in finding different resolutions to cultural intangibles and motivations.

Since the culture of any group is abstract and ineffable, one must rely on cultural expressions as the overt evidence for differing ideas and of cultural identities. Different ways of perceiving wild animals, as well as different theories, knowledge, and management suggest new ways of synthesis and of putting programs together (American Folklife Center 1983). Given these distinctions, I suggest that expressions of concern for biological diversity must include and be seen to include (Hane's phrase) concern for cultural diversity and identities.

Some Agendas

As a counterweight to the long history of top-down development, initiative of self-help and bottom-up approaches should be encouraged. Granted this objective, the way is opened for new agendas for research and synthesis. Such initiatives include the identity of local organizations and forms that may sustain and enforce regulations meaningful at the local level.

The lives and livelihoods of local people should be discussed and tackled with the same fervor spent on conservation of wildlife. The changes and continuities of past history have implications for all subsequent development projects and consequently must not be lightly dismissed. My argument is that devolution must be more inclusive than heretofore and must include knowledge and perspectives meaningful at each level. Devolution must be based on interpretations of political, cultural, and economic landscapes, in addition to ecological landscapes, including the identification of groups and individuals that are to provide support, the levels of that support, and timing.

I suggest local hunters as an appropriate group for organization and assistance. An active interest in wild animals can be inferred from their persistence, yet their history with outside authorities has been one of intense conflict and subversion. At issue is new knowledge and cultural identity. New knowledge calls for new ways of perceiving development and for whom. While recognizing cases to the contrary, I argue that local residence implies a degree of sophistication about what goes on in the neighboring social and biological spheres that defies the professional trappings of outside managers. The challenge becomes one of recognizing potentialities for cooperation and conflict while working toward their resolution, or at least their recognition. As a study of adjustment, process, and fine tuning, ecological wisdom and oral culture may be untranslatable into "science"; they must be given recognition if projects are to become meaningful locally. Such knowledge and local skills consist of confidence in the present, not necessarily survivals from the distant past. Keeping local-level skills alive and meaningfully embedded in cultural identities, while creating and building institutions to match and to support them, seems an appropriate way to sustain development goals.

A commitment to share authority with local participants and to recognize the value of different ideas and aspirations might begin with the restructuring of local committees. One positive step in this direction could be to divest the committees of so many transient civil servants and include more locals with known interests in wildlife. Resident hunters might be organized into cooperatives or guilds and given priority rights for managing, harvesting, and protecting wildlife.

Organized into cooperatives and given certain priority rights in managing and harvesting wildlife which, if desirable, suggests research into the question of wildlife ownership and tenure. If successful, the organization and development of local hunter guilds might prove an economic and cultural bastion against overwhelming outside influences. Wildlife policies that include property rights and incentives to local people should prove more promising and sustainable than strict preservation policies in which enforcement depends upon constant state intervention and repression.

A Closing Precautionary Tale

Having opened with reflections on the history of a small place, I close with another precautionary tale from the same setting. During the 1960s, expatriate biologists promoted wildlife cropping in the game reserves to demonstrate to the newly independent Zambian government the economic and tangible importance of the valley's wildlife. They knew that Western intangible values were insufficient to convert Zambian politicians, then riding a tidal sweep of nationalistic enthusiasm. In their efforts, these biological managers found support in international experts whose motivation for action was based on the need to reduce the dense concentration of elephants to save the habitat for other species. Elephants and hippos cropped were to feed urban residents and thereby generate revenue for government. There are many wrinkles to the story of why this cropping experiment failed and was stopped abruptly in the early 1970s (S. A. Marks 1984). One interpretation is that the operation was suspended by the personal intervention of influential wildlife people horrified by the prospects of killing wildlife in areas designated for national park status. The project was by then already a dismal financial failure.

Barely a decade later, the same densities of elephants and rhinos were devastated by outsider groups from the plateau, sometimes in collusion with locals. Although greatly reduced in numbers and in tusk size, elephants are still found; rhinos are rarely seen. The tragedy is that "others," not government nor locals, profited from this treasure trove when government political will and finances failed.

Although local participation and different tenurial strategies may avoid some pitfalls and help to circumvent some blind spots in current projects, they are no panacea. A strategy befitting some circumstances may be undermined in time by other forces, by changes in personnel, or by strong insider or outsider interest groups. Wildlife and community life are fluid and both consist of tangible and intangible values. Recognizing the linkages between nature and society implies provisions for the preservation of both, particularly the encouragement of "traditional" (or other) forms of expressive behavior and for the products of that behavior. In this view, provisions to preserve wildlife recognize and involve the affected human community. Wildlife is not just a commodity to be preserved; it is also a process of ongoing evaluations and options.

The end that is sought, the conservation of tangible and intangible aspects of wildlife, will be difficult to achieve. Rather than pour new wine in old skins, perhaps it's time to invest in the production of new conceptual schemes in keeping with the tempo of distant times and places.

Part Seven   AN INTEGRATED CONCLUSION

Children at
Peace Point, a
small Cree
community on
the north shore of
the Peace River,
Wood Buffalo
National Park,
Canada.

Introduction   In the concluding chapter, we the editors attempt, by using a comparative perspective, to integrate the various issues and lines of analysis presented in this book. While drawing on concepts presented in chapter 1, our primary emphasis in this comparative analysis will be on the content of case study chapters and related case study examples found in parts 2–6. This will be supplemented with comparative case studies from other published sources.

Throughout this chapter recommendations for further research and policy are presented, based in part on this comparative analysis. However, the authors of the various chapters should not be held accountable for these recommendations, because they represent our interpretation of the integrated findings based also in part on a set of values that may or may not be fully shared by other authors. For instance, it has now become part of the new conventional wisdom in international conservation circles to view primitive, traditional, tribal groups as compatible with protected area objectives. But the status of marginal peasant populations, and both tribals and peasant peoples who wish to use "nontraditional" technologies of resource extraction, are still suspect. In our frame of values, shared by some but not all our authors, these peoples deserve equal consideration. Even those who are negatively termed "squatters" are in reality impoverished, often landless peasants who have nowhere else to go and thus, in our view, deserve careful consideration. In sum, the issues of rural development among all the rural poor in and around protected areas will receive equal attention as cultural preservation amongst what Dasmann (1984) has romantically termed "ecosystem" peoples.

29 National Parks, Protected Areas, and Resident Peoples: A Comparative Assessment and Integration

Patrick C. West and Steven R. Brechin

There is no way that all the detailed information and perspectives from the foregoing chapters can be recounted and integrated in a concluding summary such as this one. Thus we will attempt to keep our eye on key aspects and dimensions by organizing this analysis around the four basic questions posed in the introduction as being most central and critical to the issue of resident peoples. These again are:

1. Whether or not resident people living in and near protected areas should be displaced and relocated; under what conditions this should or should not be permitted (and if permitted, how it should be done to minimize negative social impacts).
2. To what extent and in what ways resident people residing in or near protected areas should be permitted to utilize natural resources of the area.
3. Under what conditions (if any) the preservation of natural ecosystems, without allowing human use, is necessary for *local* rural development (i.e., local ecodevelopment), and if it is necessary in what specific documented ways.
4. What types of planning, conflict resolution, and decision processes have been or should be established in dealing with these issues on a case-by-case basis.

For each of these major categories we will use the framework of social impact analysis in assessing implications for cultural preservation and rural development, and the relationship and tension between cultural preservation and development. In this regard we will return to Goodland's analysis of the prerequisites for ethnic identity and survival developed in chapter 25, and the three main perspectives on rural development posed in chapter 1, which again are the "top-down," "basic needs," and "bottom-up" strategies for rural development. It has been our working hypothesis that the "bottom-up" strategy holds the greatest potential for integrating conservation and development and for integrating cultural preservation and development objectives. It also provides the best framework for assessing the viability of the "ecodevelopment paradigm" in relation to *local* rural development.

The bottom-up strategy takes as its guiding principles the careful involvement of the rural peoples involved and stresses the direct, pragmatic improvement in ongoing economic production sectors with which they are involved in a way that will be sustainable. More often than not, in rural areas this implies prudent use of local renewable natural resources on a sustainable basis. With respect to rural development, in particular, this perspective has been characterized by Korten and Klauss (1984:2–3) as "a 'growth with equity' strategy directed at expanding the productive use of resources in small-scale agriculture . . . focused on increasing the access of the small farmer and the self-employed to land, water, credit markets and other facilities that would allow them to increase their productivity."

Methodological Considerations

Before embarking on this formidable task of integration, a few observations on the comparative methodological approach are needed for context. We will be seeking to compare and contrast the case studies in this volume and from the broader literature, both to develop some tentative generalizations across cases and to draw out key comparative contrasts among them. For instance, we will seek to understand the key factors that contribute to positive benefits of tourism to local rural development in some cases, and negligible or negative impacts in others.

Cross-national comparative institutional analysis is an important yet difficult task common to many of the social sciences, including sociology, anthropology, history, political science, and economics. Under even the best of methodological circumstances, comparative institutional analysis is strewn with difficulties, especially in relation to "positivist" criteria (Vallier 1971). In this case there are special difficulties imposed by the fact that the case studies we will be comparing are often based on qualitative, impressionistic evidence that various analysts might interpret differently, and by the fact that the case studies were not coordinated to include a consistent set of questions, hypotheses, variables, or measurement indicators. However, this is simply the state of the art at this stage, which we have to live with and yet still hope to learn from. This is the price we pay for placing our primary emphasis on seeking to understand the complex social, historical, and ecological particulars of each institutional case study, in contrast to other attempts to study international protected areas from a comparative perspective using available quantitative data that are always limited (Buttel 1974), or questionnaire survey data of one or a few individual park managers (Machlis and Tichnell 1985) that yield quantified comparative breadth but little depth of understanding of the complex dynamics of each case.

On any given issue we will be comparing different subsets of cases that are judged to be roughly comparable. With respect to some aspects, only one, or several cases, will readily illustrate particular points. Results of this analysis will thus represent qualitative leads and insights, rather than confirmed, proven relationships. At times, however, we will be able to triangulate these conclusions with similar comparative analyses elsewhere in the literature that should strengthen our confidence in the findings. For further discussion and illustration of this qualitative comparative institutional analysis of natural resource policies with a small number of cases, see West (1982a). We begin our comparative analysis with the issue of displacement of resident peoples.

Displacement and Relocation

In chapter 1 and the introduction to part 3 we support the perspective that displacement and relocation can cause severe negative social, economic, and cultural impacts, and thus, should not be done automatically because of exclusionary definitions of national parks or other protected area categories. Rather, it should be used only as a last resort after careful study and planning, and only in situations where it is clearly documented that resident peoples are truly detrimental to park protection objectives *and* where there are adequate alternatives, circumstances, or mitigating measures for relocation that will minimize negative social impacts.

Different parks and protected areas have adopted widely varying policies with respect to the displacement and relocation of peoples residing within, and in some cases near, their boundaries. Some countries will automatically displace resident peoples due to statutory definitions especially for the national parks categories. Uganda (Calhoun, chapter 4), Costa Rica (Kutay, chapter 10), and Ecuador (Bailey, chapter 16) represent examples of this type of across-the-board exclusionary policy with respect to the national parks category. In other countries, peoples are displaced from selected parks where it is felt there is documented evidence of incompatibility with park preservation objectives. Ironically, Gir National Park in India (Raval, chapter 6) is one of the clearer examples of this in our case studies, though it would seem that this action was mistakenly taken based on incorrect assumptions about damage to park wildlife. In other situations, people who lived adjacent to park boundaries were displaced. For instance, in Royal Chitwan National Park in Nepal (Mishra 1982) adjacent villages were relocated to deal with conflicts between local people and wildlife who strayed over the borders of the park.

While countries that displace resident peoples often do so because of emulation of the United States model of national parks embodied in IUCN definitions, it should be recalled from Tucker's historical view (chapter 3) that countries such as India have long been displacing resident peoples from protected areas (in the case of India going back to 1910) before there ever was an IUCN to proselytize the concept. It should also be recalled that the IUCN has backed away from a strict exclusionary policy demanding automatic displacement, especially in the case of primitive tribal societies. At its September 1975 meeting on human rights in Zaire (Kutay 1984), the IUCN stated that "'indigenous' peoples should not normally be displaced from their traditional lands."

Korea (Woo, chapter 17), following the English (Harmon, chapter 2) and Japanese models, presents a primary example of general policies to leave peoples in national parks because of high human density and intensive land use. It should be noted that these are primarily ethnic peasant peoples who have worked and husbanded the land, often for centuries. Other countries have made individual exceptions to a general policy of displacement. For instance, Brazil made special exception to leave the very primitive tribe of the Xingo within a national park (Brechin and Harmon 1983; Bodley 1982). National parks in Australia (Weaver, chapter 26) governed by the outcome of Aboriginal land claims also leave the resident Aboriginal peoples in the park and allow resettlement of other Aboriginals back into these parks.

Some national parks, such as Kinabalu National Park in Malaysia (Jacobson, chapter 21) were situated in areas of low population density and thus did not need to consider the issue of displacement of resident people because none were residing within the boundaries of the park. Others, such as Lake Malawi National Park in Malawi (Croft, chapter 12), redefined the boundaries to exclude settlements of residents.

As noted above, one of the key factors that should be considered in decisions of whether to displace resident peoples is detailed documented evidence that resident peoples are or will irrevocably damage key park resources. The burden of proof should be on the park authorities and the conservation community to demonstrate where this is the case. The case of Gir National Park in India (Raval, chapter 6) illustrates this most clearly. Here, studies conducted indicated that cattle-grazing by the Maldharis in the park was limiting the population of wild ungulates, the natural prey of the Asiatic lion, and therefore was limiting the lion population in the park. Other research, however (Berwick 1976), indicated convincingly that the cattle were not responsible. This research provides documentation that the cattle were grazing on the ground cover, not a major part of the wild ungulates' foraging patterns which were typically the browsing of understory vegetation.

The evidence from the Raval research is clearly strong enough that, at least, the park authorities should have conducted more research to test these findings before they moved unilaterally to displace the Maldharis and restrict their use of the grazing resources.

This case also poignantly illustrates the second major condition that should be met before seriously considering displacement—the availability of suitable conditions and resources that would minimize social impact on the displaced peoples. The Maldharis were displaced to adjacent lands that were insufficient to meet their grazing needs, lands that were also coming "under extensive agricultural operations" and hence, between the park and the expanding agricultural settlements, were squeezing the Maldharis out. This, in turn, caused severe and totally unnecessary social, economic, and cultural impacts on the Maldharis.

Perhaps the most extreme social impacts from displacement represented in the foregoing pages is the case of the Ik in Uganda (Calhoun, chapter 4), which has been also referenced repeatedly in this volume. The relocation of the Thakuri and Chetri peoples from the Rara Lake Wildlife Sanctuary reported elsewhere in the literature (Thompson et al. 1986:54) presents an equally chilling spectacle of disastrous social consequences:

> On the banks of Rara Lake there used to be two medium-sized Thakuri and Chetri settlements. . . . Neither had encroached on the surrounding forests, and the cultivation of crops of barley and potatoes utilized only a small area. The lake was full of fish which the local people caught only by spearing. Such was the position in the early 1970s. When a wildlife sanctuary was established, the inhabitants of the two villages, who had lived there for many generations, were forcibly evacuated and moved from an environment situated at 10,000 feet above sea level to the lowlands of the Terai without being provided with adequate aid for their resettlement. It is reliably reported that the communities disintegrated and many perished within a short span of time (Furer-Haimendorf 1983, pers. comm.).

The critical issue, however, is to move beyond the documentation of such disastrous impacts, and specify the nature of the conditions under which displacement will have greater or lesser social impacts on displaced people. It is not enough to summarily proclaim that a given displacement and resettlement was a "success" if it is not specified how cultural systems were protected, how rural development potential was maintained or improved, and how those who were resettled felt about the move. While we have no rigorously quantified evaluation studies of relocations from protected areas, we will draw on the case of Malolotja National Park, Swaziland, as one of the better examples of more successful displacement (Ntshalintshali and McGurk, chapter 5). A number of key factors and conditions that were critical for successful relocation will be discussed using comparative references to other cases on key dimensions. The factors that led to a successful relocation with fewer social impacts in this case included the following:

1. The displacement involved a well-assimilated farming community with extensive contact with the broader society and the region they were to be relocated to.
2. The displaced community and the receiving community were culturally and linguistically the same.
3. The move involved adequate replacement lands of better agricultural quality coupled with a desire on the part of the relocated peoples to have better quality farming land.
4. There was a better infrastructure of roads, water, and so forth, in the new location.
5. There was more careful social analysis and participatory planning involving the residents to be relocated.
6. There was careful preservation of cultural resources, especially grave sites, which people could return to visit.
7. There was strong support and legitimation from respected leaders (in this case a highly respected king.)

The importance of the fact that the community to be moved was an assimilated farming community in contact with the relocation community (number 1 above) and that the receiving community was culturally and linguistically the same (number 2 above) made for a smoother transition that ensured better cultural preservation and lessened social impacts of adjustment. This stands in stark contrast to the Ik tribe and the Rara Lake farming communities cited above that were isolated peoples and settlements that faced strong culture shock with the outside world. Jungius (1976) also identifies the degree of prior isolation among Peruvian peoples as a key variable. All of these cases and the comparative contrasts among them confirm Goodland's (chapter 25) strong emphasis on the importance of cultural attachment to place that tends to correlate with degree of prior isolation. The degree of cultural similarity or dissimilarity with surrounding relocation regions may also tend to be a contingent factor. However, this is not always the case. As Nietschmann (1984) emphasizes, many island peoples are fiercely attached to their home island, and displacement, even to a culturally and linguistically similar island nearby, can have severe social and psychological impacts.

The fact that better agricultural lands were available in the Swaziland case and that the people desired better agricultural lands was also important. The availability of equally good or better land is also cited in relation to numerous other cases of seemingly more successful relocations. These include the resettlement of shifting cultivators from national parks in Latin America (Meganck and Goebel 1979); resettlement of agricultural peasants to better, more fertile agricultural soils in Paraguay (Brechin and Harmon 1983); and resettlement of agricultural peasants from the area around Royal Chitwan Park (Mishra 1982), where there were conflicts with marauding wildlife, to new, more fertile agricultural soils in Nepal. That these peoples felt adequately compensated by receiving improved agricultural lands is perhaps one of the most critical factors in successful relocations in relation to rural development criteria. In the few areas where better agricultural soils are available, such relocations can be seen in a positive light as one form of ecodevelopment. But the problem is that all too frequently, better land in developing countries is not always available.

The Swaziland case also illustrates the importance of close involvement of the people to be relocated in the move with the officials initiating it and the importance of the support of respected leaders. This is similar to the case of Maasai displacement noted by West (1982c) and stands in contrast to numerous cases of failed relocation efforts elsewhere (West 1982c; Brechin and Harmon 1983).

However, in viewing cases of displacement and relocation on a park-by-park basis, we can easily overlook the problems of cumulative impact of multiple displacements affecting the same cultural group. West (1982c) reported the seemingly positive case of Maasai relocation in Kenya. Deihl (1985), however, taking a more regional and cumulative social impact perspective, finds that the cumulative impacts of multiple relocations of the Maasai from different parks and reserves, when taken together, restrict the range of their nomadic cattle economy and detrimentally affect both their culture and their potential for rural economic development. These regional cumulative impacts are particularly significant in that, as a whole, the Maasai are now being confined to areas that are drier year-round. Positive "ecodevelopment" benefits cannot be claimed in this context. In fact, the opposite may be true if overgrazing of the more arid land base begins to take it's ecological toll. It would be dishonest to blame the Maasai for this.

Another important consideration in relation to both cultural preservation and rural development is the nature and type of compensation provided. Here again, our guiding hypothesis is that access to and participation in "bottom-up" rural development opportunities are to be stressed more than "basic needs" compensation. In this context, this means that access to suitable productive resources, such as better agricultural land, suitable grazing pasture, and so forth, which provide continuity between prior economic modes of production and opportunities for economic improvement, should be favored over the provision of welfare services such as housing and cash payments (as emphasized in Brechin et al., chapter 1). While these may be included in packages of compensation, without the inclusion of access to productive resources, such basic needs services will likely be detrimental both to rural development and cultural preservation.

Again, we would direct the reader to the well-documented case study of this situation for the members of an Ojibway tribe in Canada, who were displaced from their traditional reserve, cut off from their traditional sustained-yield economy based on renewable natural resources, and left to disintegrate on welfare and new modern housing that did not fit their cultural patterns (Shkilnyk 1985). This form of "compensation" became, as the book title indicates, a "poison stronger than love" that ended in cultural, social, and economic disorganization symbolized by tragically high rates of child abuse and neglect, suicide, and homicide within the tribe. The case of the Ik tribe (Calhoun, chapter 4) that ended in similar social, cultural, and economic disintegration reminds us also that not just any productive resource replacements will do. The Ik, who had been a successful hunter-gatherer society, were rapidly and forcibly converted into dryland farmers in a region of frequent drought that contributed to the human tragedy of their fate. Therefore, based on the importance of the bottom-up model of rural development, a related factor that is important to consider is the relationship between the displaced peoples and their traditional resource bases in the protected area from which they have been displaced. In some areas, displaced peoples are still allowed to use resources of the reserve that can mitigate the material impacts to some degree. In many cases, as we will see in the next section, this is not the case, however, because the primary reason for displacement is usually to cut resident peoples off from access to these productive resources.

Finally, we should emphasize again that if relocation is not conducted under the more optimal conditions discussed above, with the full participation and agreement of the displaced peoples, lack of support or active resentment by local peoples can undermine the objectives of improved nature preservation due to more active poaching, sabotage, and failure to exert traditional social controls that may have helped prevent illegal resource impacts in the past. To return to Gir National Park in India, it is significant that prior to their displacement, the Maldharis had played an important role in helping to prevent and control illegal commercial poaching. After their unnecessary displacement from the park, they were neither able nor willing to play this role.

To restate our fundamental conclusion from these findings, displacement should only be considered as a last resort and only where there is sound documentation that critical resource factors, such as endangered species survival, are in jeopardy *and* where there are viable relocation options in conformance with the above factors and principles.

There is a strong need for systematic research on both the social impacts and mitigating measures in relation to resettlement from protected areas and a strong need for a more sound research base in conservation biology so that this option will be exercised only where absolutely necessary. However, improved science alone will not resolve tough dilemmas. There may be cases where critical resources are threatened and there are no optimal alternatives and conditions for displacement and relocation. We will return to this fundamental moral dilemma in the conclusion of this chapter after we have examined in further detail the issue of access to protected area resources.

Access to Protected Area Resources

In this section we discuss the role of continued uses of renewable resources in protected areas by resident peoples who either reside in the reserve, live adjacent to the reserve, or who have been relocated out of the reserve but continue to use resources in the reserve. We will conclude from this analysis that access to sustained-yield harvest of renewable natural resources, including forest resources, grazing, fisheries, wildlife, agriculture, and other resource uses, should be allowed in protected areas for "traditional users in rural poverty using appropriate technologies" (not necessarily traditional primitive technologies). This access should be allowed on as much of the protected area acreage as possible and consistent with critical protection objectives, except under the following conditions: 1) where use limitations are needed to maintain sustained yield; 2) where selected closures are needed to regain sustained yield potential; or 3) where critical protection objectives involving rare and endangered species and the protection of genetic diversity are at stake or where resource preservation measures are needed to protect documented ecodevelopment objectives of direct benefit to local people *if certain criteria are met*. These criteria should include: 1) burden of proof that these resources are indeed threatened by the specific renewable resource use or uses under question; 2) adequate study to determine that such closures would not be counterproductive by eliminating ecological conditions necessary to preserve specific species and maintain genetic diversity traditionally found in the protected area; 3) soundly designed good faith efforts to gain sufficient voluntary improvements in resource harvest or land-use practices have been tried; 4) availability and adequate provision of replacement resources are available *in kind* if at all possible. Under all conditions warranting resource regulation or closure, involvement of the affected peoples should be mandatory, with sharing of power in a conflict-management process to determine specific areas and time frames for closure, and specific written agreements with respect to replacement resources or compensation. In some cases this may result in less than perfect achievement of resource protection or preservation objectives.

As with displacement policy, current policies and practices with respect to continued utilization of protected area resources vary widely from country to country and amongst different categories of protected areas or different models of a given category, such as national parks. On the whole, there is a greater tendency to allow continued use of resources on a regulated basis in developing countries than in the developed countries following the U.S. National Parks model. As Machlis and Tichnell (1985:17) observe:

In contrast to the life style in industrialized regions of the world, which includes a higher per capita income and standard of living, the short-term subsistence needs of indigenous people in developing regions are today acute. Hence, political and public support for parks in these areas often depends more on their contribution to local socioeconomic development than it does in developed regions.

While there are ways in which strict resource preservation and resource exclusion can contribute to *local* ecodevelopment (discussed below), the primary way in which protected areas in the developing world can constructively contribute to local ecodevelopment is through the careful and judicious continuity of access to renewable natural resources in protected areas on a sustained-yield basis in ways that are compatible with the protection objectives of these reserves. As Nietschmann (1984) emphasizes, the range of specific resource needs is often far broader in local cultures than is recognized by outside scientists and resource managers. Thus, careful social assessment must be done to determine the range and priority of needed resources.

Usually, however, the primary resource uses at stake are forest resources for fuelwood, poles, and other uses; grazing; agriculture; wildlife; fisheries and other marine resources; and water resources. Other resources include thatch grass (Royal Chitwan National Park; Mishra 1982); berry agriculture (Pinelands New Jersey; Hales, chapter 20); piped water for Maasai livestock from Amboseli National Park, Kenya, to compensate the Maasai for displacement from grazing resources (Western 1982); coconut harvesting in zones of low tourist use (Cahuita National Park, Costa Rica; Kutay, chapter 10); medicinal plant harvesting by local people (Annapurna National Park, Tibet; Bunting et al., chapter 14); and others. Policies and practices with respect to access to these resources vary widely. Some types of resources, such as fishing, seem to be more widely allowed; others such as forest resources, grazing, and wildlife harvesting uses are permitted in some protected areas but not in many others.

Forest Resources With respect to forest resources, in some protected areas, access to them is denied, as in, for instance, Kinabalu National Park, Malaysia (Jacobson, chapter 21), while Lake Malawi

National Park, Malawi, permits subsistence forest uses (Croft, chapter 12). In Annapurna National Park (Bunting et al., chapter 14) fuelwood extraction is to be prohibited in a core preservation zone and to be compensated by fuelwood plantations in an "influence zone," while in Michiru Mountain reserve, Malawi (Hough, chapter 11), temporary closure for fuelwood has been instituted until fuelwood plantations are ready for sustained yield harvest.

Grazing

Policies and practices with respect to grazing in protected areas also vary widely. Grazing is permitted in some land use zones, at least, for instance, in the Mapimi Biosphere Reserve in Mexico (Halffter 1981); Annapurna National Park, Nepal (Bunting et al., chapter 14); Mt. Kulal Biosphere reserve, Kenya (Lusigi 1983); Ngorongoro Crater, Kenya; Lapp grazing of reindeer in Swedish national parks; and in Peruvian national parks (Jungius 1976). Grazing is prohibited, for instance, in Amboseli National Park, Kenya (Western 1982); Cahuita National Park, Costa Rica (Kutay, chapter 10); and Kinabalu National Park, Malaysia (Jacobson, chapter 21).

In some protected areas where we find grazing, it exists only because park officials have not been able to eliminate it, while in other areas grazing is officially welcomed as a means of local ecodevelopment, following more on the European model of national parks. In the Annapurna National Park, in Nepal, for instance, Bunting, Sherpa, and Wright (chapter 14) emphasize that "in a region of limited land resources and where animals are an important symbol of wealth, the challenge is to ensure that grazing use is sustainable, not eliminated."

Wildlife Cropping

Wildlife harvesting by local people is still banned in many national parks and protected areas in the developing world, but in a surprising number of cases it is allowed on a controlled basis, usually in specified zones. For instance, in Lake Malawi National Park, Malawi (Croft, chapter 12), Annapurna National Park, Nepal (Bunting et al., chapter 14), Peruvian National Parks (Jungius 1976), Canadian National Parks in the Northern Territories (East, chapter 27; Lawson 1985), and Cahuita National Park, Costa Rica (Kutay, chapter 10). In other protected areas park officials crop wildlife to

give or sell to local people, usually at reduced prices. This is
the case, for instance, in Malolotja National Park, Swaziland
(Ntshalintshali and McGurk, chapter 5); Zimbabwe (Child
1984); and in several other areas in Africa (Myers 1972).

In some places where ecodevelopment research has been
done on wildlife harvest potential, for instance, with certain
species of monkeys in Central America, research has shown
insufficient sustained yield potential to make harvesting
worthwhile (Bruce Woodward, pers. comm.). And in other
areas, such as the Gir National Park in India, where the
local people, the Maldharis, are vegetarian, there is little
need for wildlife harvesting. But in other areas where wildlife harvesting has been made illegal, reduced access to traditional sources of protein has caused hardship for local
peoples. Marks (chapter 28) tells of local frustrations due to
government elimination of wildlife hunting. Ironically, in
one Kenyan park where antipoaching laws eliminated local
hunting, an overpopulation of elephants occurred and subsequently had to be cropped (Machlis and Tichnell 1985;
Gomm 1974).

Agriculture   While a large number of protected areas, especially national
parks, continue to prohibit agriculture, there is again an
increasing number that are permitting agriculture in restricted zones. In Costa Rica, for instance, it has long been
national park policy to eliminate agricultural land uses. But
with growing population pressures they have found this policy too costly and socially disruptive. While no management
plan has been approved, there is an administrative agreement that now permits traditional agriculture within zones
of Cahuita National Park where agriculture has traditionally been practiced (Kutay, chapter 10). Other protected
areas that permit agricultural land uses by traditional users
include Korea (Woo, chapter 17), Lake Malawi National
Park, Malawi (Croft, chapter 12), and Kuna Yala Biosphere
Reserve, Panama (proposed) (Wright et al. 1985). In some
areas agricultural enterprise to utilize local market demand
is being actively encouraged. For instance, in Annapurna
National Park, Nepal (Bunting et al., chapter 14), small-
scale agriculture, orchards, and poultry farming are being
encouraged as ancillary ecodevelopment projects to meet
tourism demand for food.

Issues of agricultural encroachment by nontraditional users and shifting agriculture remain thorny problems. It is important that protected areas not be left to fend for themselves with respect to agricultural encroachment, but it is also important that they participate with other relevant agencies and organizations in working out integrated regional agricultural development policies and plans in which protected areas may need to play a role. The special case of shifting agriculture will be taken up in other sections below.

Impacts of Prohibiting Renewable Resource Use

Where such resource uses are denied and few replacement resources are available, hardship and even malnutrition (Machlis and Tichnell 1985:18) can result, along with bitter conflicts between protected area managers and local people. This has occurred in Ethiopia, for instance, where violent conflict broke out after policies were imposed to restrict firewood cutting from Simien National Park (Clad 1982), or where other closures of access to renewable resources in other protected areas have caused serious, though usually less violent, conflict with local peoples creating local "legitimacy" problems for protected areas, such as Royal Chitwan National Park in Nepal (Mishra 1982). In Cahuita National Park in Costa Rica, Kutay (chapter 10) observes that "resource conflicts have intensified to the point where a working relationship between park authorities and local people has completely broken down." When relations deteriorate to this degree, they are very hard to rebuild. However, in some areas, such as Kinabalu National Park, Malaysia (Jacobson, chapter 21), where resource-use closures are in affect, there is a notable absence of conflict. In this case, there was no displacement of local people, because none were living in the park, and thus resource-use issues were not as controversial there.

It needs to be emphasized that access to renewable natural resources is important to local people, not only in an economic sense, but also as an important element in cultural identity and continuity. The reason that Goodland (chapter 25) specifies property rights control and self-determination as two central prerequisites to cultural survival is that viable cultures not only depend on a viable economy, but that the social institutions in which that economy is rooted embody a cultural way of life, central to identity and well-being.

As Nietschmann (1984) emphasizes: "Resource exploitation by indigenous peoples represents more than securing just the resource. It is a part of socialization, moral education, teaching of social and economic responsibilities, and an expression of skill and ability. As a result, limitations on resource use imposed by outsiders may be strongly contested."

Usually a combination of multiple resources is necessary for sustainable ecodevelopment following the bottom-up approach to rural development in ways that are compatible with and supportive of local cultures. The fact that Royal Chitwan allows an annual harvest of thatch grass from the park is often cited as a prime example of local ecodevelopment (Mishra 1982). However, not cited as often is the fact that local people are closed out of all other renewable resource uses that are equally or more important to their cultural patterns and rural economies. Thus the cumulative impact of the combination of allowed and disallowed uses is critically important to consider.

Subsistence versus Commercial Resource Use

One major distinction that is often made in deciding what types of resource use to allow in protected areas is the distinction between "subsistence" and "commercial" resource uses (Nietschmann 1984). Yet as Kutay (1984) emphasizes, it is not always easy to distinguish between these categories as there is a gray area of gradual transition between the two. Where in this dichotomy does the common pattern of domestic commodity production for combined subsistence and local market economies fit? As Kutay (1984) argues, "A money economy is an important component in the relationship between rural populations and the natural environment (Plog et al. 1976). Whereas the absence of a market demand limits production to needs only, most rural cultures experience a combination of self-reliance and subsistence, with some degree of economic ties to the outside world."

For this reason Kutay has adopted Weeks' (1981) terminology of "traditional usage" of protected areas that can include both subsistence and small-scale production for markets accompanied by "monitoring the impact of changing resource use on the local ecosystem and working with local inhabitants to set management policy consistent with conservation objectives." But the term "traditional usage" has its problems as well; many large commercial enterprises, such as ranching interests for instance, have traditionally used range resources that have become protected areas as well. An example of this is Mexico's Mapimi Biosphere reserve (Halffter 1981). Are these to be included as well? We would suggest, therefore, that the definition of "traditional usage" be modified to apply primarily to traditional usage by the rural poor living in and around protected areas. While there is no clear dividing line between "poor" and "not poor," this definition provides a clearer guideline in relation to rural development objectives embodied in the "growth with equity" model of bottom-up development and the basic principles of ecodevelopment ideology that stress emphasis on ecodevelopment efforts aimed primarily at the rural poor. In Glaeser's (1984:1) words: "By ecodevelopment we mean an alternative policy of economic development that takes care of environmental limits and that is ecologically sound. It is widely agreed that ecodevelopment contains the following elements [including] . . . the satisfaction of basic needs, *especially those of the poorest parts of the population, which are most in need* [emphasis added]."

In making this distinction between traditional resource uses from protected areas by the rural poor on a sustained yield basis, we are carefully distinguishing this form of "multiple use" policy from, for instance, the multiple use national forests in the United States that stress large-scale commercial exploitation that tends to squeeze out, both economically and politically, the marginal poor and subsistence users (see West 1982a). In some protected areas, where sustained yield access for the rural poor is a major objective, traditional access by larger commercial interests may need to be curtailed to allow increased access to the rural poor within the limits of sustained yield. This is the case in many ocean fisheries, such as the San Miguel Bay case in the Philippines studied by Bailey (1984:97–103). In other words, sticking to the equity principles and commitments in the rhetoric of ecodevelopment may necessitate coalitions of conservation interests and local rural poor to confront the power of other local, regional, national, and international commercial interests. It is in situations such as this that we will see the degree of actual commitment behind international conservationists' rhetoric about ecodevelopment. We have seen this type of commitment primarily to date in coalitions of conservationists and traditional peoples dependent upon tropical forest habitat to ward off clearing of tropical forests by large-scale international timber interests (Clad 1982).

Technology and Voluntary Primitivism

Another dimension related to the subsistence-commercial continuum is the issue of the level of traditional versus modern extractive technology that is permitted. There is a growing consensus that traditional peoples using traditional technologies appear compatible with protected area objectives. Biosphere reserves are now often defined in terms of preserving "representative ecosystems and man's traditional relationship to them" (Wright et al. 1985). But what happens when a traditional society wishes to adopt more modern means of harvesting resources? In areas where "traditional resource uses" are permitted, such uses are frequently permitted only through the use of "traditional" means. In Peru for instance (Jungius 1976), tribes permitted to stay in protected areas are allowed to hunt with bow and arrow but not with guns. In Cahuita National Park in Costa Rica, traditional practices of cacao and coconut agriculture, grazing, and subsistence fishing are now allowed in areas of customary occupancy under an administrative agreement as long as they do not "change their traditional methods of work" (Kutay, chapter 10). In Clad's (1982) essay on the harmony of interests between conservationists and traditional peoples, Clad observes that the coalition develops strains when tribals adopt modern technology to exploit resources. Yet is all this romantic primitivism really necessary, in light of the supposed commitment to the rural development of the poor found in the guiding principles of ecodevelopment cited above? It may be true that it is easier to maintain sustained yield under conditions of less efficient technology, but this doesn't mean that sustained yield cannot be maintained. If we were to respect resident peoples' desire to slowly acculturate new ways of harvesting traditional resources, and work with them to gain cooperation in maintaining sustained yield and avoid overexploitation, might this be more consistent with the principles of ecodevelopment? Harvesting an equal amount of resource in less time is no more damaging to the natural system, and thus frees productive labor for other ecodevelopment activities within or adjacent to the reserves.

Of course, there are some technologies, such as the reported use of explosives to stun-kill fish by Maori tribes in New Zealand (Clad 1982), that would have broader detrimental environmental impacts on marine ecosystems and could not be allowed in marine protected areas. But is anything really lost if a wood cutter uses a chain saw *but* does not overcut? Clad (1982) indicates, for instance, that the international conservation movement frowns on the use of chain saws in clearing forests for shifting agriculture. However, in some cases the use of modern technologies would make shifting agriculture more ecologically compatible with protected area objectives. For instance, Firey (1960) documents the case of the Bemba tribe in the old Belgian Congo, who traditionally practiced shifting cultivation. When mines in the region began drawing young men away from their tribal home, however, only older men and women were left to do the hard work of clearing land and "pollarding." Because they did not have more modern technologies, they were forced to farm plots more intensively, leading to impoverishment of the soil, ecological impacts, economic decline, and cultural disintegration.

The distinction between "enforced primitivism" and "voluntary primitivism" may be of help in sorting these issues out (Brechin et al., chapter 1; Goodland, chapter 25); but if by "voluntary primitivism" we mean that "you are free to go elsewhere if you want to change, but you can stay in the reserve only so long as you conform to our primitive myths about you," then it's not really voluntary. Voluntary primitivism must include the right, within protected areas, to slowly acculturate newer appropriate technologies within the bounds of ecological impact and sustainability.

Sustained-Yield Limits

What if local peoples, primitive or not, wish to exploit resources beyond the limits of ecological sustainability, as often occurs? In Lake Malawi National Park, for instance (Croft, chapter 12), the objectives of the park plan included a goal of meeting traditional subsistence needs for building materials and fuelwood for cooking and smoking fish. However, at current exploitation rates, existing supplies would be depleted in thirty years. Thus, restoring full sustainable potential following overexploitation may involve exclusionary preservation until resources recover or supplemental fuelwood plantations mature, as has occurred in the Michiru

Mountain case in Malawi (Hough, chapter 11). Here it was necessary to impose controls, but efforts were also made to educate the local people about the reasons for the closure *prior to the closure* in relation to their own long-term self-interests. This led to much higher compliance than would otherwise have occurred.

Because local resource needs may outstrip sustainable-yield potential, extra efforts should be made to enhance sustainable supplies within protected area zones or in the region surrounding the reserve. This is demonstrated most notably in efforts around many protected areas to develop plantations of firewood to replace sources foreclosed due to preservation policies where woodcutting is prohibited, or where demand exceeds sustainable supply in protected areas where wood-cutting is permitted. This is illustrated in numerous reserves, including Michiru Mountain, Malawi (Hough, chapter 11), La Planada Biosphere Reserve, Colombia, (Glick and Orejuela, chapter 13), and Annapurna National Park, Nepal (Bunting et al., chapter 14).

Whether to maintain or build sustained-yield potential, or to replace forest resources lost to closure for preservation zones, the development of forest management plans should draw on any existing local institutions for regulating wood-cutting, or seek to revive these institutions where they have atrophied due to nationalization of forest lands in years past (Bunting et al., chapter 14; McNeeley 1985; Berreman 1972; Tucker 1982). These had been known in the Himalayan region as the "shinganaua" institutions, organized as "indigenous village firewood resource management committees" (Bunting et al., chapter 14). Where they have fallen into disuse, it has usually been because of local bitterness over the loss of sovereignty when forests were nationalized (Berreman 1972), and hence, they may be difficult to revive due to continued resentment toward national authorities. The only way they could be revived would be to ensure power-sharing, joint-management arrangements that ensure local control.

Another important consideration is whether or not such replacement fuelwood projects for preservation, or for sustainable production, face the difficulty of the time lag between planting of replacement resources and their maturation. There are no easy answers to this problem, but some combination of fast-growing species and replacement resources in the interim needs to be provided.

Using fast-growing fuelwood species can shorten the time during which supplements are needed. However, this creates an additional problem of the appropriateness of using fast-growing exotics in a protected area, a point raised by Bunting, Sherpa, and Wright (chapter 14) with respect to the Annapurna reserve in Nepal, and discussed in general by Muller (chapter 15). Here the solution may be to use fast-growing exotics outside the protected area and in buffer zones, as occurred for instance in the "influence zones" of La Planada Biosphere Reserve (Glick and Orejuela, chapter 13). This can be coupled with the identification of faster-growing indigenous species in zones where exotics would not be compatible. There are many indigenous species that resident peoples often utilize that are not as well known to foresters, and yet may have good potential for use as firewood species. The genus *Combritum*, for instance, is being considered in this way in Niger, West Africa (West and Ariza-Nino undated).

Replacement Resources

Even with the use of fast-growing species, some form of replacement resources or alternative energy source needs to be provided. Hough (chapter 23) considers a number of options including temporary intensive management of forest resources in the reserve to bridge the gap, and the provision of subsidized replacements of firewood, charcoal, paraffin, or other energy supplements. All of these have negative consequences, but are preferable to no action at all in order to fill the gap, which can create violations of regulations (with subsequent unregulated damage to the reserve), rapid deforestation elsewhere, and loss of local support for the protected area (Hough, chapter 23; Nzima 1986).

Nevertheless, the social impacts of potential alternatives need to be considered as carefully as the social impacts of resource use closures. Alternative energy sources such as solar, kerosene, and mini-hydroelectric projects have been tried in areas of the Himalaya's where firewood pressure for trekking tourism and local use has been intense (Bunting et al., chapter 14; Weber, chapter 18; Coburn 1985). Where firewood bans are in place, and alternative energy sources made available, negative socioeconomic impacts can result especially on the very poor who cannot afford alternatives, or whose survival depends upon cutting wood for sale (see Bunting et al., chapter 14). The characteristics of alternative resources and technologies can also be maladaptive to cultural patterns.

**Improving
Resource Use
Practices**

The strategy of introducing and gaining adoption of alternative energy sources raises the broader issue of seeking changes in natural resource use practices within protected areas in ways that will make them more compatible with protected area objectives. This general strategy has not received much attention in the protected area and resident populations literature, and yet it holds great potential for improving compatibility between resource use and protected area objectives.

Glick and Betancourt (1983:5) discuss the potential of eco-development research to develop a better scientific base for improving land use practices within tropical protected areas. However, the discussion in the book's introduction of this potential is the only place in the volume where this approach is dealt with in any detail. For example, strategies associated with the "diffusion-adoption" approach to altering land use processes could be one area of research. The area of soil erosion control is one of the more important applications of this perspective in relation to protected areas. If agricultural land use practices that reduce soil erosion could be adopted by resident peoples, then these more ecologically sound agricultural resource uses may be more favorably considered for inclusion in protected area land uses, at least in certain more intensive land use zones. Research work on diffusion of soil conservation practices in general (e.g., Heffernan and Green 1986; Lovejoy and Napier 1986), and amongst peasant farmers in developing countries (e.g., Ashby 1982, 1985; West and Light 1978:367–68) provide a rich base of theory and research from which to draw.

Bunting, Sherpa, and Wright (chapter 14) call attention to the importance of using local agricultural extension services for agricultural development efforts within protected areas in Annapurna National Park (Nepal); these agricultural extension activities could be expanded to include programs to reduce soil erosion and to gain adoption of other land use practices that would enhance protection objectives of the area. These practices, in turn, would also be likely to improve the long-run viability of local economies. Thus, before conservationists can claim that resource use practices are harming protected area resources and must therefore be terminated, there should first be a good faith effort to try to gain adoption of improved land use practices using state-of-the-art community change strategies for maximizing adoption rates. It is recognized, however, that to have significant reduction in environmental impacts on area resources high rates of adoption by the entire community must be achieved. This may or may not be possible under any given set of cultural and field conditions. For instance, with respect to the diffusion-adoption of alternative energy resources in Sagarmatha National Park, Weber (chapter 18) observes that "alternative energy sources such as kerosene . . . have all been attempted, but not delivered at a level to have significant ecological impact. To date, these innovations have had negligible collective impact on escalating wood consumption."

The Role of Resource Use by *Homo Sapiens* in Preservation

Often the elimination of resource uses is done on the basis of untested assumptions that the use of "wild ecosystems" by resident peoples will *ipso facto* harm the multiple objectives of ecosystem preservation, protection of rare and endangered species, and the protection of natural genetic diversity. The reader will recall, however, that at numerous points in this book case histories and research have documented numerous cases where the elimination of resource uses by resident peoples (*Homo sapiens*) has been detrimental to the very ends managers sought to preserve. It turns out that the ecosystems that modern "man" is now trying to protect have been occupied by *Homo sapiens*, sometimes for thousands of years. *Homo sapiens* has been a part of these ecosystems and the "balance of nature" represented there, and thus the composition and diversity of species within these ecosystems have been affected by *Homo sapiens* as much as *Homo sapiens*, with its patterns of foraging, mating, reproduction, and adaptation, have been affected by those ecosystems. Thus it should come as no surprise that when modern *Homo sapiens* take steps to remove fellow members and their foraging patterns from those ecosystems, that those ecosystems might change, endangering in some instances the very values they sought to protect. This applies not only to primitive species variants of *Homo sapiens*, but also to more modernly adapted variants who, like the Israelites of Palestine, have been part of that ecosystem for thousands of years, even as their adaptive patterns have changed in the course of their evolution.

Whether it is the endangering of virgin Red Pine (*Pinus*

resinosa) in Itasca State Park in Northern Minnesota due to the elimination of human-caused fire, or the decline of rare orchids due to banning grazing and charcoal forestry in the Batha Nature Reserve in Israel (Rabinovitch-Vin, chapter 7), we should have learned by now to be more watchful for such ecosystem interactions, and therefore to plan better, based on sound ecological research, before summarily eliminating resident peoples and their traditional patterns of resource use from protected areas. The longer they or other peoples with similar foraging patterns have been occupying the same niche in an ecosystem, the more suspicious we should be; the more we should look before we leap.

Our main case study of these ecological relationships is the above-mentioned grazing and charcoal forestry ban in Israel that led to declining populations of rare orchids in the reserve. The Nature Authority then reintroduced grazing and charcoal forestry on a controlled basis (Rabinovitch-Vin, chapter 7). But we also can observe similar ecological dynamics with respect to the role of human-caused fire in maintaining rare and endangered species in the Pinelands of New Jersey (Hales, chapter 20); the role of the Maasai burning practices in maintaining grassland successional stages necessary for certain wild herbivores (Deihl 1985); the role of the annual thatch grass harvest in maintaining grassland conditions for park herbivores in Royal Chitwan Park, Nepal (Mishra 1982); the role of human-caused fire in maintaining grasslands, and the role of shifting agriculture in maintaining genetic diversity among early successional species in the Rio Platano Biosphere Reserve (Glick and Betancourt 1983:168–173). With respect to shifting cultivation, Glick and Betancourt observe that their migrating agriculture has left several small tracts in various stages of succession. These tracts of disturbed forest attract many plant and animal species distinct from those of the primary woodland, adding diversity to the reserve's genetic pool. Perhaps these findings should be cause to do further research before shifting agriculture is automatically banned or discouraged in protected areas (Meganck and Goebel, 1979; Jacobson, chapter 21). Similarly, settled agriculture has been shown to be central to maintaining ecological and species diversity in the Parc National des Cévennes in France (Beede, chapter 8).

Here, park officials are actively seeking to retain and increase rural agricultural populations, including technological modernization assistance to try to reverse the rural population decline in the park and help to maintain a desired balance of ecological stages of succession.

Elsewhere in the literature, Hatley and Thompson (1985:369) report that research on the conservation biology of the rhesus monkey in the Galis Forest of Pakistan indicates an ecological symbiosis between monkey and man. Summarizing research by Dewer et al. (1981), they indicate that food sources for the rhesus monkey depend in large part on changed habitat conditions in the Galis Forest due to human occupation and use.

Machlis and Tichnell (1985:23) observe that when managers of protected areas discover such ecological relationships after banning resident people from their reserves, their frequent response is to artificially imitate indigenous resource practices "in an attempt to sustain the desired conditions." This may make sense in the case of the controlled reintroduction of fire, but in the case of grazing, charcoal production, shifting agriculture, forest uses that sustain the rhesus monkey, and other extractive uses, is there any reason why the resident people that filled that niche in the protected ecosystem cannot be permitted to continue doing so, at least in a regulated way, in certain zones to maintain an ecological balance? Would this not conform more closely to the espoused principles of ecodevelopment? Wouldn't it be nice if, in such situations, resident peoples could give something back to nature for the bounty she could share with them? As Hatley and Thompson (1985:369) observe with respect to wildlife conservation:

If man's impact is sometimes positive, then man and animal can sometimes become caught up in a positive sum game; both can become better off as a result of an interaction that is generally assumed always to be detrimental to one, the other, or both. If such an unexpected positive sum pocket exists in the midst of all these negative sum interactions, then the development trick will be to encourage those interactions that are already in the pocket and to try to steer into it those that are not.

Natural Area Preservation as a Means of Ecodevelopment

In the above section we saw how natural area preservation can sometimes depend on the continuity of active human use. In this section we discuss ways in which strict exclusionary preservation can be important for ecodevelopment in surrounding local communities. The general concept of ecodevelopment usually involves active human use of renewable resources (Glaeser 1984), but within the international protected area movement it has come to have a particular meaning in which the strict preservation of natural areas without human use is seen as functional to sustainable economic development. As we noted in Brechin et al. (chapter 1), the general preservation of watersheds and gene pools can have important economic development implications, but there are few well-studied cases in which strict natural area preservation has been directly functional to development that directly benefits local resident peoples.

In our various case studies there are only a few clear cases of this. Hales (chapter 20) observes that the strict preservation of natural conditions in protection zones is a critical ecological condition for the long-term viability of cranberry agriculture in resource use zones. Similarly, Wright et al. (1985) indicate that the protection of steep mainland forested slopes from deforestation is critical to the viability of the marine-based fishery for the Kuna Yala peoples in the Caribbean. Nietschmann (1984) discusses traditional conservation methods that include protected zones for fish spawning that are critical to sustained yield use in other marine zones. Halffter (1981) also discusses the role of ecodevelopment research, based on protected area natural systems for improving the local cattle-grazing economy. Similarly, Hough (1989) describes research by Human in protected areas in Northern Benin (West Africa) on wildlife domestication that can be important to both local and national agricultural development. This case, more than any other we have encountered, holds potential for demonstrating the importance of the preservation of genetic diversity for viable ecodevelopment for local resident peoples.

All of these cases represent promising ways in which strict preservation zones can contribute to local ecodevelopment. However, there needs to be more careful evaluation research on these and other potential cases in order to document carefully, and critically evaluate these functions. This is critical in the general sense of moving from rhetoric toward reality in documenting local economic development benefits of protected areas and their strict preservation zones. And in a more specific sense, it is important that these benefits be clearly documented as a basis for gaining the support of local peoples for the values of preserving some natural area zones that exclude human use. It is important that this research be rigorously objective and honest with respect to the limitations of these natural area functions. Overselling these notions where they are not, in fact, warranted will only be counterproductive in the long run, leading to cynicism amongst local people and rejection of findings about natural area functions that may be truly beneficial to local ecodevelopment.

The special case of "tourism" and its general dependence on natural area preservation that limits other resource uses is a classic case in point. Too often when national parks have been established under strict exclusionary preservationist policies, claims that this preservationist policy will lead to local ecodevelopment through tourism revenues have been an empty promise. In the numerous cases documented here and elsewhere in the literature, there are perhaps some cases in which this has involved active deception; more often it has rested on a failure to appreciate the special conditions under which tourism will or will not contribute constructively to local rural development without negative consequences for cultural preservation objectives. In the following section we give detailed attention to these contingent conditions using our comparative case approach.

Tourism as Ecodevelopment

The general objective of preserving the integrity of natural areas can play a major role in the attractiveness and viability of protected areas for tourism, but the assumption that this tourism potential will benefit local economic development is often unwarranted. Numerous authors warn of the often empty promises of tourism development (Kutay 1984; Brechin and Harmon 1983; Brechin et al., chapter 1; Bailey, chapter 16; Woo, chapter 17); and across many of the case studies we have included in this volume there are some sharp contrasts in the degree to which tourism-based ecodevelopment has benefited local people in rural poverty. While potential tourism benefits were used to "sell" the idea for Royal Chitwan National Park in Nepal (Mishra 1982), very few of the tourism benefits "trickled down" to the rural poor: "Tourism has not generated local jobs despite the tourist industry's promises. Most of the well-paying jobs are taken by qualified and experienced people from outside Chitwan, or even from outside Nepal." Similarly, the vast majority of Maasai in East Africa have not benefited from international tourism, though a small number have capitalized and become quite wealthy (Deihl 1985). In the Galapagos Islands National Park, tourism is largely monopolized by large-boat tourism companies based on the mainland who again hire primarily mainland people and get their food and supplies from the mainland (Bailey, chapter 16). Park policy explicitly restricts competition from small-boat owners in direct opposition to the principles of ecodevelopment stressing rural development for the rural poor. We see in these and other examples a strong tendency for tourism benefits to be monopolized by larger-scale private companies. As noted in the introduction, this form of tourism development represents the top-down model of rural development in which economic benefits are supposed to trickle down to the poor, but rarely do (Korten and Klauss 1984; Nugent and Yotopoulos 1984).

This pattern of centralized and highly capitalized tourism development is rooted in easy availability of capital, competitive advantage, power in the political economy, and compatibility with the interests of central governments in efficient "shearing of the tourist sheep" to maximize foreign exchange. In the Galapagos Islands it is also rooted in the desire of park officials and conservation scientists in controlling tourism impacts on the park (Bailey, chapter 16; de Groot 1983). Its prevalence as a dominant model of tourism development is well known, and has been repeatedly documented and analyzed in the wider literature on the social science of tourism (e.g., de Kadt 1979; Organization for Economic Cooperation and Development 1980; Machlis and Burch 1983; MacCannell 1976), and thus, should come as no surprise to the international conservation community. Yet advocates of protected areas continue blindly to promise economic cornucopia to local residents from tourism revenues (e.g., Sankhala 1969; Villa and Ponce 1984) without appreciation of this fact or understanding of the social structural conditions under which tourism can provide benefits to local people.

In sharp contrast to Royal Chitwan Park, for instance, both Sagarmatha National Park and Annapurna National Park in Nepal are able to generate greater local benefits because of the trekking form of tourism that can be monopolized by multiple small operations run by local Sherpas (Weber, chapter 18; Bunting et al., chapter 14). Where this can be achieved it corresponds more closely to the bottom-up model of rural development and the espoused principles of ecodevelopment. Following MacCannell's (1976) analysis, Kutay (1984) discusses social conditions necessary to achieve this: "If the tourists come in advance of outside entrepreneurs, a cottage tourist industry has a chance to develop which creates a more direct link between receipts from tourism and benefits of economic development to local people."

Even where the small-scale local tourist industry gets a head start, Machlis and Burch (1983) argue that there is an almost inevitable evolutionary tendency for large-scale tourism to enter local markets and to displace the "mom and pop" cottage industry tourism.

While there is a strong tendency for this to happen due to the factors cited above (competitive advantage, power in the political economy, and central government interests in foreign exchange), it is by no means inevitable. There are at least three structural conditions that can prevent this. First, there are tourism situations, such as the decentralized trekking tourism in Annapurna and Sagarmatha parks in Nepal (Bunting et al., chapter 14; Weber, chapter 18), where small trekking firms can maintain their own competitive advantage, or at least monopolize skilled trekking experience in working for larger firms. This is also true to some extent for Inuit outfitters in Northern Territory parks in Canada (Lawson 1985). Second, not unlike the spread of McDonald's franchises only to small towns with sufficient markets, large tourism firms will enter local markets only where there are sufficient tourist "sheep to shear," and hence large profits to be made.

Third, international conservationists and protected area managers can, by merging their interests with local resident peoples, form coalitions to develop and enforce policies that will favor small, local "cottage industry" tourism (Woo, chapter 17). Thus in the proposed management plan for Cahuita National Park in Costa Rica, Kutay (chapter 10) advocates a specific policy to give preference to local people in the operation of tourist concessions, plus programs to provide credit and technical assistance to improve small-scale tourist infrastructures. Similarly, Lake Malawi National Park in Malawi favors small-scale local tourist development in part to generate local benefits and in part to minimize impacts of tourism on the park (Croft, chapter 12). While the Annapurna plan does not go that far, it does propose to stimulate local ancillary tourism industries such as farms, orchards, poultry, and handicrafts to service the larger tourist industry.

Protected area policy makers and managers will need to strongly assert this type of policy in most protected area situations if local ecodevelopment benefits of tourism are to be realized. This will frequently entail confrontation with powerful interests, including elements within their own bureaucracies that find it convenient to favor large-scale tourism for foreign exchange and for controlling impacts on parks as in the case of the Galapagos (Bailey, chapter 16). It is here that we will see the degree of true commitment to the rhetorical principles of ecodevelopment in the international conservation community. As Bunting, Sherpa, and Wright (chapter 14) observe in a more general sense, this type of political commitment has not often been forthcoming. "What has been lacking has been the political will of many governments to mobilize the resources—human, financial, cultural, and moral—to ensure the integration of ecological principles with economic development."

In the absence of this kind of understanding and political will, tourism benefits in most areas will tend to be captured by large-scale external interests. This tendency for external capture of benefits is frequently accompanied by a variety of negative economic, social, and cultural impacts that add more than insult to injury. Numerous case studies in the book emphasize that tourism fuels local inflation, with resultant negative impacts on local residents (Mishra 1982; Woo, chapter 17). With respect to tourism in the Himalaya's, McNeely (1985:27) discusses a variety of other negative economic impacts including:

The lure of cash encourages villagers to sell their best food, such as eggs and chickens, to tourists, thereby reducing the supply of protein for the village; perhaps worse, farmers may sell their surplus productivity to tourists rather

than donating it to the village temple where it used to be distributed to other villagers in need.
Unequal distribution of income from tourism can lead to social instability at both national and village levels.

McNeely (1985:27) and various case studies in this volume (Weber, chapter 18; Bunting et al., chapter 14) point also to the tourist demand for firewood, which increases prices and reduces availability of supply for local subsistence. Finally, it is well known that seasonality of tourism can create economic hardship especially on the rural poor. In developing countries the seasonality of economic activity such as tourism can be especially debilitating on the very poor at the margins of existence (Chambers et al. 1984).

Tourism development can also have detrimental social and cultural impacts. Culture contact with more isolated traditional societies are especially vulnerable (Goodland, chapter 25), but even more well-assimilated peasant cultures such as Korean farmers (Woo, chapter 17), and Costa Rican ethnic groups (Kutay, chapter 10). Cultural and religious institutions can also be impacted, resulting in negative consequences for resident peoples. Such was the case in Korea when Buddhist temples were turned into tourist attractions (Woo, chapter 17). In some protected areas, tourist visitors still come largely from within the home country and thus cultural differences and resulting culture contact impacts are less than in areas where international tourism predominates. This is the case, for instance, in Kinabalu National Park in Malaysia (Jacobson, chapter 21). In general, it might be said that the more traditional and isolated a local culture is, the greater the potential negative cultural impacts on local peoples will be, especially if tourists are more culturally dissimilar. Under these conditions it is imperative that tourism development seek to prevent contact between tourists and local people not directly involved in the tourist economy through land use zoning and other buffering strategies (Woo, chapter 17; West 1982c).

In summary, there are only certain conditions under which the positive economic development benefits will flow to local people. Further, there exist only certain conditions and planning actions that can minimize negative economic, social and cultural impacts on resident peoples. In light of these understandings, the local "hard sell" of tourism as a blanket solution to local people to compensate them for the loss of residence and traditional economic uses of reserves will only be counterproductive in the end, as local people become embittered and distrustful in the face of empty promises. Those in the international conservation community who are indeed sincere about the true intent of ecodevelopment tourism need to operate with a clearer social scientific understanding of the conditions necessary to achieve these objectives for the rural poor, and a coordinated political will to resist the tendencies in the political economy that can tend to thwart those objectives.

"Hire the Natives"

One of the first things to be mentioned as compensation for displacing resident peoples from protected areas and denying them traditional access to natural resources is the promise to hire them to work for the park as compensation for their losses. This is done in most protected areas and is discussed, for instance, in relation to Costa Rican Parks (Kutay, chapter 10), Royal Chitwan Park, Nepal (Mishra 1982), and Latin America (Meganck and Goebel 1979). While this is one valuable step, by itself it does not begin to adequately compensate local people for their losses for the simple reason that only a few members of the community can be hired and thus benefit from this form of compensation. Quite clearly, employment is no substitute for sustainable access to resources.

The "hire the natives" approach to compensation also tends to create a small salaried class of locals at the same time that exclusionary policies are negatively impacting the economic situation of the remainder of the community, which can, in turn, have negative social implications both for the local community and for relations between the park and the local community.

Because of these limitations another reason is frequently given for hiring local people—that it will be an important means by which local people can participate and influence park policies and management. But this rationale is frequently oversold too, for as Lawson (1985) observes in relation to Inuit participation in Canadian parks, "Inuit hold positions which implement management policies rather than determine them." This leads us into our last major issue in this conclusion—the role of local participation in the planning process.

**Local
Participation in
the Planning
Process**

There is hardly a chapter in this book and in other recent writings on protected areas and resident peoples that does not emphasize the importance of participation by local people in the planning process for determining management policies for protected areas. Yet in many cases, actual practices on the ground are far from this ideal. Kutay (chapter 10) observes in Costa Rica, for instance, that "involvement of local people in planning and management is perhaps the most important variable determining the outcome of the plan. . . . There has been little formal opportunity for local communities to make recommendations or comment on the current proposed plan."

It is ironic that such should be the case in one of the few societies in Central America that is a relatively stable democracy, for it is our own values of democracy we wish to have adopted along with our myths of the wilderness. And in many of the societies we are concerned with, the rights of free speech we take for granted are not embedded in their societies, and hence in a nonpermissible institutional climate it is perhaps amazing that the resident peoples speak out as much as they do even when given a chance in the formal planning process.

Neither should we be naive by failing to recognize the common functions of public participation where they do occur. We seem to be more concerned sometimes that participation rituals function to educate the local people and facilitate implementation of our plans, rather than to serve as a vehicle for true participation and power sharing in determining the basic policies of protected areas that will affect their lives. While seductive, these functions are frequently counterproductive. We noted, for instance, that one of our draft chapters was withdrawn by the authors because things weren't working out as well as it was originally hoped with the local people. Yet they had talked of solid community support through an active participation program. But looking more carefully we see that this assessment was based on the perception that the park administrators had done a good job of communicating the purposes of the reserve *to* the people. This confuses public relations with true participation; mistakes communication *to*, for communication *with*. Thus, it should come as no surprise that things are not working out. Similar "public relations" approaches to local participation failed miserably, leading to severe conflict in the case of Royal Chitwan Park (Mishra 1982). This is not to suggest that education and communications to local people cannot play a constructive role within the context of a broader conception of local participation. This is illustrated, for instance, in the case of Michiru Mountain protected area in Malawi (Hough, chapter 11).

Even when park administrators and planners really do listen to local concerns, it is often to let them blow off steam in the hopes of deflating conflict. Selznick (1949), in his classic study of the TVA, called this "formal cooptation"—the formal involvement of constituencies to deflect conflict by granting responsibility without power. Yet in many cases this has the reverse effect of leading to raised hopes and then dashed expectations followed by cynicism and heightened conflict, as illustrated by Marks (chapter 28).

True participation must involve a give and take and a sharing of decision-making power. This theme, too, is sincerely advocated by many of our authors but is rare in actual practice on the ground (e.g., Raval, chapter 6; Weaver, chapter 26; Marks, chapter 28; Lawson 1985). In the case of the Kuna Yala in the Caribbean (Wright et al. 1985) note that in the designation of a biosphere reserve, "the ultimate decision will rest firmly with the Kuna themselves." Perhaps it will in this case, but in numerous other cases where this seemed to be the case, a more careful assessment determined otherwise. Thus Hill (1983) and Weeks (1981) proclaim that Kakadu National Park was proposed by the Aboriginals and that they have veto power over management policies. Yet Weaver's anthropological research (chapter 26) indicates that this is not the case. Recent shifts in Canadian National Park policy have promised greater power sharing in joint management systems in the Northern Territories. East (chapter 27) clearly sees progress in Canada, although he admits that native groups do not have complete control over the land and states they probably never will. Lawson (1985), however, is critical of the progress to date.

True joint management involving true sharing of decision power on central issues of vital concern to resident peoples is thus an unfulfilled agenda with which the conservation community will need to come to grips (see Marks, chapter 28). It is important to note that total decision power should not be handed over to full local control, for it is true, as Lusigi

(1983:4) observes, that in relation to sustained-yield regulation "some items of obvious importance are absent from the people's list primarily because they have no experience of their value. Such are the needs for grazing control." But there is need for local participation and power sharing in determining how grazing will be regulated to ensure long-term viability as Bunting, Sherpa, and Wright observe for Annapurna (chapter 14).

Another danger of full local control is that powerful members of a given local community may capture the reins of power to the detriment of the rural poor whom the objectives of ecodevelopment are intended to favor (Burch 1971; West 1982a; Marks, chapter 28). This seems a clear danger in the granting of local control of the Mapimi Biosphere Reserve in Mexico where the large cattlemen may dominate over a powerless peasantry (Halffter 1981). Grindle's (1977) analysis of the political economy of Mexico indicates that such relations between powerful local interests and government bureaucracies are even more rampant than in developed country democracies. In these and other situations it is clear that a balance of power with institutional checks and balances may represent the optimal model, and that improved interactive planning and conflict mediation processes discussed by Bidol and Crowfoot (chapter 24) should be utilized in working through the operation of these checks and balances on any given policy issue. However, this is easy to say and hard to do. For, as we emphasized in the introduction, to implement such an approach will involve confrontation with powerful interests, not the least of which is the autonomy of the international conservation community itself. And it will take a stronger political will and resolve by that same conservation community to bring this about. Will the World Wildlife Fund grant protected area grants only on the condition of demonstrated viability of power sharing joint management? Will IUCN withhold its sanctioning of official protected area status until such institutions are guaranteed, and revoke official status when formal commitments to these institutions are eroded on the ground? Will rhetoric become true commitment and then reality? On the outcome of such questions will rest the future of resident peoples in and around protected areas, and the fate of the important values the conservation community hopes to ensure.

The Tasks and Challenges Ahead

We have sought in this volume to represent a cross-section of the state of the art in thinking, research, and practice in wrestling with the dilemmas posed by the conflicting objectives of protection, cultural preservation, and rural development. In this concluding chapter we have examined these dilemmas with respect to the specific issues of displacement, resource utilization, functions of strict preservation for local ecodevelopment, and the role and importance of local participation in the planning process. Within each of these we have sought to crystallize key conclusions and implications for rethinking these issues and devising improved solutions. But at each step along the way we were limited by an incomplete understanding of how things are really working out on the ground. Relatively few of the observations and interpretations in this book and elsewhere in the literature are based on rigorous quantitative evaluation research. This presents both limitations to our current understanding that we need to acknowledge and a challenge for the future. Thus the next major task in this arena is to undertake major programs of rigorous quantitative evaluation of the promising experiments reported in this volume and elsewhere. This will require major interdisciplinary research efforts spanning the natural and social sciences and an ability to integrate these in improved understandings and applied strategies within a framework of interactive planning processes in the search for ways to reconcile protected area objectives with the legitimate needs of resident peoples. In conjunction with these careful evaluation studies there should be careful pre-project assessments of social, economic, and ecological considerations prior to each major protected area decision. The rigorous evaluation studies of past plan implementation should be used to inform this analysis and increase the predictive power of environmental and social impact assessments that are used to guide the development and implementation of proposed plans.

However, no matter how well we are able to accomplish this scientific and integrative planning agenda it will not banish tragic conflict and hard choices among conflicting moral imperatives. We can reduce the degree of conflict and increase compatibility by careful scientific analysis and planning. We can manage the remaining conflict by improved techniques of local participation, alternative dispute resolution approaches, and institutions of checks and balances within power sharing joint management. But we will still face hard choices in the end.

We noted in the concluding synthesis that displacement should only be done where damage to park resources is scientifically established, and where more optimal social conditions for relocation are available. But what do we do when we've studied and planned and people are damaging critical resources and there are not adequate viable alternatives for relocation and equivalent replacement resources consistent with the prerequisites for cultural preservation and bottom-up rural development? What do we do when species are endangered by human use and there is no viable alternative for compensating resident peoples? Many authors in this book and in the wider literature preface their concerns for resident peoples with the notion that resident peoples should be accommodated only as long as this is consistent with critical natural protection objectives. And it is here that many of our authors would leave off when we go on to suggest that in some cases, perhaps in many cases, we should carefully consider the option of sacrificing selected protection objectives for the sake of a prolific yet fragile species whose various populations have depended on and been a part of the many varied ecosystems we seek to protect: populations of a species for whom we should have greater empathy, for they are our common humanity, and therefore ourselves.

Such a sacrifice of one moral imperative for the sake of another involves a painful choice among competing values and cannot be resolved by science. However, it can be guided, in part, by science in a deliberate and planned-for way. For instance, preservationists, not knowing fully the critical factors for species survival, run helter-skelter to try to save a species everywhere across its range, and most fervently where it is locally endangered. Conservation biologist Terry Root (pers. comm.) has suggested that realistically, this is both impractical and unnecessary. Instead of focusing such efforts on regions where a species is rare, the focus should be on critical regions where there are peak populations of the species within its range, thus ensuring its conservation there. Such a perspective, backed by sound scientific analysis, can suggest priorities where protection objectives, in irreconcilable conflict with resident peoples' needs, could be selectively sacrificed.

If the international conservation community is willing to accommodate resident peoples only where they do not damage optimal protection objectives, then the future of such conservation is bleak. For then, as Stuart Marks prophesied in the introduction, the forces of human history may mandate such alternatives, but in a far less planned-for way with far greater ecological impact, against an embattled opposition who will have lost the moral higher ground, and thus its most precious commodity, its legitimacy in the eyes of the resident peoples and in the eyes of the world.

BIBLIOGRAPHY

Abbreviations

ANPWS   Australia National Parks and Wildlife Service
IUCN   International Union for the Conservation of Nature
        and Natural Resources
JBNHS   *Journal of the Bombay Natural History Society*

Abdulali, H. 1942. "Partridge Snaring by Wandering Tribes."
    JBNHS 43:659.
Agarwal, A. 1986. Bulldozing the poor. *Resurgence* 116:8–13.
American Folklife Center. 1983. *Cultural Conservation*. Publica-
    tion of the American Folklife Center No. 10. Washington,
    D.C.: Library of Congress.
Annis, S. 1987. "The Next World Bank: Can It Finance Develop-
    ment From the Bottom-up?" Paper presented to the sub-
    committee on International Development Institutions and
    Finance, U.S. Congress, House of Representatives, April 23,
    1987.
(Anonymous). 1926. "Jurisprudence van de Zuidwestereilanden
    (1923)." *Adatrechtbundels* 25:415–421.
(Anonymous). 1947. *Report of the Terai and Bhabar Development
    Committee*. Allahabad: Government Press.
(Anonymous). 1973. *Report of the Commission of Enquiry into
    Land Matters*. Port Moresby.
Ashby, J. A. 1982. "Technology and Ecology: Implications for In-
    novation Research in Peasant Agriculture." *Rural Sociology*
    47:234–250.
————. 1985. "The Social Ecology of Soil Erosion in a Colombian
    Farming System." *Rural Sociology* 50:377–396.
Australia. National Parks and Wildlife Service (ANPWS). 1980.
    Kakadu National Park Plan of Management. Canberra:
    ANPWS.
————. 1986. *Kakadu National Park Plan of Management*. Can-
    berra: ANPWS.
Australia, Statutes. 1975. *National Parks and Wildlife Conser-
    vation Act 1975*. Canberra: Australian Government Publica-
    tions Service (AGPS).

Ayres, R. L. 1981. *Banking on the Poor*. Cambridge, Mass.: MIT Press.

Bacow, L. S., and M. Wheeler. 1984. *Environmental Dispute Resolution*. New York: Plenum Press.

Bailey, C. 1984. "Managing an Open-Access Resource: The Case of Coastal Fisheries." In D. C. Korten and R. Klauss, eds., *People-Centered Development: Contributions Toward Theory and Planning Frameworks*, 97–104. West Hartford, Conn.: Kumarian Press.

Baker, H. G., and G. L. Stebbins. 1965. *The Genetics of Colonizing Species*. New York: Academic Press.

Bandyopadhyay, J., N. D. Jayal, U. Schoettli, and Chhatrapatisingh, eds. 1985. *India's Environmental Crises: Issues and Responses*. Dehra Dun: Natraj Publishers.

Barry, T. 1987. *Land and Hunger in Central America*. Boston: South End Press.

Bazzaz, F. A. 1986. "Life History of Colonizing Plants: Some Demographic, Genetic, and Physiological Features." In H. A. Mooney and J. A. Drake, eds., *Ecology of Biological Invasions of North America and Hawaii*, 96–110. New York: Springer-Verlag.

Bedi, R., and R. Bedi. 1934. *Indian Wildlife*. New Delhi: Brijbasi Printers.

Bel, F. 1979. "L'Intérdependance des Systémes Écologiques et des Systémes D'Activités Économiques: Essai à Propos de la Lozère et des Cévennes," *Annales du Parc National des Cévennes*. Grenoble: Université des Sciences Sociales, Institut de Recherche Économique et de Planification.

Bell, R.H.V. 1986. "Monitoring Public Attitudes." In R.H.V. Bell and E. McShane-Caluzi, eds., *Conservation and Wildlife Management in Africa*, 441–450. Washington, D.C.: Peace Corps.

Berger, T. 1977. *Northern Frontier: Northern Homeland*. Proceedings of the Northern Canada Pipeline Inquiry. Toronto: James Lorimar and Company.

Berreman, G. D. 1972. *Hindus of the Himalayas*. Berkeley: University of California Press.

Berwick, S. 1976. "The Gir Forest: An Endangered Ecosystem." *American Scientist* 64:28–40.

Bezruchka, S. 1985. *A Guide to Trekking in Nepal*. Seattle, Wash.: Mountaineers Press.

Bidol, P. 1987. "Actualizing Synegistist Multi-cultural Training Program." In W. B. Reddy and C. C. Henderson, Jr., eds.,

Training Theory and Practice. Arlington, Va.: N.T.L. for Applied Behavioral Science, University Association, Inc.

Bjorness, I. 1979. "Impacts on a High Mountain Ecosystem: Recommendations for Action in Sagarmatha (Mount Everest) National Park." Unpublished paper, quoted in Garratt, 1981.

Blacksell, M. 1982. "The Spirit and Purpose of National Parks in Britain." *Parks* 6 (4): 14–17.

Boardman, R. 1981. *International Organization and the Conservation of Nature.* Bloomington, Ind.: Indiana University Press.

Bodley, J. H. 1975. *Victims of Progress.* 1st ed. Menlo Park, Calif.: Cummings Press.

———. 1982. *Victims of Progress.* 2d ed. Menlo Park, Calif.: Cummings Press.

Brechin, S. R., and D. Harmon. 1983. "People and Protected Areas: Management Concepts and Issues." Unpublished paper. Ann Arbor: University of Michigan, School of Natural Resources.

Brechin, S. R., and P. C. West. 1990. "Protected Areas, Resident Peoples and Sustainable Conservation: The Need to Link Top-Down With Bottom-up." *Society and Natural Resources* 3(1): 77–79.

Bright, J. 1982. "Cross-Cultural Transfer of Parks Technology." Paper presented at the World National Park Congress, Bali, Indonesia.

Broadus, J. M. 1987. "The Galapagos Marine Resources Reserve and Tourism Development." *Oceanus* 30 (2): 9–15.

Broadus, J. M., I. Pires, A. Gaines, C. Bailey, R. Knecht, and B. Cicin-Sain. 1984. *Coastal and Marine Resources Management for the Galapagos Islands.* Technical Report WHOI-84-43. Woods Hole, Mass.: Woods Hole Oceanographic Institution.

Brooke, J. 1988. "Niger Works to Save a Species and Bolster a Tribe." *New York Times.* May 9.

Brotherton, D. I. 1982. "National Parks in Great Britain and the Achievement of Nature Conservation Purposes." *Biological Conservation* 22 (1): 85–100.

———. 1985. "Issues in National Park Administration." *Environment and Planning* 17: 47–58.

Buckner, E. N., and W. McCracken. 1978. "Yellow Poplar: A Component of Deciduous Forests?" *Journal of Forestry* 76: 421–423.

Burch, W. R., Jr. 1971. *Daydreams and Nightmares: A Sociological Essay on the American Environment.* New York: Harper and Row.

Burdon, J. J., and G. A. Chilvers. 1977. "Preliminary Studies on a Native Australian Eucalypt Forest Invaded by Exotic Pines." *Oecologia* 31:1–12.

Burrough, J. B. 1978. "Cabbages, Conservation and Copper." In M. Luping, W. Chin, and E. R. Dingley, eds., *Kinabalu: Summit of Borneo,* 75–90. Sabah Society Monograph. Malaysia: Kota Kinabalu.

Burton, R. W. 1950. "A Bibliography of Big Game Hunting and Shooting in India and the East." *JBNHS* 49:222–241.

———. 1951a. "Wild Life Reserves in India: Uttar Pradesh." *JBNHS* 49:749–754.

———. 1951b. "The Protection of World Resources: Wild Life and the Soil." *JBNHS* 50:376.

———. 1952. "A History of Shikar in India." *JBNHS* 50:843–869.

———. 1953. *The Preservation of Wild Life in India.* Bangalore: Bangalore Press.

Buttel, F. H. 1974. "Cross-National Patterns of Habitat Preservation: A Test of Hypotheses From U.S. Research." *Humboldt Journal of Social Relations* 2 (1):11–17.

Calhoun, J. B. 1972. "Plight of the Ik as a Chilling Possible End for Man." *Smithsonian* 3 (8):19–23.

Canada. 1978. *Parks Canada Policy.* Ottawa: Department of Environment.

———. 1985a. *Living Treaties: Lasting Agreements.* Reports of the Task Force to Review Comprehensive Claims Policy. Ottawa: Department of Indian Affairs and Northern Development.

———. 1985b. *The Western Arctic Claim: The Inuvialuit Final Agreement.* Ottawa: Department of Indian Affairs and Northern Development.

———. 1987. *Comprehensive Claims Policy.* Ottawa: Department of Indian Affairs and Northern Development.

Carrier, J. G. 1981. "Ownership of Productive Resources on Ponan Island, Manus Province." *Journal de la Société des Océanities* 37:205–217.

Centre for Science and Environment (CES). 1985. *The State of India's Environment, 1894–1985.* The Second Citizen's Report. New Delhi: Centre for Science and Environment.

Cernea, M. M., ed. 1985. *Putting People First: Sociological Variables in Rural Development.* Published for the World Bank. New York: Oxford University Press.

Chaitnya, K. 1982. "Toward Recovery of Old Perception." *India International Quarterly* 9 (3 and 4). Special issue on Environment India.

Chambers, R. 1974. *Managing Rural Development: Ideas and Experience from East Africa.* Uppsala: Scandinavian Institute of African Studies.

Chambers, R., R. Longhurst, and D. Bradley. 1984. "The Seasons of Poverty." In D. C. Korten and R. Klauss, eds., *People-Centered Development: Contributions Toward Theory and Planning Frameworks,* 128–132. West Hartford, Conn.: Kumarian Press.

Chapin, M., and P. Breslin. 1984. "Conservation Kuna-Style." *Grassroots Development* 8:2.

Cherry, G. E. 1985. "Scenic Heritage and National Parks Lobbies and Legislation in England and Wales." *Leisure Studies* 4:127–139.

Child, G. 1984. "Managing Wildlife for People in Zimbabwe." In J. A. McNeely and K. R. Miller, eds., *National Parks, Conservation and Development: The Role of Protected Areas in Sustaining Society,* 118–123. Proceedings of the World Congress on National Parks, Bali, Indonesia, 11–22 October 1982. Washington, D.C.: Smithsonian Institution Press.

Clad, J. C. 1982. "Conservation and Indigenous Peoples: A Study of Convergent Interests." Paper presented at the World National Parks Congress, Bali, Indonesia.

Coburn, B. 1985. "Energy Alternatives for Sagarmatha National Park." In J. A. McNeely, J. Thorsell, and S. Chalise, eds., *People and Protected Areas in the Hindu Kush-Himalaya,* 71–72. Proceedings of the International Workshop on the Management of Parks and Protected Areas in the Hindu Kush-Himalaya, 6–11 May 1985, Kathmandu: King Mahendra Trust for Nature Conservation and International Centre for Integrated Mountain Development (ICIMOD).

Colletta, N. J. 1975. "The Use of Indigenous Culture as a Medium for Development: The Indonesian Case." *Indonesian Journal of Social and Economic Affairs* 1 (2): 60–73.

———. 1977. "Folk Culture and Development: Culture Genocide or Reconstruction Mentality?" *International Journal of Adult Education* 10 (2): 12.

Conservation Commission of the Northern Territory (CCNT). 1984. *Cobourg Peninsula Sanctuary Plan of Management: Draft for Discussion Only.* Darwin: CCNT.

Consultora de Investigaciones para el Desarrollo Urbano Regional. 1983. *Necesidades Educativas Básicas del Cantón Isabela-Galapagos. Investigaciones para el Desarrollo Urbano Regional.* n.p., n.d.

Countryside Commission, The. 1977. *Ninth Report, 1976–1977.* London: Her Majesty's Stationery Office.

———. 1978. *Tenth Report, 1977–1978.* London: Her Majesty's Stationery Office.

Crawley, M. J. 1986. "The Population Biology of Invaders." *Philosophical Transactions of the Royal Society of London (Phil. Trans. Soc. Lond.)* B314:711–731.

———. 1988. "What Makes a Community Invasible?" In A. J. Gray, M. J. Crawley, and P. J. Edwards, eds., *Colonization, Succession and Stability,* 429–453. 26th Symposium, British Ecological Society. London: Blackwell Scientific Publications.

Cremer, K. W., R. N. Cromer, and R. G. Florence. 1978. "Stand Establishment." In W. E. Hillis and A. G. Brown, eds., *Eucalypts for Wood Production,* 81–135. Australia: Commonwealth Scientific and Industrial Research Organization.

Crocombe, R. G., and R. L. Hide. 1971. "New Guinea: Unity in Diversity." In R. G. Crocombe, ed., *Land Tenure in the Pacific,* 292–333. London: Oxford University Press.

Cumming, P. 1985. "Canada's North and Native Rights." In B. W. Morse, ed., *Aboriginal Peoples and the Law: Indian, Metis, and Inuit Rights in Canada,* 695–731. Ottawa: Carleton University Press.

Dandekar, H. C. 1986. *Men to Bombay, Women at Home.* Ann Arbor: University of Michigan, Center for South and South-East Asian Studies.

Dasmann, R. F. 1975. "Difficult Marginal Environments and the Traditional Societies Which Exploit Them: Ecosystems." *News From Survival International,* no. 11.

———. 1984. "The Relationship Between Protected Areas and Indigenous Peoples." In J. A. McNeely and K. R. Miller, eds., *National Parks, Conservation and Development: The Role of Protected Areas in Sustaining Society,* 667–672. Proceedings of the World Congress on National Parks, Bali, Indonesia, 11–22 October 1982. Washington, D.C.: Smithsonian Institution Press.

Davies, G., and J. Payne. 1982. *A Faunal Survey of Sabah.* Kuala Lumpur: International Union for the Conservation of Nature and Natural Resources/World Wildlife Fund (IUCN/WWF) Project No. 1692.

de Groot, R. S. 1983. "Tourism and Conservation in the Galapagos Islands." *Biological Conservation* 26:291–300.

Deihl, C. 1985. "Wildlife and the Maasai." *Cultural Survival Quarterly* 9 (1): 37–40.

de Kadt, E. 1979. *Tourism: Passport to Development?* New York: Oxford University Press.

Department of Indian and Northern Affairs. 1978. Communique: Faulkner Announces Public Consultation for Six Artic Wilderness Areas in the National Park System. Jaunuary 23.

Desai, J. R. 1976. "The Gir Forest Reserve: Its Habitat, Faunal, and Social Problems." In Sir Hugh Elliot, IUCN, ed., *The Second World Conference on National Parks,* 193–198. Morges, Switzerland: IUCN.

Dewer, R. E., S. Goldstein, and A. F. Richard. 1981. "Anthropogenetic Alteration of a Himalayan Temperate Forest." Paper presented at the Annual Meeting of the American Association of Physical Anthropology, Detroit, April.

Dharmakumarsinhji. 1982. "The Lions of Gir." *Sanctuary* 2 (4): 326–341.

Dirección de Turismo del Litoral. 1980. *Informacion Turistica Galapagos.* Cuenca, Ecuador: Dirección de Turismo del Litoral.

Dobyns, H. F., and R. C. Euler. 1971. "The Havasupai People." *Indian Tribal Series.* Phoenix, Arizona: Center for Anthropological Studies.

Dower, J. 1945. "National Parks in England and Wales." *Reports from Commissioners, Inspectors and Others, 1944–1945,* Cmd.; 6628. London: His Majesty's Stationery Office.

East, K. 1986. "Resource Co-Management in Wood Buffalo National Park: The National Parks Perspective." In *Native People and Renewable Resource Management, 86–95.* Proceedings of the 1986 Symposium of the Alberta Society of Professional Biologists. April 29–May 1. Edmonton. Symposium Series no. 10. Edmonton: Alberta Society of Professional Biologists.

Eidsvik, H. K. 1979. "The Biosphere Reserve and Its Relationship to Other Protected Areas." IUCN, Morges, Switzerland.
———. 1985. "Biosphere Reserves in Concept and Practice." In J. D. Paine, ed., *Proceedings of the Conference on the Management of Biosphere Reserves.* Great Smokey Mountains National Park, Gatlinburg, Tenn. Uplands Field Research Laboratory, Smoky Mountains National Park Biosphere Reserve.

Epton, N. C. 1974. *Magic and Mystics of Java.* London: Octagon.

Euler, R. C. 1979. "The Havasupai of the Grand Canyon." *American West* 16 (3): 12–65.

Farmer, B. 1974. *Agricultural Colonization in India Since Independence.* Oxford: Oxford University Press.

Feit, H. A. 1983. "Conflict Arenas in the Management of Renewable Resources in the Canadian North: Perspectives Based on Conflicts and Responses in the James Bay Region, Quebec." In *National and Regional Interests in the North,* 435–458. Proceedings of the Third National Workshop on People, Resources, and the Environment North of 60. Ottawa: Canadian Arctic Resources Committee.

———. 1988. *Self Management and State Management: Forms of Knowing and Managing Northern Wildlife.* Traditional Knowledge and Renewable Resource Institute, Publication No. 23. Edmonton.

Finsterbusch, K. 1977. *Methods for Evaluating Non-Market Impacts in Policy Decisions, with Special Reference to Water Resources Development Projects.* Fort Belvoir, Va.: Institute for Water Resources.

Finsterbusch, K, L. G. Llewellyn, and C. P. Wolf, eds. 1983. *Social Impact Assessment Methods.* Beverly Hills: Sage Publications.

Firey, W. 1960. *Man, Mind, and Land: A Theory of Resource Use.* Glencoe, Ill.: Free Press.

Ford-Robertson, F. C. 1936. *Our Forests.* Allahabad: Government Press.

Foresta, R. A. 1984. *America's National Parks and Their Keepers.* Washington, D.C.: Resources for the Future.

Foster, J. 1979. "A Park System and Scenic Conservation in Scotland." *Parks* 4 (2):1–4.

Foster, J., A. Phillips, and R. Steele. 1982. "Limited Choices: Protected Areas in the United Kingdom." Paper presented at the World National Parks Congress, Bali, Indonesia.

Fox, A. 1983. "Kakadu is Aboriginal Land." *Ambio* 12 (3/4): 161–166.

Fox, J., R. W., G. H. Kelleher, and C. B. Kerr. 1977. *Ranger Uranium Environmental Inquiry: Second Report.* May 17, 1977. Canberra: Australian Government Publishing Service.

Frankel, O. H., and M. E. Soule. 1981. *Conservation and Evolution.* Cambridge: Cambridge University Press.

Freudenburg, W. R. 1986. "Social Impact Assessment." *Annual Review of Sociology* 12:451–478.

Fundación para la Educación Superior (FES). 1983. *Plan Operativo, 1983–1985, Reserva Natural la Planada.* Cali, Colombia: FES.

Garces, F., and J. Ortiz. 1983. *Diagnóstico de la Actividad Turística en la Provincia de Galápagos y Sus Impactos Sociales y Ecológicos.* Quito, Ecuador: Instituto Nacional Galápagos.

Garratt, K. J. 1981. "Management Plan for Sagarmatha National Park." Kathmandu, Nepal: National Parks and Wildlife Conservation Office.

———. 1984. "The Relationship Between Adjacent Lands and Protected Areas: Issues of Concern for the Proteced Area Manager." In J. A. McNeely and K. Miller, eds., *National Parks, Conservation, and Development: The Role of Protected Areas in Sustaining Society,* 65–71. Proceedings of the World Congress on National Parks, Bali, Indonesia, 11–22 October 1982. Washington, D.C.: Smithsonian Institution Press.

Geartz, C. 1986. "The Uses of Diversity." *Michigan Quarterly Review* 25 (1): 105–123.

Gee, E. P. 1950. "Wild Life Reserves in India: Assam." *JBNHS* 49:82.

Gillespie, D. 1983. *The Rock Art Sites of Kakadu National Park.* Special Publication no. 10. Canberra: ANPWS.

Glaeser, B. 1984. *Ecodevelopment: Concepts, Projects, Strategies.* Oxford: Pergamon Press.

Glick, D. 1981. "Honduras Biosphere Reserve." Masters thesis, School of Natural Resources, University of Michigan.

Glick, D., and J. Betancourt. 1983. "The Rio Platano Biosphere Reserve: Unique Resource, Unique Alternative." *Ambio* 12:168–173.

Gomm, R. 1974. "The Elephant Man." *Ecologist* 4 (2): 53–57.

Goodland, R. 1982. *Tribal Peoples and Economic Development.* Washington, D.C.: International Bank for Reconstruction and Development.

———. 1985. "Tribal Peoples and Economic Development." In J. A. McNeely and D. Pitt, eds., *Culture and Conservation,* 13–32. London: Croomhelm.

Government of Gujarat. 1975. *Gir Lion Sanctuary Project.* Gandhinadar, India: Forest Department, Government Central Press.

———. 1981. Development of Community Forestry in Gujarat. Vadodara, India. Government Press.

Government of India. 1986. *Strategies, Structures, Policies: National Wastelands Development Board.* New Delhi: National Land Use and Wastelands Development Council.

Gradwohl, J., and R. Greenberg. 1988. *Saving the Tropical Forests.* Washington, D.C.: Island Press.

Gray, A. J., M. J. Crawley, and P. J. Edwards. 1987. *Colonization, Succession, and Stability.* 26th Symposium, British Ecological Society. Boston: Blackwell Scientific Publications.

Greenbaum, R. A. 1982. "The Pinelands and the 'Taking' Question." *Columbia Journal of Environmental Law* 7 (2): 227–249.

Griffith, R. 1987. "Northern Park Development: The Case of Snowdrift." *Alternatives* 14 (1): 26–30.

Grindle, M. S. 1977. *Bureaucrats, Politicians, and Peasants in Mexico: A Case Study in Public Policy.* Berkeley: University of California Press.

Guha, R. 1983. "Forestry in British and Post-British India: A Historical Analysis." *Economic and Political Weekly,* October 29:1882–1896; November 5–12:1940–1947.

Gunn, A., G. Arlooktoo, and D. Kaomayak. 1988. "The Contribution of the Ecological Knowledge of Inuit to Wildlife Management in the Northwest Territories." In M.M.R. Freeman and L. Carbyn, eds., *Traditional Knowledge and Renewable Resource Management in Northern Regions.* Edmonton, Boreal Institute Occasional Publication #23.

Hakone Accommodation Association, ed. 1986. *The History of Sakone Hot Springs.* Tokyo: Gyosei.

Hales, D. F. 1978. Testimony Before the U.S. Senate Concerning the Pine Barrens, New Jersey. Washington, D.C.: USGPO.

———. 1984. "The World Heritage Convention: Status and Directions." In J. A. McNeely and K. R. Miller, eds., *National Parks, Conservation, and Development: The Role of Protected Areas in Sustaining Society,* 744–750. Proceedings of the World Congress on National Parks, Bali, Indonesia, 11–22 October 1982. Washington, D.C.: Smithsonian Institution Press.

Halffater, G. 1981. "The Mapimi Biosphere Reserve: Local Participation in Conservation and Development." *Ambio* 10 (2–3): 93–96.

Halffater, G., and E. Ezcurra. 1987. "Evolution of the Biosphere Reserve Concept." Paper presented at the Fourth World Wilderness Congress, Estes Park, Colorado, September.

Harmon, D. 1987. "Cultural Diversity, Human Subsistence, and the National Park Ideal." *Environmental Ethics* 9:147–158.

Hatley, T., and M. Thompson. 1985. "Rare Animals, Poor People, and Big Agencies: A Perspective on Biological Conservation and Rural Development in the Himalaya." *Mountain Research and Development* 5:365–377.

Heady, H. F. 1988. "Valley Grassland." In M. G. Barbour and J. Major, eds., *Terrestrial Vegetation of California,* 491–514. California Native Plant Society, Special Publication No. 9, Davis, California.

Heffernan, W. D., and G. P. Green. 1986. "Farm Size and Soil Loss: Prospects for a Sustainable Agriculture." *Rural Sociology* 51:31–42.

Heymans, J. C. Undated. Extrait des Reglements de la chasse. Mimeo, FSA, National University of Benin.

Hickson, S. J. 1886. "Notes on the Sengirese." *Journal of the Anthropological Institute* 16:136–142.

Hill, M. 1983. "Kakadu National Park and the Aboriginals: Partners in Protection." *Ambio* 12 (3–4):158–167.

Hirst, S. 1985. *Havsuw 'Baaja: People of the Blue Green Water.* Havasupai Tribe, Supai, Arizona.

Hobhouse, Sir A. (chairperson). 1947. "Report of the National Parks Committee (England and Wales)." *Reports from Commissioners, Inspectors and Others, 1946–1947.* Cmd. 7121. London: His Majesty's Stationery Office.

Hodd, K.T.B. 1969. "The Ecological Impact of Domestic Stock on the Gir Forest." *Proceedings of the IUCN 11th Technical Meeting at New Delhi, India,* 259–265. 1 sec. D(2). Morges, Switzerland: IUCN Publications.

Holloway, C. W., G. B. Schaller, and A. R. Wani. 1969. "Dachigam Wild Life Sanctuary, Kashmir: Status and Management of the Kashmir Stag *Cervus elephus hanglu*: Report." *IUCN Eleventh Technical Meeting,* vol. 3. New Delhi: IUCN.

Hough, J. L. 1986. "A Framework for Valuing Wildlands in the Miombo Woodland Biome of Southern Africa." M.S. thesis, University of Michigan.

———. 1988. "Obstacles to Effective Management of Conflicts Between National Parks and Surrounding Human Communities in Developing Countries." *Environmental Conservation* 15 (2):129–136.

———. 1989. "National Parks and Local People Relationships: Case Studies From Northern Benin, West Africa, and the Grand Canyon, USA." Ph.D. diss., University of Michigan.

Hough, J. L., and M. N. Sherpa. 1989. "Bottom Up vs. Basic Needs: Integrating Conservation and Development in the Annapurna and Michiru Mountain Conservation Areas of Nepal and Malawi." *Ambio* 18(8): 434–41.

Inkeles, A., and D. H. Smith. 1974. *Becoming Modern: Individual Change in Six Developing Countries*. Cambridge, Mass.: Harvard University Press.

Instituto Nacional Galapagos (INGALA). 1981. *Indicadores Regionales—Provincia de Galapagos*. Quito, Ecuador: INGALA.

———. 1982. *Plan Operativo INGALA; 1983, 1984*. Quito, Ecuador: INGALA.

International Institute for Environment and Development (IIED) and World Resources Institute (WRI). 1987. *World Resources 1987*. New York: Basic Books.

International Union for Conservation of Nature and Natural Resources (IUCN). 1975. *World Directory of National Parks and Other Protected Areas*. Gland, Switzerland: IUCN.

———. 1980a. *World Conservation Strategy: Living Resource Conservation for Sustainable Development*. Gland: IUCN, United Nations Development Program (UNDP), and World Wildlife Fund (WWF).

———. 1980b. "How Conservation: Discussion Between Professor E. Salim, Dr. Omo Fadaka, and D. Schultze-Westrum." Gland, Switzerland: IUCN Commission on Ecology.

———. 1985. *1985 United Nations List of National Parks and Protected Areas*. Gland, Switzerland, and Cambridge, U.K.: IUCN.

IUCN and Commission on National Parks and Protected Areas (CNPPA). 1984. "Categories, Objectives and Criteria for Protected Areas." In J. A. McNeely and K. R. Miller, eds., *National Parks, Conservation, and Development: The Role of Protected Areas in Sustaining Society*, 47–53. Proceedings of the World Congress on National Parks, Bali, Indonesia, 11–22 October 1982. Washington, D.C.: Smithsonian Institution Press.

IUCN and Conservation Monitoring Centre. 1987. *Protected Landscapes: Experience Around the World*. Gland, Switzerland: IUCN.

Jacobson, S. K. 1985. *Kinabalu Park*. Sabah Parks Publication No. 7. Sabah, Malaysia.

———. 1987. "Conservation Education Programmes: Evaluate and Improve Them." *Environmental Conservation* 14 (3): 201–205.

Jefferies, B. E. 1982. "Sagarmatha National Park: The Impact of Tourism in the Himalayas." *Ambio* 11 (5): 274–281.

Jenkins, D. V., F. Liew, and P. Hecht. 1976. *A National Parks Policy for Sabah*. Sabah, Malaysia: Government Printing Office.

Johannes, R. E. 1978. "Traditional Marine Conservation Methods in Oceania and Their Demise." *Annual Review of Ecology and Systematics* 9:349–364.

———. 1981. *Words of the Lagoon*. Berkeley: University of California Press.

———. 1982. "Traditional Conservation Methods and Protected Marine Areas in Oceania." *Ambio* 11 (5): 258–261.

Joslin, P. K. 1969. "Conserving the Asiatic Lion." *Proceedings of the IUCN 11th Technical Meeting at New Delhi, India*, 24–33. 2 sec. 1b. Morges, Switzerland: IUCN Publications.

Junguis, H. 1976. "National Parks and Indigenous People: A Peruvian Case Study." *Survival International Review* 1 (14): 6–14.

Kandari, O. P., and T. V. Singh. 1982. "Corbett Park, India: An Exploratory Survey of Habitat, Recreational Use and Resource Ecology." In T. V. Singh et al. (eds.), *Studies in Tourism, Wildlife Parks and Conservation*, 244–246. New Delhi: Metropolitan Press.

Kellert, S. R. 1986. "Public Understanding and Appreciation of the Biosphere Reserve Concept." *Environmental Conservation* 13 (2): 101–105.

Kolff, D. H. 1840. *Voyage of the Dutch Brig of War Dourga*. London: Madden.

Korten, D. C., and R. Klauss, eds. 1984. *People-Centered Development: Contributions Toward Theory and Planning Frameworks*. West Hartford, Conn.: Kumarian Press.

Kun, S. 1979. "An Overview of Canada's National Parks." Paper presented at the 14th International Seminar on National Parks and Equivalent Reserves, Jasper, Alberta, August.

Kutay, K. 1984. "Cahuita National Park, Costa Rica: A Case Study in Living Cultures and National Park Management." Masters thesis, School of Natural Resources, University of Michigan.

Lahav, H. 1988. "Regeneration of Vegetation After Fire in Natural Pine Forest on Mount Carmel." M.S. thesis, Department of Botany, Tel Aviv University.

Lang, R., and A. Armour. 1981. *The Assessment and Review of Social Impacts*. Ottawa, Canada: Federal Environmental Assessment and Review Office.

Laue, J. H., and G. Cormick. 1978. "The Ethics of Intervention in Community Disputes." In G. Bermant, H. C. Kelman, and D. P. Warwick, eds., *The Ethics of Social Intervention*, 205–232. Washington, D.C.: Halsted Press.

Lawson, N. 1985. "Where Whitemen Come to Play." *Cultural Survival Quarterly* 9 (1): 54–56.

LeBar, F. M. 1972. *Ethnic Groups of Insular Southeast Asia.* Vol. 1: *Indonesia.* New Haven, Conn.: Human Relations Area Files.

Lehmkuhl, J. F., R. K. Upreti, and U. R. Sharma. 1988. "National Parks and Local Development: Grasses and People in Royal Chitwan National Park, Nepal." *Environmental Conservation* 15 (2): 143–148.

Leipziger, D., ed. 1981. *Basic Needs and Development.* Cambridge, Mass.: Oelgeschlager, Gunn and Hain Publishers.

Leonard, P. 1980. "Agriculture in the National Parks of England and Wales: A Conservation Viewpoint." *Landscape Planning* 7 (4): 369–386.

Levitus, R. 1982. *Everybody Bin All Day Work: A Report to the Australian National Parks and Wildlife Service on the Social History of the Alligator Rivers Region of the Northern Territory, 1869–1973.* Canberra: Australian Institute of Aboriginal Studies. February 1982.

Lewis, H. T. 1989. "Ecological and Technical Knowledge of Fire: Aborigines versus Park Rangers in Northern Australia." *American Anthropologist* 91:940–961.

Ley de Parques Nacionales y Reservas, Decreto no. 1,306 de 27 Agosto, 1971, Registro Oficial no. 301, 2 de Septiembre, 1971: Providing for the Creation and Administration of National Parks and Reserve Zones, Including Marine Parks. Ecuador: Government of Ecuador.

Lovejoy, S. B., and T. L. Napier, eds. 1986. *Conserving Soil: Insights from Socioeconomic Research.* Ankeny, Ia.: Soil Conservation Society of America.

Loza, H. P. 1981. *Ecologia Humana para las Islas Galapagos.* Puerto Ayora, Santa Cruz, Galapagos Islands, Ecuador: Charles Darwin Research Station.

Lusigi, W. J. 1983. "Mt. Kulal Biosphere Reserve: Reconciling Conservation with Local Human Population Needs." First International Biosphere Reserve Congress (UNESCO), Minisk/BSSR-USSR, September 26–October 2.

———. 1984. "Future Directions for the Afro-Tropical Realm." In J. A. McNeely and K. R. Miller, eds., *National Parks, Con-*

servation and Development: The Role of Protected Areas in Sustaining Society, 137–146. Proceedings of the World Congress on National Parks, Bali, Indonesia, 11–22 October 1982. Washington, D.C.: Smithsonian Institution Press.

MacCannell, D. 1976. *The Tourist.* New York: Schocken Books.

McCormick, J. 1982. Review of *National Parks: Conservation or Cosmetics?* by Ann MacEwen and Malcom MacEwen. *New Scientist* 1 April, pp. 33–34.

McCormick, J. F., and R. B. Platt. 1980. "Recovery of an Appalachian Forest Following the Chestnut Blight, or, Catherine Keever—You Were Right." *American Midland Naturalist* 104:264–273.

McCredie, D. W. 1973. "Mt. Kinabalu and Development in Peripheral Districts in Sabah: A Review of Progress of the Sabah National Parks." *Symposium of Biological Resources and National Development,* 5–7 May 1973. Kuala Lumpur, Malaysia: Malayan Nature Society.

MacEwen, A., and M. MacEwen. 1982. *National Parks: Conservation or Cosmetics?* London: George Allen and Unwin.

Machlis, G. E., and W. R. Burch, Jr. 1983. "Relations Between Strangers: Cycles of Structure and Meaning in Tourist Systems." *Sociological Review* 31 (4): 665–692.

Machlis, G. E., and D. L. Tichnell. 1985. *The State of the World's Parks: An International Assessment for Resource Management, Policy and Research.* Boulder, Colo.: Westview Press.

Mack, R. N. 1985. "Invading Plants: Their Potential Contribution to Population Biology." In J. White, ed., *Studies on Plant Demography,* 127–142. London: Academic Press.

MacKenzie, John M. 1988. *The Entire of Nature: Hunting, Conservation and British Imperialism.* Manchester: Manchester University Press.

McNeely, J. A. 1985. "Man and Nature in the Himalaya: What Can Be Done So Both Can Prosper." In J. A. McNeely, J. Thorsell, and S. Chalise, eds., *People and Protected Areas in the Hindu Kush-Himalaya,* 25–30. Proceedings of the International Workshop on the Management of Parks and Protected Areas in the Hindu Kush-Himalaya, 6–11 May 1985, Kathmandu. King Mehendra Trust for Nature Conservation and International Centre for Integrated Mountain Development.

Manring, N., P. C. West, and P. Bidol. 1990. "Social Impact Assessment and Environmental Conflict Management: The Potential for Integration and Application." *Environmental Impact Assessment Review* 10(3): 253–65.

Marks, P. L. 1974. "The Role of Pin Cherry (*Prunus pen-sylvanica L.*) in the Maintenance of Stability in Northern Hardwood Ecosystems." *Ecological Monographs* 44:73–88.

Marks, S. A. 1976. *Large Mammals and a Brave People.* Seattle: University of Washington Press.

———. 1984. *The Imperial Lion: Human Dimensions of Wildlife Management in Central Africa.* Boulder, Colo.: Westview Press.

———. 1988. "Common Property Regimes and Traditional Management: Methodology, Concepts, and a Review of Current Projects." Rome: Consultants' Report to the Food and Agriculture Organization of the United Nations.

———. 1990. *Southern Hunting in Black and White: An Interpretation of Roles and Rituals in a Carolina Community.* Princeton, N.J.: Princeton University Press.

Martin, J. F. 1987. *The Havasupai.* Flagstaff, Ariz.: Museum of Northern Arizona.

Meganck, R. A., and J. M. Goebel. 1979. "Shifting Cultivation: Problems for Parks in Latin America." *Parks* 4 (2): 4–8.

Merritt, J. 1983. "A Review of Federal Land Claims Policy." *National and Regional Interests in the North,* 71–86. Proceedings of the Third National Workshop on People, Resources and the Environment North of 60. Ottawa: Canadian Arctic Resources Committee.

Miller, K. R. 1978. *Planning National Parks for Ecodevelopment: Methods and Cases From Latin America.* Ann Arbor: Center for Strategic Wildland Management Studies, School of Natural Resources, University of Michigan.

———. 1980. *Planificación de Parques Nacionales para el Ecodesarollo en Latinoamérica.* Madrid: Fundacion para la Ecologia y la Proteccion del Medio Ambiente.

———. 1982. *Planning National Parks for Ecodevelopment: Methods and Cases From Latin America.* Ann Arbor: Center for Strategic Wildland Management Studies, School of Natural Resources, University of Michigan.

Mills, S. 1982. "An Endangered Species," review of *The Economy of Rural Communities in the National Parks of England and Wales,* by Brian Duffield, Roger Vaughn, et al. *New Scientist,* 1 April, p. 33.

Mishra, H. R. 1982. "Balancing Human Needs and Conservation in Nepal's Royal Chitwan Park." *Ambio* 11 (5): 246–251.

Mohamad, S. 1983. "Road Development and Rural Change in Sabah." In H. M. Dahlam, ed., *Sabah: Traces of Change.* Sabah, Malaysia: Universiti Kebangsaan Malaysia-Yayasan.

Mooney, H. A., and J. A. Drake. 1986. *Ecology of Biological Invasions of North America and Hawaii*. New York: Springer-Verlag.

Moody, M. E., and R. N. Mack. 1988. "Controlling the Spread of Plant Invasions: The Importance of Nascent Foci." *Journal of Applied Ecology* 25:1009.

Moss, W. 1985. "The Implementation of the James Bay and Northern Quebec Agreement." In B. W. Morse, ed., *Aboriginal Peoples and the Law: Indian, Metis and Inuit Rights in Canada*, 684–693. Ottawa: Carleton University Press.

Munro, D. 1984. "Global Sharing and Self-Interest in Protected Areas Conservation." In J. A. McNeely and K. R. Miller, eds., *National Parks, Conservation, and Development: The Role of Protected Areas in Sustaining Society*. Proceedings of the World Congress on National Parks, Bali, Indonesia, 11–22 October 1982. Washington, D.C.: Smithsonian Institution Press.

Myers, N. 1972. "National Parks in Savannah Africa." *Science* 178: 1255–1266.

———. 1979. *The Sinking Ark: A New Look at the Problem of Disappearing Species*. New York: Pergamon Press.

Nader, L., and H. E. Todd, Jr. 1978. *The Disputing Process: Law in Ten Societies*. New York: Columbia University Press.

Naik, V. A. 1981. *Man and the Universe: A New Philosophy of Science*. Pune: Shubhada-Saraswat.

Nash, R. 1970. "The American Invention of National Parks." *American Quarterly* 22 (3): 726.

National Parks Act of Canada. R. S. c.N-13, Amended by 1974, c.11.

National Research Council. 1986. *Proceedings of the Conference on Common Property Resource Management, April 21–26, 1985*. Washington: National Academy Press.

Nature Conservation Bureau, Environment Agency, Government of Japan. 1981. *The Administrative History of Nature Conservation*. Tokyo: Daiichi Hoki Shuppan.

Naveh, Z. 1973. "The Ecology of Fire in Israel." Proceedings. Annual Tall Timbers Fire Ecology Conference 13th; 1973. Tallahassee, Fla.: Tall Timbers Research Station, pp. 131–170.

Neidjie, B., S. Davis, and A. Fox. 1985. *Kakadu Man: Bill Neidjie*. Canberra: Mybrook Inc., Allan Fox Associates.

Nevis, E. C. 1983. "Cultural Assumptions and Productivity: The United States and China." *Sloan Management Review* 24 (3): 17–19.

Newby, J., and J. F. Grettenberger. 1986. "The Human Dimension in Natural Resource Conservation: A Sahelian Example from Niger." *Environmental Conservation* 12 (3):249–256.

Newmark, W. D. 1985. "Legal and Biotic Boundaries of Western North American National Parks: A Problem of Congruence." *Biological Conservation* 33:197–208.

Nietschmann, B. 1984. "Indigenous Island Peoples, Living Resources, and Protected Areas." In J. A. McNeely and K. R. Miller, eds., *National Parks, Conservation, and Development: The Role of Protected Areas in Sustaining Society,* 333–343. Proceedings of the World Congress on National Parks, Bali, Indonesia, 11–22 October 1982. Washington, D.C.: Smithsonian Institution Press.

Noble, I. R., and R. O. Slatyer. 1980. "The Use of Vital Attributes to Predict Successional Changes in Plant Communities Subject to Recurrent Disturbances." *Vegetatio* 43:5–21.

Nugent, J. B., and P. A. Yotopoulos. 1984. "Orthodox Development Economics Versus the Dynamics of Concentration and Marginalization." In D. C. Korten and R. Klauss, eds., *People-Centered Development: Contributions Toward Theory and Planning Frameworks,* 107–120. West Hartford, Conn.: Kumarian Press.

Nzima, H. E. 1986. "Law Enforcement and Public Relations: A Case History." In R.H.V. Bell and E. McShane-Caluzi, eds., *Conservation and Wildlife Management in Africa,* 381–386. Washington, D.C.: Peace Corps.

Ogden, F.G.D. 1942. "Partridge Snaring by Wandering Tribes." *JBNHS* 44:299.

Olwig, K. R. 1980. "National Parks, Tourism, and Local Development: A West Indian Case." *Human Organization* 39 (1): 22–31.

Orejuela, J. 1981. "Project Report to World Wildlife Fund." Unpublished paper.

Organization for Economic Cooperation and Development (OECD). 1980. "The Impact of Tourism on the Environment." General Report. Luxemburg.

Osherenko, G. 1988. "Can Comanagement Save Arctic Wildlife?" *Environment* 30 (6):6–13, 29–34.

Penfold, A. R., and J. L. Willis. 1961. *The Eucalypts.* New York: Interscience Publishers.

Perlez, J. 1988. "In Rwanda, No Tourists, No Park." *New York Times,* December 28.

Phillips, A. 1988. "Protected Landscapes in the United Kingdom." In J. Foster, ed., *Protected Landscapes: Summary Proceedings of an International Symposium.* Symposium held in the Lake District, U.K.: International Union for Conservation of Nature and Natural Resources, Countryside Commission, and Countryside Commission for Scotland.

Phythian-Adams, E. G. 1893. "Nilgiri Game Association Report." *JBNHS* 8:535.

———. 1927. "Game Preservation in the Nilgiris." *JBNHS* 32:339–343.

———. 1929. "Game Preservation in the Nilgiris." *JBNHS* 33:947–951.

———. 1939. "The Nilgiri Game Association, 1879–1939." *JBNHS* 41:374–396.

Pinelands Commission. 1980. *New Jersey Pinelands Comprehensive Management Plan.* Vols. 1 and 2.

Pinkerton, E. 1987. "Intercepting the State: Dramatic Processes in Assertion of Local Comanagement Rights." In B. M. McCay and J. M. Acheson, eds., *The Question of the Commons,* 344–369. Tucson: University of Arizona Press.

Plog, F., C. Jolly, and D. Bates. 1976. *Anthropological Decisions, Adaptation, and Evolution.* New York: Knopf.

Polunin, N.V.C. 1983. "The Marine Resources of Indonesia." *Oceanography and Marine Biology Annual Review* 21: 455–531.

———. 1984a. "Do Traditional Marine 'Reserves' Conserve? A View of Indonesian and New Guinean Evidence." *Senri Ethnological Studies* 17:267–283.

———. 1984b. "Traditional Marine Practices in Indonesia and Their Bearing on Conservation." In J. A. McNeely and D. Pitt, eds., *Culture and Conservation,* 155–179. London: Croomhelm.

———. In press. "Marine Regulated Areas: An Expanded Approach for the Tropics." In J. I. Furtado and K. Ruddle, eds., *Tropical Resources Ecology and Development.* New York: Wiley.

Polunin, N.V.C., M. K. Halim, and K. Kvalvagnaes. 1983. "Bali Barat: An Indonesian Marine Protected Area and Its Resources." *Biological Conservation* 25:171–191.

Poore, D., and J. Poore. 1987. *Protected Landscapes: The United Kingdom Experience.* Manchester: Countryside Commission, Countryside Commission for Scotland, Department of the Environment for Northern Ireland, and International Union for Conservation of Nature and Natural Resources.

Prakash, I., and P. K. Ghosh. 1976. "Human-Animal Interactions in the Rajasthan Desert." *JBNHS* 75:1260.

Price, D. 1977a. "Acculturation, Social Assistance and Political Context: The Nambiquara in Brazil." *Proceedings of the XLII International Congress of Americanists,* 603. Paris.

———. 1977b. "Comercio y Aculturación Entre los Nambecuara." *American Indígena* 37 (1): 123–135.

Prime Minister's Office, Government of Japan. 1980. *The 100 Year History of Tourism Administration and the 30 Year Progress of the Tourism Policy Council.* Tokyo: Gyosei.

Putney, A. D. 1982. *Reformulación del Plan de Manejo: Parque Nacional Galápagos.* Borrador Informe de Consulta. Puerto Ayora, Santa Cruz, Galapagos Islands, Ecuador: Comisión por el Plan Maestro de Galápagos.

Rabinovitch, A. 1982. "The Influence of Fire in the Mediterranean Maquis." *Teva va'Aretz* 24:201–205. In Hebrew.

Rabinovitch-Vin, A. 1983. "Influence of Nutrients on the Composition and Distribution of Plant Communities in Mediterranean-Type Ecosystems of Israel." In F. I. Kruger, D. F. Mitchell, and J.U.N. Jarvis, eds., *Mediterranean-Type Ecosystems: The Role of Nutrients.* New York: Springer-Verlag.

Ramos, A., and K. Taylor. 1976. *The Yanoama in Brazil.* IWGIA Document no. 37. Copenhagen: International Workgroup for Indigenous Affairs.

Ramsay, Sir J. D., F. F. Darling, D. G. Moir, and P. Thomsen. 1945. "National Parks: A Scottish Survey." *Reports from Commissioners, Inspectors and Others* 1944–1945. Cmd. 6631. Edinburgh: His Majesty's Stationery Office.

Randle, E. M. 1982. "The National Reserve System and Transferable Development Rights." *Boston College Environmental Affairs Law Review* 10:183–241.

Raval, S. R. 1986. "Minimum Viable Population: A Study of Asiatic Lions." Unpublished manuscript. Ann Arbor: School of Natural Resources, University of Michigan.

Raven, P. H. 1986. "The California Flora." In M. G. Barbour and J. Major, eds., *Terrestrial Vegetation of California,* 109–137. California Native Plant Society, Special Publication No. 9.

Reck, G. K. 1983. *The Coastal Fisheries in the Galapagos Islands, Ecuador.* Doctoral diss., Christian-Albrechts-Universität zu Kiel, Kiel, Bremerhaven, West Germany.

Reck, G., and T. W. Rodriguez. 1978. "Informe Sobre Pesca de Bacalao y Especies Afines, 1977–78." Unpublished report. Guayaquil, Ecuador: Instituto Nacional de Pesca.

Rhodehamel, E. C. 1973. *Geology and Water Resources of the Wharton Tract and Mullica River Basin*. Special Report No. 36. New Jersey Department of Environmental Protection.

Richards, J. F., et al. In preparation. *Land-Use and Vegetation Changes in South and Southeast Asia, 1700–1980*.

Risk, M., M. Murillo, and J. Cortes. 1980. "Observaciones Biológicas Preliminares Sobre el Arrecife Coralino en el Parque Nacional de Cahuita, Costa Rica." *Revista Biológico Tropical* [San José, Costa Rica] 28 (2): 361–372.

Robinson, A. H. 1975. *Recreation, Interpretation and Environmental Education in Marine Parks*. Working Paper No. 4. IUCN Publications, n.s., no. 37. Morges, Switzerland: IUCN Publications.

Robinson, G. 1983. "The Marine Park in Galapagos: A Case Study." Unpublished report. Puerto Ayora, Santa Cruz, Galapagos Islands, Ecuador: Charles Darwin Research Station.

Robinson, W. L., and E. G. Bolen. 1989. *Wildlife Ecology and Management*. New York: Macmillan Publishing Co.

Rodriquez, P. W. 1984. "Estudio preliminar para evaluar las caracteristicas biologicas pesqueras de *Mycteroperca olfax* en las Islas Galapagos (Ecuador)." *Boletin Cientifico y Tecnico*. Guayquil: Instituto Nacional de Pesca.

Runte, A. 1979. *National Parks: The American Experience*. Lincoln: University of Nebraska Press.

Rutgers, The State University of New Jersey. 1978. *A Plan For a Pinelands National Reserve*. New Brunswick, N.J.

Rutter, O. 1922. *British North Borneo: An Account of Its History, Resources, and Native Tribes*. London: Constable and Co.

Sabah State Government. 1980. Siaran Perangkaan Tahunan. Kota Kinabalu, Sabah, Malaysia: Government Printing Office.

———. 1983. Siaran Perangkaan Tahunan. Kota Kinabalu, Sabah, Malaysia: Government Printing Office.

Saharia, V. B. 1982. "Human Dimension in Wildlife Management: The Indian Experience." In J. A. McNeely and K. R. Miller, eds., *National Parks, Conservation, and Development: The Role of Protected Areas in Sustaining Society*, 190–196. Proceedings of the World Congress on National Parks, Bali, Indonesia, 11–22 October 1982. Washington, D.C.: Smithsonian Institution Press.

St. John, S. 1862. *Life in the Forests of the Far East*. Vol. 1. London: Smith Elder and Co.

Salvat, B. 1981. "Preservation of Coral Reefs: Scientific Whim or Economic Necessity?" *Proceedings of the Fourth International Coral Reef Symposium* 1: 225–229.

Sankhala, K. H. 1969. "National Parks of India." In *Proceedings of the IUCN 11th Technical Meeting at New Delhi, India,* 11–26. 3 sec. A (1). Morges, Switzerland: IUCN Publications.

Sax, J. L. 1982. "In Search of Past Harmony." *Natural History* 91 (8): 42–51.

———. 1984. "Do Communities Have Rights? The National Parks as a Laboratory of New Ideas." *University of Pittsburgh Law Review* 45 (3): 499–511.

Sayer, J. A. 1981. "Tourism or Conservation in the National Parks of Benin." *Parks* 5 (4): 13–14.

Seley, J. E. 1983. *The Politics of Public-Facility Planning.* Lexington, Mass.: Lexington Books.

Selznick, P. 1949. *TVA and the Grass Roots.* New York: Harper and Row.

Seshadri, B. 1969. *The Twilight of India's Wildlife.* London: J. Baker.

Sherpa, M. N. 1987. "People, Park Problems and Challenges in the Annapurna Conservation Area in Nepal." Paper presented at the International Symposium on Protected Landscapes, Grange-over-Sands. Cumbria, England. 5–10 October 1987.

Sherpa, M. N., B. Coburn, and C. P. Gurung. 1986. "Annapurna Conservation Area, Nepal, Operative Plan Based on Findings of a Feasibility Study of Protected Status and Community Involvement." Unpublished report of the Annapurna Conservation Study Project, January 1986.

Sherpa, N. W. 1979. "A Report on Firewood Use in Sagarmatha National Park, Khumbu Region, Nepal." Kathmandu, Nepal: His Magesty's Government (HMG), Nepal National Parks and Wildlife Conservation Office.

Shkilnyk, A. M. 1985. *A Poison Stronger Than Love: The Destruction of an Ojibwa Community.* New Haven, Conn.: Yale University Press.

Singh, K. S. 1982. *Tribal Movements in India.* Vol. 1. New Delhi: Manohar.

Skeen, J. N., M.E.B. Carter, and H. L. Ragsdale. 1980. "Yellow-Poplar: The Piedmont Case." *Bulletin of the Torrey Botanical Club* 107: 1–6.

Smyth, D., P. Taylor, and A. Willis, eds. 1986. *Aboriginal Ranger Training and Employment in Australia: Proceedings of the First National Workshop, July 1985.* Canberra: ANPWS.

Spier, L. 1928. "Havasupai Ethnography." *Anthropological Papers of the American Museum of Natural History* 29 (3): 81–408.

Stebbing, E. P. 1922–1926. *The Forests of India.* Vol. 1 of 3 vols. London: John Lane.

Stracey, P. D. 1963. *Wild Life in India: Its Conservation and Control.* New Delhi: Department of Agriculture.

Sullivan, H., ed. 1984. *Visitors to Aboriginal Sites: Access, Control and Management.* Proceedings of the 1983 Kakadu Workshop. Canberra: ANPWS.

Susskind, L., and C. Ozawa. 1983. "Mediated Negotiation in the Public Sector: Planner as Negotiator." Cambridge, Mass.: MIT-Harvard Negotiation Project.

Tatz, C. 1982. *Aborigines and Uranium.* Melbourne: Heinemann Educational Australia.

Thompson, M., M. Warburton, and T. Hatley. 1986. *Uncertainty on a Himalayan Scale: An Institutional Theory of Environmental Perception and a Strategic Framework for the Sustainable Development of the Himalaya.* London: Milton Ash Editions.

Tico Times. 1983. San José, Costa Rica. April 6, 1983.

Tucker, R. P. 1982. "The Forests of the Western Himalayas: The Legacy of British Colonial Administration." *Journal of Forest History* 26 (3): 112–123.

———. 1986. "The British Empire and India's Forest Resources: Assam and the United Provinces, 1914–1950." In J. F. Richards and R. P. Tucker, eds., *The World Economy and the World's Forests in the Twentieth Century.*

Tucker, R. P., and J. F. Richards, eds. 1983. *Global Deforestation and the Nineteenth-Century World Economy.* Durham, N.C.: Duke University Press.

Turnbull, C. M. 1972. *The Mountain People.* New York: Simon and Schuster.

Uluru Katatjuta Board of Management and ANPWS. 1986. *Uluru (Ayers Rock–Mount Olga) National Park: Plan of Management.* Canberra: ANPWS.

U. S. Department of Agriculture (USDA), Southwestern Region, Kaibab National Forest. 1982. *Range Capacity and Terrestrial Ecosystem Evaluation of the Havasupai Traditional Use Lands.* Washington, D.C.: USGPO.

U. S. Department of Commerce, International Trade Administration. 1983. *Foreign Economic Trends and Their Implications for the United States: Ecuador.* International Marketing

Information Series. September 1983. Washington, D.C.: USGPO.

United States Department of the Interior (USDI). 1980. *Final Environmental Impact Statement, Pineland National Reserve.* Washington, D.C.: USGPO.

————. 1982. *Secretarial Land Use Plan for Addition to Havasupai Indian Reservation.* Washington, D.C.: Secretary of the Interior and the Bureau of Indian Affairs, in Consultation with the Havasupai Tribe.

————. 1983. *Grand Canyon National Park: Backcountry Management Plan.* Washington, D.C.: USDI, National Park Service.

————. 1984. *Grand Canyon National Park: Natural and Cultural Resources Management Plan, April 1984 Revision.* Grand Canyon National Park, Arizona. Washington, D.C.: USDI, National Park Service.

Usher, M. B. 1986. "Invasibility and Wildlife Conservation: Invasive Species on Nature Reserves." *Philosophical Transactions of the Royal Society of London, Biology (Phil. Trans. Soc. Lond. Bio.)* 314:695–710.

Usher, P. J. 1983. "Property Rights: The Basis of Management." *National and Regional Interests in the North,* 389–416. Proceedings of the Third National Workshop on People, Resources and the Environment North of 60. Ottawa: Canadian Arctic Resources Committee.

————. 1987. "Indigenous Management Systems and the Conservation of Wildlife in the Canadian North." *Alternatives* 14 (1): 3–9.

Vallier, I., ed. 1971. *Comparative Methods in Sociology: Essays on Trends and Applications.* Berkeley, Calif.: University of California Press.

Van Der Sande, G.A.J. 1907. "Ethnography and Anthropology." *Nova Guinea* 3.

Van Hoevell, G.W.W.C. 1890. "De Kei-Eilander Tijdschrift Voor Indische Taal." *Land en Volkenkunde* 33:102–159.

Vayda, A. P. 1976. *War in Ecological Perspective.* New York: Plenum.

Villa, J. L., and A. Ponce. 1984. "Islands for People and Evolution: The Galapagos." In J. A. McNeely and K. R. Miller, eds., *National Parks, Conservation, and Development: The Role of Protected Areas in Sustaining Society,* 584–587. Proceedings of the World Congress on National Parks, Bali, Indonesia, 11–22 October 1982. Washington, D.C.: Smithsonian Institution Press.

Vitousek, P. M. 1986. "Biological Invasions and Ecosystem Properties: Can Species Make a Difference?" In H. A. Mooney and J. A. Drake, *Ecology of Biological Invasions of North America and Hawaii,* 163–176. New York: Springer-Verlag.

Wales Tourist Board. 1974. *Tourism in Gwynnedd: An Economic Study.* Cardiff: Wales Tourist Board.

Waquin, A. 1986. "Resource Co-Management in Wood Buffalo Park." In *Native People and Renewable Resource Management,* 86–95. Proceedings of the 1986 Symposium of the Alberta Society of Professional Biologists, April 29–May 1. Symposium Series No. 10. Edmonton: Alberta Society of Professional Biologists.

Weaver, S. M. 1984. "Indian Government: A Concept in Need of a Definition." In M. Boldt, J. A. Long, and L. Littlebear, eds., *Pathways to Self-Determination: Canadian Indians and the Canadian State,* 65–68. Toronto: University of Toronto Press.

Weeks, N. C. 1981. "National Parks, Native Peoples: A Study of the Experience of Selected Other Jurisdictions With a View to Cooperation in Northern Canada." Montreal: Parks Canada.

Wellington, G. M. 1974. "Una Descripción Ecología del Ambiente Marino y Ambientes Asociados en el Monument Nacional de Cahuita." San José, Costa Rica: Servicio de Parques Nacionales, Ministerio de Agricutura y Ganaderia.

———. 1976. "A Prospectus: Proposal for a Galapagos Marine Park." *Noticias de Galápagos* 24:9–13.

———. 1984. "Marine Environment and Protection." In J. E. Treherne and R. Perry, eds., *Key Environments Series: Galapagos Islands.* Oxford: Pergamon Press.

West, P. C. 1982a. *Natural Resource Bureaucracy and Rural Poverty: A Study in the Political Sociology of Natural Resources.* Ann Arbor: School of Natural Resources, Natural Resources Sociology Monograph Series, monograph No. 2.

———. 1982b. "Tribal Control and the Identity-Poverty Dilemma." In C. C. Geisler, R. Green, D. Usner, and P. C. West, eds., *Indian SIA: The Social Impact Assessment of Rapid Resource Development on Native Peoples,* 80–92. Natural Resource Sociology Monograph Series, Monograph No. 3. Ann Arbor: School of Natural Resources, University of Michigan.

———. 1982c. "Resident Populations and National Parks in Developing Nations: Sociological Perspectives and Policy Implications." Unpublished paper. Ann Arbor: School of Natural Resources, University of Michigan.

———. 1986. "Max Weber's Human Ecology of Historical Societies." In V. Murvar, ed., *Theory of Liberty, Legitimacy, and*

Power: New Directions in the Scientific and Intellectual Legacy of Max Weber, 216–234. London: Routledge and Kegan Paul.

West, P. C., and S. Light. 1978. "Community Level Change Strategies." In K. H. Shapiro, ed., *Science and Technology for Managing Fragile Environments in Developing Nations,* 322–378. Ann Arbor: School of Natural Resources, Office of International Studies, University of Michigan.

Western, D. 1982. "Amboseli National Park: Enlisting Land Owners to Conserve Migratory Wildlife." *Ambio* 11 (5): 302–308.

Whiting, A., S. A. Weber, and P. D. Seaman, eds. 1985. *Havasupai Habitat.* Tucson, Ariz.: University of Arizona Press.

Whittington, M. S. 1985. "Political and Constitutional Development in the N.W.T. and Yukon." In M. S. Whittington, ed., *The North,* 53–110. Toronto: University of Toronto Press.

Woo, H. T. 1980. "A Study on the Public Policy, Planning, and Management of Korean National Parks for the Future." Master's thesis, School of Horticulture, Chiba University, Matsudo-City, Japan.

World Bank. 1988. *World Development Report 1988.* New York: Oxford University Press.

World Commission on Environment and Development. 1987. *Our Common Future.* New York: Oxford University Press.

World Resources Institute, International Institute for Environment and Development, and United Nations Environmental Program. 1988. *World Resources 1988–89.* New York: Basic Books.

Wright, R. M., B. Houseal, and C. DeLeon. 1985. "Kuna Yala: Indigenous Biosphere in the Making?" *Parks* 10 (3):25–28.

Zinser, C. I. 1980. *The Economic Impact of the Adirondack Park Private Land Use and Development Plan.* Albany: State University of New York Press.

ABOUT THE CONTRIBUTORS

Editors
Patrick C. West is an Associate Professor of Natural Resources/ Environmental Sociology, and Samuel T. Dana Professor of Outdoor Recreation at the University of Michigan, School of Natural Resources. He has worked for many years on sociological and interdisciplinary aspects of domestic parks and protected areas and in the sociology of natural resources and rural development. As a staff member on the International Seminar on National Parks and Equivalent Reserves for three of its last ten years, West has long been involved with the issues of resident peoples and national parks in developing countries. Most recently, he has been involved with research on this topic in Northern Benin, West Africa.

Steven R. Brechin is presently a post-doctoral Research Fellow, The University of Michigan, School of Natural Resources where he received his Ph.D. He is interested in applying social science perspectives to international and domestic environmental and resource issues. Topics of special interest include population-environment interactions, sociological perspectives to international and nongovernmental organizations, and sustainable development. In collaboration with Indonesian counterparts, Brechin is currently researching resident peoples and forest reserve conflicts and their solutions in South Sumatra, Indonesia. He will join the Sociology Department and Center for Energy and Environmental Studies, Princeton University, fall 1991.

Authors
Conner Bailey's professional interests include the sociology of natural resource management and the political economy of development. Prior to joining the faculty at Auburn University in 1985, he worked at the Marine Policy Center, Woods Hole Oceanographic Institution, and at the International Center for Living Aquatic Resources Management (ICLARM). Bailey has conducted field research in Malaysia, the Philippines, and Indonesia, as well as in Ecuador. Among his publications are *The Sociology of Production in Rural Malay Society,* and numerous journal articles, book chapters, and research monographs on problems of coastal and marine resource management. He received his Ph.D. in rural sociology from Cornell University.

Susan F. Beede is the EPA Region I (New England) Program Manager for the joint state and federal Long Island Sound Study. Previously, she served as the Public Outreach Coordinator and Program Assistant for all three of the federally supported New England estuary projects. Beede has also worked for the State of Massachusetts' Department of Environmental Management and the National Park Service in Glacier National Park. Professionally she has had a long-standing interest in exploring ways to reconcile the objectives of conservation and development. As a researcher in 1983–84, she conducted a study in Africa and France of biosphere reserves and other multiple use protected areas. Beede received her Masters in Natural Resource Science from the University of Michigan and her B.A. from Bryn Mawr College.

Patricia Bidol-Padva has worked with urban and rural organizations and communities so that they can institute social changes with a minimum of disruption to the life-styles of the impacted populations. During the last twenty-five years she has worked with Native American, Hispanic, African, Caucasian, and Asian populations in the United States, Canada, and Israel. Her professional interests include designing systems to ensure the protection of cultural diversity and implementing collaborative conflict management approaches for natural resource and multicultural disputes. She received her Ph.D. in individual, group, and organizational change from the University of Michigan.

Bruce W. Bunting is the Vice President of World Wildlife Fund's Asia/Pacific Program. He is responsible for the development of a comprehensive Asian conservation program that encompasses projects in Bhutan, Indonesia, Malaysia, Nepal, the Philippines, and Thailand. Prior to his position with the Asia Program, Bunting worked for TRAFFIC (U.S.A.), WWF's illegal wildlife trade monitoring unit. He has consulted on trade issues and the conceptual development of a computer data base of animal species protected by various international agreements. Bunting received his B.S. in zoology and his doctorate in veterinary medicine from Michigan State University.

John B. Calhoun, ecologist and psychologist, National Institute of Mental Health, focused his research on role development and utilization of resources in natural and designed environments with respect to crowding, cooperation, and changes in population density. In the "Album of Science, the Biological Sciences," Calhoun is included as one of ten individuals, starting with Sigmund Freud and Margaret Mead, who developed major new approaches and concepts related to inquiry about human and animal behavior in the twentieth century.

Trevor A. Croft is a geographer and town planner by background, and has particular interests in conservation-related land use. Following a period as Planning Officer with the Countryside Commission for Scotland he spent six years in Malawi under the UK Government's overseas aid scheme. As Park Planner with the Department of National Parks and Wildlife, Mr. Croft had an active interest in the development of tourism in ways which respected the social and natural environment of the Malawians. He joined the National Trust for Scotland as Head of Policy Research in 1982 and is now the Trust's Regional Director for Central and Tayside Region.

James E. Crowfoot, Professor and former Dean of the School of Natural Resources at the University of Michigan, became interested in conflict processes by working on problems of urban high school disruptions in the late 1960's. Since the late 1970's his research has focused on environmental dispute resolution. He is currently a member of the interdisciplinary Program on Conflict Management Alternatives at the University of Michigan.

Ken M. East is Superintendent of Wood Buffalo National Park, Canada's largest national park. In addition to administering the park, Mr. East is involved in the negotiation of native land claims affecting national parks in the North. He has also had extensive experience in the design and implementation of "co-management" arrangements to provide for native involvement in the planning and management of Wood Buffalo and other national parks. Mr. East's training and past experience is in the field of natural resource management with particular emphasis on coastal zone and natural hazard management. He holds an M.A. in Geography from the University of Windsor.

Dennis Glick is the Director of the Greater Yellowstone Tomorrow project of the Greater Yellowstone Coalition in Bozeman, Montana. Previously, he was the Senior Program Officer for Central America and Codirector of the Wildlands and Human Needs Program at the World Wildlife Fund–U.S. He spent several years working in Latin America including two years at the Wildlands Management Unit of CATIE in Turrialba, Costa Rica. He assisted in the development of the management plan for the La Planada Reserve and in carrying out a Latin American–wide workshop on sustainable rural development for wildland managers held in La Planada in 1988. His principal conservation efforts continue to focus on integrating natural area protection with meeting the human needs of rural populations.

Robert Goodland is a tropical applied ecologist working for the World Bank in Washington, D.C. where he is Chief of the Environment Division for Latin America. Before going to the Bank in 1978, Dr. Goodland set up the ecology department at the then-new University of Brasilia in 1969–71; and created the first post-graduate course of tropical applied ecology at INPA in Manaus in 1974. He assisted with the environmental sections of the Third Malaysia Plan and helped start up the Ministry of Environment in Indonesia. He has developed environmental policies for the World Bank, including its "Tribal Peoples" policy from which this chapter is condensed. He has published a dozen books in his field.

David F. Hales is much more of a practitioner than a scholar of natural resource management. His chapter grew out of experiences during his tenure as Deputy Assistant Secretary for Fish, Wildlife, and Parks, U.S. Department of Interior, when he coordinated international programs for the U.S. Fish and Wild Service, the National Park Service, and the Heritage Conservation and Recreation Service. Mr. Hales is currently Director of the Michigan Department of Natural Resources.

David Harmon has written on international environmental issues, nature's place in literature, and the history of conservation. He has also been a consultant to the World Resources Institute of Washington, D.C. for the *World Resources Report*. He recently edited the anthology *Mirror of America: Literary Encounters with the National Parks*.

John Hough is a wildland management specialist with a particular interest in the role of protected areas in development and the problems of implementing integrated conservation and development projects at the site level. In addition to planning and managing the Michiru Mountain Conservation Area in Malawi,

Central Africa, he has worked as a conservation project manager in Britain, with the International Park Seminar in the USA, Canada, and Costa Rica, and has taught Wildland Management at the University of Michigan School of Natural Resources. He has conducted research on national park–local people relationships around the Pendjari Biosphere Reserve complex in northern Benin, West Africa, and around the Grand Canyon National Park in the USA. He is currently Chief Technical Adviser to the World Wide Fund for Nature's (WWF) conservation and development project at Montagne d'Ambre in Madagascar. Hough received his Ph.D. from the School of Natural Resources, The University of Michigan.

Susan Kay Jacobson is presently coordinator of the Program for Studies in Tropical Conservation and a research scientist with the Department of Wildlife and Range Sciences at the University of Florida. She has conducted field work in Kenya, Malaysia, Costa Rica, and Belize. Her research interests include the human dimensions of wildlife management, national park development and environmental education/communication, and resource ecology and biological conservation. She has a Ph.D. from Duke University.

Kurt Kutay is the director of Wildland JOURNEYS, an adventure travel tour company based in Seattle, Washington. He completed an M.S. degree in Natural Resource Management at the University of Michigan, School of Natural Resources after conducting field research as a planner for the National Park Service of Costa Rica. Kutay is also codirector of the Earth Preservation Fund, a nonprofit organization which supports conservation and community development through adventure travel. He has published articles on low impact nature tourism as a basis for conservation and rural economic development.

Stuart A. Marks was reared on a development frontier in Central Africa, and still returns there occasionally for research. His latest research in Zambia was supported by a Fulbright grant and by the National Geographic Society. He is currently completing another long-term study of wildlife and development in the southern United States which helps him keep a perspective on environmental issues in the Third World. Stuart Marks is an independent scholar and consultant who resides in Raleigh, North Carolina.

Carmelita McGurk has been a naturalist and public relations specialist for several state park systems; she is currently employed as a park manager with the Minnesota State Park system. Ms. McGurk received her M.S. in Natural Resources from the University of Michigan in 1987.

Robert N. Muller is an Associate Professor at Forest Ecology at the University of Kentucky, where he teaches undergraduate and graduate courses in forest ecology, community ecology, and ecosystem analysis. His research addresses ecosystem-level implications of community and population processes in temperate zone forests. He has had prior research experience at Argonne National Laboratory in air pollutant effect on productivity of agricultural crops. He recently served as a consultant to forestry education programs in Indonesia. Professor Muller obtained his doctorate from Yale University.

Concelia Ntshalintshali is currently employed by the Ministry of Education in Swaziland, her native country, where she is working to integrate environmental education into the national school curriculum. She has also taught geography and has held the position of school principal in the Swaziland school system. She received her M.S. in Natural Resources from the University of Michigan.

Jorge Orejuela is Chief of Environment and Natural Resources at the Fundacion para la Educacion Superior (FES) in Cali, Colombia. Since 1983 he has been involved in the establishment and development of private nature reserves in Colombia. His work at La Planada Nature Reserve, an integrated nature conservation and sustainable development project in southwestern Colombia, has increased his interest in the relationship of human societies with their living resources. He has been a faculty member at the Universidad del Valle and a researcher with World Wildlife Fund. He earned a Ph.D. in Biology at New Mexico State University.

Nicholas V.C. Polunin is an ecologist who has worked in Britain and the Indo-Pacific, on wetlands and coral reefs. His research is focused on the biology of marine fishes, and he is interested more generally in the ecology and environmental management of coasts. Having been a consultant for IUCN in Indonesia, and an academic in Papua New Guinea, he is now a lecturer in marine biology at the University of Newcastle Upon Tyne.

Avia Rabinovitch-Vin is Chief Scientist for the Israel Nature Reserves Authority. Her Ph.D. training focused on the influence of rock types on soil composition and plant communities. Her current interest and research center on the effects human activities, particularly grazing, cutting, and burning, have on different ecosystems, and on the management of nature reserves and open spaces involving local residents and their animals. She also teaches these subjects at the Technion, Haifa.

Shishir R. Raval's professional interests are in the field of landscape, land use planning and design with special interest in Human Ecology and Environmental Psychology. His work includes research and fieldwork in landscape planning for semiarid towns, pilgrimage places, and wastelands; social forestry programs and protected area planning in India; and Lakeshore development and wilderness area planning in the U.S.A. He is currently a doctoral candidate in the Landscape Architecture program at the University of Michigan's School of Natural Resources.

Mingma Norbu Sherpa is the Asia Program Officer for the World Wildlife Fund's Nepal and Himalayan program. He is responsible for development and oversight of a variety of projects, including the Annapurna Conservation Area Project (ACAP) and management of Shey Phoksundo National Park. Mingma has been an integral part of ACAP since 1985 when he served as a principal investigator for the feasibility study of the Annapurna area, and later its director. Mr. Sherpa received his diploma from Lincoln College in New Zealand in 1980, and a M.A. in Natural Resource Management from the University of Manitoba in 1985. In 1987 he was awarded a Fulbright Scholarship to study at the School of Natural Resources, University of Michigan.

Richard P. Tucker is Professor of History and Asian Studies at Oakland University and Adjunct Professor of Natural Resources, The University of Michigan. His research centers on ecological change in India and the Himalayan mountains. He chairs an international project on the history of tropical deforestation, and is preparing a book on the United States and the environmental history of the Third World.

Sally M. Weaver is a professor in political anthropology at the University of Waterloo (Canada). Her approach to resource management came from her more general interest in power-sharing in policy development between national governments and indigenous peoples in western democracies. She has published in the field of federal policy making with and for indigenous peoples in Canada and Australia. Her specific interest in self-management and aboriginal empowerment resulted from her work on the role of Aboriginal peoples in the operation of national parks in northern Australia.

Will Weber is director of Journeys International Inc.(Ann Arbor, Michigan), a tour operator which emphasizes traveler participation in nature and culture-oriented preservation projects in Asia, Africa and Latin America. He worked in the Nepal National Parks and Wildlife Conservation Department as a Peace Corps Volunteer, and then completed graduate studies at the University of Michigan School of Natural Resources. His current interests include working with local villages in Madagascar, Rwanda, Papua New Guinea, Myanmar and Ladakh to develop personal, international, cross-cultural involvement in nature conservation programs.

Hyung Taek Woo recently received his Ph.D. in landscape architecture at the University of Michigan. His major interests include land use planning and management of protected landscapes in different countries and their international comparison. His analytical focus has been the integration of political, public policy, and resource management perspectives in relation to land use planning and management. He has conducted research in Britain, Japan, South Korea, and the United States.

R. Michael Wright is vice president and general counsel of World Wildlife Fund – U.S. He initially directed WWF's Park Program and developed WWF's Wildlands and Human Needs Program linking conservation and human development. He is now Director of the Osborn Center for Conservation and Development, a joint program which includes all of World Wildlife Fund and the Conservation Foundation activities addressing issues of sustainable development. He was selected for *National Leaders of American Conservation* (1985) and received a FUNEP 500 Award for 1988 from Friends of the UN Environmental Programme. Mr. Wright has a law degree from Stanford University.

INDEX